## DATE DUE

# FIVE PLAYS

# BOOKS BY EDMUND WILSON

I THOUGHT OF DAISY

POETS, FAREWELL!

AXEL'S CASTLE

THE AMERICAN JITTERS

TRAVELS IN TWO DEMOCRACIES

THE TRIPLE THINKERS

TO THE FINLAND STATION

THE WOUND AND THE BOW

NOTE-BOOKS OF NIGHT

THE SHOCK OF RECOGNITION

MEMOIRS OF HECATE COUNTY

EUROPE WITHOUT BAEDEKER

CLASSICS AND COMMERCIALS

THE SHORES OF LIGHT

FIVE PLAYS

# FIVE PLAYS

By EDMUND WILSON

---

Cyprian's Prayer

The Crime in the Whistler Room

This Room and This Gin and These
Sandwiches

Beppo and Beth

The Little Blue Light

---

FARRAR, STRAUS AND YOUNG
NEW YORK
1954

*Printed in Great Britain by the*
*Camelot Press Ltd., Southampton*
*for the publishers,*
*Farrar, Straus and Young, Inc., New York*

# CONTENTS

CYPRIAN'S PRAYER
[*page 9*]

THE CRIME IN THE WHISTLER ROOM
[*page 129*]

THIS ROOM AND THIS GIN AND THESE
SANDWICHES
[*page 211*]

BEPPO AND BETH
[*page 313*]

THE LITTLE BLUE LIGHT
[*page 417*]

# PREFACE

THIS preface is frankly a sales talk. For years I have been writing plays. Two of them have been produced, and this has encouraged me to continue— though I should probably have gone on writing them in any case, since I have always been particularly susceptible to the theater, and the stories that take shape in my imagination are likely to do so in dramatic form. This in some ways has perhaps been unfortunate. Few people care to read printed plays unless they have been very successful, and even fewer publishers care to print them. If my plays had been novels instead, they would at least have had some circulation. As it was, when I published three of them— into which I had put, as it seemed to me then, some of my best work—in a volume which was called, from a key-phrase in one of them, *This Room and This Gin and These Sandwiches*, with the imprint of the *New Republic*, in the latter's series of Dollar Books, it was acknowledged in the Press by, so far as I remember, only two notices: an unsigned and extremely disagreeable note in the New York *Evening Sun* and an appreciative review in the *Nation* by Mr. Kenneth Burke, who would undoubtedly never have heard of the book if he had not happened himself to have brought out a book in that series.

This volume of three plays was introduced by the following note: "These three variations on the same theme represent three successive stages of the artistic and moral revolt which had its headquarters in New York after the War." I thus claimed for them, and still claim for them, a certain historical and critical interest as attempts to

7

dramatize the mentality, the characteristic types and the various milieux of the twenties and the early thirties. *The Crime in the Whistler Room* is a fantasy of our first liberation from the culture and convention of the previous era; *This Room and This Gin and These Sandwiches* (in the earlier collection called *A Winter in Beech Street*) shows the movement consolidated and concentrated in the Greenwich Village section of New York; and *Beppo and Beth* is a comedy of New York "sophistication" reeling from the Stock Market crash. Later on, after the second world war, I went on to write *The Little Blue Light*, which was published in 1950 by Farrar, Straus. This attracted more attention than my earlier plays and was produced both in New York and in Cambridge, Mass. *The Little Blue Light*, though it is laid in the future, is really another instalment of the same historical chronicle, another panel in the same sequence—since it deals with the same sort of people in a later and even more desperate phase; so I have here made it follow the others.

*Cyprian's Prayer*, which is new, is a play of a different kind, and I have written for it a separate foreword.

So I dump the whole lot in your laps, at the risk of having you dump them right off. Is it possible to read continuously a volume of five modern plays that are not by Chekhov or Shaw? Would it be possible even with Chekhov or Shaw? I don't know; but I hope that such people as have lately been reading my other books will not hesitate to bite into this one. Since I am publishing these plays in a volume, I have let them run rather long— especially *This Room and This Gin*, which I seem to have aimed to make, as a *tableau de moeurs*, almost encyclopaedic. If you get through *This Room and This Gin*, you might take a long rest, then go on to the other two. Cuts supplied on application.

8

# Cyprian's Prayer

Cyprian } *Sons of a Small Tenant Farmer*
Cyrus

Their Mother

Their Father

Rodolphe de Tancarville, *a Feudal Baron*

The Moonlight Drunkard, *an Apparition*

Merlin, *an Aged Magician*

Janet, *his Daughter*

Claude, *his Assistant*

Mr. B., *a Reformed Devil*

A Girl Who is in Trouble

A Would-be Poisoner

A Vampire

A Steward

Luigi, *a Major-domo*

Slingo
Stingo } *Imps*
Bongo

Buster, *a Mohammedan Genie*

The action takes place in France in the sixties of a fabulous fifteenth century—the reign of Louis XI.

This play, though it was recently written, had long been building up in my head. As a child, I used to read and reread, in an old bound volume of *St. Nicholas,* a story by Frank Stockton called *The Magician's Daughter and the High-born Boy* (published also, in 1881, in a collection of Stockton's stories called *The Floating Prince and Other Fairy Tales*), which delighted me and stayed in my mind. I have borrowed from this my magician's daughter, who is left by the death of her father with a staff that she cannot control and an equipment she does not understand, as well as her queue of clients and the study in which they are received. This idea became later associated in my mind with the theme of the Sorcerer's Apprentice—a legend which first occurs in one of the dialogues of Lucian, which Goethe, finding it there, used for his ballad *Der Zauberlehrling,* giving it a Faustian touch, but which is probably best known as the subject of Paul Dukas's dramatic scherzo. To all this, at some point, attached themselves certain incidents from Michelet's volume on the reign of Louis XI, which I had read at the end of the first World War; and later, in 1935, while quarantined in a hospital in Odessa, I occupied some dreary hours by working out the first two acts of this play pretty much as I finally wrote them. I also planned at that time the later invocation of the genie, but I conceived him then as merely unmanageable— devious, obstructive and sly—and not so ferocious as he has now become.

Two years later, in 1937, Jean Cocteau produced and published a highly entertaining play called *Les Chevaliers de la Table Ronde,* in which Guinevere, bewitched by Merlin and animated by an alien and evil spirit, is made to shift back and forth between two contrasting roles which must have offered the actress great possibilities. I had already then invented Jezebel-Janet, and I doubt whether I owe to Cocteau anything except stimulation to try my hand at something similar. The witch who changes her shape to masquerade as somebody's sweetheart had figured already in Ben Jonson's *The Sad Shepherd* and John Marston's *Sophonisba*, neither of which I had read at that time, and I must have picked up the idea, as these earlier writers did, from old stories of demonic possession and of elf-women disguised as mortals.

The intimate relation between body and soul of which Cyprian has an inkling was perceived, at a date slightly later than that at which the play is supposed to take place, by the thaumaturge Paracelsus, who, like Cyprian, mixed science with magic. He anticipated the modern conception which has produced the word *psychosomatic*.

The imprisonment of the genie in the bottle as a penalty for belonging to the wrong sect comes simply from the *Arabian Nights*, though of course it might equally apply to the early stages of Russian Communism—or to those of Christianity, for that matter.

# ACT I

## SCENE I

*The inside of a tenant's cottage, which shows, for the peasantry of the time, a fairly high standard of living. A door on the left that leads out of the house; small windows without glass in the left and back walls, and underneath these a bench, on which lie a few articles of clothing; in the right back corner, a fireplace, the hearth of which extends into the room farther than that of a modern one and the chimneypiece of which resembles the roof of a shed rather than a modern mantelpiece; on the right wall, pots and pans, some hung up by the handles, others arranged on a shelf; below them, big crocks and a copper cauldron. A goodlooking woman not far under forty sits on a stool by the fire, baking loaves in the coals. She is dressed in an apron and cap and wears blunt-toed leather shoes with bows; but she is obviously conscious of her prettiness, and there is something of coquetry about her. At her girdle hangs a mirror of polished silver. In the middle of the room, a plain wooden table, with three stools clustered around it. Cyprian, a young man of twenty, sits behind it, facing the audience, intent on a folio, which he reads by the light of a candle. He is dressed in a smockfrock, stockings that come up to his knees and black leather shoes without soles that are split at the ankle like half-fastened goloshes.*

*A late afternoon at the end of September.*

THE MOTHER. Cyrus isn't going to like it when he finds you burning that candle.

CYPRIAN. It's getting too dark to read.

THE MOTHER. This fire gives plenty of light.

13

CYPRIAN. I can't read when you're baking.

THE MOTHER. Your brother's not going to like it.

CYPRIAN. Please, Mother, let me alone.

*She looks in her little mirror and tucks the hair in under her cap. Cyprian watches her.*

CYPRIAN. I always know what that means.

THE MOTHER. I thought you wanted to study.

*He returns to his book.*

*The Father and Cyrus come in. The Father is a restless little man, wiry, wizened and bent, who peers and pokes about. Cyrus is two years older than Cyprian. They are dressed like Cyprian, but wear dark soft brimless hats with long flaps that cover the backs of their necks. They take their hats off and throw them down on the bench.*

THE FATHER (*to the Mother and Cyprian*). It feels like a frost to-night, and the sowing's not half done. (*He sits down to the left of the table and takes his shoes off.*)

CYRUS (*glancing at Cyprian*). If we'd had a little assistance, we could easily have cleaned it up.

THE FATHER. Never mind: when Cype is a full-fledged priest, he'll make it up in other ways. He'll get all our sins forgiven.

CYRUS. Only God can do that.

THE FATHER. If Cyprian's a saint like his namesake, we'll at least have a friend at court.

CYRUS. That's a frivolous way to talk, old man, and sometimes there's a very thin line between frivolity and blasphemy.

CYPRIAN. Did you pick that up at the castle?

CYRUS (*looking over Cyprian's shoulder*). That's not a work of piety you're reading.

CYPRIAN. How do *you* know?—you can't read.

CYRUS. I can see by the queer pictures that it isn't a religious book. (*Pointing at the page*) It's got something to do with the Devil.

14

CYPRIAN. Isn't the Devil a part of religion?

CYRUS. Who loaned it to you?

CYPRIAN. None of your business.

CYRUS. You're just wasting your time on rubbish—if you're not doing something worse.—And candles! (*He blows the candle out.*) I've told you, and your mother has told you: no candles before nightfall!

*Cyprian slams the book and stands up.*

CYPRIAN (*in a voice at once aggrieved and belligerent*). If you want me to go to the monastery, why don't you tell me so? But you don't—you don't want to let go of me: you think that it's going to be useful to you to have a priest in the family. (*A hunting horn is heard outside, and he pauses for a moment, then continues.*) You'll expect me to beg for you at the castle—and yet you want to nag me at home!

*The horn is heard coming closer.*

THE FATHER (*to Cyrus*). Do you hear that? It's coming our way.

CYRUS (*to Cyprian*). Are the sheep in?

CYPRIAN. No: why should they be? The sun's not setting yet.

CYRUS. Nor the chickens, I suppose.

CYPRIAN. No.

*During the dialogue that follows, the Mother returns to her mirror.*

CYRUS. You ought to have known he'd be hunting today.

CYPRIAN. What do I know about when he hunts?

CYRUS. He's usually out on Saturday—if the weather's as fine as this.

CYPRIAN. I don't study his habits as you do.—I see that Mother's got out her mirror.

*The hunt is heard nearer at hand: barking of hounds and shouts of the hunters. The Father peers out the window at the back on the right-hand side.*

15

THE FATHER. They're coming right across our field. There goes all our work today!

*Cyrus looks out the other back window. Bleating of sheep and cackling of chickens.*

THE FATHER. Why, in the name of God, do we have to have a baron like that? He hasn't even got the sense to have his dogs taught not to kill sheep!

*Intensified tumult and squawking.*

CYPRIAN (*rushing out and calling as he reaches the door*). Get out of those vegetables! What are you doing?

CYRUS (*starting after him*). Stay inside—you can't talk to them like that! (*He stops this side of the door.*)

THE MOTHER (*going to the window through which Cyrus has been looking out*). He's coming in here, I think.

THE FATHER. A little informal call!

*Tancarville appears at the door, dragging Cyprian by the arm. He is a tall but potbellied man in his forties, with a red drinker's face. He wears high boots and a plumed hat and carries a long boar-spear. The Father slips out the door.*

TANCARVILLE (*to the Mother*). Lottie, tell this brat of yours that when orders are to be given in Tancarville's fief, they'll be given by Tancarville.

THE MOTHER (*making a curtsy*). Be gracious, my lord, and forgive the boy!

TANCARVILLE. If he didn't belong to you, I'd string him up in a minute! (*He contemptuously flings Cyprian away.*)

THE MOTHER. What's all the rumpus out there that your lordship is pleased to make?

TANCARVILLE. Why, a goddam son of a bitch of a hare just ran down through your garden and bolted into the house!

CYRUS (*very respectfully*). We have seen no hare, my lord.

TANCARVILLE. Well, *I* saw it!—it ran in the door.

THE MOTHER (*with a smile that shows a certain familiarity*). The excitement of the hunt, my lord!——

16

TANCARVILLE. D'ye mean to suggest that I'm drunk?—that I don't known what I'm seeing?

THE MOTHER. Oh, no, my lord! You know very well that I never should want to displease you!

*Squawking of chickens outside.*

CYPRIAN. Would it be too much, my lord, to ask you to call off your huntsmen? Those dogs are killing our chickens.

TANCARVILLE. Use them for chicken-pie. I've got to have my hare!

CYPRIAN. The hare is not here, sir, the door was shut.

TANCARVILLE. I tell you I saw where it went: it's here and I'm going to find it—a son of a bitch of a hare—a goddam sly peasant hare! Maybe he's a friend of yours! (*He picks up the book from the table.*) Maybe he reads books! (*He throws the book into the fire, from which Cyprian makes haste to retrieve it.*) It ought to be easy to find him: there isn't much room in this hovel. (*He turns over the cauldron with a jab of his spear and goes on to knock down the crocks.*) We'll just go through these pots and pans!

THE MOTHER (*smiling*). You were kind to us once, my lord.

TANCARVILLE. Can't lose my hare, Lottie—and I *think* he's hiding here. (*He sweeps the saucepans down and prods at the fireplace.*) He might be in one of these boots! (*He picks up the Father's shoes and holds them upside down, then flings them away in disgust.*) Phew! No self-respecting hare would nest in a hole like that!

*The Father comes in, with an arrow in his hand.*

CYPRIAN. You see there's no hare here.

TANCARVILLE. To hell with it! I say it *is* here! (*He thrusts his hand down the neck of her dress.*) Maybe it jumped in here, eh?

THE MOTHER (*not entirely displeased*). Please, my lord! What are you doing?

17

*The Father comes behind him and jabs him in the behind
with the arrow; then drops it and dodges aside.*

TANCARVILLE (*turning around*). Who did that? (*Seeing the
old man and guffawing*) Why, you damned little biting
weasel! (*He reaches for the Father, who evades him.*)

THE FATHER (*pointing at the arrow*). It was an arrow from
one of your own men, my lord. They're shooting down
our poultry like pigeons.

TANCARVILLE. By God and by Jesus, why shouldn't they?
It'll keep the weasels from getting them. I sometimes hunt
weasels, too. Did you ever see a dog shake a weasel?

*He lunges at the Father with his spear; Cyprian interposes
the folio. The Mother comes up to the Baron and forces herself
on his attention.*

THE MOTHER (*in a low voice, exercising all her wiles*).
May I have a word aside with you, my dearest lord?

TANCARVILLE. Come to the castle and say it! (*To Cyprian,
pushing her aside*) Throw that book in the fire! Who told
you you could be a priest, you sour little half-baked
peasant! (*As Cyprian stands obstinate, with the book under
his arm*) Burn that book up, I say! or I'll have you on
a rope before sunset!

CYRUS. Do what his lordship says.

THE MOTHER. Please, Cyprian: don't be stubborn.

*Cyprian puts the book in the fire.*

TANCARVILLE. Put it where it'll burn—let me see it burn!

*Cyprian gives it a shove with his foot, pretending to push it
nearer the coals, then conceals it by planting himself in front
of the fire.*

TANCARVILLE. If I find you reading again, I'll have both
your eyes out!

THE MOTHER. Be merciful, my lord! (*Lowering her voice*)
When would you like me to come?

TANCARVILLE (*loudly, without discretion*). When I'm back
from the hunt—not too late. I'll make you amends for

18

your livestock. I'm a good natured fellow, Lottie—you know that goddam well. Even when some fool makes me furious (*glaring at Cyprian*), my heart's in the right place! (*Clapping his hand to the right side of his chest.*)

CYPRIAN. The other side.

TANCARVILLE. The hell you say! Shall I cut you open and check on that?

THE MOTHER. Spare the boy, please, your lordship: study has crazed his brain. Now that his book is burned, I'm sure that he'll be much better.

TANCARVILLE. I'll spare him for your sake, Lottie. (*Going to the door and calling to the men outside*) All right, boys, let's be off! Where the hell is that boar you promised me?

*His exit leaves them silent. Cyprian gets the book out of the fireplace, knocks the ashes off it and looks to see how much it has been damaged. The Mother puts back the pans; the Father examines the crocks; Cyrus, again at the window, watches the departure of the hunt.*

THE FATHER (*breaking the silence*). Four sheep and God knows how many chickens!

THE MOTHER. He told me he'd make us amends.

CYPRIAN (*with insinuation*). There's no doubt that he likes you, Mother. I heard what he said just now. I think he came here to see you.

THE MOTHER. He hasn't spoken a word to me in years.

CYPRIAN. It must have been a pleasure today!

THE MOTHER. He can be nice when he isn't drinking.

CYPRIAN. Which is never, so far as is known. Even the nobles call him Rody the Rumpot.

CYRUS (*turning from the window*). You're not to talk about him like that. He's our liege lord: we're bound to respect him.

CYPRIAN. I'm impressed by your self-restraint. Since you're doomed to have your life and your work and everything you've got in the world at the mercy of this drunken scoundrel, it's a very good thing you were born respectful!

CYRUS. The Baron is a strong man. He's held his own against his neighbors—who are wolves if there ever were wolves.

CYPRIAN. He also poisoned his brother and put his father to die in a dungeon.

CYRUS. We haven't any proof of that.

CYPRIAN. I know what makes you stand up for him. I've never said it before—but I've known all along what you thought, and, from what happened here today, I haven't a doubt you're right.

CYRUS. Be careful.

CYPRIAN. I'm through being careful. You think that you're Tancarville's son.

THE MOTHER. Oh, Cyprian, please don't!

CYPRIAN. Everybody knows about how Mother had to go up to the castle to give him the privilege of the first night.

THE MOTHER. This isn't respectful to your father.

THE FATHER. Oh, don't mind about me!—it's too late in the day to begin.

CYPRIAN. —And she's often been back since.

CYRUS. That'll be enough, Cyprian.

CYPRIAN (to Cyrus). So you've always adored old Rumpot, because you're just as big a blockhead as he is. And Mother adores him, too. That's the only thing you people admire: you don't give a straw for my brains!

CYRUS. Your conceit is absolutely insufferable!

CYPRIAN. I think you even get a kind of kick out of seeing him make a shambles of our barnyard! You're willing to take anything from him!

THE FATHER. What else can we do, Cype? The lords will always be on top.

CYPRIAN. But we can get out from under if we've got

enough gumption to. I'll be damned if *I'm* going to go on like this—and when I say I'll be damned, I'm willing to mean it *literally*.

THE MOTHER. Oh, Cyprian: what are you saying?

CYPRIAN. I'm not going to be a priest, I may as well tell you now—I'm going to work for Merlin.

THE MOTHER (*crossing herself*). Oh, Cyprian!

CYRUS. I knew that that book was Black Art!

CYPRIAN. It's power—the only kind of power that's open to people like us.

CYRUS. Merlin is an evil spirit.

CYPRIAN. So is Rody the Rumpot—and evil spirit for evil spirit, I'd rather be Merlin's man, because Merlin has more brains.

THE MOTHER. Do you want to work for Satan, Cyprian?

CYPRIAN. Why not? If Satan will help us, why shouldn't we be his vassals? It's plain enough that God won't protect us——

THE MOTHER. Cyprian!

CYPRIAN. —Jesus Christ is not on our side——

CYRUS. Hold your tongue!

CYPRIAN. —if our priest is his agent on earth—Father Fatso is hand and glove with old Rumpot.

CYRUS. I suspected, when you were out all night, that you were going to those Black Sabbaths!

CYPRIAN. *W*e call them People's Rallies. It's the only place a peasant is free. We say whatever we like and we enjoy ourselves however we like.

THE MOTHER (*sinking to a chair*). Oh, don't let him do it: we'll all be hanged!

CYPRIAN. Listen, Mother: I made him so sore tonight that who knows but he may hang us, anyhow. When I'm gone, all you'll have to do is tell him I've been a bad boy and that I've run away and good riddance.

THE MOTHER. What if it got back where you were?

CYPRIAN. I won't compromise you: I'll take a false name.

CYRUS. Let him go. We'll be better off without him.

CYPRIAN. Let me take this bread, Mother: it's all I need. (*He picks up the loaves from the hearth and stuffs them into his pocket.*)

THE MOTHER. You haven't any clean clothes.

CYPRIAN (*picking up his hat and coat from the bench*). I don't care so much about clothes as you. (*Embracing the old man*) Goodby, Father: I wish I could help you. May God protect you!—(*He pulls himself up, then gives them a black look.*) I ought to say, may Somebody Else protect you!

*He goes out.*

THE MOTHER. Oh, Cyrus: what shall we do?

CYRUS (*coming over to comfort her*). It's all for the best, I think. There's no telling what might have happened.

THE FATHER (*looking out the door*). Ha! that one is mine all right!

SCENE 2

*A clearing in the forest: a background of trees. On the left a large tree-trunk rises, with a dim mass of leaves above; on the right a full moon in the sky, and bright moonlight over everything. Cyprian comes in on the right.*

CYPRIAN. Those mountains are farther away than you think—I ought to have brought more to eat. I'll look like a tramp when I get there. (*He sits down against the trunk of the tree.*) And what if he turns me away? What real qualifications have I? A smattering of magic that I got from books. We didn't have real magic at our Sabbaths —I know that perfectly well. What we tried to pretend was Satan was just old Matt Fox, the cobbler, blacked up, with a couple of phony horns and a false face on his behind. If Merlin won't give me a job, I'll just have to take to the roads. I've got nobody to turn to now.

A VOICE (*silvery, sweet and mild*). Why don't you turn to the moon?

CYPRIAN. Who is that?

*A figure that has been lying on the ground on the other side of the stage lifts itself to a partially sitting posture, propping itself behind with its arms, as if unwilling to rise from its recumbent position. It has a masculine but soft and pale face and is dressed in pale clothes, which shine with a greenish radiance. There is a pillow behind him on the ground.*

THE FIGURE. A devotee of the moon.

CYPRIAN. What good can the moon do you?

THE FIGURE. What good? You can bathe in the moonlight till it soaks you to your inmost soul.

CYPRIAN. Does the moonlight have—magic properties?

THE MOONLIGHT DRUNKARD. Magic properties? Oh, dear, yes! It charms you—it utterly enchants you: you never need to worry about anything.

CYPRIAN. But what do you eat out here?

THE MOONLIGHT DRUNKARD. Fruits and nuts in season.

CYPRIAN. You don't hunt or fish?

THE MOONLIGHT DRUNKARD. Oh, dear, no: I never do anything so active. In the daytime I sleep and at night I bask. I hardly ever stir from my clearing here.

CYPRIAN. What do you do when the moon is waning?

THE MOONLIGHT DRUNKARD. I look forward to its swelling again. It gives life a delightful rhythm.

CYPRIAN. But what if the weather is bad?

THE MOONLIGHT DRUNKARD. That just postpones the enjoyment: it gives one the touch of uncertainty without which no pleasure is perfect.

CYPRIAN. But what do you do with your mind?

THE MOONLIGHT DRUNKARD. My dear boy, I indulge my reveries—I steep myself in wonderful dreams—and no one ever comes to destroy them.

CYPRIAN (*after a moment's thought*). Do you really find that that's enough?

THE MOONLIGHT DRUNKARD. Oh, someday, of course, I'm going back—when I've drunk in enough of the moonlight. I'll be luminous, I'll shine for them then—they won't be able to reject or deny me. (*Getting up*) You can see that I'm beginning to glow already?

CYPRIAN. Will that really give you power?

THE MOONLIGHT DRUNKARD. Power of a kind, yes—or call it sanctity, rather.

CYPRIAN. Sanctity isn't enough: the holiest priest in our province was burnt as a heretic.

THE MOONLIGHT DRUNKARD. Well, what can one hope for? The strong are the strong—the vulgar are the vulgar. They'll always make the wars and the laws——

CYPRIAN. That's what my father says.

THE MOONLIGHT DRUNKARD. But *we* can always evade them.

CYPRIAN. That's just what I told him, but, after all——

THE MOONLIGHT DRUNKARD (*coming over to him*). I'm sure that you've had the idea—I can see you're a solitary: a being who can do without other people. Do let me persuade you to join me here. (*Taking him by the arm*) You couldn't begin on a better night. See how perfectly divine it is! We can just lie and drench ourselves. I don't think you'd bore me—but, of course, if you did, you could go to another clearing.

CYPRIAN (*getting up*). I've got to be on my way—I'm going to Merlin's castle.

THE MOONLIGHT DRUNKARD. A dreary old man and a fake, besides! You mustn't believe in Merlin. (*Taking him by the arm and leading him away from the tree*) Come out from under that tree—you're missing all the good moonlight.

CYPRIAN. It isn't enough to evade them: you have to oppose them, too.

THE MOONLIGHT DRUNKARD. Why oppose them? One has always one's own domain—the only domain that counts—(*tapping his forehead*) in here.

CYPRIAN. What do you do when they hunt?

THE MOONLIGHT DRUNKARD. Oh, I hide, and they don't harm me.—Don't you feel it?—how relaxing it is? Just lie down for a moment and see how it soothes one—how it melts all one's stubborn resistance.

CYPRIAN. I don't want to hide from them—I want to stand up to them!

THE MOONLIGHT DRUNKARD. I can't see that point of view: it's certain to end in defeat—especially for a sensitive boy like you—you don't look like much of a warrior.

CYPRIAN. There's another kind of power—there's Merlin.

THE MOONLIGHT DRUNKARD. Oh, cleverness can get you a certain way, but you have to keep it up all the time, and I find it such a strain to be clever. In any case, I can tell you that Merlin's distinctly *not*.

CYPRIAN. Well, I've made up my mind to try it, and I want to do some more miles tonight.

THE MOONLIGHT DRUNKARD. I'm sorry to have you go, but of course one doesn't need companions: one is thoroughly happy alone.

CYPRIAN. Goodby. Pleasant dreams!

THE MOONLIGHT DRUNKARD. Thank you. You may care to come back in time. If you do, you might bring a pillow-case—that's the only convenience you'll need. (*He holds up his pillow and fluffs it out.*) You can stuff it with grass and leaves. *I* prefer feathers, but soft leaves and grass will do for a country boy like you. (*He puts the pillow down and prepares to stretch out again.*) I admire you

25

tremendously, you know, making all that long trip alone, but the same thing that takes you there may eventually bring you back—and I'll always be glad to see you.

*The background becomes dark. Cyprian stands in a spotlight.*

CYPRIAN. What use are my mind and my will if I can't find a fulcrum to move things? I might better be buried in some monastery than to stupefy myself like him and to lose all the sense of debasement or pride, powerlessness or strength! Let it never be said of *me* that I stood neither with God nor His enemies!—Satan: Great Rebel Angel! I choose you for my patron: hear my prayer. Bring me to Merlin's castle—teach me those secrets of power that can make me the equal of barons and bishops—let me share them all with all their penalties!

## SCENE 3

*Merlin's waiting-room. A door in the right-hand wall admits the magician's clients; another, right of center in the back wall, leads into Merlin's study. A young man, a rather dull-looking blond, sits at a little table, to the right of this second door, on which are a strip of parchment, a sand-shaker and an inkpot with a long quill pen. At his left, facing the audience and further front, is a long bench with a back, on which four clients are sitting. The first three, from right to left, are a pale and worried young woman of about the same social status as Cyprian; a sullen elderly man, booted and bearded and of rough stock; and a pretty anemic woman, better dressed than the other two. These three are sitting side by side, but a considerable space has been left between the anemic woman and her neighbor on the other side, who sits close to the end of the bench. This person is tall and well-built, with an aquiline face and completely black skin.*

26

*He is naked to the waist and wears only dark green trunks. He
has pointed ears, long sharp claws on his hands and large cloven
hoofs for feet. These hoofs are immediately striking, because—
though the other visitors are nervously sitting up—he has
settled himself, quite free from self-consciousness, with one
knee crossed over the other, so that his feet are thrust into
the foreground. His demeanor is dignified and his aspect rather
saturnine, but he is alert, with an accent of irony, to everything
that is going on.*

*A knock is heard at the visitors' door.*

THE YOUNG MAN AT THE TABLE. Come in.

*Cyprian timidly enters. His clothes are the worse for travel,
and he looks very shabby beside the others. He carries his hat
in his hand.*

THE YOUNG MAN. You want to see the magician?

CYPRIAN. Yes, sir.

THE YOUNG MAN. Your name?

CYPRIAN (*pulling himself up after the Christian name and
carefully enunciating his alias*). Cyprian—Leclerc.

*The Young Man, who has heard many bogus names, gives
Cyprian a shrewd look.*

THE YOUNG MAN (*repeating the name with a mocking
implication*). Cyprian—Leclerc. (*He gestures with his pen
toward the bench.*) Take a seat over there.

*Cyprian, acutely self-conscious, goes over and, seeing the
Black Man, conceals his astonishment but hesitates a moment,
then sits down beside the Anemic Woman. She has been watching him since he came in and at once shows a lively interest,
smiling and displaying, as she does so, two sharp rodentlike
incisors. He tries to return her smile, then glances aside at the
Black Man, who regards him with an experienced impassive eye.
Cyprian drops his gaze to the Black Man's feet, which he has
not noticed before, stares for a moment, then looks away. The
Anemic Woman catches his eye.*

THE ANEMIC WOMAN (*being charming*). A stranger here?

CYPRIAN. Yes, ma'am.

THE ANEMIC WOMAN. From far?

CYPRIAN. It's about sixty leagues.

THE ANEMIC WOMAN. I hope you've found a place to stay.

CYPRIAN. Not yet, ma'am—but I'm told there's an inn.

THE ANEMIC WOMAN. Not a decent one—absurd though it seems when one thinks what a lot of great people come here to see the magician.

CYPRIAN. Oh, anything will do for me.

THE ANEMIC WOMAN. I don't think you'd be happy there. The bad thing about the inn is that one can't be sure of getting out alive.

CYPRIAN. I'm glad to know that: I'll avoid it.

THE ANEMIC WOMAN. I'm staying here with relatives, not far away, and I'm sure that they'd be glad to put you up.

CYPRIAN. Thank you very much, ma'am, but I'm used to sleeping out of doors, and the nights are still quite warm.

THE YOUNG MAN (*his attention attracted by the sound of this conversation—to Cyprian*). You must take your place at the end of the line. (*He points with the end of his pen.*)

*Cyprian, much embarrassed—as the woman gives him a quick sympathetic smile—gets up and goes to the end of the bench. The Black Man moves to make room for him.*

*The door to the study opens, and a young girl comes in: Janet, the magician's daughter. She is pretty, neat, businesslike, brisk; from her waist hangs a mirror on a cord and a bunch of large keys. Everybody turns to look.*

JANET (*to the young man at the table*). Don't let in any more people. He's not a bit well today.

*He nods and hands her the parchment. She comes over to the girl at the right of the bench.*

JANET (*consulting the list*). Isabeau Minguet?

28

THE GIRL (*getting up*). Yes, miss.

JANET. What do you want to see the magician about?

THE GIRL. Could I speak to you alone, please, miss?

*Janet leads her away from the bench in the direction of the study door, and their conversation is seen but not heard. The girl, in great agitation, explains something with vehement gestures; Janet answers briefly, with composure, or merely shakes her head.*

THE BLACK MAN (*who has been watching this—to Cyprian*). He won't do abortions. She won't get anywhere with that.

CYPRIAN. Oh, really?—of course—I see.

*The girl begins to weep, and her pleading becomes more passionate; Janet cuts her short with a word not unkind but decisive.*

THE BLACK MAN. That's Janet, the magician's daughter. She goes through the applicants first and weeds out the cases they won't take.

CYPRIAN. I see.

*Janet dismisses the girl, who goes out in bitter disappointment. Janet comes back to the bench and interrogates the bearded man.*

JANET (*consulting her list*). Mathurin Leboeuf?

THE BEARDED MAN (*standing up*). Yes, miss.

JANET. What do you want?

THE BEARDED MAN. I've got an old sick horse, miss, and I just want a dose of something strong to put him out of his misery.

JANET. Why don't you kill him some simpler way?

THE BEARDED MAN. I couldn't bear to: he's like a friend; it would be like killing one of the family. I just want to put him to sleep.

JANET. We can't give out deadly drugs except in very special cases. We can't give you poison for a horse.

*She turns away.*

THE BEARDED MAN. It will break my wife's heart!——

*She pays no attention to him, and he has to go.*

29

JANET (*to the Anemic Woman, who quickly rises*). Valérie de Châteaumort?

THE ANEMIC WOMAN. I should like to get a sleeping-draught—nothing deadly (*smiling*): just something to quiet my nerves.

JANET. You have difficulty in getting to sleep?

THE ANEMIC WOMAN (*smiling, but under a strain*). I literally haven't had a night's sleep for almost two months now, and I really don't think I can stand it much longer.

JANET. Why have you been so nervous?

THE ANEMIC WOMAN. Our part of the world has been very unsettled—peasant uprisings and that sort of thing. My husband was murdered last summer. I've come on here for a visit to relatives to get away for awhile—and of course I've heard about Merlin, and I thought he might give me a sedative.

JANET. You may go in—but please don't stay too long: the magician has been ill.

THE ANEMIC WOMAN. Thank you.

*She goes into the magician's study.*

JANET (*nodding in a friendly way to the Black Man, who does not rise*). Hello, Mr. B. You may go in when she comes out. (*Passing on to Cyprian*) Cyprian Leclerc?

CYPRIAN (*standing up*). Yes, miss.

JANET. What do you want to see the magician about?

CYPRIAN. I—I came about a job.

JANET. I'm afraid there's no opening here: we have all the staff we need. What sort of work do you want?

CYPRIAN. I'd like to learn the profession.

JANET. Oh, my father has a pupil already—(*indicating the young man at the table*) Mr. Claude is my father's assistant.

CYPRIAN. He wouldn't take on an apprentice?

JANET. You read and write?

CYPRIAN. Oh, yes.

JANET. What languages?

CYPRIAN. Latin as well as French. I thought I might have some qualifications. I've studied the subject a little.

JANET. You can talk to him about it, but don't stay too long.

*She turns and goes over to Claude. She checks through the list with him, explaining each name.*

MR. B. (*to Cyprian*). Look out for that woman who was sitting beside you: she's a vampire, and she thinks you're a juicy item. Don't on any account spend a night under the same roof with her.

CYPRIAN. I see—— (*After a moment's pause, not wanting to expose his ignorance*) I wasn't sure.

MR. B. She's evidently on a hot spot at home—they've probably got wise to her there. She's desperate: she wants her blood badly. She's trying to get a sleeping-draught to put her victims to sleep. The young girl knew that very well, but they don't like to offend such creatures. The magician will give her something that will keep her prospects awake instead of knocking them out. (*Cyprian is impressed, but does not know what to say.*)—That farmer wanted to poison his wife.

CYPRIAN. Are you—in the profession, too?

MR. B. Magic? No: not exactly; but I know something about such things.—You come from Tancarville way?

*At this point, Janet has reached Cyprian on the list; she looks over toward him, and Claude looks around at him with an interest that he has not shown before.*

CYPRIAN. Yes, I do. (*Made uneasy by this stroke of insight*) How did you know?

MR. B. They all have that whine in their voices.

CYPRIAN. Yes: I suppose we do.

MR. B. You not so much as the others.—You're not fortunate in your liege lord, I understand.

CYPRIAN (*with a sneering smile*). No: we're certainly not.

*The Vampire comes out of the study, clasping a little bottle and obviously much elated.*

THE VAMPIRE (*smiling and nodding to Janet*). Thank you so much.

*Janet, in a businesslike way, nods back. The woman goes out through the other door.*

MR. B. (*to Cyprian*). She's all set up, you see.

JANET. All right, Mr. B. (*She returns to the table.*)

MR. B. (*getting up, to Cyprian*). You've made the best choice, if you can carry it through. This girl (*nodding toward Janet*) is the one to stand in with. Claude, the young man at the table, has been picked to take over when Merlin dies, but Janet is supposed to marry him, and she'll still be the brains of the business. Good luck.

CYPRIAN. Thank you, sir.

*The Black Man nods and goes in, immediately followed by Janet. A moment after the door is shut, Claude, who has been annotating the list, glances in Cyprian's direction.*

CLAUDE. You ought to have cleaned your boots before you came to see the magician.

CYPRIAN. I'm sorry, sir: I did my best. I've come a long way on foot.

*Claude returns to his writing; then, without raising his eyes, speaks again.*

CLAUDE. You wouldn't go to see your liege lord in your working clothes like that, and in such an unkempt state, and you oughtn't to come here.

CYPRIAN. I'm sorry. These are all I have.

*Claude is shaking sand on the fresh ink. He neither glances at Cyprian nor answers, but picks up the parchment and blows off the sand with a puff that suggests contempt.*

## SCENE 4

*The magician's study: a great Gothic room. On the right, a stone fireplace; in the back at the extreme right, a large open double door that gives on a stone terrace, upon which falls the light of an autumn morning; high ogival windows in the back wall; a door in the left-hand wall into the waiting-room. Below the windows in the back wall there are formidable tiers of shelves that are partly filled with bulky folios, partly with globes, retorts, pestles and mortars, bottles and glass jars with dubious-looking objects inside; on top are a stuffed owl and the mounted skeleton of a monkey. Between these shelves and the double door is a tapestry with the figure of the Arthurian Merlin; to the right of the fireplace, a portrait of Albertus Magnus. Above the stone mantel itself hangs the head of a gigantic elk: the animal's naked skull, with wild glass eyes and branching antlers, mounted on a dummy neck. On either side of the door in the left-hand wall hang an astrological chart with the signs of the Zodiac, and a mycological chart, depicting in vivid colors the various kinds of mushrooms. From the ceiling a large stuffed crocodile is suspended by the tail and neck, with a spidery wrought-iron lamp dangling on a chain from its middle. Dark carved high-backed chairs: two at the left and one standing against the tapestry, directly in front of the figure of Merlin. There is a table of medium size up against the right-hand set of shelves; and in front of the fireplace, a large work table or desk, half-facing the audience, with, behind it, a kind of carved throne, in which the magician sits.*

*Merlin is a dry old man, with a small and well-trimmed white beard, wearing a skull-cap and a long black robe that has collar and cuffs of fur and a cabalistic design in brocade.*

*Janet ushers in Mr. B.*

JANET. You know Mr. B., Father.
MERLIN. Ah, yes—come in. (*Mr. B. bows.*) Pray sit down.

*He indicates the visitors' chair, in which Mr. B. sits. Janet takes her place at her father's left, behind the end of the table. The magician's tone to his visitor is patronizing, a little malicious.*

MERLIN. I'd been wondering how it was going with you. A devil who reforms in earnest, that's a very uncommon thing—a case that I watch with interest. I suppose that your charming—er—companion has made the step quite worthwhile? I haven't the honor of knowing her.

MR. B. It's impossible for me to speak of my wife. You know that I'm not equipped to do justice to that kind of beauty.

MERLIN. A paragon, I understand. It was her pitying you, wasn't it? that touched you so. Yes, that's something that few women would be capable of.

JANET. That's not very kind, Father.

MERLIN. Oh, I didn't mean it in that way! But when women fall in love with devils, they usually like them because they're bad, not because they're sorry for them.

MR. B. She has nothing but love in her heart—that's something I'd never found and that of course I can hardly grasp. I can only perceive that it's true and be amazed that your fallen humanity has been able to produce this wonder.

MERLIN. And you're able to enjoy that, eh?—with such a different—moral background. You're never dissatisfied?

MR. B. Dissatisfied, no—I have chosen it. One does feel a little empty at times. For her to be generous and gentle is to realize her own nature—but, in my case, I can only refrain—refrain from the opposite qualities—and it does make one's life rather negative. Of course I was always negative, but I was negative before, as you'll understand (*with a deprecatory smile*), in a more active and positive way.

34

MERLIN. Very curious! An odd situation!—And what brings you here today?

MR. B. (*somewhat embarrassed*). My wife—is ill.

MERLIN. Oh! Have you any idea what it is?

MR. B. I'm afraid I know only too well what it is.

MERLIN. And what is your diagnosis?

MR. B. I hate like heaven to admit it, but I don't think there's any doubt . . .

MERLIN. Pray tell me.

MR. B. The hoof and mouth disease.

MERLIN. The cattle plague? (*Hardly repressing a grin and glancing at the visitor's feet*) Ah, that would be a most peculiar hazard of your most peculiar case.

JANET. How dreadful for you, Mr. B.!

MR. B. (*to Janet*). It's not a fatal disease, of course, but it reminds us both of what I am—and there's already enough to remind her.

MERLIN. Though you did cut off your horns, didn't you?

MR. B. And I tried wearing clothes for awhile. But that kind of thing's a mistake. It's bound to be degrading, I found, to pretend to be something one isn't—even though what one is is—unpopular. So I go about frankly like this. Nobody, of course, will come near us, but then, they wouldn't before.

JANET. How mean of them! and she'd done so much for them!

MR. B. (*shrugging*). They've been told they ought to shun the Devil. But what worries me is that, if people find out, they may treat her like a kind of leper and even drive us away. There's been some talk of that already.

MERLIN. And you've come to me for a cure?

MR. B. I hoped you might know some remedy—though, of course, if my wife's disease is something that's been sent by *Him* (*jerking his head toward the heavens*), there's nothing one can do about it. He may think that I'm trying to evade my doom.

MERLIN. It would be painful to have to face that. In justice to her, you'd have to leave her.

MR. B. But that would present a problem—with everybody here against her. She'd have to go somewhere else.

JANET (*to her father*). How about that new ointment?

MERLIN. No reason he shouldn't try it: we've sometimes had good results—(*to Mr. B.*) but I can't guarantee anything.

JANET. He's not well himself, Mr. B.—I mustn't let him talk too long.

MR. B. (*getting up*). I'm sorry to hear that.

MERLIN. Oh, I'm quite all right. I get a bit faint at times, but I think it's just the dull old world that's losing its interest for me and that's finally fading out. One has seen things so often at my age—though I must say, in all my experience, I've never had a case like yours. I really should like to live long enough to hear what happens about it. Please let me know how it goes. Put the ointment on twice a day. I hope that your determined effort —but I suppose I mustn't say that: if it is part of the Divine Justice for God not to let you repent, I suppose that I oughtn't to say that I hope your wife will recover.

JANET. *I* hope so, Mr. B. I'll bring the ointment myself and tell her what to do.

MR. B. Better not; she'd be very glad to see you, but it would get you badly thought-of, if people knew.

MERLIN (*to Mr. B.*). Tell Claude to make you up some double digamma.

MR. B. (*bowing to Merlin*). Thank you, sir. Good morning.

MERLIN. Good morning.

*He goes out through the waiting-room.*

JANET. I think I ought to go to see her.

MERLIN. You mustn't think of going.

*Janet glances after Mr. B. and waits till he is out the door.*

JANET. You weren't very sympathetic.

MERLIN. *Can* one be sympathetic with devils?

JANET. *I am* with him—and then, his wife.

MERLIN. What is she like, his wife?—to give her that courtesy title. Is she beautiful, as he says?

JANET. She's the most extraordinary woman. She's not beautiful in the ordinary sense. In fact, I suppose she's ugly. She has a long pointed nose and clear little yellow eyes and several large warts on her face. She's big-boned, and she looks ungainly, but she always moves around with ease and she has rather small hands and feet. People have always wondered about her—she's much the cleverest person in the village, and they thought she might be a witch, but really she's a perfect angel, and they've had to recognize that—at least, they did before she married Mr. B.

MERLIN. She can't be as good as he thinks. He represents absolute evil himself, and of course he can't accept Christ, so he comes across a woman as ugly as himself and imagines she's absolutely good. I'll wager she makes him pay for everything she's suffered on his account.

JANET. I don't believe she does.

MERLIN. Women always do.

JANET. I know that you're bitter because Mother left you, but I'm sure she really loves Mr. B.

MERLIN. Bitter? I've got along better alone.

JANET. Not quite alone. How about me? Poor Mr. B. has no daughter.—And, Father, I do think you might spare him your smugness about the Divine Justice, when, after all, our own position isn't exactly regular.

MERLIN. It's as respectable as I can make it, and I don't want you getting involved with that devil and his paramour.

JANET. It's not *their* fault they couldn't get married. A devil can't go into a church.

37

MERLIN. Anybody else today?

JANET. Just one—a young man who wants a job.

MERLIN. There's no point in seeing *him*.

JANET. Well, we do really need someone else—with me doing so much of your work and Claude doing so much of mine.

MERLIN. The time has come, I think, to give Claude a little more responsibility. He was complaining the other day.

JANET. I am: I've been having him make outside calls.

MERLIN. And if you're actually going to marry him, I wish you'd do it before I die. He lacks finesse, of course, but he won't do anything silly.

JANET. Eventually, you know, Father, after you're gone, we *shall* have to have a new man—Claude will need an assistant. And this young fellow seems rather bright. He says that he knows Latin.

MERLIN. All right: let's have a look at him.

JANET (*in the doorway, to Cyprian, outside*). You can come in now.

*Cyprian appears at the door, and Janet leads him to Merlin's desk.*

MERLIN. Well, young man, what can you do? What we need here, if we really need anything, is somebody to trim the hedges.

CYPRIAN. I think I could do that, sir: I've had some experience as a gardener. But what I wanted to ask about was whether you'd take an apprentice. I've had some training as a scholar.

MERLIN. I've never had a real apprentice, and I don't believe I want one now.—*Te dícis erudítum ésse. Loquerísne Latíne?*

CYPRIAN. *Latíne sáne lóquor. Líbros mágicos légi.* (*Nodding toward the portrait*) *Albértum Mágnum béne cognósco.*

MERLIN. *Écce fília méa Latíne légit et lóquitur.*

CYPRIAN. *Itáne est?*

JANET. *Íta.*

MERLIN. And why is your heart set on studying magic? You imagine it's a glamorous profession?

CYPRIAN. Because it gives knowledge and power.

MERLIN. Not so much as you think, my boy. A few drugs that do very simple things: make you dizzy or make you sleepy—and a few that can cure certain ailments —though you can't absolutely depend on them.

CYPRIAN. But there *are* supernatural forces?

MERLIN. Do you think so?

*He reaches down and turns a handle set in the side of his chair. A skeleton, with a shrill gibbering shriek, leaps into the double doorway, dances a moment, then disappears.*

MERLIN (*grinning*). Scare you?

*Cyprian cannot help glancing at the handle on Merlin's chair.*

JANET (*to Cyprian*). You saw the wires.

CYPRIAN. No, I didn't.

JANET. Of course, you did.

MERLIN. Just to make an impression, you know—get rid of persistent callers.

JANET (*to Cyprian*). He didn't mean that for you. He just uses it for simple people.

MERLIN. Sit down, boy—that chair over there. (*He indicates the chair which stands with its back against the tapestry.*)

CYPRIAN. Thank you, sir.

*The magician turns another handle, and a pair of stuffed gloves with long fingers shoot out from two slits in the tapestry and clasp themselves on Cyprian's face. He starts up; the hands go back.*

MERLIN. A little more convincing, eh?

CYPRIAN (*anxious to play up to Merlin*). That really scared me to death!

*Janet smiles to let Cyprian understand that she considers these devices childish and that she knows he was not frightened.*

MERLIN. But there's always a gimmick you'll find. It's all just a bag of tricks. You mustn't overestimate us, my boy.

CYPRIAN. But in Hermes and Albertus and the Cabala you read about authentic spirits.

MERLIN. Oh, that's all in the books, I know—I've got it all there on the shelves. But I've never cared to do very much with it. One can have most unpleasant experiences —if anything happens at all—as the magician before me here did. Those creatures get out of hand—and it's not really worth the risk. In fact, the whole literature of magic is a veritable *Historia Calamitatum*, eh? And the Philosopher's Stone and alchemy, that you read about in those writers—that's all absolute nonsense. Nobody has ever succeeded in making gold out of the baser metals, and nobody ever will! All those old retorts and things (*gesturing toward the shelves*) are nothing but curiosities. I've never had the mania for miracles, as some of my confrères have. I'm not the real Merlin, you know: he died long ago, if he ever lived. Merlin is just a trade-name. Such power as a wizard has nowadays is mainly a matter of pure prestige —and the most worthwhile thing he can gain in this agitated chaotic age, is just to get people to let him alone. One does enjoy a certain position: even the nobles respect one——

*A tumult at the door of the waiting-room.*

TANCARVILLE'S VOICE (*bellowing*). "Wait"? Why should I wait? I come first, and don't you forget it!

CLAUDE'S VOICE (*expostulating*). Allow me to announce you, my lord.

*Tancarville, followed by Claude, bursts in. Claude, during the first part of the scene that follows, keeps safely in the background, not far from the door.*

TANCARVILLE. There you are, you village quack! What kind of a goddam magician are you! That love-philtre you gave me was lousy—it wouldn't raise a lech on a monkey!

MERLIN (*rising behind his desk*). What is the matter, my lord.

TANCARVILLE. I've just told you what was the matter! I asked you for an aphrodisiac to work on the Lady Elinor, and she's taken the whole bottle and is just as standoffish as ever.

MERLIN. You're sure that she's really taken it?

TANCARVILLE. Didn't I bribe her maid? She's had it three nights in her posset—and when I took her out hawking this morning, she couldn't have been blinder to me if she'd been wearing a goddam hood like the hawks!

MERLIN. She may be anemic, my lord. In such cases, our potions are powerless——

TANCARVILLE. Anemic, my eye: she's as juicy as a beef-steak! She's got me steaming and seething. If you could see her hips when she's sitting her horse, you wouldn't talk about anemic!—and her bubbies just like great big plum-puddings bursting right out of her bodice!—I wake up in the morning and think about them, and oh-h-h! (*He gives a roar.*)

MERLIN. My daughter is present, my lord!

TANCARVILLE (*glancing at Janet*). Well, that little old maid is no good to me. I hope you don't call *those* breasts! And she's probably got extra tits turning up on the wrong parts of her body the way they say these witches all have. I don't want your broom-handle daughter: what I want is the Lady Elinor. Somebody has put a hex on her so she won't give me a tumble—and you've goddam well got to take it off! Hex her the other way!

MERLIN. I don't know about that, my lord——

TANCARVILLE. You don't? Why the hell don't you? If you're a wizard, you can do it—if you can't, you're a fraud—and I'll have your liege lord, who's a friend of mine, take your crazy little castle away and string you up on your own turret!

MERLIN. You're a famous hunter, my lord. Do you see that stag up there? (*Showing him the mounted head above the fireplace*) He was given me by the Wild Huntsman— you've heard of the Wild Huntsman?—Well, *he* happens to be a friend of *mine*——

TANCARVILLE (*staring at the head in a daze and momentarily given pause*). That's not a real stag!

MERLIN. The Wild Huntsman's not real either, in the commonplace sense of the word—that is, he's not flesh and blood. But offend him, and I give you warning that your own flesh and blood will feel it: the Huntsman can curse and can kill! You've heard the story of St. Hubert— how he was hunting and met a great stag with a crucifix between its horns, and how this stag brought his soul to God. Well, if you don't show respect to magicians, you're going to meet a different kind of stag (*nodding toward the head*), who'll take you straight to the Devil!

TANCARVILLE (*softening his tone*). All right, but listen here: I tell you this thing is destroying me—it's frustrating me and making me brutal, it's making me drink too much! —It's got me so goddam hot I go out and grab the peasant wenches the way I haven't done in years, and that's ruining my authority in my own fief! If you stand in with all these devils, why can't you make Elinor love me?

MERLIN. My lord, let me give you a piece of advice. There's no spell in the magician's armory that can operate contrary to Nature. If you want to please the Lady Elinor, you must be gracious and gentle with her.

TANCARVILLE. What the hell do you mean, "gentle"? I'm a baron, ain't I? That's gentle.

MERLIN. I mean you must try to charm her. Surprise her by turning up sober. Make her feel you are heart-broken about her. Don't be sulky—just sigh and look sorrowful.

TANCARVILLE. You want to make a monkey out of me?

MERLIN. Better a monkey than a drunken bear—I speak harshly, but I'm trying to help you.

TANCARVILLE (*after a moment of stupor, bursting out again*). Do you dare to talk to Tancarville like that, you swindling old doddering faker? (*Leaning across the table and taking him by the throat*) Give me something that will do the trick or I'll tear out your impudent tongue!

*Cyprian and Janet rush to intervene, he going around the nearer end of the table and seizing the Baron's hands and she, on the other side, pulling at his right arm. Claude runs up to the table, but not in time to accomplish anything.*

JANET. Stop that at once! He's got a weak heart, and if you kill him, you'll get nothing done.

*Tancarville lets go of Merlin, who falls back into his chair, dropping his head on the table.*

TANCARVILLE (*planting himself in the chair in front of the tapestry*). I'm going to sit right here till you give me some satisfaction!

JANET (*to Cyprian*). *Maní́culam vérte!—maní́culam vérte!*

TANCARVILLE. What's the matter with a sleeping-draft? Don't tell me you haven't got that! I can have her when she passes out.

*Cyprian turns the handle on Merlin's chair, and the hands shoot out of the tapestry and clasp the Baron's face.*

TANCARVILLE (*leaping out of the chair*). God's wounds! (*He turns around and sees no one there.*)

JANET (*standing over her father*). If you want to leave this castle alive, you'd better go right away. (*To Cyprian*) *Álteram maní́culam vérte.*

*She lifts the old man from the table and makes him sit back in the chair. He is limp, and his eyes are closed. She loosens his gown and his shirt at the throat and tries to check on his heart. Claude comes around and helps her.*

CYPRIAN. I'll see that he leaves! (*He gets hold of the other handle.*)

TANCARVILLE (*to Cyprian*). Haven't I seen you before? By God, it's that booklearned brat whose mother I've just been to bed with!

CYPRIAN (*speaking toward the tapestry, as if he were summoning a devil*). All right, let him have it, Astaroth: we've got to pay him for that! (*In the direction of the double doors*) You, too: come along, Cannagosta!

TANCARVILLE (*falling back*). You filthy witches and ghouls!

CYPRIAN. Come on, boys: go for him, throttle him! Give him the bum's rush!

TANCARVILLE (*on his way out, protecting his throat with his hands*). I'll have you drawn and quartered, you apes!

*He retreats through the waiting-room, Cyprian following after.*

JANET (*to Claude*). Get some brandy.

*He takes down a bottle from the shelves.*

*She picks up the mirror at her girdle and holds it to Merlin's lips.*

JANET. I'm afraid he's gone. (*She takes the brandy and tries to pour some down his throat, while Claude helps her to hold him.*) Can you drink this, Father?—Can you hear me? —He can't take it—his teeth are set.

*They stand looking down at the inert body. Cyprian comes back.*

JANET (*to Cyprian*). He's dead: that beast has killed him. —Claude, go and get the priest.

CLAUDE (*on his way to the door*). We can't be sure that he'll come.

JANET. Try to make him: we've done him some favors, and he knows we don't practise Black Magic.

*Claude goes out.*

JANET (*to Cyprian*). Poor father! He sounded second-rate just now, but he was really a good man.

CYPRIAN. He certainly stood up to that bullying lout.

JANET. He was shrewd about handling people, and he never would take any nonsense. This was really the first time he ever failed. It was just that his strength had given out.

CYPRIAN. I was very much impressed by him today.

JANET. You weren't really, were you? I thought you were disappointed. It's true he didn't like to take chances, and that kept him from doing original work.—I must put him in his room. Will you help me?

*They pick up Merlin's body, she taking it under the arms and he lifting the feet.*

JANET. We've got all the equipment, of course.

CYPRIAN. For burying him, you mean?

JANET. No: for the other kind of thing—the magic that's supernatural.

CYPRIAN (*excited*). You have?

JANET. Oh, yes: of course.

CYPRIAN. That's what I want to learn!

JANET (*steering toward the double door*). Let's carry him out through here.—He never cared about real magic. Poor father!

# ACT II

*Merlin's study: late morning of New Year's Day the following January. The double doors are closed, and there is a fire in the fireplace. The chair which was formerly in front of the tapestry has been moved—for the accommodation of visitors— to the opposite side of the desk from that where the magician sat. Merlin's cap and robe hang on a peg in the right corner; a long ruler and a string with a piece of chalk attached are lying on the table against the wall. Cyprian and Claude at the desk—Claude in Merlin's place, Cyprian at the end of the table that is farthest away from the audience. They have strips of parchment before them. Cyprian is now more correctly dressed.*

CYPRIAN.—And now, what drugs do we need?

CLAUDE (*consulting a list*). We're almost out of bella-donna—mandragora and cinquefoil, too.—We've been out of bats' blood for a long time now, and we ought to get some right away.

CYPRIAN. Do you really think bats' blood's important?

CLAUDE. It's needed for Number 19 and some of the other formulas.

CYPRIAN. I have a feeling that that's one of those witch's ingredients that's just put in for effect.

CLAUDE. It's always been regarded as basic.

CYPRIAN. Janet is of my opinion—about bats' blood and snakes' tongues and all that. Why don't we try it without them and see whether the drugs don't work just as well?

CLAUDE. Janet is a woman and squeamish. She didn't

46

like to catch the bats. But now you can do that. There are plenty in the tower.

CYPRIAN. Very well: why not make an experiment? Why not try out Number 19 with and without bats' blood and see what results we get? (*Referring to his list*) Well, that seems to be all, doesn't it? One thing, though: it's New Year's today, and Janet and I were thinking that it might be a good idea to inaugurate the year 1464 by cleaning the place up a bit.

CLAUDE (*suspiciously*). What do you mean precisely?

CYPRIAN. Why, getting rid of some of this old paraphernalia. That skeleton, for example. (*He goes out through the double doors and brings the skeleton in.*) It's so old that it's ready to fall apart.

CLAUDE. The old master always had it. There are times when it's very useful. It helped us get rid of that ruffian.

CYPRIAN (*laying the skeleton across the desk*). It may make some impression on Rody when he's absolutely pie-eyed, but it wouldn't impose on an intelligent child. It's such an obvious fake that it makes our whole business look phony. The new learning has made a big difference: people aren't so naïve as they used to be. Janet tells me that Merlin had been losing his clientele among the more advanced people. We can't afford to be taken for quacks.

CLAUDE. They still expect spooks on occasion, and I do *not* think the skeleton should be removed.

*Janet comes in through the waiting-room door. She is a little more smartly and less soberly dressed than she was in the first act.*

CYPRIAN (*to Janet*). I'm trying to persuade Claude that we ought to retire Old Bones.

JANET. I'm going to clean out this whole place. It hasn't really had an overhauling since Father first took over the business, and it's full of the most awful junk. Those things in those jars are disgusting!

CLAUDE. I think it would be a mistake to do anything to destroy the old atmosphere.

CYPRIAN (*to Janet, indicating the crocodile*). What do you think about that?

JANET. I wanted Father to take it down long ago. It's splitting along the seams.

CLAUDE. That's precisely the thing, I can tell you, that the simpler people are most impressed by. They expect to see it when they come here. They'd lose confidence if they found it gone. We call it the Hermetical Dragon.

CYPRIAN. But actually it's just a stuffed crocodile, and it hasn't any actual use.—I should think that we could do without that elk's head, too.

CLAUDE. Don't say "we": speak for yourself.

JANET. I thought that we could fix up the big front hall as a sort of museum of magic. We could put all those old things down there.

CYPRIAN. A brilliant idea! (*To Claude*) Don't you think so? Then the simpler sort of people could see them and feel that they were getting their money's worth, while the scholars would read the labels and know that they were not being cheated. If we're going to branch out now and go in for more serious magic, that will make quite impression enough.

CLAUDE. You know that I don't approve of our meddling with forbidden things.

CYPRIAN. Who forbade them?

CLAUDE. It's dangerous and most unwise. And I'd like to remind you of something that seems to have been forgotten. I agreed to stay on here a year ago, at the time I was offered a job as clerk of the Abbéville court, because the old master asked me to and promised I'd be his successor. Well, I expect the bargain to be kept, and when Janet and I are married—as I want to be as soon as her mourning is over—I'm sure we can manage the business without any third person.

JANET. You agreed to have Cyprian stay.

CLAUDE. For a limited time, as a paid assistant. I didn't agree to allow him to decide on questions of policy.

JANET. We talked about the possibility of taking him in as a partner.

CLAUDE. The old master knew nothing about this youth. He saw him for the first time only a few minutes before he died—and he certainly would not have approved of what you want to let him do.

CYPRIAN. After all, I'm the person who's taking the risks.

CLAUDE. It's risky for all of us—(to Janet) you know that. When your father's predecessor, the previous Merlin, was fooling around with those spells, there were two very serious fires, and something else happened here that your father never wanted to talk about.

JANET. But we've got to do *something* now about all that equipment and the magic books. We ought either to make use of them ourselves or sell them to that wizard from Toledo who's been so anxious to buy them. In any case, we've got to make an inventory and find out about the subject enough so that we know what the stuff is worth.

CLAUDE. What I don't like—I've told you before—is committing ourselves to the Black Art.

CYPRIAN. It's all Black Art more or less—at least, that's what people call it.

CLAUDE. But you're going to invoke the Devil.

CYPRIAN. That doesn't commit us to anything—we ought to know how it's done. We're not even sure that it *can* be done. And if anybody suffers, it's bound to be me. If I should be carried off, it will show you what to avoid.

CLAUDE. That isn't the way it works—I know (to Janet)

from hearing your father talk. When a magician starts dabbling in the Black Art, he may think he knows what he's doing, but once he lets those forces loose, he can never be sure of controlling them. This may mean the damnation of all of us!

CYPRIAN. That's a notion invented by ignorant priests!

CLAUDE (*to Janet*). You see what a crackpot he is? How can you let him behave in this irresponsible way?

*Cyprian, ignoring this, goes to the bookcase and gets out a book. He sits down at the desk, looks something up and begins attentively reading.*

JANET (*to Claude*). I'll keep track of what he's doing. You'll admit that we ought to find out——

CLAUDE. I don't admit it at all. I'd rather we sold everything to that Spaniard—then we shouldn't have to worry about it.—And sold the castle, too. It's gloomy to live in the forest—it cuts us off so from the world. It's giving you queer ideas. A lot of people think you're a witch—and there's a rumor that *I've* got the evil eye.

JANET. Oh, surely they know you're harmless.

CLAUDE. They'll never believe that we're harmless unless they see us living like everybody else. If you're going to strip the castle of its mystery, we might just as well do as I once suggested: buy that nice little four-room house that we saw at the edge of the forest and just settle down to dispensing drugs.

JANET. Oh, come: you enjoy the castle—you like being important, you know you do!

CLAUDE. I don't know: I sometimes wish that I could just have gone on raising goats the way my father did.

JANET. After all, I'm not a dairymaid.

CLAUDE. Yes: learning to read and write unfits one for that kind of life.

JANET. Come: we're neglecting our duties! There won't be any clients on New Year's Day, but you ought to go over to Abbéville to look at that child with the King's Evil—and the woman with fits, too. And I want to get the waiting-room swept.

CLAUDE. You're determined to go ahead—with that dangerous thing tonight?

JANET. He's just going to try out a spell.

CLAUDE. God protect us! God pardon us! We might better call upon *Him*! I'm still going to Mass, I can tell you, though nobody else here does—and it's in church— in church before the priest that I'm going to have you stand up beside me. You'll have to begin thinking *then* about making a home for your children. We can't bring them up in a place where devils are popping about. I hope you'll consider that—when you've satisfied your morbid curiosity. (*Janet, who wants to escape, moves away to the desk and picks the skeleton up, attracting the attention of Cyprian.*) And I shouldn't like to have them grow up even the way that you did—like an alien, almost an outlaw. They'd have a much better chance in a nice little house like that —a little house at the edge of the wood!

JANET (*coming back, with the skeleton over her arm*). Go along, if you're so eager to give out drugs. Your patients are languishing for you.

*He goes out. She is about to follow him, but, seeing some- one in the waiting-room, stops in the doorway and greets him.*

JANET. Oh, come in. (*To Cyprian*) It's Mr. B.

*Mr. B. enters. Janet drops the skeleton on a chair near the door.*

JANET (*curtsying*). Welcome, sir—and happy New Year.

MR. B. }
CYPRIAN } Happy New Year.

MR. B. I hope you'll have the goodness to pardon me for coming to you on business on New Year's Day.

JANET. Yes: do sit down, Mr. B.

*He seats himself in the visitors' chair; Cyprian stands up, against the bookcase; Janet sits down on the left.*

JANET. Is your wife not well again?

MR. B. No: she is worse.

JANET. The ointment didn't help?

MR. B. No. The truth is *He's* sent us this plague, and He won't let up till I leave her.

CYPRIAN. Are you sure of that?

MR. B. I know how He works. You see, it's my guilt that she has to share, and it's not merely a question of illness. She's always been so brave and self-confident, and now she's getting nervous and frightened. I can't stand to see her like this, and I've made up my mind to free her. But she can't live alone here now, and nobody—not even her own sisters and brothers—would be willing to take her in.

JANET. I'd be glad to have her here——

MR. B. It's something I've been loth to suggest—I know that you have problems of your own—but it's the only place I'd feel she was safe. I'd hesitate to put her in a convent. And I'll really have to go quite away: she must get well and have her own life again.

JANET. The only thing is—I ought to explain that we thought we'd experiment a little with—certain things that Father neglected——

CYPRIAN (*helping her out*). We want to try some of the bigger stuff.

MR. B. Ah, I see.

JANET. We're not going to go too far, but I'm not sure we'd have the approval of—the Power you're trying to placate.

MR. B. If you're planning to do business with my former chief, it wouldn't do at all, of course.

JANET. You don't think that the disease might run its course? I hate to see you give up like this. Why should He persecute you so when you're doing your best to—to please Him?

MR. B. You see, I was one of the leaders of the revolt in Heaven against Him.

CYPRIAN. Were you really?

JANET. But that was so long ago!

MR. B. What seems a long time to you means nothing to us who must live for ever. And, besides, I had rather an important rank in the kingdom that we afterwards founded; and from the time that you men became civilized, that Kingdom was of vital importance to Him. The whole prestige of the higher regime now depends on the stability of the lower one, and it won't do, from *His* point of view, to have Satan's morale shaken (*with a sad but sardonic smile*) by the voluntary resignation of one of his top men.

CYPRIAN. That seems extremely unfair!

MR. B. I can no longer venture to criticize. I can only accept my position if the decree is relentless against me. —Because what can I do? It's my nature itself that's infecting her and making her waste away—my negative loveless nature. I thought at first that I was moved by love— but it was only *her* love that moved me. My cold heart was just the same. I could admire: I'm a prince, after all, and I recognize all that is excellent. But I couldn't give back her love, and my contact is killing her now.

JANET. That can't be correct, Mr. B. If you were really as loveless as that, you wouldn't be worried about her. I think that you're very unselfish. There's something— something noble about you.

CYPRIAN (*to Janet, becoming uncomfortable at the note of admiration for Mr. B.*). Don't you think it might be worth while to talk to him about our experiments?

JANET. *You* talk to him: I have to clean house. (*She gets up.*) But what about your wife, in the meantime?

MR. B. I'll have to think of something else. After all, there's always the convent. But I can't take her there myself.

JANET. *I'll* take her, Mr. B.—I'd be glad to. I'll come down tomorrow morning—if everything's all right up here.

MR. B. I shan't count on you—but thank you for your kindness. I value it all the more because you know I can never repay it. I can't give you back good for good.

JANET (*curtsying to Mr. B.*). Don't worry about that, Mr. B. It always does us good to see you.—I hope that the New Year will bring you more luck than the last.

MR. B. (*rising and bowing*). I can at least return your kind wishes.

*Janet goes out through the waiting-room door, on her way picking up the skeleton.*

MR. B. (*to Cyprian, smiling*). This is one of the only holidays that a devil can legitimately celebrate.

CYPRIAN. Oh, because they're all saints' days! Well, you don't miss much: our so-called holy days are mostly just excuses for the priesthood to shake down their congregations!

*Cyprian goes over and seats himself in the chair in which Janet has been sitting. Mr. B. resumes his seat.*

MR. B. So you're going in for real magic.

CYPRIAN. Yes—the old man had dropped all that—and we thought that we ought to find out—what it was all about.

MR. B. Beginning with what exactly?

CYPRIAN. Well, we thought that we ought to know something about—what's vulgarly called the Black Art.

MR. B. I'm afraid I can't advise you there.

CYPRIAN. No, of course—I suppose not.

MR. B. You understand my position——

CYPRIAN. Yes: of course—I didn't mean——

MR. B. I don't work with them any more; but on the other hand, it wouldn't be proper for me to give their secrets away.

CYPRIAN. I didn't mean to be indiscreet, but you know you *did* give me some good advice the first day I saw you here.

MR. B. Not on anything of official importance. Now, tell me: are you going to take over?

CYPRIAN. You mean for what we're doing today.

MR. B. No: the business.

CYPRIAN (*hastily*). Oh, no: I'm just helping out.

MR. B. It oughtn't to be difficult for you to have the field to yourself.

CYPRIAN. I don't want to—I don't think I ought to: after all, Claude got here first. Merlin had promised it to him.

MR. B. And promised him Janet.

CYPRIAN. Yes.—It would be wrong of me to take it away from him.

MR. B. Wrong?

CYPRIAN. I've thought it all over carefully, and I can't—it's out of the question. I can't commit such an injustice.

MR. B. What do you mean, an injustice?

CYPRIAN. Why, I came here—deserted my parents—to get away from our brute of a baron. He poisoned his brother for the title, and he's made all his vassals loathe him. How can I do the same thing to Claude? I resent his attitude toward me, but at the same time I'm abler than he is, and I don't want to abuse my advantage. I don't want to base my power on cruelty to people who are weaker than I.

MR. B. You do want a position of power?

CYPRIAN. Yes, of course; but I'll learn the trade here and then set up on my own.

MR. B. Do you think you'll be able to work with them, your relationships being what they are? Claude will be jealous of you.

CYPRIAN. I'm not trying to get him out—I'm not making love to Janet. I'm sure she wouldn't want me if I did.

MR. B. What makes you so sure of that?

CYPRIAN. Why, women don't like me, and I don't like them. My own mother didn't like me. She only adored my brother—who is one of the stupidest men alive—because she thought that our baron was his father.

MR. B. You'll live like a celibate?

CYPRIAN. Yes: why not? There are priests who can do it, so why can't I? I've got my career to make, and that I can best do alone.

MR. B. (*getting up*). As I told you, I can't advise you. (*Smiling*) I'm in a state of suspended maleficence, but I oughtn't to work for the other side—and in your case I wouldn't know what to say. You seem to be invoking the gospel of—His Deputy, your so-called Savior, and that's something I can't understand. You mix it with other things that seem to be completely at odds with it. I can bow to a soul like my wife's: her love is a natural force, like the sun; but this doctrine of pity of yours that complicates the impulse to power——

CYPRIAN. I don't believe in Christian doctrine—I'm ready to accept Satan.

MR. B. That won't set you free from these problems. We always talked morality to our prospects. We argued with them exactly like the churchmen. But enough! that's the kind of thing I oughtn't to say.—I'll watch what you do with much interest.

CYPRIAN. I hope that your wife gets well.

MR. B. Thank you. (*Bowing*) And now goodby. I'll leave you to your researches.—But be careful!

CYPRIAN (*bowing and awkward*). I'll try to.—Come back again.

MR. B. Thank you.

CYPRIAN. Goodby.

*Mr. B. goes out: Cyprian stands looking after him, rather puzzled by what he has said. Janet comes in through the double doors, carrying a bag with something in it, a black bowl and a large knife.*

JANET. Was he helpful?

CYPRIAN. No.—He says he can't talk.

JANET. We ought to start right away if we're going to get it over before Claude comes back. He'll accept it if we've already done it and nobody's any the worse.

CYPRIAN. Yes.—I've got the things all ready. I was just going to draw the figure.

*He picks up the open book from the desk and the ruler and the chalk on the string from the table against the wall, and sits down on the floor in the middle of the room, where, copying from the book, he begins to trace a magic figure: a star of David that consists of two triangles, with a circle at the points of the triangle and mystic characters in the center of the figure and inside each of the points of the star. The diameter of the circle is about four feet.*

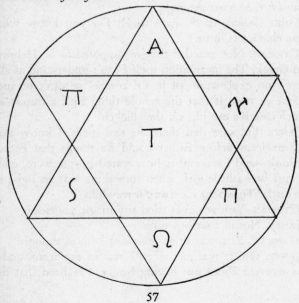

JANET. You're sure it's all right at this time of day. I thought you had to do it at midnight.

CYPRIAN. That's not the modern way, it seems. This book says that midnight and graveyards and gallows-trees and all that are just hokum for the superstitious. The formula's supposed to work at any time. Well, we'll soon find out.

JANET (*holding up the bag*). Here's the black hen. I thought it might be a good idea to have the bowl black, too.

CYPRIAN. Thank you.

JANET. It will make a mess on the floor, but it's easy enough to clean up.—You're sure you don't want me to stay here?

CYPRIAN. No. (*He has come to drawing the circle.*) Will you just hold this down with your finger while I make the circle around it?

*She kneels and holds one end of the string while, walking around her, he traces the circle.*

JANET (*looking at the open book*). Do you know what these characters mean?

CYPRIAN. Not exactly: they're supposed to be Hebrew and Greek. The incantation itself I can't understand at all: there's no explanation of it. Of course we can't be sure till we've tried it that the whole thing isn't a fraud—in which case we can just eat the chicken.

JANET. I'm sure that there *are* real spells. I know that the magician before Father could do things that Father couldn't—and I remember how scared people were, once when I was a little girl, when something was let loose in the castle. They sent me away for awhile.

CYPRIAN. You've never tried any magic yourself?

JANET. Not in a serious way.

CYPRIAN. You *have* done *something* with it, though?

JANET. Oh, it was just when I was in my teens, and I was worried about not having beaux. I realized that the boys kept away from me because they were frightened of me. So I tried to work an ancient charm that was supposed to bring you a lover.

CYPRIAN. What happened?

JANET. Claude appeared.

CYPRIAN. So it did work.

JANET. Yes, perhaps.

CYPRIAN. You've never seen anything queer yourself?

JANET. I don't know—I don't think so.

CYPRIAN (*stopping and looking up at her*). There *has* been something queer?

JANET. I'm not sure—it may just have been nightmares. But ever since Father died I *have* been having some very queer dreams that seemed almost as if they were real.

CYPRIAN. What were they?

JANET. Well, I wasn't going to tell you, but now that you're going to try this, perhaps it would be just as well.

CYPRIAN (*again looking up*). Yes: tell me.

JANET. Well, the first time it happened it seemed to me that a young man came into my room. I thought it was you at first, and I didn't know what you were doing. I don't remember falling asleep. Then I saw that he was dressed like a courtier. He spoke to me and said that, since Father was dead, I ought to apply to the King and get a patent to practise magic. He said the most unpleasant things about Claude and you both—all in a polished way —and he told me that I needed a husband, somebody who was really a man—and then he tried to make love to me, and I fought him off.—I know that this sounds rather silly, but it wasn't just an ordinary dream.

CYPRIAN. What did he say about me?

JANET. He said you were a half-baked peasant, who wouldn't have the nerve to put anything through, and he made me look into a mirror, where I saw a kind of living picture of you. You were standing in a forest somewhere, hobnobbing with a kind of spook.

CYPRIAN. What did the spook look like?

JANET. He was thin and had pale clothes and a soft-looking pale face.

CYPRIAN. Was it night—were we standing in the moonlight?

JANET. Yes, it must have been moonlight. What was it?

CYPRIAN. It may have been something that happened when I was on my way here.—Now tell me what else you saw.

JANET. Well, the young man appeared three times. The last time was quite a tough struggle, but I finally got him out. Then the next night a woman came. She said she was a woman magician—that she was interested in my situation and had projected herself here to see me. She told me what a bright girl I was and said that she'd teach me her secrets—that women like her and me didn't need to be dependent on men. She said she'd be glad to guide me if I'd put myself completely in her hands.

CYPRIAN. Don't do it!

JANET. Of course not, but the curious thing was that I half believed what she said and told her she could come again. She was handsome, though she made one uncomfortable.

CYPRIAN. Don't let her come again. You can handle all this yourself.

JANET. I'll try to if *you'll* stand by me.

CYPRIAN (*who has now finished, getting up and brushing the chalk from his hands*). Of course I will.—You know I admire you, Janet. You're the most capable girl I've ever seen. You've got no nonsense about you!

JANET. It's not true you have—other commitments?

CYPRIAN. To what?

JANET. It's not true you'll let me down? That was what that courtier said.

*She goes to the peg in the corner and takes down the magician's robe.*

CYPRIAN. Why should I let you down? You mustn't take dreams too seriously. There must be all kinds of spirits trying to get in here now. I've been having some queer dreams, too. Last night I dreamt that Claude was beheaded.

*She gives him a quick look, then holds up the robe.*

JANET. You'd better wear this.

CYPRIAN. Oh, no. I have no right to: those are Claude's.

JANET. You ought to assume authority if you're going to perform this spell.

CYPRIAN. It would make me feel like a usurper.

JANET. They've always been used for real magic. I'd feel much better about you.

CYPRIAN. All right, if you want me to. (*He lets her help him on with the robe.*)

JANET. You're going to look splendid in it. It was a little too gorgeous for Father—that's why he let it get so shabby. But I've mended it and had it washed.

CYPRIAN (*buttoning the front, pleased with himself but protesting*). I feel like an impostor.

JANET (*handing him the cap*). You mustn't. You've got to be the real thing. If *you* don't master our big magic, I don't know who's ever going to. I don't think a woman can do it, in spite of what that creature said—she's bound to get too much involved—that's what I'd be afraid of. It would make one a kind of witch instead of a lady magician.—(*Smiling with excitement*) It's going to be fascinating now to see what we've got in that storeroom. You know there's a genie in a bottle.

CYPRIAN. Yes: I saw it.

JANET. I wonder whether we could get him to work for

us—as a regular servant, I mean. We do need more servants badly, and it's so hard to get anybody to stay up here.

CYPRIAN. Wouldn't he frighten people too much?

JANET. He might, I suppose. What we really need is some kind of major-domo, who would take all the house-keeping off my hands: I want to give more time to the business—and we ought to have a boy or two to work around the place and run errands.

CYPRIAN. What about that Italian who wrote you, with all those distinguished references?

JANET. I told him to come to see me. If he seems to be any good I'll send him up and you can see what you think.

CYPRIAN. Claude ought to see him, too.

JANET. Yes.—Well, shall I leave you now?

CYPRIAN. Yes.

JANET. Do you want me to look in later?

CYPRIAN (*after a moment's hesitation*). Not for about an hour—better make it an hour and a half.

JANET. You'll be wanting something to eat. Don't you want a little lunch first?

CYPRIAN. No: I'd rather go through with it right away.

JANET. I'll bring you up something in about an hour and leave it outside the door.

CYPRIAN. You'd better not knock, though.

JANET. No.—Don't be nervous. The great thing with the spirits, they say, is just to remember that *you're* the master. You mustn't let them flatter you or bully you. It seems that they can't do anything that you don't consent to yourself.

CYPRIAN. What was it that went wrong before?—when they had those fires and things?

JANET. I don't know. The trouble is apparently that they sometimes get people confused, so that they ask for the wrong things.

CYPRIAN. I'll try to make myself very plain.

JANET. What *are* you going to ask for?

*She looks in her mirror to tidy her hair.*

CYPRIAN. It's better for you not to know.

JANET (*glancing around from the mirror*). I thought we were going to work together.

CYPRIAN. I don't want you to be involved if anything gets out of hand.

JANET (*going back to her mirror*). I hoped we could trust one another——

CYPRIAN (*reminded of his mother as he sees her with the mirror and impatiently interrupting her*). Must you be primping? If you play the siren, no wonder the devils are after you! You've got your best dress on, too.

JANET. A woman is always in a weaker position if she looks a positive fright.

CYPRIAN. Why not leave the tempting to them?

JANET. Now, don't be nervous.

CYPRIAN. I'm not.

JANET. I'll leave the doors open, shall I?

CYPRIAN. No, of course not: they ought to be closed.

JANET. Don't bolt them from the inside.

CYPRIAN. You must really leave this part to me.

JANET. But *please* don't bolt them.

CYPRIAN (*impatiently*). All right.

JANET. Well, I'll leave you. Good luck.

CYPRIAN. Don't worry.

*She goes out, shutting the door behind her. He looks around toward the double door and has a moment of awkwardness, as he faces the chalk figure and the other apparatus for the ritual. He picks up the bag with the hen, hesitates as to what to do with it, then drops it and picks up the book, comparing the figure with the diagram. He now kneels down with the chalk and touches up the mysterious characters. Then he puts down the bowl inside the circle, sticks the knife under his arm, and, determinedly but with evident distaste, takes the hen out of the bag. Its feet are tied together and it does not move. He puts the book down beside him on the floor, and, kneeling in the circle with his back to the audience, is seen to be cutting the head off the hen and holding it to bleed into the bowl. In the silence, the hen squawks horribly.*

CYPRIAN. *Eloim, Essaim, frugativi et appellavi.*—(*To himself*) That Latin is completely cockeyed!

*He looks up and glances around, as if in fear that he has committed an impiety. Then he puts down the hen, picks up the bowl, and, still kneeling, turns around toward the audience. He lays the book open in front of him.*

CYPRIAN (*to himself*). I don't know how to pronounce this language, and you're supposed to have everything perfect. Well, I'll follow it with a prayer of my own. I'll appeal directly to Satan, to let him know that I'm not just a dabbler, that I am a rebel, too. Well, here goes! (*He holds up the bowl with both hands and reads from the book on the floor.*)

> Bagabi laca bachabe
> Lamac cahi achababe
> Karrelyos
> Lamac lamec bachalyas
> Cabahagy sabalyos
> Baryolas
> Lagoz atha cabyolas
> Samahac et famyolas
> Harrahya.

(*Launching into his own appeal*) I kneel to you, Satan: accept my prayer. Let me prosper in knowledge and power. As you fought the oppression of Heaven, so help me to revenge my injuries against the oppressions of earth, of the lords of misrule of this world that imprison and cripple and crush. Let me vindicate against their injustice my dignity as an individual, and let me do it in such a way as not utterly to crush, myself, the dignity of other individuals. I long to be master here, but I would not destroy my rival, as my villainous baron would do. And grant me the hardness to stand alone. (*Dropping his voice, as if talking to himself*) My mother never gave me her love, and I learned to get on without it. I can get on without Janet's love. I learned to live day after day with the scorn my mother had for my father, and compelled myself not to feel it—I can live with Janet's contempt for the miserable bargain she's getting. I can be strong in my work in this castle, and (*raising his voice, addressing Satan again*) I can serve you if you stretch out your hand—I can fight against the dark forces of ignorance—or piety, of fear, of subservience—that are breaking men's self-respect, that are blinding them against the light. Tell me, Satan, how we may serve one another! Let me stand with you face to face—let me speak to you as soldier to captain! . . . (*To himself*) I don't know how to close: Amen won't do.— Accept my allegiance, Satan.

*Still holding the bowl, he looks down for a moment, then straightens up and waits. He glances about him on either side and sets the bowl on the floor; waits a few seconds more, with his head bowed. A knock at the waiting-room door. He looks quickly in that direction, not able to decide what to do. The knock is repeated. He gets to his feet and makes a movement as if to go to the door, but then remembers the circle and decides that he ought not to step out of it.*

CYPRIAN. Come in.

*The door opens, and a lean old man appears. He is dressed with some distinction in black and has long silvery hair that comes down to his collar. He is swarthy, with a long nose and a mobile Italian face. He approaches Cyprian with deference, and his manners show a certain courtliness.*

THE VISITOR (*bowing low and speaking with an Italian accent*). Luigi Malacoda, at your service, my lord: an applicant for a place in your household.

CYPRIAN (*much embarrassed*). I'm busy at the present time——

LUIGI. Pray forgive me if I discommode you, but her ladyship told me to come to you——

CYPRIAN (*surprised*). She told you to come to me now?

LUIGI (*with smiling deference*). She wanted you to see me, and if you did not disapprove, she was good enough to say she would give me a trial. If I come at an inopportune moment, of course, I'll retire at once—I'll merely leave you my recommendations. (*He glides forward, producing a handful of letters, while Cyprian still stands in the circle.*) I don't know whether you read Italian.

CYPRIAN. Never mind. If Miss Janet approves, that's all that's necessary.

LUIGI (*holding up the letters*). The Romani, the Ursini, the Colonna—I've worked for them all in my time—the great families of Rome, as you know. With the La Scala I spent seventeen years—always in positions of trust.

CYPRIAN. I'm sure that your references are satisfactory. Tell Miss Janet that I can't see you now.

LUIGI (*bowing*). Thank you, my lord. (*He glances toward the figure on the floor.*) I see that I *have* intruded at an inauspicious moment. Pray forgive me, but would you allow me to make one little suggestion? I hope you will not think me impertinent, but I have had some experience in these matters—and from the way you have drawn this figure, I should say you were not an old hand. These characters are a little equivocal. One has to be very exact with the curlicues of these queer old letters. (*He picks up the chalk and, kneeling, corrects some of Cyprian's signs.*)

CYPRIAN. That may be why I've had no results.

LUIGI. I'm not sure that it's serious enough for that, but carelessness in preparation may have rather annoying consequences.

CYPRIAN. What is likely to happen?

LUIGI. Why, sometimes they like to disconcert one with roughish practical jokes.—You have finished the invocation?

CYPRIAN. Yes—a moment ago.

LUIGI. Then there's no need to stay in the circle.

CYPRIAN. I didn't know. (*He steps out.*)

LUIGI. I don't want to seem officious or to push myself indiscreetly, but if you haven't got the hang of these practices, I might perhaps be useful to you. We had a good deal of this in Italy in those households in which I had the honor to serve. I can tell you that it needs a cool head and a very steady hand—if you want to hold your own. If you give them a finger, you know (*smiling*), you'll find that they're trying to take the hand—and then the arm, and then, you know what!

CYPRIAN (*rather unnerved*). How should one go about it?

LUIGI. I'll tell you. To begin with, it's vital to insist on the minimum terms that they'll give you. They'll try to take advantage of your innocence to make you go the whole hog—it's their own inelegant expression. But such a *coup* would only be possible with some clodhopper greedy for power. In my dealings with my masters in Italy, such a thing would not even have been suggested. Lorenzo de la Scala, my gracious prince, knew almost as much about the Old Boy's game as the Old Boy did himself. They sold him up, I fear, in the end, but in the meantime he'd had his money's worth—and what a rich life his was!

CYPRIAN. What *are* the minimum terms?—Please sit down.

*Cyprian goes behind the desk and sits in the magician's chair while Luigi takes the visitors' seat, turning it around toward the desk.*

LUIGI. Thank you, my lord.

CYPRIAN. I'm not a lord.

LUIGI. But a magician has a very high position, and you, sir, if you will pardon my speaking with the frankness in which my late master indulged me—you, sir, show the natural qualities of one born to shine and command. A little experience of the great world, a little more polish and *savoir faire*——

CYPRIAN. Please tell me about the contract. What are the minimum terms?

LUIGI. Six months is the least they will do.

CYPRIAN. And what is the—price they ask?

LUIGI. You must insist on the easiest arrangement. The most important thing is not to give them any sort of claim on you that will still remain in force after their part of the bargain is over. They can make it very nasty for you by turning up and exacting their payment at some moment when you can least afford it and when they'll try to take advantage of the situation to blackmail you into another bargain.

CYPRIAN. What would you recommend?

LUIGI. Six months, and pay as you go.

CYPRIAN. What does that involve precisely?

LUIGI. You sweat it out as you go along—to use their own rather squalid expression.

CYPRIAN. But what does the sweating-out consist of?

LUIGI (*smiling*). That depends on your condition and character. But the process of payment is light in proportion to the limited term of the loan.

CYPRIAN. And what do you get in return?

LUIGI. Whatever you ask for—that is, to the value of six months.

CYPRIAN. Knowledge and power?

LUIGI. Oh, yes—of course, in a worldly way.

CYPRIAN. That's all that I want.

LUIGI. Quite.—(*Moving his chair to the desk and picking up the pen and a strip of parchment*) Now, this is the sort of arrangement that I'd like to take the liberty of suggesting. (*Writing*) "I, Cyprian"—I haven't the privilege of knowing your full name——?

CYPRIAN. Leclerc.

LUIGI. "I, Cyprian Leclerc, petition you, Lord Satan, to grant me whatever I crave of those benefits that are in your power and in the manner in which you can bestow them—for the space of six months. In return for which I accept the condition that I pay for these gifts as I get them in any way demanded by you, provided that this payment be not of a kind to prejudice the ultimate fate of my soul." (*He pushes the parchment toward Cyprian.*)

CYPRIAN. Is that all that's necessary?

LUIGI. The simpler the contract, the better. With an inexperienced petitioner, they will put in a multitude of clauses that they count on his not understanding and that will let him in for things that he doesn't expect.

CYPRIAN (*examining the contract*). That doesn't say precisely what I'm getting.

LUIGI. You must check on that directly with Satan.

CYPRIAN. But Satan has not appeared.

LUIGI. Satan is here: he has heard you. Ask him to accept the pact.

CYPRIAN. Satan, are you here? Have you heard me? Do you consent to accept this pact?

A VOICE (*somber and deep*). Do you, Cyprian, of your own free will, give me power over body and soul?

LUIGI (*reassuring Cyprian*). It's only for six months. (*He picks up the knife from the floor.*)

CYPRIAN. As defined in the contract, yes. In return for certain benefits.

THE VOICE OF SATAN. The power to work wonders.

CYPRIAN. Yes.

THE VOICE OF SATAN. The power to revenge yourself against the oppressions of earth.

CYPRIAN. Yes.

THE VOICE OF SATAN. Immunity from the envy of your rival.

CYPRIAN. I don't want to destroy him, though.

THE VOICE OF SATAN. Immunity from the charms of this lady.

CYPRIAN. Yes.

THE VOICE OF SATAN. All these gifts you shall have. Sign!

*Cyprian reaches for the ink, but Luigi holds up the knife.*

LUIGI. The signature must be in blood. The wrist will do. Allow me. (*Cyprian holds out his right wrist.*) The left. (*Cyprian holds out the left.*) Better write with the point of the knife. You shouldn't mix the blood with ink. (*Cyprian takes the knife and traces the signature.*) As clearly as you can. It's difficult to write with a knife. A clean pen is better—but never mind.—There!

THE VOICE OF SATAN. The pact will be kept. Farewell.

CYPRIAN. Farewell—I am grateful, Lord Satan!

LUIGI (*producing a bandage from his pocket*). Allow me to bind this up. (*He ties up Cyprian's wrist.*)

CYPRIAN (*trying to shake off the spell by taking a lighter tone*). How gloomy he sounds! I'd imagined him—more fiery, more defiant. I should think he'd be proud and exult.

LUIGI. He's very correct, Lord Satan. He'd think it indecent to gloat. That's something he leaves to his subordinates. (*He laughs, and Cyprian eyes him uneasily.*) And besides, of course, this, you know (*with a shade of malicious patronage*), is very small business for him.

CYPRIAN. Yes, of course.

LUIGI. And now, shall I begin my duties?

CYPRIAN. Report to Miss Janet for that. And please tell her I'd like to see her.

LUIGI. Very good, sir. I am infinitely grateful—I hope I shall give satisfaction.

CYPRIAN. How did you come to leave your family in Italy after working for them so many years?

*Luigi shakes sand on the signature.*

LUIGI. Oh, they'd virtually exterminated themselves. Brother against brother, you know—mother against daughter—that sort of thing. And the whole thing made worse, I'm afraid, by a certain amount of incest. (*He quietly picks up the pact and slips it into his pocket.*)

CYPRIAN (*a little apprehensively*). I see.—Here, don't take away that contract!

LUIGI. I shall keep it under lock and key.—And now, I can't say that I hope that you will never regret this bargain: there will be moments, I fear, when you *will*—but I am happy to have been of service in assisting you to put it through. (*He bows and is about to retire.*)

CYPRIAN (*getting up and coming out from behind the desk*). Please give me that parchment back.

LUIGI (*smiling*). It is impossible, of course, for such contracts to remain in the possession of the applicant. They have to be always available for the party of the Second Part. I shall keep it quite safe, I assure you: you may ask to see it at any time. (*Bowing again with perceptible mockery*) At your service, my respected Lord Cyprian: your obedient major-domo—for a six months' trial, shall we say?

*He goes out through the waiting-room door. Cyprian stares after him, annoyed and puzzled, then looks down at the things on the floor. He picks up the bowl and then the hen, sets the bowl on one of the shelves and looks around for a place to put the hen, then, abruptly, with an impulse of repugnance, flings it into the fireplace and turns to pick up the book. The hen, as if hurled by an unseen hand, is immediately ejected from the fireplace and lands in the middle of the room. It is followed by an ugly black imp, who stands a moment, arms akimbo, on the hearth, then jumps upon the magician's desk. He is carrying a big sling-shot.*

SLINGO (*in a squeaky voice*). Don't you trow tings at me, boss! I can trow tings, too!

*He shoots pebbles at Cyprian, who has to duck.*

CYPRIAN. Stop that! Who the devil are you?

SLINGO. You watch your language, boss! Don't you talk dat way about our chief!

*Cyprian makes a plunge after Slingo, who leaps down from the desk and escapes. The double doors are rudely thrown open, and two more little devils come in, carrying a large tray, on which are set a covered dish, a napkin, a knife and fork, a goblet and a flagon of wine.*

STINGO AND BONGO (*in unison*). We've brought you your luncheon, boss! (*They march over to the table against the back wall, chanting Chopin's Funeral March.*) Da da-da-da, da-da-dada-da-da-da! (*They set the tray on the table and stand one on either side of it, like butlers.*)

STINGO (*bowing low*). Miss Janet sent it up to you, boss.

BONGO (*bowing low*). She hopes you find it tasty, boss.

CYPRIAN (*after his first astonishment, attempting to collect himself*). Thank you: you can go now. (*Turning to Slingo, who is aiming at the crocodile*) And you, too.

*Stingo, bowing again, proffers Cyprian the knife and fork, while Bongo takes the cover off the dish. The severed head of Claude is seen standing upright on the platter, with its eyes open as if it were alive. From the moment the cover is removed, the head begins to speak, saying over and over again the last words of Claude's final speech. He repeats them with the same intonation with which they were originally uttered and with the monotony of a metronome.*

CLAUDE'S HEAD. A little house at the edge of the wood . . . a little house at the edge of the wood . . . a little house at the edge of the wood . . .

*Stingo and Bongo squeal with laughter; Slingo, seeing the head, joins in. Janet appears at the waiting-room door, followed by Luigi.*

JANET. You wanted to see me?

CYPRIAN (*indicating the head*). What's this?

JANET (*smiling with malice*). That was what you wanted, wasn't it?

CYPRIAN. I said I didn't want to destroy him.

LUIGI (*smiling*). You see that he still lives.

*Cyprian looks at them a moment in amazement, then snatches the dish-cover from Bongo and puts it over the head.*

CYPRIAN (*to Luigi*). So this is the beginning of the price I pay!

LUIGI. It also fulfils your wish.

CYPRIAN (*to Janet*). Did you know about this?

JANET. I do now. It's what you intended, isn't it?

CYPRIAN. Don't make fun of me, Janet. You're not on their side, are you?

JANET. You didn't want to love me, you know.

CYPRIAN. You're not one of them?

JANET. I don't understand you, Cyprian. These are my new staff. You asked to have things made convenient for me, so I got what I wanted, too. They have sent me my major-domo (*Luigi bows*)—and these boys to run errands for me.

LUIGI (*indicating the Little Devils, each of whom, as he is named, clicks his heels, presents his appropriate instrument, then salutes and stands to attention*). Slingo, Stingo and Bongo— three brisk little imps at your service.

CYPRIAN. All right: you can all go now. Not you, Janet—you please stay here.

*Bongo takes the cover off the head.*

CLAUDE'S HEAD. A little house at the edge of the wood . . . a little house at the edge of the wood . . .

SLINGO, STINGO AND BONGO. Da da-da-da, da-da-da da-da-da-da! . . .

*They all burst out laughing at Cyprian—the Little Devils gleefully and shrilly, Luigi more discreetly, Janet with girlish malevolence.*

73

LUIGI (*silencing the Devils with a gesture of his hand and speaking loudly in order to be heard above the voice of Claude's Head*). But, sir, you must try your new powers.

CYPRIAN. Can I heal without drugs?

LUIGI. Of course. Touch that wound in your wrist three times with your fingers crossed like this (*crossing his middle and index fingers*) and say: "Satan, make me whole again." Then take the bandage off.

CYPRIAN (*touching the wound*). Satan, make me whole again.

*He takes the bandage off, as the others, grinning slyly, watch him. No trace of the wound remains. Though puzzled and disturbed, he smiles.*

CLAUDE'S HEAD. A little house at the edge of the wood . . . a little house at the edge of the wood . . .

# ACT III

*The same room, three months later. The furnishings are mostly the same as before; the full weeding-out projected by Janet has never been carried through, but some of the shelves have been cleared of their miscellaneous objects and are now filled with Cyprian's pharmacy: neat rows of bottles and boxes. The lunch tray with Claude's covered head is still on the smaller table. It is a mild morning early in April, and the left-hand half of the double door has been left partly open, but a coldness in the stage lighting suggests an atmosphere of damnation. Slingo, Stingo and Bongo are clustered about the desk—Bongo sitting on the end nearest the audience while the other two stand on either side, Slingo on his right, Stingo on his left. He is leading them with his fists as they sing. The three little devils should never be so comic as to cease to seem disagreeable. Slingo talks tough; Bongo is more refined; Stingo is intensely malignant in a more rudimentary way.*

Slingo, Stingo and Bongo.
  Boola-boola boola-boola
  Boola-boola
  Boola-boola

  Boola-boola boola-boola
  Boola-boola
  Boola $\left\{ \begin{array}{l} \text{BOO!} \\ \text{BLAH!} \\ \text{BAH!} \end{array} \right.$
    *The last boo is a discordant yell.*

75

SLINGO.

Now, Prezz-bo Brox talked hard as rocks,
　　But he had one tender passion:
He loved the Gorgon Glamorpuss—
　　He loved her in his fashion.


ALL.

Yes, he loved her in his fashion!


SLINGO.

Now, Glamorpuss isn't good for us—
　　She's no biscuit tortoni—
A single buss from Glamorpuss
　　Can turn poor devils stony.


ALL.

With a hótotototó and a hátatatá
And a hákkamákka jákkamákka joney!
　　A single buss from Glamorpuss
　　　Can turn poor devils stony.


STINGO.

Said Prezz-bo Brox to Curlylocks,
　　"I'll take you on, my siren!
My heart's cuirass is a triple brass,
　　And my nerves are made of iron."


ALL.

Yes, his nerves were made of iron!


STINGO.

"My grasp you'll feel like a clasp of steel,
　　Though your snakes be squirmy-slimy.
You may stare and stare with your Gorgon glare,
　　But you'll fail to petrify me."

ALL.

With a hótotototó and a hátatatatá
And a hákkamákka jákkamákka jymie!
"You may stare and stare with your Gorgon glare,
But you'll fail to petrify me."

BONGO (*speaks instead of singing, with portentous and ghoulish ferocity*).

So face to face in a locked embrace,
He crushed his lovely Gorgon,
Till his mind grew dazed and his eyes grew glazed:
She'd paralyzed every organ!

ALL (*singing*).

Yes, she'd paralyzed every organ!

BONGO.

Now Prezz-bo Brox is immune to shocks:
He's had his load of glamor!
Yes, Prezzo-Brox is hard as rocks—
You can ring him with a hammer!

(*singing the last line*)

*Bongo illustrates this by hitting Stingo on the head with his mallet. Stingo reels for a moment, then turns quickly and jabs him with his skewer. Bongo jumps down, and they fight, each trying to wrest away the other's weapon.*

STINGO (*squealing*). You dirty little backhanded bopper!

BONGO. Mad as a hornet, eh?

SLINGO. Hey, guys: break it up! You know what Uncle Luigi says. Don't scratch each udder's eyes out: save it for de common enemy! (*He shoots at them with his sling, and they go after him and chase him around the table.*) Hey, look out: dere's somebody comin'! (*They look toward the waiting-room door.*) Get back into de act!

ALL (*resuming the song*).
With a hótotototó and a hátatatatá
And a hákkamákka jákkamákka jammer!
Yes, Prezzo-bo Brox is hard as rocks—
You can ring him with a hammer!

*They parade around the stage in single file, singing* Boola-boola *as before—Slingo first, Stingo holding his tail and Bongo holding Stingo's tail. Cyprian, accompanied by Luigi, enters from the waiting-room. Cyprian is wearing his gown and cap; he is harried, unsmiling and jumpy.*

BONGO. We've got a new song, Uncle Luigi!
LUIGI. Well, don't be too long about it.

BONGO (*to the same tune as before*).
Oh, what a man was Cyp-ri-an!
He tried to help the Devil.
Yes, Cyp-ri-an spoke man to man—
He was always on the level.

ALL.
He was always on the level!

BONGO.
He said, "I'll bust or be bad and just—
Especially the latter."
But he lost his broad, and we brought him Claude
With parsley on a platter.

ALL.
With a hótotototó and a hátatatatá——
LUIGI (*laughing indulgently*). That's enough, you rascals!
Scram!
SLINGO. We got some more, Uncle Luigi!
CYPRIAN (*morosely, to Luigi*). Get those devils out of here.
LUIGI (*to the Little Devils*). Never mind any more.
Skedaddle!

SLINGO. Okiedoke, Uncle Luigi.

*Slingo darts into the fireplace, Stingo behind the tapestry, and Bongo out behind the closed right-hand half of the double door. Bongo, on his way, adroitly lifts the cover from the dish with Claude's head.*

CLAUDE'S HEAD. This may mean the damnation of all of us! . . . This may mean the damnation of all of us! . . . This may mean, etc.

*Cyprian, surprised at this new refrain, looks at the head a moment, then puts the cover back, as if he were performing mechanically an action that had become habitual.*

CYPRIAN. Claude's got a new tune.

LUIGI. Even more of a bore than the other. What a pity you couldn't have chosen a more entertaining victim!

CYPRIAN. What he's saying is rather against your interests, isn't it?

LUIGI. Oh, he's not merely our puppet, you know. He's still alive and can say his say.—But don't worry about our interests—they take care of themselves!

*They settle down at the desk, Cyprian behind it, Luigi at the upstage end.*

CYPRIAN. Before we proceed to business, I want you to answer a question, Luigi, that you've always hitherto evaded. Answer me yes or no: What's the truth about the Philosopher's Stone? Is it or is it not possible to make gold out of the baser metals?

LUIGI. What need have you, sir, for the Philosopher's Stone when you can have gold from *us* for the asking?

CYPRIAN. In the first place, it's not in our contract.

LUIGI. It would be easy to arrange a new one.

CYPRIAN. In the second place, I don't want gold.

LUIGI. Do you not make a mistake to disdain it, when it could bring you so many things? I wonder that you don't care to travel.

*The Little Devils, at this hint of temptation, look out from their hiding-places.*

CYPRIAN. The only thing I care about at present is learning the magician's trade.

LUIGI. But frankly, my dear young sir, you labor under a great disadvantage: you know nothing as yet of the world. And you're not getting your money's worth: your time is half up today, and you haven't had any of the things that a young fellow like you could profit by: the refinements and the gaieties of court-life, the freedom of the great ducal libraries—and the women—you know nothing of women—if you could see our Italian beauties! (*He kisses his hand to the air.*) Their flesh as gamy as pheasant! Their flashing illicit glances! (*Cyprian gives him a sour look.*) All this you could have for gold—given your looks and distinction—and you could always fill your purse by a prayer.

THE LITTLE DEVILS (*popping out*). Moola-moola moola-moola!——

LUIGI. Hush up, you little wretches!

*They hide again.*

CYPRIAN (*irritably*). Those imps are getting more and more out of hand. If the customers get a glimpse of them, it will be the end of our business.

LUIGI. Don't worry about that, my lord: the wrong people never see them. And don't let their nonsense annoy you: I was serious in what I was saying.

CYPRIAN. So was I. I don't want your luxuries. I don't want to mix with the rich. I came here to learn how to compete with them on an entirely different ground. And you people haven't taught me a single thing about anything I want to know.

LUIGI. Please tell me what you'd like to learn.

CYPRIAN. Oh, I've told you a dozen times! (*Getting up to expostulate*) I want to know the principles of Nature.

I've only begun since I've been here to see what the problems are. I've been trying, for example, as you know, to find out about the human body. How does our blood heat us? How do we fuel ourselves with food? What contrivances do we carry in our heads to solve problems and perform calculations? Of what does the soul consist and where does it have its lodging?

LUIGI. I've provided the dead bodies you asked for and kept them from going to pieces.

CYPRIAN. But otherwise, you're not of the slightest use. You don't know a thing about anatomy, and you don't seem to have any way of finding out. The truth is that you agents of Satan are just as limited in your way as the priests. You sit at my elbow prescribing spells that will guide people to find lost objects—which are usually much better lost—to know things that are happening at a distance or that haven't happened yet—and that only make trouble when they're known—or to help some young girl attract a man or some old man to get a girl—though, as soon as the spell wears off, they're in a worse situation than ever. The cures that we do are illusions——

LUIGI. You ought not to blame *us* if you limit yourself to these trivia. I've told you you were far too cautious.

CYPRIAN. I haven't the slightest interest in performing mischievous tricks—and I've found out that the greater the magic, the more mischief it's likely to cause.

LUIGI. You take a conventional view of our work.

CYPRIAN. So do you. You're completely conventional, with the conventions turned upside down. You people don't have any real moral courage. You haven't a spark of intellectual audacity. Satan, so far as I can see, knows nothing about philosophy whatever! He may be cunning the same way that you're cunning, but, if *you* represent his deficiencies, he's a Philistine and an ignoramus!

LUIGI. I can't hear my master insulted—and by one

who is scarcely a novice. You mustn't expect too much (*smiling*) for six months of light damnation.

CYPRIAN. You mean that I could learn something more if I took on a heavier commitment?

LUIGI. Of course—and though it's against my own interests—in such matters I've always been candid—in Italy it earned me some credit as a detached and reliable advisor—I should say that you oughtn't to hesitate to enter into a longer contract. You have a stubborn independence of character which, in centuries of varied experience, I have hardly, if ever, seen equalled. A weaker or more frivolous man of such—let me say, unprivileged origin, would have been wallowing in self-indulgence.

*Janet appears in the waiting-room door. Her manner and appearance have somewhat changed: she seems hard and a little vulgar, and her costume is a little flashy.*

JANET. Aren't you ready to begin seeing people? It's almost ten o'clock.

*She produces a small box of rouge from the pocket of her apron, and, holding up her mirror, applies it to her cheeks.*

CYPRIAN (*with acid sarcasm*). There must be somebody you find attractive!

JANET. Do you know what I see in this mirror? A moonlight night in the woods, with a boy who's escaped from the priests falling into the arms of the puffballs.

*Cyprian gives her a sulky glance; Luigi discreetly smiles.*

CYPRIAN. Who's first?

JANET. The steward from the castle. Not a bad-looking man, if it wasn't for his scars from King's Evil.

CYPRIAN. Send him in.

JANET (*nodding to someone in the waiting-room*). You can go in.

*She returns to the waiting-room. A man of about forty enters —his neck is disfigured by scrofula. Cyprian gets up from the desk and comes forward to examine him.*

CYPRIAN. Sit down there.

*The Steward sits down in the visitors' chair. Cyprian looks at his scars.*

CYPRIAN. How long have you had these?

THE STEWARD. Since childhood, Master.

CYPRIAN. Have you ever had anything done about it?

THE STEWARD. No, Master. I'd always heard that only the King could cure it, but my liege lord says *you* can cure it. He gave me this letter to show you.

*Cyprian takes the letter and puts it on the table behind him without looking at it.*

CYPRIAN. You're lucky to have a master who worries about your welfare. (*Feeling the glands in his neck*) Does that feel sore where it's swollen?

THE STEWARD. Yes, Master.

CYPRIAN. Open your shirt.

*The Steward opens his shirt. Cyprian goes to the shelves and takes down a round box.*

LUIGI. Don't you want the mirror?

*He picks up a mirror, breathes on it and makes a quick pass with his left hand. Cyprian, returning from the shelves, reaches out his hand and takes it, without looking at Luigi.*

CYPRIAN (*listening at the Steward's chest*). Now breathe deeply.—All right. (*Making a gesture for him to fasten his shirt and putting his hand on the man's abdomen*) Soreness in the bowels?

THE STEWARD. Yes, Master.

*Cyprian touches the scars, makes a pass and hands the man the mirror.*

THE STEWARD (*in amazement, as he looks in the mirror*). It's gone!

CYPRIAN (*giving the Steward the box*). Take this in hot wine every night just before you go to bed—and come back to see me in a month.

THE STEWARD (*looking in the mirror again*). The first time

I've ever looked like other men! Oh, Master: a thousand thanks!

CYPRIAN. Unfortunately, it won't last—so don't forget to take the powder.

THE STEWARD. My lord bids me tell you he is suffering from another attack of gout. He bids me say he is in horrible pain.

*Luigi, who has been watching the interview, now picks up the letter and reads it.*

CYPRIAN. Tell my lord I much regret to hear of it—that I say he should follow the same regime—cut down on wine and red meat and rub his feet with some more of this salve. (*He gives the Steward another box.*)

THE STEWARD. Yes, Master. Could you not come to the castle and touch it?

CYPRIAN. My touch is powerless against the gout.

*He nods: the man bows and goes out.*

CYPRIAN (*to Luigi*). The trouble is you can't make them diet.

LUIGI. You didn't take account of this letter. (*He reads.*) "This steward of mine is a bad number. He robs me, and I think he's a spy. I've sent him to you for treatment for the King's Evil, but please give him something to finish him off—if possible, without too much howling." As you were saying, the man's very fortunate to be bound to so kind a master. (*Getting up*) I'll bring him back.

CYPRIAN. Sit down: let him go. I'm not my lord's executioner—and I'm interested in these cases. This makes three I've got under treatment.

LUIGI. You can't afford to displease our patron.

CYPRIAN. I'll see him and make it all right. I've always found him perfectly reasonable.

*Janet appears at the door.*

JANET. There's a man here who says he's your brother.

CYPRIAN (*in surprise*). My brother?

JANET. Your brother Cyrus.

CYPRIAN. Well—(*Hesitating*) All right: have him come in.

*Janet turns back to the waiting-room.*

CYPRIAN. You can go now, Luigi.

LUIGI. Don't you think it might be useful to have me here?—in case he wants to ask for something.

CYPRIAN. You heard what I said: now go.

LUIGI. I must remind you that breaches of courtesy are sometimes repaid in kind. With your brother coming to see you, you ought to appear at your best, and you don't want your interview spoiled by interruptions from these impudent children.

*The Little Devils stick out their heads. Cyprian gives Luigi a hostile look. Cyrus appears at the door, dressed better than in Act I and with riding-boots.*

CYPRIAN. Well, Cyrus: what brings you here?

CYRUS. I'm happy to see you, brother. A very fine place you've got!

*Cyprian comes out from behind the desk; they exchange salutatory kisses. Luigi also rises, with a demeanor of extreme deference.*

CYRUS (*admiring his brother's costume*). A full-fledged magician, eh?

CYPRIAN. Not quite. (*Nodding towards Luigi*) This is Luigi, my major-domo—and confidential assistant.

*Cyrus and Luigi bow. Cyprian gestures toward the visitors' chair and goes back behind the desk. They all sit.*

CYPRIAN. I'm surprised that you should venture here.

CYRUS. Many things have changed since you saw me last.

CYPRIAN. You've evidently prospered.

CYRUS (*rather smug*). I haven't done so badly, Cyprian.

CYPRIAN. What's happened? Has the Baron taken you up?

CYRUS. No, Cyprian: he's let me down. I'm sorry to

say you were right about him: I'll have to admit it now.

CYPRIAN (*a little ironical*). What's brought you to that conviction?

CYRUS. I don't want to dwell on the subject—but I was married a month ago——

CYPRIAN. And your wife went up to the castle for the privilege of the first night.

CYRUS. It was a little too much to bear.

CYPRIAN. How did Mother feel about it?

CYRUS. I think she was deeply hurt—though she did her best to take it as a matter of course. Of course, I could hardly do that.

CYPRIAN. No, I suppose not.—How is Father?

CYRUS. He's all right. He sent you his love—he told me to tell you he was proud of you. Everybody's been favorably impressed by the way you've been getting ahead.

CYPRIAN. I haven't really got very far.

CYRUS. But you've taken Merlin's place? You're master of the castle here?

CYPRIAN. Merlin's daughter is the owner of the castle. I'm merely the acting magician.

CYRUS. The whole thing, I understand, is on a thoroughly reputable basis.

CYPRIAN. We're protected by our local lord.—Now tell me what brings you here. You came on a horse like a gentleman?

CYRUS. I think I may say that my horse is one of which no gentleman would be ashamed.

CYPRIAN. Whom do you work for now?

CYRUS. It's become very plain to me, Cyprian, that there's only one side to be on!

CYPRIAN. You're in the King's service?

CYRUS. I am—and *you* ought to be, Cyprian. There's going to be a showdown soon between the King and the lords. You know that he's been cracking down on them?

CYPRIAN. Some rumors of it had reached me.

CYRUS. Did you know that he'd abolished the right to hunt that used to play such havoc with us?

CYPRIAN (*impressed by this*). Has he really? I'm surprised he should go so far. How does old Rody take it?

CYRUS. He blusters, but he keeps to the castle.

CYPRIAN. What about Charles the Bold? *There's* a vassal who wants to be king himself—and who fears neither God nor (*stopping himself as he glances at Luigi*)—sovereign.

CYRUS. Charles is a mutinous hothead—his projects are quite unsound. His Majesty is shrewd and farseeing and will know how to strike when the time is ripe. But he depends on the burgesses to back him up.

CYPRIAN. Are we burgesses?

CYRUS. We're not simple peasants.

CYPRIAN. Yes, of course; in your case, there's a difference.—Do you think there'd be a title in it for you?

CYRUS. It's not beyond the bounds of the possible. His Majesty has had the grace to ennoble persons of baser birth.

CYPRIAN. I see. Well, I wish you luck.

CYRUS. That must wait. In the meantime, my only aim is to serve His Majesty's cause.—And I want you to help me, Cyprian.

CYPRIAN. What can *I* do for Louis?

CYRUS. You possess certain powers, I understand.

CYPRIAN (*shrugging*). Only to a limited extent.

LUIGI (*with a smile, to Cyrus*). If you will permit me, sir: Master Cyprian is far too modest.

CYRUS (*after taking this in, to Cyprian*). The King, you know, is strong on magic. He keeps an astrologer at court.

CYPRIAN. Astrology has always bored me: I'm not sure there's anything in it.

CYRUS. That wasn't what I had in mind. I've heard on the highest authority that there might be a place at court for a mage of another kind. The inevitable day is coming when Louis must meet Charles in the field. Now, if Charles could be sent adverse weather—or a pestilence to weaken his troops—or even a fatal stroke in one of his fits of temper!—I don't know what your magic can do . . . ? (*He looks inquiringly toward Luigi.*)

LUIGI. A mage of Master Cyprian's caliber can command almost infinite powers if the proper conditions are met.

CYPRIAN. How could I serve the King and keep my liege lord's protection? He belongs to the nobles' league, too.

CYRUS. That doesn't sound like you, Cyprian! You never liked to owe anything to the nobles.

CYPRIAN. This one's a brilliant exception: a patron of the new learning, a humane and enlightened man.

LUIGI (*smiling slyly*). With occasional lapses perhaps.

CYPRIAN. I'm perfectly satisfied.

CYRUS. Take the King for your patron, Cyprian—our protector against feudal privilege!

LUIGI (*to Cyprian*). You wanted revenge, you know.

CYPRIAN. I've got to learn my business first.

CYRUS. This is the moment, Cyprian: the struggle will soon be decided.

CYPRIAN. Come back in three months' time—come back when you can tell me exactly in what way I could be useful at court and whether the King would receive me.

LUIGI. If the crisis arises sooner?

CYPRIAN (*getting up*). It will have to be decided without me. Come back the first week in July. That's all I can say at the present time.—And now I must see my clients. These are my office hours.—(*Not urging him very warmly*) You'll stay with us, won't you?

CYRUS. I can't tonight: I must get on to Abbéville on business of vital importance. But I'd like to lie down for an hour. (*Yawning*) I've been riding most of the night.

88

CYPRIAN. Yes, certainly.—(*To Luigi*) Will you please ask Miss Janet to come in here?

LUIGI (*obsequiously*). Yes, Your Excellency: at once.

*He goes out into the waiting-room.*

CYRUS (*looking around*). You're living devilish well here, Cyprian——

CYPRIAN (*nervously*). What?—Oh, yes.

CYRUS. —though your furnishings are a bit peculiar. (*Seeing the tray on the table*) A snack always handy, eh? (*He starts to lift the cover to see what is underneath.*)

CYPRIAN (*catching him just in time*). Don't touch that! Put it down!

CYRUS (*hastily dropping the cover*). What is it?

CYPRIAN. It's magic—it's not really a lunch. You mustn't fool with things around here.

*Janet comes in with Luigi.*

CYPRIAN. But you'll be all right in your room. (*To Janet*) This is my brother Cyrus. (*To Cyrus*) This is Miss Janet, Merlin's daughter. She is the châtelaine here. (*She curtsies; Cyrus bows.*) Cyrus has been riding all night and wants to lie down for a nap. Will you have a room made ready?

JANET. The room in the north tower is always prepared for guests, if your brother will please to accept it.

LUIGI. May I have the honor of escorting him?

CYPRIAN. I'll show him the way myself. (*To Janet*) Are there any more people out there?

JANET. Only one: Mr. B.—our ever-returning petitioner.

CYPRIAN. Have him come in—I'll be back in a moment.

*He takes Cyrus out through the double doors. The latter bows deeply to Janet.*

JANET. You can go, Luigi.

LUIGI. This brother was sent by our people. It carries out part of the pact, you know, and it's time that we got him hooked. He's getting bored with his conjuring-tricks.

89

JANET (*walking to the waiting-room door*). I know all about that. You can go.

*He withdraws through the double doors.*

JANET (*at the waiting-room door*). Come in, please.

*Mr. B. enters. During the conversation that follows, the Little Devils look out of their hiding-places, astonished to see Mr. B. and at first very much in awe of him.*

JANET. And how is your good wife?

*He turns away.*

JANET. Not dead already?

MR. B. Yes.

JANET. What a pity when you wanted so to love her! So *she* never got the love, and *you* have lost your idol.

MR. B. I am greatly to blame—I should never have tried.

JANET. We must practise humility now!

MR. B. With her I was always humble. How else could I have given up my throne and gone with her to live in the forest?

JANET. *You* humble! *You* playing the penitent! The most arrogant devil in Hell! You thought that it wasn't enough to challenge the Powers Above: even when you'd been damned to eternity, you dared to rebel against Hell—to pretend to the honors of sainthood!—and now that you haven't succeeded, you're whining like a dirty Franciscan!

*The Little Devils show signs of delight.*

MR. B. Beware of moral scorn, Miss Janet: it doesn't hurt *me*, but it's harmful to *you*. It's an emotion we used to encourage.

JANET (*laughing*). Harmful for me, is it? Miss Janet thanks Mr. B.!—He's too thoughtful for that darling Miss Janet who was always so nice to his wife—but then, there's another Miss Janet who rejoices to hear of her death!

MR. B. Oh, it's you! (*He takes her by the shoulders and looks into her eyes intently.*) I thought there was something wrong! How did you get in here, Jezebel?

JANET. That young pedant did nothing to prevent it. He actually left the door half-open.

MR. B. This is rather small time for you!

JANET. I picked the assignment on purpose. I wanted to enjoy your fiasco.

MR. B. So I've earned the vengeance of Hell as well as the vengeance of Heaven.—(*Bitterly and fiercely*) Well, I'm ready to stand up to both!

JANET. You presumptuous twice-damned fool! What will you try to do now? You can hardly go home again: you won't find them very cordial.

MR. B. When was Hell ever cordial?

*The Little Devils, emboldened now, come out and begin to jeer at him in their native diabolic language.*

BONGO. *Mákka-nánya oónya gígna-weésta!*

STINGO. *Mákka-nányi gánzi gleésta-gleésta!*

SLINGO. *Gánza wíddi-wíddi skímba-nímbi!*

ALL (*pointing and prolonging the vowels in a final intensive insult*). *Nímba-nambáyanyi-neeésta-neeésta!* (*They break into derisive laughter.*)

JANET (*to Mr. B.*). Why don't you make them be quiet? *The Little Devils stop laughing.*

MR. B. I've given up my authority now—I'm not going back to Hell.

JANET. Turning the other cheek! I thought you had guts at least!

*The Little Devils, thus encouraged, begin to snicker again. Slingo slaps Stingo on the cheek, and Stingo turns the other cheek, meekly rolling up his eyes and, his skewer under his arm, joining his hands in a pose of prayer. Bongo raises his mallet to hit Stingo on the head, but Stingo sees this and dodges away and falls upon Bongo with his skewer. Slingo seizes Stingo by the tail in order to pull him off.*

JANET (*to the Little Devils*). *Gyench-gónchamyank-gónya-gyench!*

*They cease fighting and scamper to their places, from which, however, they continue to peer. Mr. B. goes over to the waiting-room door and looks out as if to check on something.*

JANET (*to Mr. B.*). You've got to expect this. But don't think that *I'm* going to jeer at you.

MR. B. (*ironic*). Kind of you, Jezebel!

JANET. I've already had my revenge—and you really can't blame me, can you? After centuries we'd spent together!

MR. B. Who am I to blame you?

*The Little Devils shriek with laughter at this.*

JANET (*nodding toward the waiting-room door*). You've got the body out there?

MR. B. Yes.

JANET. A problem for you, I can see. What will you do with her now?

MR. B. That's no concern of yours.

*Bongo darts over behind the desk and whispers to Slingo and Stingo. They eagerly fall in with his suggestion, and all, without Mr. B.'s seeing them, creep across the back of the stage and out into the waiting-room. Cyprian comes in from the porch.*

CYPRIAN (*to Mr. B.*). I'm sorry to keep you waiting, but my brother has just arrived. How have things been going with you?

MR. B. My wife is dead.

CYPRIAN (*after a moment's shocked silence, with sincerity*). I'm sorry—I'm terribly sorry. (*To Janet*) You didn't tell me how ill she was.

JANET. I wasn't able to get to see her.

CYPRIAN (*to Mr. B.*). If you'd only come back to see me! I had something that might have helped her!

MR. B. Nothing would have helped. It was sent by *Him*. But I want to ask you one favor.

CYPRIAN. Yes, of course: what is it?

MR. B. Well, you know the new priest here: he's a fool,

an insane fanatic. He wouldn't let her be buried in the churchyard—which, after all, is understandable—but when I made her a grave in the forest, he preached to the village people that they ought to go out and dig her up and drive a stake through her body. He told them she was a vampire and would rise from the grave.

CYPRIAN. I'm not sure that she'd be safe here. You know that we——

MR. B. I know about that.

CYPRIAN. But still, if she died a Christian, I doubt whether they could harm her.

MR. B. She tried to, but I can't be sure. The priest, of course, wouldn't come near her—and she refused to repudiate her love for me—which of course was completely irregular—though I did my best to persuade her.

CYPRIAN. Won't somebody intercede?

MR. B. (*ruefully shrugging his shoulders and nodding toward the heavens*). You'd imagine that Somebody would if Their principles are what They pretend.

CYPRIAN (*to Janet*). Could we put her in the family vault?

JANET. There's no room. It was full up when Father died.

CYPRIAN. There's still room between the niches. The devils wouldn't dare disturb her—(*to Mr. B.*) Where is she?

MR. B. I brought her—in a kind of coffin. I didn't want to leave her in the forest.

CYPRIAN. You brought it to the castle here?

JANET (*nodding toward the door on the left*). He left it in the waiting-room. A delightful surprise for our clients!

MR. B. It looks like a travelling chest. Nobody would know it's a coffin.

*Cyrus comes in through the double doors in a state of restrained agitation. The Little Devils creep in behind him and listen with evident glee. Luigi discreetly follows.*

CYRUS (*to Cyprian*). I don't know whether you know it, Cyprian, but that bed's got a dead woman in it.

CYPRIAN. What, the bed in your bedroom?

CYRUS. Yes.

CYPRIAN. It was all right when I was there. I made a point of looking through the curtains.

CYRUS. It may have happened after you left. I was out of the room for a while. A little black page appeared and said he'd been sent by you to show me the grounds.

*Cyprian glances toward the Little Devils, who quickly pull in their heads.*

CYPRIAN. You're sure it was not a dummy or a mere empty simulacrum?

CYRUS. I'd say it was perfectly real and that it needed immediate attention. She was pretty far gone around the mouth.

MR. B. (*to Cyprian*). Take me to the room, please.

*Cyrus, looking around at Mr. B. and taking in his strange appearance, is more flabbergasted than ever.*

CYPRIAN (*moving toward the door, to Cyrus*). I'm sorry about it, Cy. We've had some mischievous spirits here—though our friend Mr. B. isn't one of them.

JANET. I doubt whether Cyprian would notice whether a bed had a woman in it—or whether she were alive or not!

*Cyprian goes out to the porch, followed by Mr. B.*

LUIGI (*coming forward, to Janet*). Those young ruffians will have to be dealt with. One would think it was Halloween! (*To the Little Devils*) Away with you!—I'll make you say the Lord's Prayer backwards five hundred and fifty-nine times.

*They retreat through the double door.*

LUIGI (*to Cyrus*). Can we hope that you will pardon us, sir? You will have a poor opinion, I fear, of the hospitality of the castle. How a person of your gentle birth must have shuddered at this disgusting incident!

CYRUS. I cannot claim gentle birth.

LUIGI. But your dress, your demeanor, your conversation, all—if you will pardon my saying so—unmistakably proclaim noble blood.—We must trust to your knowledge of the world, if not to condone, then at least to comprehend, that—distasteful though we always find it —we are sometimes compelled to resort to rather unsavory agents. Even His Majesty must sometimes do that!

CYRUS. His Majesty's agents are all loyal subjects.

LUIGI (*with a deprecatory laugh*). Well, I can't say so much for our own. But what we aim at is to get results, and we cannot afford petty scruples.—I was fascinated by your subtle ideas for demolishing Charles the Bold. To the modern magician, such projects present an exciting challenge.

CYRUS. Could it be done?

LUIGI. There's no doubt that it *could* be done, but the cost would be rather high.

CYRUS. His Majesty can meet any cost.

LUIGI. It would be necessary for Master Cyprian—or for somebody empowered to act for him—to wait upon the King himself.

CYRUS. I am prepared to secure such an audience.

LUIGI. It ought, of course, to be done at once.

CYRUS. That's just what I was trying to tell him!

*Cyprian and Mr. B. return through the double doors. Mr. B. is carrying a long chest, which he sets down just inside the room; he stands in front of it with folded arms.*

CYPRIAN (*to Cyrus*). Don't think me inhospitable, Cyrus, but perhaps it is just as well for you not to try to stay here at present.

CYRUS. Don't say a word, old boy! I appreciate the situation perfectly. It's a ticklish business, I know—but the big results are what count, eh?

CYPRIAN (*taking Cyrus by the arm*). I'll go down and have your horse brought round.

CYRUS. Your counsellor here has suggested that, if anything is going to be done in the way of approaching the King, it ought to be done at once.

LUIGI (*to Cyprian*). Let me remind you, sir, that if you wait till our agreement ends, you may no longer have the power to act.

*Cyprian, impressed by this, stands silent a moment, thinking.*

CYPRIAN (*to Cyrus*). Come in on your way back from Abbéville.

LUIGI (*to Cyprian*). I should be happy to represent you, if you feel, sir, that you cannot leave the castle.

CYPRIAN. If anything's to be done, I'll do it myself.

LUIGI (*smiling to himself*). Very good, sir.

CYRUS. It's a chance of a lifetime, Cyprian! It's the biggest thing since the Crusades! If Louis falls, then France is lost, and that would sound the knell of Christendom. The Sultan's at the gates of Venice, and Venice is the gate to Europe!

CYPRIAN. I congratulate you, Cyrus.

CYRUS. You may, indeed! Am I not defending our Holy Faith—the Cross against the heathen Crescent!

*Luigi, at the mention of the Cross, shudders and bites his lip; Cyprian looks away.*

CYPRIAN. I meant, on having found a new source for eloquent readymade phrases.—But come in on your way back.

CYRUS. Right you are, Cyprian. And now I'll be off. (*Kissing Janet's hand*) At your service, my lady. (*Bowing low to Luigi*) Your servant, sir.

CYPRIAN (*turning to Janet*). Will you get me the key to the vault?

*He steers Cyrus toward the waiting-room door. Luigi follows.*

JANET. I don't know where it is—I've mislaid it.

LUIGI (*speaking to Cyprian just as Cyrus goes out*). You

know this is just what you asked for: a chance to get back at the Baron.

CYPRIAN (*on his way out*). You don't need to tell me, Luigi.

*He goes out, and Luigi follows.*

MR. B. (*stepping forward as Cyrus leaves the room*). Give me the key: you've got it there.

JANET (*clutching the bunch of keys that hangs at her belt*). I'll give it to you on one condition.

MR. B. I don't accept any conditions.

JANET. In that case, you can no longer command me.

MR. B. (*moving toward the chest, as if to pick it up*). Quite true: well, do as you please.

JANET (*holding out the key*). Bury your saint if you like but then come back to *me*.

MR. B. I've told you, I'm done with all that. I'm sick of the traffic in souls. It can no longer nourish my pride.

JANET. It did in those days in Provence when you and I were working together. You were brilliant when you talked over the Albigensians and got them all burned as heretics! What a great lark that was! Not only were the heretics damned but we pulled in the monks as well. How we laughed when those Inquisitors were dying and thought they were going to their just reward, and then found a beady-eyed devil waiting to whisk them below.

MR. B. Yes: that was a dirty business! The best of those heretics were holy men. It was they who should have gone to Heaven. He leaves it to the churchmen to decide about doctrine and then damns them for their sins of ambition and spite.

JANET. Well, you see what you get by criticizing. You were once the most envied of all the devils—the most dashing figure in Hell. They talked about your exploits in Heaven. And what are you now? Nothing: a laughing-stock to Hell and Heaven both!

MR. B. I carried such exploits as far as they could go. Doing evil is a blind alley.

JANET. Did you know that the King was available?—Louis, their French King? That brother who was here has a plan to reach him. He's crafty and deceitful, Louis. They say that he's pious and superstitious, but with the superstitious kind of piety, it's never hard to turn it the other way.

MR. B. That sordid schemer and traitor!—I don't even want to know him.

JANET. What a lofty moral tone for a devil as black as Sin!

MR. B. I can make my own choice of evils.

JANET. Oh, *can* you? You tried to repudiate your people, and what happened?—you sent your ugly mistress to Hell——

MR. B. Is she there?

JANET. Of course she's there. Didn't she give herself to you?—And you're stuck with her nasty remains, going around begging favors of mortals, with no home and no occupation. It's an impasse: you'll have to go back.

MR. B. I want neither Heaven nor Hell.

JANET. Why don't you fly to Arabia and bury your darling there in the earth of the unbelievers?

MR. B. I won't use diabolic powers—it would make me a devil again. I want to rejoin mankind.

JANET. But why?

MR. B. There's the germ of some new power in them—a power that may shatter our universe.

JANET. I can't imagine what you mean; but in any case you never can join them.

MR. B. After all, their Savior, His son, did.

JANET. Oh, so that's it!—I hadn't guessed. You want to compete with *Him*! You can't rest till you're crucified!

MR. B. (*smiling*). I know who would drive the first nail.

JANET. Oh, oh, that's too much! Old Crucified! Old Hornless carrying a coffin!—Well, you can't leave your coffin here. Even our little imps can knock it around, you see!

MR. B. The bodies of mighty magicians lie under a spell in that vault. Your hoodlums won't dare go near it.

JANET. I'll tell you what I'll do then, and this you won't like! That young idiot is crazy for corpses—he cuts them up for his medical studies, and I'll give him your late wife as a subject. He's already so much under my influence that he hasn't even noticed yet that Jezebel isn't Janet, and the slightest suggestion from me would soon have him hauling out that cadaver and scrouging at her liver and lights.

MR. B. (*suddenly furious*). Be still! I command you— begone!

*He seizes Janet by the upper arms and bends over her with fierce eyes, while she tries to avoid his gaze, threshing from side to side.*

MR. B. Look at me, you miserable succuba! I make myself your master again. Get out of this good girl's body and let her return to herself! (*She convulsively strains her head away, but he grasps it and holds it before him.*) Your master commands you: go!

*He slaps her on either cheek, and she utters a hateful cry that prolongs itself and sinks to a moan, as he drops her into a chair to the left of the double doors, her eyes staring fixedly and her body held rigid, as if in a cataleptic fit. Mr. B. stands over her, ferocious; then, glaring, looks away at the coffin; then becomes aghast at himself.*

MR. B. That's bad: the first time I've relapsed! I must curb it: I might have been cruel (*looking at Janet in the chair*)—I might have spat on the coffin or kicked it (*turning away toward the chest*)—I might have flamed up and flown back to Hell. But no: I can hold, still. (*He carefully picks up the coffin and balances it on his shoulder.*) Neither Satan nor the Other shall judge me, for I can judge myself. I will keep my oath to myself though I carry this coffin forever!

*He goes out through the double door.*

JANET (*gasping in her own voice, like a sleeper crying out from a nightmare*). Cyprian—oh, Cyprian, help me!

*Cyprian comes in from the waiting-room, does not notice Janet at first and looks around for Mr. B., then sees that the coffin is gone. He goes to the double doors and out on the stone porch.*

CYPRIAN. Mr. B.!—oh, Mr. B.! (*He returns, sees Janet, but goes on to the desk, hardly glancing at her, and, busying himself with papers, speaks to her with casual coldness.*) Did you drive him away? What did you do?—pretend you couldn't find the key?—I don't understand you, Janet. You used to be so considerate, and now you seem so hard. You're as cutting and cold as your father was.—I thought at first that, no matter what happened, I'd always have a supporter in you—and now I don't feel that you're with me at all. There's nobody I can count on—not a soul! The worst of it is that I'm not even sure that any of us has got a soul.

JANET. This is my soul, Cyprian!

CYPRIAN. What? (*He looks over and sees her strange attitude, then comes to her and stands before her.*) Are you ill? What's the matter?

JANET (*gasping*). I can't wake up—from the nightmare. I've been—asleep—too long.

CYPRIAN (*shaking her*). Your eyes are open. Wake up!——

JANET. I can't—get control—of my body.

CYPRIAN. What's happened? Come: try to move!

JANET. You—banished me. You thrust me—away.

CYPRIAN. I'm here with you now.

JANET. Are you?

CYPRIAN. Yes, of course.—You sound like your old self again!

JANET (*speaking somewhat more easily, her face becoming responsive and her hands making freer gestures, though she still remains stiffly seated*). An alien spirit was in me.

CYPRIAN. What spirit?

JANET. That woman I told you about.

CYPRIAN. They bewitched you!

JANET. I'm not free yet.—Why did you have them do it?

CYPRIAN. I didn't.

JANET. You asked not to love me.

CYPRIAN. But not to dislike you.

JANET. It has to be one or the other.

CYPRIAN. Not always.

JANET. If people want one another.

CYPRIAN. I didn't know what would happen.

JANET. Try to break the spell.

CYPRIAN. How can I? I've signed a pact, and it's still got three months to run.

JANET. They're trying to make you sign another.

CYPRIAN (*realizing the situation*). So they are! They were almost succeeding! What's happened to me? I've not been myself.

JANET. Try to fight them with some other kind of magic.

CYPRIAN. But what?

JANET. Try the genie in the bottle.

CYPRIAN. Could a genie destroy the pact?

JANET. It's supposed to be the strongest thing.

CYPRIAN. All right—*by God*! I'll try it!

JANET. Better hurry! I don't want them to take me back. In the storeroom: the closet on the left.

CYPRIAN. I know where it is!

*He dashes out to the porch. She tries to gain control of herself and succeeds, holding on to the arms, in partly getting up from the chair. Luigi hurries in through the double doors, followed by the Little Devils.*

LUIGI (*to Janet*). Jezebel! . . . What's this? are you here?
*Janet does not answer.*

LUIGI. That renegade has sent her away! . . . (*Looking around the room*) Jezebel, are you here?

JANET. Keep away: I don't want you near me!

*Luigi comes around to face Janet and makes rapid signs in the air. She sinks back into the chair, stiffening and staring again.*

LUIGI (*hypnotic and soothing*). Abátha amátha-náthas. (*Peremptorily and sharply*) Jezebel, amákkin-tákkyulak knáthas!

*The Little Devils cluster around to see what is going to happen.*

JANET. Go away, go away! I hate you!

*Luigi signals to Stingo, who leaps upon Janet's lap and holds his skewer against her heart.*

LUIGI (*almost shrieking with vehemence*). Yield!—you must yield to Jezebel! Do you feel this poniard at your heart? In a moment it will pierce you through. Satan is not mocked!

JANET. Kill me and free my spirit!

LUIGI. *Knáthsa bemblóso-bássa! amássa strúmpstharso, Iezebel!* (*Stressing the syllable* strumpsth) Now, yield to her!

*Janet is shaken as if by a sudden jolt and sits forward, pushing Stingo off her lap.*

*Cyprian comes back through the double doors, carrying a round copper bottle. Seeing Luigi and the Little Devils clustered around Janet, he rushes over and, taking Luigi by the arm, violently flings him aside.*

CYPRIAN. Get away from her, you filthy fiend!

LUIGI (*seeing the bottle and pointing at it*). What's that?

CYPRIAN. We're soon going to see!

LUIGI (*servile again*). Oh, I beg you, sir, don't open that bottle! It's dangerous to mix two magics!

CYPRIAN. Dangerous to you, perhaps.

LUIGI. But the game we play has certain rules—both sides must abide by the rules. You accepted our terms and you must stick to them!

CYPRIAN. I never promised not to summon new forces. And, frankly, I'm bored with you, Luigi—I don't fall for your banal temptations, and I'm sick of the confusion here: personalities going to pieces, dead people in the beds! Even my work is all mixed up with charlatanry, and I'm not making any progress!

LUIGI. You have only three more months of your bargain.

CYPRIAN. Here's something that will help me get through them. (*He holds the bottle up and reads an inscription on it.*) "Giant oriental genie: impervious to Western magic; capable of immense labors. Does everything on a colossal scale, so be careful not to ask too much."

*The Little Devils slink out through the double doors. Janet is now possessed again by Jezebel, and starts up from the chair with a shriek.*

JANET. A genie? Oh, *no!*

*She rushes out through the waiting-room.*

LUIGI. You don't know what you're doing, sir. He could pick up this whole castle, just the way an eagle does a tortoise, and smash it on the earth below!

CYPRIAN (*goes on reading*). "Be sure to make bargain with genie before letting him out of bottle."

LUIGI. My good sir, you won't be able to control him! It takes a wizard of exceptional powers.

CYPRIAN (*still reading*). "Real name is"—I can't pronounce it—"but he answers to the name of Buster"——

THE GENIE (*in a high thin voice*). There is no God but Allah, and Mohammed is his prophet!

CYPRIAN (*to the Genie*). Will you do what I ask if I let you out?

BUSTER. I swear it by the beard of the Prophet!

*Cyprian takes out a knife and begins to scrape away the wax with which the stopper is sealed.*

LUIGI (*in desperation*). Do you realize that this genie is a Mohammedan? Do you want to let Islam in?

CYPRIAN (*straining at the stopper, as he holds the bottle against his thigh*). Better Mohammed than Satan!

*Luigi gasps for a moment as if to start a new remonstrance, then swiftly glides out through the double doors.*

*The stopper comes out with a loud report. Darkness: a hissing sound, as if of steam escaping. Then the Genie is seen in a spot-light, towering in the center of the stage and facing toward Cyprian at stage left. He has oriental eyes, swarthy skin, hair that stands straight up on his head and a mustache that resembles Stalin's. He is dressed in oriental costume.*

BUSTER (*in a guttural voice*). My liberator, how can I serve you?

CYPRIAN. This castle has been taken by Satan. I cannot expel him yet. But help me to hold him in check—help me keep order here.

# ACT IV

*The study, three months later: the night of the last day of June. The double doors are open on darkness and a sky where a few stars appear. The magician's robe and cap are back on their peg in the corner. Buster is sitting behind the desk, leaning back in his chair, with his left foot up on the desk-top. He has finished his day's work and is enjoying a moment of recreation. The skeleton has been hung from the shelves to the right of the tray with Claude's head, and Bongo is playing on its ribs with his hammer, as if it were a xylophone. His back is presented to the audience, and he is seen to have lost his tail, of which only a stump is left, with a bandage tied around it. The tune is* Au Clair de la Lune. *At the end of the last line —Pour l'amour de Dieu—he strikes a sour note. Buster looks around with a frown.*

BUSTER. What kind of music is that?

BONGO. It's a much-admired melody, Your Radiance— but we don't like the last word, so we give it a touch of dissonance.

BUSTER. Disgusting European stuff! The art of the West is putrescent! Give me something gay from the East.

BONGO. Yes, Your Radiance.

*He begins to play some hootchy-kootchy music: Buster sits back and smiles. Stingo comes in briskly from the porch and stands at attention beside the desk. Bongo looks around from his xylophone; Buster with a gesture bids Bongo stop, and he stands at attention with his hammer in both hands.*

BUSTER (*to Stingo*). Well, what is it?

STINGO (*making a low salaam and presenting a piece of parchment but looking at Buster with hatred*). Master Cyprian just got this letter.

BUSTER (*scanning the letter*). What's he doing?

STINGO. Just the same thing as usual: mucking around with dead rabbits.

BUSTER (*throwing down the letter*). Tell him to come here at once.

STINGO (*salaaming*). Immediately, Your Radiance.

*He goes out through the back, and at the same moment Slingo comes running in. He has been flying and has just alighted. He hurriedly salaams.*

BUSTER. You're late. What's the reason?

SLINGO. I'm sorry, boss: I couldn't make it no faster.

BUSTER. It oughtn't to take you twelve hours to pop down to Constantinople!

SLINGO. I can't seem to fly like I used to, boss.

BUSTER. That's not the way to address me!

SLINGO. Excuse it, please, Commander of the Faithful.

BUSTER. And *why* can't you fly like you used to?

SLINGO. It seems like I'm losing my power, boss—— (*catching himself up*) Bright Shining Sun. It must be those Mohammedan prayers you make us say every day. They kinda take the zingo out of us.

BUSTER. Be still, you little infidel flea that doesn't even know how to hop!

SLINGO. Yes—Center of the Universe.

BUSTER. What message did the Sultan give you?

SLINGO. He told me to inform Your Radiance that he figures it won't be long now. It seems as though Venice was knuckling under.

BUSTER. What else?

SLINGO. Mm. Seems like he didn't say no more.

BUSTER. He must have said something more.

SLINGO. Seems like my memory is going, too.

BUSTER. Was your memory sufficiently retentive to convey to him the message I gave you?

SLINGO. I told him, like you told me, that the princes of Europe are all at one anudder's t'roats—so deh can't carry on no new crusade.

BUSTER. All right: go and get a rest, and then make another effort to remember what the Sultan said.

SLINGO. Can I skip the prayers tonight, boss?

BUSTER. Are my orders to be questioned?

SLINGO. No, boss—but I can tell you that my old chief in Hell ain't gonta like it much if he t'inks I'm disloyal to him. He's gonta turn off my current, he's gonta let me fade away.

BUSTER. What do you mean, "disloyal"? Mohammed is your only chief! Say it after me: Allah is the only God.

SLINGO. Allah is the only God!

BUSTER. "And"—go on! "And"——

SLINGO. And Mohammed is his prophet.

BONGO (*producing a scrap of parchment*). I wonder whether this might help to explain. I found it in Slingo's writing. It raises a suspicion of sabotage.

BUSTER (*taking the slip and reading aloud*).

"Oh, Buster Big is a very big pig,
But he came from a very small bottle."

(*He gives Slingo a terrible look.*)

"He tried to boss the demon force—
He tried to make them grovel"——

SLINGO. I didn't write dat, boss! I can rhyme better dan dat!

BUSTER. Ha! A formalist, eh?

SLINGO (*pointing at Bongo*). *He* wrote it—*he* wrote it—he wrote it himself!

BONGO. Everybody knows that Slingo has been writing all our songs.

SLINGO. You dirty little squealer! *you* write dem!

BUSTER (*to Slingo*). Do you know what happened to Bongo for running away last night? (*To Bongo*) Show him your rump, you rat!

*Bongo turns around and sticks out his behind, displaying the pathetic stump. Slingo, with an instinctive movement, puts his hand to his tail.*

*Cyprian and Luigi come in by way of the door on the left. Cyprian is dressed in his working clothes.*

BUSTER (*to Luigi*). Luigi, take this little black ape and clip him like the other one. (*Illustrating with his right hand brought down like a cleaver on to his left palm*). Chop, chop!

LUIGI (*salaaming*). Your order shall be executed, Commander of the Faithful.

BUSTER. He's a poet, our little Slingo! Let him write a nice hymn to Buster—and Bongo will set it to music! (*He makes a gesture for them to go.*)

*Luigi salaams again and leads Bongo and Slingo out by the back, dragging them by the arms.*

CYPRIAN (*to Buster*). Well, what is it? It's got to be important. I told you not to disturb me at night.

BUSTER (*holding up the letter*). No visitors, Master Cyprian! Your brother must not come here.

CYPRIAN. You're spying on my correspondence! I thought our understanding was that you were to run the castle and I was to be left in peace!

BUSTER. Has anyone interfered with your work?

CYPRIAN. These devils are a damned nuisance! I can't leave my room a minute without having an imp creep in.

BUSTER. I ordered them to be very quiet.

CYPRIAN. I don't want them around at all!

*Slingo screams shrilly outside. Cyprian turns with a frown.*

BUSTER (*with a too friendly smile*). Security, good Master Cyprian: we have to take proper precautions! It wouldn't do to have it known that you're harboring a Mohammedan here.

CYPRIAN. We shan't need precautions now. You'll be free to go home tomorrow. My agreement with Satan expires at twelve o'clock noon.

BUSTER. I'm quite comfortable here, Master Cyprian, and I don't think you ought to be hasty in dismissing our helpful devils. I've brought them to heel, as you see. They can profitably serve us both, and my presence here gives you protection. Have I not established order, as you bade me?

CYPRIAN. I shan't need you for that any more.

BUSTER. But how can you pursue your studies without an Arabian mentor? Arabia is the mother of medicine——

CYPRIAN. Not quite: there were also the Greeks.

BUSTER. Oh, no, no, no, Master Cyprian! All the vital discoveries in the healing art were made by the race of the Prophet. Have you read the treatise I gave you?

CYPRIAN. I can tell you that the Arabs are out of date. Their use of drugs even is obsolete, and what interests me most—anatomy—is a subject they've never touched.

BUSTER. Anatomy is an unclean study. The Koran forbids us to tamper with corpses. No, your work should be with drugs, Master Cyprian. The countryside is ringing with your marvellous cures—all of which you owe to Arab science!

CYPRIAN. The fact remains, Buster, that you leave tomorrow.

BUSTER. I am not at your orders, Master Cyprian—you summoned me here in the first place and you cannot expel me now. Christendom is crumbling while its rulers quarrel. Do you know that with one blow of my fist (*he brings it down on the table*) I could smash this little castle to atoms?

CYPRIAN. I wonder that you haven't snatched Paris and presented it on a platter to the Sultan!

BUSTER. That will come, Master Cyprian. The sword of Allah will conquer—and in the meantime our interests, yours and mine, are absolutely one and the same. Are we not both the sworn foes of Christendom? You have spat upon its fraudulent God——

CYPRIAN. Not to take on your even more fraudulent one.

BUSTER (*roaring*). Blasphemer!—be respectful to Allah or I'll slit your unbelieving throat! Get back to your laboratory—throw out your disgusting dead bodies and give me prescriptions for the healing of wounds! In this war we are waging on Europe, we shall need to save horses and men.

*Janet has appeared from the waiting-room.*

JANET (*to Buster*). You'd better go to Luigi on the porch. A messenger from Hell has arrived to send him on to another assignment when his time is up here tomorrow.

BUSTER. The old reptile! He told me he was free to stay. (*To Janet*) Don't *you* come—you keep away!

*He hurries out through the doorway at the back.*

CYPRIAN (*to Janet*). Can a genie get the better of the Devil?

JANET. That's what I want to see.

CYPRIAN. What I don't understand is how Buster has been getting all you people to submit to him.

JANET. The way he gets Luigi to submit to him is by promising the old fool to have him admitted to the Mohammedan paradise. He's told him that a devil who accepts their faith can blossom into a blessed spirit, and Luigi's been so long in Italy tempting people to sensual pleasures that he couldn't enjoy himself that he fell for (*ironically*) all those fountain-sprayed gardens and beautiful black-eyed houris and non-alcoholic drinks that the faithful are supposed to get.

CYPRIAN. Have the imps been converted, too?

JANET. They have to take orders from Luigi.

CYPRIAN. And how about you?

JANET. I'm not working for Buster. There's nothing in it for me.

CYPRIAN. Why not?

JANET. You know what they think of women!

CYPRIAN. Why does Buster want to stay in Europe? The way he was talking just now, I almost thought he was a Mohammedan agent.

JANET. Of course he's a Mohammedan agent. He thinks he's preparing the conquest of Europe. Some sultan shut him up in a bottle a couple of centuries ago for belonging to the wrong sect—that's the worst thing that can happen to a Mohammedan—and now he's working his silly fat head off trying to show how loyal he is. This castle is their headquarters in France now.

CYPRIAN. I never know when you're lying.

JANET. You don't need to worry in this case. I don't want Islam to win: it would mean the end of my freedom.

CYPRIAN. Then why did you tell Buster the messenger was here?

JANET. I wanted to see which was the stronger.—Look out now and tell me what they're doing.

*Cyprian goes to the doorway and, keeping out of sight, watches.*

JANET. I'm worrying because Luigi and his imps have been losing their vitality lately. This Mohammedanism is making them impotent.

CYPRIAN (*reporting on the scene outside*). It looks as if Buster was winning.

JANET. How disgusting! They'll want you to sign a new pact. He'll be constantly needing new devils, because working for him makes them go dead.

CYPRIAN. I'll tell you they won't succeed.

JANET. They're in the strong position.

CYPRIAN. They've evidently agreed on something. The messenger is going now.

JANET. I'll be furious if I have to stay on here bedevilling an untonsured monastic like you! Oh, for a decent assignment, with a victim one can get one's teeth into!

*Buster and Luigi come in. Janet gives them a look and goes out through the waiting-room.*

BUSTER (*to Cyprian*). An emissary from Luigi's sovereign. I believe we can work together—we must have your consent to a new agreement.

LUIGI. It's a question of renewing the pact—for a couple of years, let us say.

CYPRIAN. The pact will be over tomorrow!

LUIGI. Pray listen to me, Master Cyprian. If you will stay with us a little longer, your position will become supreme. The combination of your medical skill and the prodigies of our magic have already made a great impression. Why should you not continue? You can become the most brilliant physician in Europe.

CYPRIAN. I'm tired of playing the charlatan.

BUSTER. You need not even lack opportunity for your favorite study of anatomy. It is true that the dissection of corpses is implacably forbidden by the Prophet, but we have nothing against vivisection, and in the war that is to burst on Europe, there will be plenty of wounded persons who will be certain to die of their wounds and who might as well serve your science.

CYPRIAN. I shan't need the permission of the Prophet.

BUSTER. You are very unwise, Master Cyprian. Don't you know that I can hand you to the hangman? If your neighbors or even your patron were to be told that you are served here by devils as foul as the midden of Hell, your life would not be worth a fig.

CYPRIAN. The devils will be gone tomorrow.

BUSTER. The alarm will be given tonight.

CYPRIAN. By whom? They can't disobey me as long as our bargain lasts, and *you're* in no position to show yourself.

BUSTER. By Miss Janet, who is not in your service. She will go to the village at once and tell them you are sold to the Devil—she will herself lead a mob to the castle. You will be lucky if you reach the gallows.—Now enough. I dislike to threaten. Think it over for an hour, Master Cyprian.—Come, Luigi: let us draft the agreement.

*They go out through the waiting-room.*

*The Moonlight Drunkard appears, bathed in his lunar radiance, standing in the door to the porch.*

CYPRIAN (*left alone*). She'd like nothing better! If she gets me killed, she can go on to some livelier assignment!

THE MOONLIGHT DRUNKARD (*in a croaking voice*). That's just what they all want to do, dear boy! You'd much better leave them alone.

CYPRIAN. Oh, it's you.

THE MOONLIGHT DRUNKARD. I just looked in for a moment to see how you were getting on. I've been hearing about your wonderful work, but somehow I've had the impression that you weren't really happy up here.

CYPRIAN. How did you hear about me?

THE MOONLIGHT DRUNKARD. Oh, we gossip a good deal out there.

CYPRIAN. Have you got companions now?

THE MOONLIGHT DRUNKARD. Oh, yes, indeed, dear boy. There's quite a colony of us out there now: all the rarest and purest souls who have learned how to slip from the century and yet avoid the rigors of a monastic life. And we're glowing brighter and brighter. Don't you see how much brighter I'm glowing?

CYPRIAN. A little, perhaps—but you're hoarse: you must catch cold staying out all night.

THE MOONLIGHT DRUNKARD. A very small price to pay for our freedom from all *your* vexations—from the worry of deciding which side to be on, from all those annoying factions, those princes and priests and people who are always trying to make one do things or prevent one from doing things!

CYPRIAN. I can't seem to get free of them now.

THE MOONLIGHT DRUNKARD. Why not? Why not just steal away? You can slip over the wall as I did.

CYPRIAN. I've made such a mess of things here—I don't want to run out and leave it.

THE MOONLIGHT DRUNKARD. You can always put the past to sleep. If you'll only relax with us in the moonlight, you'll find that all those nasty mishaps hardly trouble your sleep as uneasy dreams.

CYPRIAN. I can't do without my work—I can't simply be idle like you.

THE MOONLIGHT DRUNKARD. Oh, our brains are not idle, dear boy. We've been doing some of the loveliest things with thought! There's one chap with a brilliant intellect who interfuses Aristotle with Plato—and a marvellous theologian who's woven something absolutely shimmering out of the dual nature of Christ. A little bit unorthodox, perhaps, but nobody needs to know!

CYPRIAN. Those things are not in my line, but the kind of thing I do want to do I don't get a chance to do. I have a theory that matter and spirit are actually all the same substance, and that if only you could find out how that substance works, you could minister to body and soul both at the same time.

THE MOONLIGHT DRUNKARD. What a charming idea! —and so *simple*!

CYPRIAN. It's not really simple—that's the trouble: it's so complicated it's all one can do even to get hold of the problem. And the naggings and spyings and threats that go on in the castle now are making it impossible for me to concentrate.

THE MOONLIGHT DRUNKARD. I told you that the same thing that took you here would eventually bring you to us!

CYPRIAN (*in a low voice, tempted*). Where did you climb the wall?

*Mr. B. appears from the porch, still carrying the coffin on his shoulder.*

THE MOONLIGHT DRUNKARD. Is this Pan returned from the Golden Age?

MR. B. No: a devil in an age of barbarity.

THE MOONLIGHT DRUNKARD. I must shrink from you, happy or damned. (*To Cyprian*) I leave you, but you know where to find me. Farewell till we meet again.

*He retires.*

MR. B. You don't want to meet *him* again!

CYPRIAN. Yes: I'd rather see you. Come in.

*Mr. B. sets the coffin down just underneath the skeleton.*

CYPRIAN. You still have to carry that?

MR. B. What else can I do with it? He won't let it rest. If I have it buried in Holy Ground, He causes the earth to reject it. If I bury it in a secret place, He sends someone to dig it up. *Now*, who is vindictive: He or I?

CYPRIAN. I wish I could offer to help you—but I'm in a worse jam than ever.

MR. B. So I gathered when they turned me away at the gate.

CYPRIAN. I'm struggling with a genie now. He's turned out to be a Moslem agent.

MR. B. I hoped you'd last out the pact.

CYPRIAN. He's recruited the devils to the Moslem faith, and he threatens to denounce me to the village if I don't sign another agreement.

MR. B. I'm afraid you've played your cards rather badly.

CYPRIAN. I wish you'd tell me *how* to play them! Where did I make my mistake? I can't seem to think clearly nowadays about matters of right and wrong.

MR. B. That's part of the damnation, of course—and I'm hardly the person to set you right. I didn't venture to advise you before when you talked to me about your conscience. *We* only know conscience as something that can cook up good reasons for evil acts—but I wanted to give you the benefit of the doubt. It turned out that your conscience had led you astray before our people even began to work on you.

CYPRIAN. Please explain what you mean.

MR. B. Well, in the first place, you wanted to get rid of that lout who was supposed to succeed to the business, but you wouldn't admit it to yourself—and you wanted the girl, too, but you punished her for your grudge against your mother.

CYPRIAN. It isn't as simple as that.

MR. B. That's what they always say. Of course, I only know the less favorable side.

CYPRIAN. I wanted to spare Claude.

MR. B. Spare him to make an ass of himself by playing a role for which he wasn't fitted?—to marry a woman that he didn't deserve and who was falling in love with you? For the strong to yield to the weak—there's always a fallacy in it, no matter what your Gospels may say. Nobody can really believe that the greater should give way to the less. When people make a virtue of that, it's nothing but their own timidity. It was weakness, not decency, in you that made you so considerate of Claude— that was proved when the very next minute you fell a victim to that tenth-rate Italian lackey, and he gave you the uncomfortable comfort of having the poor clown suppressed.

CYPRIAN. That was stupid, inexcusable, of course—but what I don't think you understand is that I'd just given up God and that I had to preserve my own honor.

MR. B. That I do understand: that's the problem we've

got to master. But not too much self-abnegation! There's always something wrong, as I say, about the notion that the weaker should dominate. You may think that my opinion is biased, but I speak to you as honestly as I can, and I still can't believe we were wrong—in spite of the unfortunate outcome—when we rebelled against the leadership up there. When our Archon set the universe going—He Himself was only half-conscious then—it turned out to be essentially murderous. To triumph or even to remain alive one had to crush other beings. That was just as much true in Heaven as here, and when we organized a faction of angels and had a showdown with the reigning group in an attempt to get parliamentary government, we were outlawed and made the scapegoats for the general cruelty and chaos that was just as much a nuisance to Him as to us. The role of destroyers was assigned to *us* while *He* went on posing as the great creator. But at that time the human race was waking up to a moral consciousness, and He knew that a corrective was needed if mankind were to accept His rule, so He generated a half-human agent who sympathized with human beings and who made it appear that His Highness had an interest in love and peace. Yet He couldn't pull the teeth of the natural laws that He had unleashed Himself. Even His Prince of Peace had moments when he became pugnacious, and when the Prince finally staked his credit on living up to an ideal of non-resistance, he left behind him such a heritage of discord, oppression, persecution and slaughter as no purely human leader has ever bequeathed to the world.

CYPRIAN. But where shall we look for our principles? I tried to resort to the Devil, but I didn't understand his real nature.

MR. B. Yes: Satan is also false. He is doomed to pretend that the destructive force is the only effective one. It's high time that you human beings got away from both

Satan and your Savior, and learned to depend on yourselves!

CYPRIAN (*apprehensive for fear Buster will come*). But the damage is already done. I've brought in these spirits now, and my problem is how to get rid of them.

MR. B. I may be able to help you there if you'll swear to stand up for yourself and never to ask favors from the gods again.

CYPRIAN. By whom or by what shall I swear?

MR. B. You ought to know better than I. Swear by the light of the mind.

CYPRIAN. My mind is half darkened now. I can't tell true ideas from delusions. As a doctor, I'm partly a fake —I can't even be sure of my own research.

MR. B. I'm going to clear that up.

CYPRIAN. Can you violate Satan's arrangements?

MR. B. You're thinking of that scene in the Gospel where your Savior is graciously casting out devils, and the doubters are saying that his power must come from Beëlzebub. Your Savior replies that the Devil can never cast out the Devil—that he can't war against himself. (*With a touch of grimness and fierceness*) Well, we'll see what a devil can do!

CYPRIAN. Has it never been done before?

MR. B. Never yet—and the difficulty is that, to have my commands obeyed, I shall have to revert to—my appointed role.

CYPRIAN. Not forever?

MR. B. Never mind about that.

CYPRIAN. I don't want you to go back to Hell just to get me out of my mess.

MR. B. (*shrugging*). Why not? I've failed to get free of the character that has been assigned me—look at that coffin there!—and I might as well use my position to give your cause a *coup de main*!

CYPRIAN. I'm not sure that I represent a cause any more.

MR. B. Come, come, boy!—the freedom of the intellect —the overthrow of Heaven and Hell!—This will be ticklish work for *me*. I'm condemned to the negative pole, and I'll have to fight against its attraction. As soon as I summon my forces, it will be hard not to use them for harm instead of to do you a service. I must try to catch the moral split-second, just the moment when I've picked up my old power but before I've lost touch with my purpose. That moment I'll use like a razor to slice your tormentors away!—Don't be shocked, when I've called them off, if I follow them straight to Hell. Remember that *you* must stay here—you'll have to face a life of such moments.

CYPRIAN. I'm hardly in your position.

MR. B. Why, boy, you must always be choosing: how far to be ruthless and when to spare. Don't be asking what principles you should act on. You'll have to find that out as you go—and, in the meantime, you'll have to be deciding in all sorts of situations and taking a chance that you're right. But if you can learn to act correctly in these crises, you can make of us devils and our opposite numbers— and that hybrid Mohammedan monster—a flight of grotesque myths that will fade in the night of Time!

CYPRIAN. Must you fade? Can't you hope to get free?

MR. B. Never mind. That remains to be seen.

CYPRIAN. Who are you?

MR. B. What does that matter?

CYPRIAN. Belial?

MR. B. No: not Belial.

*He picks up a parchment from the desk, scribbles something on it and tosses it over toward Cyprian. Luigi and the Little Devils appear in the double doors. Slingo has lost his tail.*

CYPRIAN (*to Mr. B.*). Here they are to make me sign.

MR. B. Take it easy—and don't be scared when I change.

CYPRIAN (*reading the name and looking up at Mr. B. with awe*). The second in command!

LUIGI (*mocking Mr. B.*). Gonóstrono, Beëlzebub!

BONGO. Gonóstrono-gnáthro, Beëlzebub!

STINGO. Where are your horns, Beëlzebub?

SLINGO. Somebody's been shaving Beëlzebub!

BINGO (*singing*).
Oh, Beëlzebub got a nasty snub:
    He tried to melt and soften;
But the Powers above wouldn't let him love:
    They spliced him to a coffin!

ALL.
They spliced him to a——

MR. B. (*who has been summoning his power, suddenly cutting them short*). Skáfrum! skáfrum! stakáfrum!

*They stop at once, stunned, and huddle together.*

MR. B. Stakáp! Stakáfrum-shlee! (*He gestures toward the porch.*)

LUIGI (*now servile, spreading his hands in propitiation*). Meleé-kály-meeleékeely, padradralóni. Kanópas kaniápolos-kedreéon.

MR. B. Shtísto-stakáp—shlee!

LUIGI (*asking pardon*). Pekiásky peéty-padradralóny!

*They walk backwards into the doorway, where they pause.*

MR. B. (*with a peremptory gesture*). Zoop-zoop!

*They turn and rush away. Buster appears in the doorway, strongly illuminated.*

BUSTER (*to the Devils, roaring*). Where are you going? Get back here! (*Seeing Mr. B.*) What is this? Who are you? What are you doing here?

MR. B. (*to Cyprian*). He's impotent without his helpers. If you cease to believe in him, he'll disappear.

CYPRIAN. But I see him: he's still real!

BUSTER. *You'll* find that I'm *real*! Disbelieve and the Crescent will cut you down.

MR. B. (*to Cyprian*). An illusion!

CYPRIAN. But I summoned him here.

MR. B. Then dismiss him.

BUSTER (*laughing derisively*). Who are *you* to dismiss me? You begged me to dominate the castle, and now you can't do without me.

MR. B. Do you swallow his ridiculous creed?

CYPRIAN. No, of course not, but how can I kill it?

MR. B. Then, damn it! imagine the world for yourself—pit your mind against his!

CYPRIAN (*to Buster*). Your faith is a sterile fanaticism! your Prophet a cunning politician! I oppose to them the word that convinces!

BUSTER. *You* convince only yourself. My Master convinces millions!

MR. B. (*in a low voice, to Cyprian*). Tell him he belongs to the wrong sect.

CYPRIAN. You belong to the wrong sect!

BUSTER. I expiated that in the bottle.

MR. B. (*taking the bottle from the shelf and handing it to Cyprian*). Tell him he can't live it down.

CYPRIAN (*holding up the bottle*). That's a sin that can never be expiated! You still belong to the wrong sect. Back to the bottle, Buster!

BUSTER (*his voice breaking and reverting to its earlier thinness*). I confess my disloyalty, Allah! I accept this eternal atonement! There is no God but Allah, and Mohammed is his prophet!

*Darkness: the shrill shriek of Buster becoming fainter and fainter. When the light goes on again, Cyprian is putting in the stopper.*

MR. B. Never appeal again to a power outside yourself! That was your second mistake.

CYPRIAN. But how can I carry on here alone? I've had

to have my liege lord's protection in order to do anything at all, and now it looks as if I'd got him down on me: I refused to do a poisoning job he wanted.

MR. B. (*with harsh impatience*). If you can't hold your own with another man, peasant or liege lord, you might as well go to Hell at once!

CYPRIAN. If I only had Janet! She's still bewitched.

MR. B. Ah, Jezebel! She must go, too. Where is she?

CYPRIAN (*nodding toward the right partition*). In her room next door, I imagine—waiting to hear of my ruin.

MR. B. *I'll* attend to *that*. You stay here.—I'll send her to the grubbiest corner of Hell!

*He strides out through the double doors.*

*Cyprian looks after him a moment, then, left alone, begins to soliloquize.*

CYPRIAN. Will she hate me? Is Janet half Jezebel? Shall I ever have her with me again? Can we make our own world together alone in this castle here?—between walls built by men like me to defend us from our treacherous fellows, under this roof that keeps off the rain and that screens us from the terror of the universe? Shall we master its secrets from books that have been written by men like me, with tools we have shaped ourselves? I know that I can call on myself and summon in myself a magic that satisfies all my demands—that there are moments when the tangle of questions that were squirming like worms from my grasp lies suddenly as plain as an egg in the hand, when the fluxes of life that one never could seize stand revealed like the weave of an arras—when the very books leap from the shelves and open at the pages that speak to me, when the sentences stream from the pen to dazzle me with the new ideas that have never been given expression!—O Power that drives us and guides us! O Spirit of Man that speaks, that imagines, that plans, that contrives!—in your name (*he stumbles with the difficulty of*

*formulating his intention*) I decide that—I assert—I desire
that——

*Cyrus bursts in from the waiting-room, in riding costume as
before, but somewhat more handsomely dressed.*

CYRUS. Pardon me, won't you, old chap? There was
nobody around, so I just barged in.

CYPRIAN (*with more cordiality than he showed on Cyrus's
previous visit*). Oh, hello, Cyrus! Come in. (*A fraternal
embrace*) Sit down.

*Cyprian takes the throne behind the desk, but Cyrus, full of
his mission, continues to stand while he talks.*

CYRUS. I came a little earlier than you told me——

CYPRIAN. That's all right: it doesn't matter.

CYRUS.—but the situation is pressing. We need you
for the King's party, Cyprian!

CYPRIAN. You need me in what capacity?

CYRUS. As physician and mage to His Majesty.

CYPRIAN. What makes you think I can qualify?

CYRUS. Why, everybody from here to Tancarville is
talking about your miracles. They have even reached the
ears of the King, and he has asked me to bring you to
see him. Can you start with me tonight?—at once?

CYPRIAN. Not tonight—but we'll see about later.

CYRUS. You can't disappoint His Majesty! He spoke to
me with great condescension. It will mean a place at court
for us both.

CYPRIAN. How are Louis's affairs going?

CYRUS. Charles the Hothead has no chance against him.

CYPRIAN. What if he blockades Paris?

CYRUS. The King has God on his side.

CYPRIAN. What makes you so sure of that? The King
has done some very dark things.

CYRUS. His Majesty's exalted position exposes him to
special risks: he has sometimes to resort to desperate
measures.

CYPRIAN. He's a cooler head than our Rody, but he's not any closer to God. Rody imprisoned his father, but Louis's supposed to have poisoned his.

CYRUS. I can't let you talk like that, Cyprian! The King is our anointed sovereign.

CYPRIAN. We seem to have had this discussion before.

CYRUS. I don't understand you, Cyprian: when we argued before, *I* supported the barons but you were most bitterly against them——

CYPRIAN. I still am—I'd be glad to see Louis send them back to their kennels yelping. Even my patron here has been trying to put the screws on me to make me do some of his dirty work.

*Mr. B., returning with Janet, who, faint from the convulsions of dispossession, leans upon his arm.*

CYPRIAN (*going on to Cyrus*). Here's Janet. (*Cyrus bows.*) A good deal depends on *her*. I'll tell you something more definite later. Please leave us alone for awhile. You can wander around the place wherever you like. There's no one to bedevil you now.

CYRUS. You mustn't delay too long!

CYPRIAN. I'll try to let you know in an hour.

*Cyrus goes out through the double door.*

MR. B. (*to Cyprian*). I've brought you a companion for your solitude.

JANET (*rather dazedly*). I tried to stand by you, Cyprian: I didn't let her drive me out. I warned you about the genie.

CYPRIAN. Oh, Janet: will you try to forgive me?

JANET. Oh, yes.

CYPRIAN. Will you work with me?

JANET. Yes, of course. (*Catching sight of the cover on the tray*) But what about poor Claude?

CYPRIAN. We ought to have had the sense to let him have what he wanted: that little house at the edge of the wood.

JANET. Is it too late to save him now?

MR. B. (*picking up the cover and addressing Claude*). Snap out of that: you're liberated!

*Claude stands up behind the table.*

CLAUDE. I told you I didn't approve!

MR. B. Would you like the little house I've left vacant?

CLAUDE. No, thank you! I'm leaving the forest. I'm going back to raise goats with my father. At least, I'll be able to breathe and move, up in the mountains there. Here I've been buried alive!

JANET. Oh, Claude: I'm so sorry it didn't work out!

CLAUDE. I heard what was going on with your genies and demons and all the rest. You've all been too clever for your own good, and it can't go on like that! I can tell you that our Savior was right when he said that the meek would inherit the earth. The good plain people will have their day! Do you hear that, Beëlzebub?

*He walks toward the waiting-room door.*

MR. B. How depressing it would be if he were right!

JANET (*going after Claude*). Goodby, Claude. Let me know where you're going to live, and I'll come up and help you get settled.

CLAUDE. Please keep away! I shan't need you.

*Janet stops; Claude goes out.*

MR. B. And now, my good couple, I'll leave you.

JANET (*to Cyprian*). You won't distrust me now?

CYPRIAN. You won't despise me?

MR. B. (*in a sharp contemptuous tone that startles them and makes them look round*). That's not going to be so easy. There'll be Hell to pay in this house!

CYPRIAN. You think so?

MR. B. Oh, pay no attention: I told you I'd become unpleasant. I'll pick up my coffin and go.

*He lifts the coffin to his left shoulder.*

CYPRIAN. Don't you want to leave that here? We'll put

it away in the vault. There's no reason it shouldn't be safe now that our guests have gone.

MR. B. Haven't I told you it will never be safe? He won't allow earth to receive it. But I'll tell you what I'm going to do: I'm going to take it up there! I'm going to walk into His presence and thrust it under His nose and say to Him, "You knavish old tyrant, you've punished my wife for her pity, you've caused her to die in anguish, you've insulted her very grave! Is this your forgiveness and love? What's happened to your merciful Son? (*Pounding the table with his fist in a fit of wild fury*) This world is still your same old shambles, where dog must still chew up dog, and our people grab the hindmost—and Our Father in Heaven amuses himself by twisting the Devil's tail! Now give rest to the bones of this saint and summon her soul to your side. Are you frightened of her long inquisitive nose and her quick understanding smile? You may damn her, but it won't be the last of her: she'll look up at you with wonder from down below—just a glance of her yellow eye, and she'll make you feel a cad and a hypocrite—you'll be sickened yourself with the scandal of your bigoted rotten reign!"

*He carries the coffin to the double door and lights up when he has passed the doorway with an intensely bright rufous fire.*

CYPRIAN. Shall I wish you good luck?

MR. B. If you're not afraid.

CYPRIAN. At this moment I'm not afraid of anything!

MR. B. You men can remake the earth—and I may still harass Heaven!

*In a flash he has vanished. They go to the door and look out at the late night sky.*

JANET. Where is he? Can you see him?

CYPRIAN (*pointing*). There. He's going like lightning: look!

JANET. Isn't that the morning star?

CYPRIAN. No: it's moving.—That's the star over there.

JANET. They named it for Satan, didn't they?

CYPRIAN. "*Quomódo cecidísti, Lúcifer?*"—Lucifer, why did you fall?

JANET. What's the answer?

CYPRIAN. Through pride, is the regular answer—but of course there was something else.

JANET. I hope he makes it.—— (*Clutching Cyprian's arm*) Oh, look! What's happened?

CYPRIAN. He's falling.

JANET. Oh, poor Mr. B.!

CYPRIAN. You admired him, didn't you?

JANET. One oughtn't to, perhaps.

CYPRIAN. *I'm* going to make it, though.

JANET. You're not going to storm Heaven?

CYPRIAN. I'm going to put it through on earth.

JANET. Did your brother come to offer you something?

CYPRIAN. The post of the King's physician.

JANET. Oh, how splendid! There's no reason to refuse it now.

CYPRIAN. But I don't want to give up my own domain—the kingdom of thought and art—for a corner of Louis's court. Shall I put myself at Louis's mercy, as Beëlzebub was at God's? Not for me: I'll stay here in my castle! Let them settle their quarrels without me—Charles the Reckless and Louis the Sly, the Crescent and the Cross that are always at war and one as bloody as the other!

*Cyrus appears from the waiting-room.*

CYRUS. I'm sorry to interrupt——

CYPRIAN. I've decided not to do it, Cyrus.

CYRUS. It's your liege lord—he's down below. I think that you'd better see him. He's angry about his steward, who's robbed him and who's joined the King's party—he seems to think that you're responsible.

CYPRIAN. I see.

*Cyprian is silent a moment, then quickly goes into action.*

CYPRIAN (*to Janet, indicating the visitors' chair*). Sedílem cóntra tapétas póne.

*She moves the chair against the tapestry while he goes to get the robe and cap and hastily puts them on.*

CYPRIAN. Manículam experíre.

*She works the crank on the arm of the chair, making the hands shoot out from the tapestry.*

CYPRIAN (*to Cyrus*). Bring him up here, but not too soon. Try to stall him off a couple of minutes. Tell him I'd gone to bed and had to get dressed to receive him.

*Cyprian picks up the skeleton and begins rigging it up outside the door.*

CYRUS. It will take him some time just to get up the stairs. He's suffering badly from gout. He seems to blame you for that, too. You see that the King is our only hope. We've got to fight it out at Paris.

*He opens the door to listen.*

CYPRIAN. *My* only hope is right here! I'll fight it out in this castle!

CYRUS. Look out: he's started up already!

*A thunder of grumbling and groaning is heard from the direction of the waiting-room. Cyrus hurries out and shuts the door.*

JANET. Bóno ánimo ésto!

CYPRIAN (*coming back from the doorway*). Te magnópere ámo.

JANET. Íta véro est?

CYPRIAN (*taking her in his arms*). Mehércle, íta véro.—Da mi básium.

*She kisses him. She turns her head as the sound of the deep angry voice is heard just outside the door.*

JANET. Désine—ílle accédit!

*Cyprian moves quickly to his place at the desk, where he sits up straight in the throne and prepares a professional face with which to receive the visitor. Janet smooths her hair and dress and goes over to open the door. An atmosphere of tense expectation*

# The Crime in the Whistler Room

*The Crime in the Whistler Room* was produced in New York by the Provincetown Players at the Provincetown Playhouse in Macdougal Street, on October 9, 1924, under the direction of James Light and Stanley Howlett, with the following cast:

| | |
|---|---|
| Bill | MARY BLAIR |
| Miss Streetfield | MARY MORRIS |
| Anna | WILMA HENDERSON |
| Cousin Serena | JUDITH LOWRY |
| Mr. Streetfield | EDGAR STEHLI |
| Julia | LUCY CURRIER |
| McGee | PERRY IVINS |
| Simon Delacy | E. J. BALLANTINE |
| The Guard | ALLEN NAGLE |
| Ted | WALTER ABEL |
| The Tutor | ROMEYN BENJAMIN |
| Maud | DOROTHÉE NOLAN |

# ACT I

*A large and very pleasant sitting-room in a country house on Long Island. The house evidently dates from the beginning of the last century, but has never been allowed to tarnish and has been scrupulously weeded of the luxuriance of the Victorian era. This room, in particular, with its white woodwork and cream panelling, has been kept as clear and as light as possible to allow a small collection of Whistlers to appear to the best advantage. There are a few handsome and chaste pieces of furniture: a mahogany sofa, covered in brownish yellow, on the left rather far to the front; a closed mahogany desk, the upper part of which is a bookcase with glass doors and narrow panes, toward the back of the right wall; a silver-faced grandfather's clock, in the left corner against the back wall; a gate-leg table, with the leaves open, in the middle of the room; and four chairs, of which three are on the right and one is between the sofa and the back. At the left, about the middle of the wall, is a door leading into the dining-room; and at the right, further toward the front, a door leading into the hall. The sofa and the chairs are all turned toward the middle of the room; and in the center of the back wall is a fine Colonial fireplace, in which a fire is burning: there are brass andirons, poker, tongs and firestone, and, on the mantel, a pair of brass candlesticks with light yellow candles in them and a vase of yellow tulips between them. Over the mantel hangs a Whistler painting, a portrait of a little English girl, who has been resolved by the artist into an exquisite harmony of brown and gold. On the side walls hang Whistler etchings, from the Venetian series: there are no other pictures in the room, and not many of these. On either side of the fireplace is a French window, with the blinds open: one sees the smooth sloping shoulder of the lawn and, beyond it, the lavender of the water, now dimming in the fall of twilight but washed with the watercolors of May; it is as if the sea and the sky asked nothing better than to compose into this charming landscape and serve as panels for this bright room. There is a cashmere shawl in the chair nearest the fire-place on the right, a bag of crocheting on the table and a copy of the* Atlantic Monthly *lying on the sofa.*

*The clock begins to chime nine.*

*From the dining-room enter a lady of about forty and a girl of about nineteen, both in evening gowns. The lady is tall and thin, verging on dryness and angularity, but with fine animated dark eyes; she has the commanding force of great dignity com-bined with nervous intensity; she speaks sharply and briskly. The girl is black-eyed and black-haired, with a slim boyish figure; she stares and moves awkwardly, as if possessed by some passionate idea; one of her shoulder-straps has slipped down and a strand of her straight black hair has escaped from behind her ear.*

BILL. Well, I don't see that Simon Delacy did anything so terrible! He just got a little bit stewed! He didn't mean any harm! You ottn't all to givum the razz!

MISS STREETFIELD. *Give him*, dear.

BILL. Give him.

MISS STREETFIELD (*readjusting Bill's shoulder-strap*). Well don't worry about it any more, dear. Let Simon Delacy deal with his own difficulties. What you ought to think most about now is passing your examinations. Of course I'm very glad to have you go out and enjoy yourself, but if you really want to go to college, I don't think you ought to waste your energies. You know that I had you come down here precisely because you had so little time and Mr. Dunning is such a remarkable tutor; he got Ned Raybold into Princeton when he had flunked all his entrance examinations. But, of course, he can't do anything for you without your putting forth *your* best efforts, too.

BILL. Yes, I know: I am!

MISS STREETFIELD. Yes, you must. (*She contemplates the table.*) You know, I really can't make up my mind whether I did right to move that table out! It worries me. I lay awake last night thinking about it. (*She goes over and straightens it carefully, then stands back and looks at it again.*) What do you think? Do you think it ought to go back?

BILL. What's wrong with it where it is?

*A maid comes in from the dining-room with the coffee things: an agreeable young Swedish woman, very spare and clean.*

MISS STREETFIELD. We used to have it over in the corner, don't you know? (*she indicates the nearer end of the left-hand wall*) under that little Whistler. What do you think about it, Anna? Do you think it was a mistake to move the table?

ANNA (*setting the tray on the table: she bubbles in a sing-song Swedish voice*). I think it look very nice where it was, but now that you move it out, I think it is more handy. It's yust because you're not used to it: when you get used to it, you like it yust as well.

*Two more ladies come in from the dining-room: a pretty blonde young girl, glowing with a superb American cleanness, whose smartness and easy grace make Bill's embarrassed movements seem more awkward; and a stout elderly lady of impressive presence, buoyed up by a great amplitude of purple skirt. They are followed by a slightly-built gentleman in a dinner-jacket: he stoops a little and his features are plain, but a sort of distinction of texture is felt in even his husk-skinned bony hands and his disproportionate hooked nose, which in earlier generations may well have been formidably aggressive; he wears a small pale mustache, and his hair is turning silver. Mr.*

*Streetfield sits down in the chair furthest front, and Juliet take the chair on his right. Bill seats herself on the sofa. Miss Street-field, still standing, pours the coffee from a slender silver urn and Anna serves it, in the order: Cousin Serena, Juliet, Bill Mr. Streetfield.*

COUSIN SERENA (*picking up her crocheting from the table*) I cannot get used to that table there, Clara. I really cannot When I arrived in the house this morning it quite took my breath away! (*She picks up her shawl from the chair near the fireplace and arranges it about her shoulders; then she subsides into the chair.*)

MISS STREETFIELD. Well, we know what a conservative you are, Cousin Serena.

COUSIN SERENA. Cousin Fred always had it in the corner. and I have *not* been able to get used to it out here. I feel as if it were *crowding* me! (*She peers down from the ramparts of her bulk.*) What is your feeling about it, Schuyler? (*She begins to crochet.*)

MR. STREETFIELD. Well, I hate to see the little Whistler left suspended in the void.

MISS STREETFIELD. Can't it be rehung?

MR. STREETFIELD. That would disorganize the whole room. I really think the table ought to go back, Clara.

BILL (*as Anna offers her coffee, brusquely, as if not to be conciliated*). No thanks: I don't wahnt any!

MISS STREETFIELD. Well, you know how impossible for cards the library table is: you said yourself that it was so wide that you could hardly see your partner across it.

JULIET. I suppose there's some perfectly good reason why the library table can't come in here and the gate-leg table go into the library?

MR. STREETFIELD. The library table's much too big to have the etching over it: it would simply be crushed to death.—That would be breaking the Butterfly, not on a wheel, but on a table!

*Anna finishes serving the coffee and goes out through the dining-room.*

BILL (*abruptly*). I don't see that Simon Delacy was really a bit worse than lots of other people were last night! Just because he happened to get into a fight—!

MISS STREETFIELD (*who has taken up a dominating position in front of the fireplace*). Well, I don't think a dance is quite the place for a fight, do you? Mr. Delacy may be a very clever young man, Elizabeth, but I really think he behaved rather badly last night—and I doubt very much whether as a writer he's really very sound.

COUSIN SERENA. There are so many unsound writers nowadays. I should consider a great many of the books that you have about, Clara, absolutely unsound.

MR. STREETFIELD. I think the wittiest literary man I ever knew was Thomas Bailey Aldrich. I remember once, when he was visiting my father, we were talking about some wholesale dealer in fish who had just received a baronetcy in England, and my mother said that she didn't see why there should be so much difference between him and an ordinary fishmonger. "Why," Aldrich replied in a flash, "it must be a difference of scale!" (*All laugh, except Bill.*) Oh, Aldrich was amazingly witty! Wasn't he, Serena?

COUSIN SERENA. And so charming with children!

BILL. Don't you thinkuz books are any good then?

MR. STREETFIELD. Whose? Aldrich's?

BILL. No: Simon Delacy's.

MR. STREETFIELD. I'm afraid I've never read any of his books.

JULIET. I read one perfectly mad thing called *The Downfall of the Ritz*——

BILL. *The Ruins of the Ritz*, it is!

JULIET. Yes: *The Ruins of the Ritz*—all about a man who goes insane and thinks the Ritz is a menagerie and goes about shooting people for fear they will bite him.

MR. STREETFIELD. Perhaps Delacy himself was suffering from some such hallucination when he tried to assassinate the waiter last night.

BILL. He didn't assassinate the waiter. I don't see that he did anything so terrible. You could never get put out in Pittsburgh for just giving a waiter a bloody nose. Why, at the Hotel Carnaygie once they had a regular beat-up with champagne bawttles and eight men were knocked out cold!

MR. STREETFIELD. They do things on an heroic scale in Pittsburgh!

BILL. Why, there was one old man there—he must have been seventy-five years of age—and a boy that he tried to cut in on knockedum down a whole big flight of stairs and he cutuz head wide open.—

COUSIN SERENA. How dreadful!

BILL. And they stole all the electric light fixtures!

MISS STREETFIELD. Well, I think that was a very wasteful and a very dangerous party: I should think you would have been glad to have escaped with your life! (*Anna comes in for the coffee things.*) And now, Cousin Serena, you must tell us about Aunt Harriet. (*She sits down on the sofa at Bill's left.*)

COUSIN SERENA. Well, I assure you it was the greatest surprise to everyone. Nobody had had so much as a letter from her for it must have been nearly ten years.

MISS STREETFIELD. Yes, I know: it's quite worried me!

COUSIN SERENA. I wrote her twice at the time of Arthur's death to ask her if she wanted the old clothes-press that had originally belonged to her mother, and she replied to neither of my letters.

MISS STREETFIELD. She never does; but one ought to make the effort to go to see her just the same.

COUSIN SERENA. I did go to see her: she received me in bed, with a decanter of sherry at her elbow. I thought she was excessively unreasonable, though I told her how distressed we all had been by the attitude she had been taking toward the family. She behaved so strangely, you know, when she came up to Alice's funeral. She was only Harry's father's half-sister, in any case.

JULIET. What did she say, Cousin Serena?

*Miss Streetfield gets up and closes the blinds.*

COUSIN SERENA. She insisted that there was a conspiracy against her to exclude her from the family affairs. She even accused Arthur of having kept the old clothes-press and some soup-plates when he had no right to do so. The thing that made her particularly angry seemed to be the fact that Evadne had been asked and she not. Evadne came to the wedding, by the way, and really looked charming. She has quite taken a new lease on life since she's begun receiving her annuity.

MR. STREETFIELD. Well, that was one decent thing that Will Brewster did in his life!

COUSIN SERENA. She has had the house thoroughly renovated and a little conservatory built at the back, and she is as happy as a lark.—

MISS STREETFIELD (*going over toward the dining-room door*). I must send her some cuttings of our tea-roses. She always admires them so. (*She turns on the electric light by a button beside the door, putting an end to the twilight conversation.*)— Well, shall we have a hand of bridge?

MR. STREETFIELD. Very well.

MISS STREETFIELD. You have time, haven't you, Juliet?

JULIET. Yes, Aunt Clara.

MISS STREETFIELD. You're not too tired, are you, Cousin Serena?

COUSIN SERENA. Yes, I'm afraid I shan't be able to play: the trip down from Litchfield was very fatiguing!

MISS STREETFIELD. Won't you join us then, Elizabeth?

BILL. If you wahnt me to. I'm pretty rotten!

*Miss Streetfield goes over to the desk and gets out the cards.*

JULIET. And Aunt Harriet's Skye terriers—are they still alive?

COUSIN SERENA. I saw one—so old and feeble that it could scarcely even wheeze. Its hair had come out in great patches. I think it very unpleasant and very unwise to continue to have a dog about when it has become as old as that: she should keep it outside the house or allow it to be chloroformed. So I told her; but she won't listen to anyone.

BILL (*who has, throughout this conversation, been betraying signs of restlessness and boredom, but is now deeply touched*). Oh, I think it's a shame to kill an old dog! I had an old setter-dog named Ginger that lived to be almost fifteen!

MR. STREETFIELD. Her father, General Bullard, was exactly like that, you know. They used to call him Adamant Ben.—(*As he notices that his sister is moving the table forward.*) You're not going to play in here?

MISS STREETFIELD. Yes: don't you want to try it once?

MR. STREETFIELD. If you insist. It seems highly unnatural.

COUSIN SERENA. No one has ever played cards in here. I never remember seeing Cousin Fred play anywhere but in the library.

MISS STREETFIELD. Well, let us see if it spoils our game. —Elizabeth, will you be my partner?—

BILL. Get ready for a lot of boners!

MISS STREETFIELD. And Juliet and Schuyler play together !

*They take their seats—Miss Streetfield on the left side of the table and Bill on the right, Mr. Streetfield facing the fire and Juliet opposite him. Miss Streetfield shuffles and begins to deal.*

COUSIN SERENA. You knew that the Commodore had been ill?

MISS STREETFIELD. Yes: Grace Raybold told us.—(*Aside to Bill.*) Don't pick up your cards, dear, till they've all been dealt.

BILL. Oh, I'm sawrry! I forgot.

COUSIN SERENA. It seems that, while he was in bed, something wrong was done about his bees, and he became so anxious about them that it is believed to have brought on a relapse.

JULIET. I remember when I was up there last year they had got into the wrong kind of clover or something, so that the honey wasn't just the right color, and he was awfully bitter about it.

BILL. I didn't know that you could keep bees for pets like that!

MR. STREETFIELD. I'm afraid this table is much too high.

MISS STREETFIELD. It's only an inch higher than the other: I had Robert measure it. And the table in the library is really *much* too wide!

COUSIN SERENA. I seem to remember that Cousin Fred had it made that way on purpose, Clara. Cousin Fred, you know, was one of the best cribbage players of his time. It was said that the only man who had ever beaten him badly was afterwards expelled from his club for cheating.

MISS STREETFIELD. Let's forget about the table for the moment.

*Anna appears at the hall door.*

ANNA. Miss McGee's father is here.

MISS STREETFIELD. Oh!—Well, will you take him into the front room, Anna, and——

*But Anna is followed immediately by an elderly gentleman who looks a little like an old actor. He wears a white vest, an impressive wing collar and a large pair of horn-rimmed eyeglasses with a thick black ribbon dangling from them; his flabby cheeks appear to be rouged and his eyebrows reinforced with eyebrow-paste; but behind his laboriously composed false-face one feels a profound and appealing debility, which is betrayed by his uncertain hands and his occasional collapses of assurance.*

BILL (*springing up, dismayed*). Why, Father!

McGEE (*coming forward and kissing her profusely*). Well, Billy, old girl, how are you?

*Miss Streetfield and her brother rise.*

MISS STREETFIELD. How do you do, Mr. McGee. Mr. McGee, this is my brother, Mr. Streetfield—and Miss Raybold—and Mrs. Middleton.

McGEE. Most delightful to know you, I'm sure, Mr. Streetfield. (*He shakes hands with him heartily and bows profoundly to the others.*) Most delighted! What a beautifully appointed home you have here! I certainly consider you very lucky, Billy, to be living in such a beautiful home.

MISS STREETFIELD. Elizabeth has been working very hard. She takes her examinations next month.

McGEE. She's always had a bright mind, Miss Streetfield —just as quick and alert as she could be. And I'm sure she'll prove her appreciation of the splendid opportunities you've opened to her.

MISS STREETFIELD. It's quite an effort, of course, to do such a lot in so short a time; but I hope and believe she'll succeed. Won't you sit down, Mr. McGee?

McGEE. If I may so far intrude. I reely hope I'm not intruding!

MISS STREETFIELD. Or perhaps you'd like to talk to Elizabeth.

McGEE. Oh, no. I was just stopping in New York on some business and I thought I'd snatch a little flying visit to pay my respects to Miss Streetfield and have a look at our young scholar.

*He sits down on the farther end of the sofa. Mr. Streetfield moves back Bill's and Juliet's chairs so that they now face McGee; and Mr. Streetfield and Juliet sit down together. Miss Streetfield moves her brother's chair out so that it also faces McGee, but stands farther forward than the others.*

BILL. Where'd you get the glasses, Father?

McGee (*beaming*). Your father has a college himself now, Billy. In fact, he's a college president!

Bill (*crossing over and sitting down beside him on the sofa*). You're a college president?

McGee. Yes, Billy; I am now the President of the Roosevelt Institute of Success!

Bill. Gee, are you teaching success?

McGee. That's just what I am, Billy.

Miss Streetfield. What is your Success Institute, Mr. McGee?

McGee. The Roosevelt Institute of Success is a very inter-esting and—if I may say so—a very crucial—educational venture. It represents an attempt to educate the people at large on a scale which has simply never been dreamt of—not even in the broadest visionings of an Eliot or a Wilson.

Miss Streetfield. That sounds very interesting, Mr. McGee.

McGee. I was sure that our project would inter-est you, Miss Streetfield, knowing how much you are inter-ested in social betterment. You are familiar with the methods of the Y.W.C.A., and I should certainly be the last to forget what we owe to that very idealistic institution. (*He pats Bill's hand.*) If it were not for the Y.W.C.A., my daughter would not be here at this moment—in this delightful home, amid cultured people, with these wonderful opportunities before her. But all that the Y.W.C.A. and the Y.M.C.A. try to do for the growing girl and boy of today, that the Roosevelt undertakes to do—and to do ten times more besides.—You will ask, perhaps, "What about the public schools? Don't the public schools educate the people? Don't they supply all the training needful for the manhood and the girlhood of the nation?" And I answer, No, they do not! They do not do so for a simple and deeplorable reason: *There are not enough public schools to go round!* Still Arkansas must blush in shame for her three hundred thousand illiterates! Still Georgia comes limping to the federal councils, almost unable to speak her mother tongue! But to these backward children of the great Republic the Roosevelt will bring the best that the world has ever produced—the best in Art, the best in Science, the best in Commercial Success! Painting, Poetry, Eurhythmic Dancing; Swimming, Boxing and the Development of the Figure; Industrial Psychology, Business Morale and the Secret of Getting a Raise in Salary! All these——

Miss Streetfield. You must have a very large equipment.

McGee. We have as yet only a single room, but——

Miss Streetfield. But you will need gymnasiums and swimming-pools, won't you?

McGee. We shall need no swimming pools, Miss Streetfield, because we shall not teach our pupils to swim in swimming pools! We shall teach them to breast the breakers and to revel in the crystal rivers——

Bill. What do you mean? The Allegheny?

McGee. The activities of the Institute are not confined to Pittsburgh, my dear!

Bill. What do you do—have branches?

McGee. No: nor do we reequire any branches! Our message is conveyed through the mails.—

Bill. Aw, it's just a cawrrespondence school!

McGee. Yes, a correspondence school. But a correspondence school that differs from any other such enterprise in the world! What the Mona Lisa is to painting, what Shakespeare is to the drama, what the Parthenon is to public buildings, that the Roosevelt is to correspondence schools! We have seized upon that humble and familiar agency, the United States postal service, and we have forged it into a great instrumentality for the advancement of Knowledge and Success! As the electric current of the power-house, travelling out along its millions of wires, brings a clear bright light to a million homes that would otherwise be groping in darkness, so the Roosevelt Super-Brain in the Pittsburgh Blodgett Building flashes out to the four quarters of America——

*But someone has opened the window on the left and is peering in from behind the blind. Miss Streetfield, seeing him, has risen. Mr. Streetfield rises, also; Bill looks around and quickly springs up; and McGee, becoming at last aware of the diverted attention of the others, interrupts his oration, looks around and rises to his feet.*

THE INTRUDER. Oh, I beg your pardon! I didn't know there was anybody in here or I would have come in by the door! I was just looking for Bill.

*He is an attractive young man with a good profile, who wears a clean soft shirt and a gay summer necktie, but looks haggard and dissipated. After a moment, he lounges forward. His manner in the presence of the Streetfields alternates between too much and too little assurance, but there is something disarmingly childlike about his egoism.*

BILL (*much embarrassed*). Oh, hello!—uh— This is Miss Streetfield—uh—Mrs. Middleton. I guess you know— Miss Juliet Raybold. (*Juliet politely nods and smiles.*) And this is my father.

SIMON (*bowing*). Bill has neglected to explain that my name is Simon Delacy.

MISS STREETFIELD (*crossing over to Simon and passing behind the table*). How do you do, Mr. Delacy.

MCGEE (*shaking Simon's hand with warmth*). Most happy to know you, Mr. Delacy!

SIMON (*coming forward to Bill: they stand in front of the sofa*). I just thought you might like to go for a little ride.

BILL (*constrained*). I'm sawrry—I'm afraid I can't tonight.

MCGEE. I won't deetain you for a moment, Mr. Delacy, from the company of these delightful people—I just wanted to say one word more in regard to the Roosevelt Institute of Success—an educational idea, Mr. Delacy, which I was venturing to describe to Miss Streetfield.—I just want to acquaint you with a feature that we particularly pride ourselves on as one of our most revolutionary steps —I refer to the application of the principles of Psychoanalysis—with which I am sure you are all familiar—to the promotion of Business Success!

SIMON (*incredulous, amused*). My God: really?

McGEE. Yes: isn't it amazing. It *is* astounding reelly. We teach them to *dream* Success! For the old-fashioned dreams of erotic fulfillment—if Miss Streetfield will pardon my mentioning them—we have substituted dreams of commercial fulfillment. No longer shall our youth fall a prey to the ravages of impure fancies—in their place, by the aid of suggestion, shall come visions of the Swelling Pay-Check, the Speed-up of a Faster Efficiency!

BILL (*blushing and desperate*). Oh, Father, Mr. Streetfield doesn't wahnt to hear about your old Success Institute!

McGEE. One word more and I have done! (*He advances steadily toward Mr. Streetfield, passing in front of the table.*) The Roosevelt will not only teach Success but also practise Success! Any investment in the enterprise made now will treble its value in a year's time. Now we are offering fifty shares of preferred stock (*producing a packet of documents from his inside breast pocket*)—the most preferred stock ever issued!—

MR. STREETFIELD. Yes—well, I am very grateful to you, Mr. McGee, and very much interested in your project. But I've made it a rigid rule never to invest in any new ventures——

McGEE. A very admirable rule, Mr. Streetfield: it will save you much disappointment. Yet I think you ought to take into account, sir, the cultural objectives of the Roosevelt—I know how much you are inter-ested in culture—

that what we are doing, for the first time in human history, is *merchandising* the Seven Arts!—

Miss Streetfield (*coming forward behind the table and taking the situation in hand*). I assure you, Mr. McGee, that I have a very high opinion of the work that the correspondence schools are doing——

Simon. All education is valueless!

*As no one pays any attention to this and Miss Streetfield goes on talking, he registers a rebuff, for the benefit of Bill, by jerking his chest in and his chin down, as if he had received a blow.*

Miss Streetfield. —and I wish you all success with your enterprise. You must forgive us if we don't feel able to contribute to it. But, as you know, my own particular field is the Y.W.C.A., and——

*While she has been speaking, the clock has struck half past nine, and Bill now interrupts.*

Bill. What train are you taking, Father? You know the 9:50's the last. I wahnt to tok to you a minute before you go.

McGee (*to the Streetfields*). Of course! I mustn't deetain you any longer.—Well, I hope you will forgive me, my dear Miss Streetfield, for intruding unceremoniously like this—and let me express my most heartfelt thanks for all you have done for my daughter—and I hope that you will allow me some day to tell you a little more about the Roosevelt School and its vision, and to send you some of our literature! (*He shakes hands all around.*) Most happy to have seen you, Miss Streetfield—most happy to have met you, Mr. Streetfield—Miss . . . Mrs. . . .

Simon (*to Bill*). I felt so depressed and terrible I just had to run over. You better come out with me for a little ride.

Bill. Oh, I can't! I wish I could, but I can't!

McGee (*who has made the circuit of the semicircle*). And

goodby, Mr. Delacy! Most happy to have made your acquaintance!

BILL. You with a Success Institute! That hands me a laugh!—Listen, Father, where you living now?

McGEE. In the same old room, Bill.

BILL. Not much money in it!?

McGEE. Brighter days are dawning, Billy!

BILL. Still have to paste the punches back into the street-car transfers?

McGEE. I have never abandoned my old habits of thrift! *She pilots him toward the hall door, passing in front of the table.*

BILL (*in a low voice*). You haven't got room for me any more, huh?

McGEE (*disturbed*). You're not leaving, are you, Billy?

BILL. I just wahnted to know how you were fixed.

MISS STREETFIELD (*as they reach the door*). Don't you want to take your father into the library, Elizabeth?

BILL. Thanks, I will.

McGEE (*bowing*). Goodby! Goodby!

*He and Bill go out together.*

*In the meantime, Simon has picked up the* Atlantic Monthly *from the sofa and has been examining it. Now he throws it down emphatically on the table and addresses Mr. Streetfield.*

SIMON. What do you think of H. L. Mencken?

MR. STREETFIELD. I'm afraid I don't know H. L. Mecklin.

SIMON. He's a writer.—You write yourself, don't you?

MR. STREETFIELD. Yes—a little.

SIMON. What do you write?

MR. STREETFIELD. Just now I'm editing some old letters.

SIMON. Whose letters are they?

MR. STREETFIELD. They were written by my grandfather at the time when——

SIMON. Who was your grandfather?

MR. STREETFIELD. His name was Nathaniel Streetfield.

SIMON. I mean—I suppose he was somebody in particular, wasn't he? What was he?—was he a writer?

MR. STREETFIELD. He was our minister to France at one time.

SIMON (*blank but impressed*). Oh!—What books of your own have you written? You've written some books yourself, haven't you?

MR. STREETFIELD. I did a small biography of Gouverneur Morris a good many years ago.

SIMON. What did they think about things in your grandfather's time? They didn't think that life was meaningless then, did they?—Of course, *I* think that American democracy has just been the most complete failure!

JULIET (*rising*). I'm afraid I must go, Aunt Clara.—(*In explanation to Cousin Serena*) Mother's sailing tomorrow morning, and I have to see her tonight.

*Miss Streetfield commences immediately to pick up and put away the cards.*

SIMON (*to Juliet*). You know Katherine March awfully well, I suppose.

JULIET. Yes. Have you met her?

SIMON. I just met her this afternoon. Don't you think she's a wonder?

JULIET. She's very striking, isn't she? And she rides so awfully well.

SIMON. Absolutely marvellously! She asked me to go riding with her tomorrow morning, but I'm such a bum horseman myself that I thought it was safer to take her for a drive instead.—Gosh, I wish I could ride like that!— she seems absolutely part of the horse!—She's sort of like a horse herself—she has just the same kind of beauty!

JULIET. I think that's rather an ambiguous compliment —I don't think she'd be very much flattered to be told she looked like a horse.

SIMON. Oh, I don't mean she has a face like a horse or

anything like that! It's just that she's so straight and moves so naturally and freely. And there's something about the way she bites her hat-strap!—She's *far* the most beautiful girl I've seen down here: she absolutely fascinates me!

JULIET. Well, I think you were very wise not to let yourself in for her fences.—Good night. (*She gives him her hand.*) Good night, Uncle Schuyler. Good night, Cousin Serena. Good night, Aunt Clara. (*She kisses Miss Streetfield.*)

MISS STREETFIELD. Good night, dear.—Tell your mother, Juliet, that she needn't bother about the roses. I'm going to send Fletcher over to Huntington to get some.—She has so much to do.

*Bill comes back; Juliet shakes hands with her just as she is going out.*

JULIET. Good night, Elizabeth. I hope you'll come over to see us sometime. Do come over to lunch some day. We'd love to have you.

BILL. Thanks. Maybe I will.

*Juliet goes out through the hall. Bill remains near the door on the right. Cousin Serena rises from her chair, putting her crochet-work away and settling her shawl around her.*

COUSIN SERENA. I'm really afraid you must excuse me— my trip down was such an exhausting one. I was annoyed all the way from New York by the most ill-bred little girl. She had been occupying two seats by herself, and I had the conductor turn one over for me. But then she leaned over the back of the seat and talked to me every minute of the way. She told me that she had come on from Kansas City all the way alone.—

SIMON. My home town!

COUSIN SERENA. Well, I think it's a very long way for a small child to come alone. Her parents had simply put her on the train and given her an enormous box of jelly sandwiches. They looked horrible! She kept trying to make me take one. I should think she would be ill after such a journey—her teeth were in the most dreadful condition.—And she wanted me to read her the comic paper. (*Delacy laughs.*) I told her she shouldn't read such stuff as that. I don't know what parents can be thinking of to neglect their children in that fashion!

Miss Streetfield. Well, people of that class, you know, very often have no time for their children. Among the girls who have come to grief that we see at the Y.W.C.A., we find that in only about thirty per cent of the cases have the parents been dissipated or lazy. In most of the other cases, it is simply a question of both parents' working all day and being unable to look after the children.—Well, will you pardon us, Mr. Delacy, if we are very rude and leave you? I have letters still to be written, and I hope you will forgive me if I say good night.

*She shakes hands with him.*

Simon. Sorry to have arrived without warning like this, but I felt so absolutely rotten that I just had to see somebody!

Mr. Streetfield. I'm afraid you haven't found us very stimulating.

Simon. Oh, the way I was feeling tonight, anybody would be stimulating: I just wanted a human face!

Mr. Streetfield (*shaking hands with him*). We try to look human. Good night.

*He and Cousin Serena go out by the hall door.*

Miss Streetfield (*to Bill*). Now don't stay up too late, will you, dear?

Bill. No: I won't.

*Miss Streetfield follows the others.*

*As soon as the boy and girl are left alone together, they embrace with a sudden and powerful impact: he squeezes her tight and kisses her lavishly.*

Simon. Dearest Bill!

Bill. Hello, dear!—Gee, we haven't seen each other for a long time!

SIMON (*with humorous irony*). Almost twenty-four hours!

BILL. I thot it was a long time.

SIMON. And we parted under such tragic circumstances, too!—(*taking out a hip-flask*) Have a drink?

BILL. Oh, you ottn't to have come here tonight! The Streetfields are scandalized!

SIMON. I don't care!—they can't high-hat me!

BILL. They're sore at me about it, too.

SIMON. It wasn't your fault!

BILL. No: but I was with you at the time, and I suppose they feel that sort of invawlves them.

SIMON. Don't you want some of this?

BILL. What is it?

SIMON. Gin.

BILL. The same as you had last night?

SIMON. Uh-huh. Goes down like liquid nail-files!

BILL. Oh, that's the most terrible gin I ever tasted! I don't wahnt any!

SIMON (*drinking*). Well, you need something a little bit rough in here. Don't you ever feel like stepping on an etching or cutting your initials in the desk or something? (*He inspects the room, humming* The Sheik.)

BILL. Oh, I do enough damage to their feelings as it is. They make me feel like a regular blacksmith.—Oh, Simon, I've thot about you all day!

SIMON. That must have been delightful. Didn't you enjoy it?

BILL. I'd rather we'd been together.

*He makes her sit down with him on the sofa, on his right, and puts his arm around her and kisses her. In the conversation that follows, he sometimes, with his restless energy, rises and walks about.*

SIMON. Gosh, I thought we weren't going to make it in that pink room last night!

BILL. How did you ever get your pump back?

SIMON. Oh, I dodged in and retrieved it when whoever it was had gone.

BILL. Listen, Simon: I'm worried!

SIMON. Oh, don't worry about last night. Nobody's any the worse.

BILL. It's not that: it's something else—it's something that might be serious——

SIMON. Did you see about last night in the paper?

BILL. Gee! it wasn't in the paper, was it?

SIMON (*producing a copy of the* Daily News *and reading with burlesque grandiloquence*). Listen to this! "Delacy's Slug Fells Waiter at Society Dance. Chivalrous Young Novelist Adds Another Ruin to the Ruins of the Ritz." Now listen to this! "The squared ring lost a two-fisted fighter the day that Simon Delacy decided swinging a mean Underwood was an easier way of earning a living than throwing padded mitts. This was the unbiased opinion of the socially elite audience who saw Mr. Delacy soundly thrash a surly head-waiter at a smart dance at the home of Mr. Jethro Dorrance, prominent Long Island society leader."—

BILL. My God! Mr. Dawrnce will have a fit!

SIMON. Serves him right. If he hadn't put me out, nobody would have heard anything about it. But listen to this—here's where you come in: "A careless remark by the waiter about a woman was the match that set off the explosion."

BILL. Aw, that isn't true!

SIMON. Yes, it is, practically: that's what I gave out. I thought he was laughing at you and me when we were coming down the stairs there. I even had a sort of an idea that he was the person who tried to walk in on us—it was sort of a heavy step, don't you remember?

BILL. I bet it was at that: he had a pussy-footing look, that waiter!

SIMON. And then I asked him for a match, don't you

remember? and there was something about the way he refused it that I didn't like. I thought he was trying to ritz me.—I was feeling sort of sore last evening on account of a jam I got into at the club.—And then when he said, "You're obstructing the door, sir," don't you remember?, I just hauled him off and smashed him.—Here's how the paper describes it: "Chivalrous as any hero of his imagination, the youthful author expressed his resentment with a right cross to Mr. Head Waiter's jaw. With nary a return, he followed up with a rain of blows"——

BILL. Aw, that isn't true!

SIMON. No: but it would have been, if old Dorrance hadn't come running up.—But just let me read you the end: "In his new romance, *The Ruins of the Ritz*, starting in the *News* today, Mr. Delacy packs a wallop that you need not go to Long Island to see."—Wonderful publicity, what?

BILL. Oh, Simon, you'll get in so wrong that you'll never be able to come down here again!

SIMON. Oh, they can't high-hat me! They'll find out in a few years' time that I have as much money as any of them—and that I *am* somebody, too! (*He takes out the flask and drinks.*) Besides, I apologized to old Dorrance this morning.

BILL. They've got it in for both of us, though.—Gee, I wish Father hadn't come just tonight!

SIMON. Has your father always been in the bunk business?

BILL. You think he's pretty terrible, huh?

SIMON. No: God forgive me, I can't cast any stones. I used to lead a life of shame myself!

BILL. You really don't mean it, do you?

SIMON. Oh, I used to write captions for a film company. And I can tell you it's a damn heart-breaking thing to use up all your intellectual energy trying to think like a child of eight!—trying to make things that are so cheap already that they actually make you sick, cheap enough so that they'll satisfy the taste of the people they were too highbrow for before. (*Vehement*) Why you wouldn't believe it but actually, by the time I'd been doing movie captions a year, when I'd get out the old stories I'd written at college, instead of thinking how crude they were and how I ought to do something better, my mind would get to work automatically to think up ways to make them rotten enough for movie scenarios!—Well, I don't care now—I can tell them all to go to hell! I've proved that there's money in telling the truth—if you jazz it up enough!

BILL. Well, Father reelly beelieves in his bunk, though. That's the reason he can get away with it. There's reelly something sort of wonderful aboutum. He can charm the money right out of people's pockets. When I was a little girl, I always used to thinkovum as a kind of a magician. Why, I've knownum to come into Cincinnati with only forty-five cents inuz pocket, and inside of two weeks' time raise seven thousand dawllars!

SIMON. What did he do then?

BILL. He went back to Pittsburgh.

SIMON. I mean what was it he was selling?

BILL. Oh, it was a company for making bread without flour. It was reelly a good idea—but he never got enough money to float it.—And another time, during the War, he had a big military invention. He almost sold it to the German government.

SIMON. To the *German* government!

BILL. Yeah: he thot he was going to sell it to a German agent for fifty-five thousand dawllars. It was a new kind of explosive that was supposed to kill everything in sight.

SIMON. What happened?

BILL. Why, he started for New York to meet the German agent there, and on the way it went off innuz grip.

SIMON. Do much damage?

BILL. No: it just singeduz hair-brushes a little.—And then he had a vaudeville theater. I was one of the star acts.

SIMON. What did you used to do?

BILL. I used to come out and sing. I was only about ten.

SIMON. What did you used to sing?

BILL. It was a little song that went like this—

> Bugs! bugs! I'm bugs about you!
> Honest and true, honest and true!

SIMON. My God, what a terrible song!—How did you ever get to New York?

BILL. Oh, I finally couldn't stand it with Father any longer: he was absolutely broke. And I wahnted to get away and do something. I wahnted to go on the stage. But I never had much luck. You have to sleep with the managers to get anywhere on the stage.

SIMON. Is that so?

BILL. Yes, I should say!—Why, the first time I ever went to see a manager, it was Sam Gundelfinger in Cincinnati, and I toldum that I wanted to act and he said to me, he said, "Little girl, can you deepict love and hate?" —he said, "There's one thing that if you can't do it, you'll never be a nactress, and that's to deepict love and hate." So he took me into a room and shut the door and he said to me, "Now put your arms around me and say just as hard as you can, 'I love you! I love you!' I want to see you deepict love." So I threw my arms aroundum and I yelled out just as loud as I could, so you could hear me a block away: "I love you, Mr. Gundelfinger! I love you, Mr. Gundelfinger!"—So that was the end of that!

SIMON (*kissing her delightedly*). Oh, you're so cute!

BILL. Oh, you just think I'm cute. You don't reelly like me much.—Say, I've got to tok to you, Simon. I'm awf'ly worried about something!

Simon (*kissing her again*). Don't worry, dear! God is dead!—What happened to you after that?

Bill. Oh, I got a job in vaudeville. It was a tramp and cake-eater act—a juggling act. I was the little assistant who comes out in the white silk tights, you know, and looks pretty and smiles at everything that happens. (*She illustrates.*) And then Foley, the bum, got a crush on me, and LaFollette, who did the dude part, started drinking so that he couldn't catch the balls anymore. So the team broke up. They must have been queer.

Simon. What were you doing just recently when Miss Streetfield got hold of you?

Bill. I was working as a waitress in the Dolly Madison Tea-Room.

Simon. How did you get to know her?—in the restaurant?

Bill. No: she was working with the Y.W.C.A., and I was staying there.—I said I was a nactress because I was ashamed to say I was a waitress—and they didn't want to take me in. They won't take in any actresses. Can you imagine that?

Simon. The damned old maids!

Bill. But Miss Streetfield happened to be there, and she heard me tokking to the woman and she got me let in.

Simon. Gosh, you must have been pretty low!

Bill. Gee, I used to think some nights that I'd just turn on the old gas. That was all there was—just old green walls and an old leaky gas-jet. It was just like they gave you a room and the only thing you needed to croak.—Then Miss Streetfield rescued me. (*With irony*) I'm a rescued girl!

Simon. Is she pretty decent?

Bill. Yes: she is. But she gets a big kick out of rescuing me.—She wahnts to do good.

Simon. Something wrong with the old sex-life?

Bill. I suppose so.—She reelly hasn't got any life of

her own except keeping house for her brother, and the only way she knows to break out is trying to improve other people. I reelly feel sawrry for her.

SIMON. God, *he's* a terrible ass, isn't he? He's such a disappointment you could boot him. You think at first he's going to be distinguished, and then he only turns out to be insipid!

BILL. He doesn't like me!

SIMON. Well, you should worry! I'm sure he doesn't like me either. I think they're a pretty weak bunch down here! (*He gets up and stands behind the table.*) You'd think that, with a lot of money like that, they'd want to do something exciting with it, instead of just giving little dances where you can't even ride the waiters!—God, you don't know how wonderful it is to run into somebody like you!—somebody with real vitality where everybody else is tamed—where they've got the very servants watching you to see that you don't break the rules!—somebody who's capable of passion without worrying about whether it's correct!—somebody who can *give* herself!

BILL (*wanting him to know that she does not usually give herself so easily*). I might have made you wait from two to three weeks, if I'd wahnted to!

SIMON. It was just because you didn't that I adored you! All the rest are scared to be themselves; but *you're* a fearless living force!—(*He produces the flask again.*) Look: you *must* have a drink now!

BILL. Oh, I ottn't to, here!

SIMON. Oh, hell! Don't let them crab you! Remember you're alive and they're dead! Remember every moment of pleasure is a triumph against the forces of death! (*He gives her the flask and she drinks; then he drinks again himself.*) It's all going to be in my new book—*The Skeleton in the Taxi*—don't you think that's a swell title: *The Skeleton in the Taxi*? It's going to be about the lives these people lead

and the lives they make other people lead—the dead
coupon-clipper at one end of the line and the dead time-
clock-puncher at the other! About how they all carry
corpses around with them and pretend that live men don't
exist! (*He sits on the table, facing Bill.*) There'll be a skeleton
in a taxi, you see, that travels round New York at night.
Can't you see it rattling up Fifth Avenue when it's all
dark at night? Some innocent youth from the West—like
me—encounters this grisly spectacle and is shocked. He
begins to avoid Fifth Avenue—but by and by he meets
other skeletons: he rides in an elevator with one, coming
out of an editor's office—and then he realizes that the subways are full of them. He finally gets so exercised about
it that he complains to the Chief of Police. But the police
just give him the laugh, and so does everybody else. He
thought they would be surprised, incredulous, see, but
they knew about it all the time. That's the normal state
of things for them! Finally, he goes to the richest man in
New York—the big financier, you see—the man who
owns all the newspapers and all the public officials. The
rich man listens very politely and answers him very
seriously: "Why, Mr. Dumbell," the rich man says, "my
attention has been called to this nuisance, and I have
appointed a committee to investigate it, with Mr. Thomas
Ludlow Bones as the chairman. Believe me, no object is
nearer my heart then exterminating the live skeletons. And
we should feel ourselves more than honored if you would
consent to serve on our committee. The salary is ten
thousand a year." Mr. Dumbell, of course, accepts, smiling
from ear to ear. "Won't you let me send you home in
my car?" suggests the millionaire. "I should be delighted,"
says Mr. Dumbell. So he gets into a great big limousine—
all equipped with a pipe-organ and a pool table and everything! "Pretty soft!" thinks Mr. Dumbell. "This shows
that virtue pays in the long run." He tells the chauffeur to

drive him home to the Allerton House—and just then he happens to catch a glimpse of himself in a little looking-glass in the car, and he jumps about eight feet. All he sees is a staring skull. "Allerton House, hell!" says the driver, "your address is the graveyard now!"—Of course, that's all pretty crude—but you see the idea, don't you? Don't you think it sounds pretty good?

BILL. I think it's wonderful!

SIMON (*jumping down from the table and embracing her*). I think *you're* wonderful!

*He offers her the flask.*

BILL (*elated*). Oh, you don't reelly think I'm wonderful!

*She takes another drink.*

SIMON. Yes, I do: I think you're wonderful. I think you're the most wonderful girl down here—the most wonderful girl I know!— (*As she hands him back the flask*) The little face is beginning to light up again!

BILL. I'm still worried about something, though.

SIMON. And the reason I think you're wonderful is because you appreciate instinctively everything that's living and fine! You understood me right away though you'd never read a word I'd written!

BILL. I like things that are crazy like that. I couldn't hand those other books much. All these stories about these old dames being reepressed in Massachusetts! (*Very scornfully*) Gee whiz!

SIMON. You are right! I agree with you perfectly! This miasma of the dreary must cease! Simon Delacy will put a stop to it! I'm going to run amuck through American literature, like a satyr—like a werewolf!—Say, that's a good title for an article, isn't it?—*Simon Peter Delacy, the Werewolf of Modern Letters*!

BILL. Is a werewolf a special kind of wolf?

SIMON. Oh, didn't you ever hear of werewolves? They're people who are people during the day-time but turn into

wolves at night.— (*Going on more and more enthusiastically*)
I'm going to be the most amazing American writer since
Edgar Allan Poe—a Poe with a social conscience! No more
middle-western bohunks! No more wistful old maids!
I'll write satires—satires fantastic and savage!— (*He stops
and coughs violently.*) Gee, I'm in terrible shape! I must
go back and go to bed. I've got to be up in the morning
so that I can get the car attended to and get back to town.

BILL. I didn't know you were going tomorrow!

SIMON. Doesn't seem to be anything else to do. They
make me feel like a stray dog at the club now.—And I'm
fed up with it down here anyway.—I think I'll take a trip
to Europe soon: I think I'll go to Paris. (*He gets up, as if
to leave.*)

BILL. I thot you were going to meet me tomorrow!

SIMON. I will. What time was it we were going to
meet? It was in the afternoon, wasn't it?

BILL. No, it wasn't: it was in the morning—it was
eleven o'clock in the morning!

SIMON. Well, let's make it the afternoon: it'll take me
all morning to get the car fixed. That won't make any
difference to you, will it?

BILL. What time?

SIMON. Say two o'clock.

BILL. All right.—Gee, I didn't know you were going
so soon!

SIMON. Gosh, I was so stewed last night that I didn't
know what dates I was making! My mind's been a blank
all day. And I'm beginning to get the twitches! See that?
My left eye-lid twitches! (*He takes another drink.*)

BILL (*getting up from the sofa*). You better go home and
get slept up. (*A little plaintively*) I wish you could stay
a little longer. You only just came down yesterday. I
haven't seen you for almost three weeks!

SIMON. I'll be down again soon.

BILL. When?

MISS STREETFIELD'S VOICE. Elizabeth!

BILL. Now you better go home. (*Kissing him*) Goo
night, deerest. (*Long embrace, which she breaks off*) Now yo
go home and sleep off your jim-jams. I want to tok t
you very seriously tomorrow.

SIMON. Don't let's talk seriously. We're—much to
serious people—talk seriously!

BILL. Two o'clock then by that old bath-house.

SIMON. By the old ruined petting-house!

MISS STREETFIELD'S VOICE. Elizabeth!

BILL. Now, you must go now! Miss Streetfield's gettin
excited.

SIMON. Good night, dearest Bill!

*He engulfs her in another monstrous hug and she yield
pledging herself, to his kiss—beyond play, beyond shynes
beyond fear. But after a moment she breaks away. They ar
standing at the French window.*

BILL (*whispering*). You must go now!

SIMON (*with a gay gallant gesture*). Farewell!

*He goes off unsteadily, but humming* The Sheik. *Mis
Streetfield comes in from the hall.*

MISS STREETFIELD. Mr. Delacy has finally gone, has he

BILL. Yes: he just left.

MISS STREETFIELD. I really don't think you ought to se
too much of him.

BILL. I'm sawrry he came tonight!

MISS STREETFIELD. Well, that doesn't matter. But I d
really think you're making a great mistake in going abou
with him so much. The whole incident last night wa
most unfortunate: Mr. Delacy really behaved very badl
You know, my dear, you must learn to distinguish be
tween different sorts of people. The leaders and associate
we choose are the index to our own ideals and standard
and other people judge us by them. We must learn not t

be deceived by people of merely superficial brilliance, but to recognize the real leader, the real man of character and inspiration, who will strengthen and enrich our lives. You know what Tennyson says:

"We needs must love the highest when we see it—
    Not Lancelot nor another."

You must try to remember that—will you?

BILL. Yes: I'll reemember.—But if you really knew Simon Delacy better——

MISS STREETFIELD. —*Remember*, dear.—

BILL. Remember.

MISS STREETFIELD. Well, Mr. Delacy strikes me as a young man with no serious purpose in life, who——

BILL. Simon *has* got a serious purpose!

MISS STREETFIELD. Well, I'm very glad to hear it: what is it?

BILL. He wahnts to attack modern civilization!

MISS STREETFIELD. Our civilization has its faults—I'm keenly aware of that. But I don't think we can do any good by a purely negative attitude. The great men of the world you know, have been creators and builders—not destroyers and tearers-down. Their ideal has been Service——

BILL (*with ideas of the Dolly Madison Tea-Room*). Service?!

MISS STREETFIELD. Yes: Service to our fellow men and, through them, to God. If people care for nobody but themselves and seek nothing but their own self-indulgence, they naturally become angry with society, because it will not gratify all their whims.—It's like that dance you were telling us about tonight at which the young people became so brutalized with irresponsible pleasure-seeking that a young man actually attacked an old man and threw him down a flight of stairs!

BILL. Oh, the old man didn't mind it! There was a doctor there and he took some stitches inuz scalp, and he was back on the floor in half an hour, dancing like a regular demon—he just had this big wad of bandages sticking out on the backovuz neck, and he thot that was a big joke.

MISS STREETFIELD. But suppose he had happened to be killed!—And they destroyed all the lights, you said—just out of wantonness, I suppose—for no reason at all!

BILL. No: they didn't: they *had* a reason!

MISS STREETFIELD. What was it?

BILL. They wahnted it dark.

MISS STREETFIELD. Why couldn't they simply turn out the lights, instead of tearing down the fixtures?

BILL. They wahnted them turned out right—so as they couldn't be turned on again.

MISS STREETFIELD. What did they want to do that for?

BILL. I guess they wahnted to pet!

*A silence.*

MISS STREETFIELD. Well, I think you're very tired, Elizabeth, and you ought to get to bed as soon as possible. You were up so late last night: your nerves are all on edge from lack of sleep—and you have algebra in the morning!

BILL (*balked by Miss Streetfield's evasion and frightened at her own boldness*). I know! I'm going right up!

MISS STREETFIELD. You're sleeping down here tonight, you know, in the room across the hall. I like to give Mrs Middleton the room she's accustomed to. I think Ann has moved your things.

BILL. Yes: I know—I forgot.

MISS STREETFIELD. Well, good night, Elizabeth. (*Shaking hands with her*) I hope you will be able to sleep.

BILL. Good night.—I'll be all right.

*She goes out through the hall door.*

*When she has left, Miss Streetfield turns sharply away and goes over to the fireplace, where she energetically prods the fire and reconstructs the pile of logs.*

*Mr. Streetfield appears from the dining-room.*

MR. STREETFIELD. Well, shall we have our Trollope?

MISS STREETFIELD. If you like.

*She sets the tongs and poker in their places and goes over to the desk for the book.*

MR. STREETFIELD. I suppose we ought to ask the Fawcetts down here before it gets too hot for Alice.

*He sits down in the chair farthest forward on the right.*

MISS STREETFIELD. We must certainly do something about Aunt Harriet. Why don't you pay her a visit when you go up to town for the museum meeting?

MR. STREETFIELD. I'm afraid I shouldn't have time. It would take a whole extra day. I might stop off sometime when I'm going to Boston.

MISS STREETFIELD. You never go to Boston any more.— Well, *I* shall have to do it then. (*She has been moving the table back so that it may not stand between them.*)

MR. STREETFIELD. You see: that's the fatal difficulty about having the table out here: one has to shift it back and forth continually.

MISS STREETFIELD. That's very easily done—and there are so many things one can use it for. We've always needed a table in this room. (*She sits down on the sofa and opens the book.*) Well, where were we?

MR. STREETFIELD. We were reading the love scene, don't you know, between Mr. Arabin and Eleanor.

MISS STREETFIELD. " 'I hope we are not to part as enemies?' "—is that it?

MR. STREETFIELD. Yes—where they have the misunderstanding.

MISS STREETFIELD. " 'I hope we are not to part as enemies?' said he. 'There shall be no enmity on my part,' said Eleanor; 'I endeavor to avoid all enmities. It would be hollow pretence were I to say that there can be true friendship between us after what has just passed. People cannot make their friends of those whom they despise.'

" 'And am I despised?'

" '*I* must have been so before you could have spoken of me as you did. And I was deceived, cruelly deceived. I believed that you thought well of me; I believed that you esteemed me.' " (*She stops and listens.*) What was that?

MR. STREETFIELD. What is it?

MISS STREETFIELD. I thought I heard a sound from Elizabeth's room—it sounded like a cry. She's sleeping across the hall, you know.

MR. STREETFIELD. I shouldn't worry about her: she probably sleeps like a top.

MISS STREETFIELD. " 'Thought well of you and esteemed you!' said he. 'In justifying myself before you, I must use stronger words than those.'

"He paused for a moment, and Eleanor's heart beat with painful——" There!—I'm sure I heard her call.

*She gets up quickly and goes out through the hall door.*

*Mr. Streetfield, left alone, stares placidly into space; then, as he becomes aware of the vacant corner, he fixes it for a moment and turns around to look at the table.*

*Miss Streetfield returns.*

MISS STREETFIELD. She seems to be sleeping quietly enough: I opened the door and she didn't wake. But I thought I heard her call.—You know, I'm really quite worried about her—that Delacy boy upsets her so. The same thing happens whenever he comes down. He's so wild and such a dreadful cad—and I'm afraid she's fallen in love with him!

MR. STREETFIELD. How do you know they're not well suited to one another?

MISS STREETFIELD. No: she really has character and brains; and I want her to get an education.

MR. STREETFIELD. I always thought it was a mistake to have her here.

Miss Streetfield. It will be good for her, I think, as training.

Mr. Streetfield. What a marvelous understanding of human relations there is in this scene of Trollope's!

Miss Streetfield (*absently*). Yes.—Where was I?

Mr. Streetfield. The scruples of shyness and pride that keep human beings apart!

Miss Streetfield. "Eleanor's heart beat with painful violence within her bosom as she waited for him to go on. 'I have esteemed, do esteem you, as I never yet esteemed any woman. Think well of you! I never thought to think so well, so much, of any human creature. Speak calumny of you!' "— (*She pauses a moment and looks up, as if she heard something again.*) " 'Insult you! Wilfully injure you! I wish it were my privilege to shield you from calumny, insult, and injury. Calumny! ah me. 'Twere almost better that it were so. Better than to worship with a sinful worship; sinful and vain, also.' "

*But as she reads, the room is turning dark, and her voice fades gradually away.*

*When the stage becomes visible again, we are confronted by a dark length of corridor, which ends in a door on the left. The door is guarded by a man in uniform. Bill comes quickly in on the right, with a paper-covered bundle in her arms, and hurries along the corridor toward the door. She is dressed in the plain black dress and the white cap and apron of a waitress. At the door she is stopped by the guard.*

The Guard. Hey! you can't go through here!

Bill. I've got to! I've got to get away!

The Guard. Well, you can't go through here: this door has gotta be kept closed!

Bill. But I wahnt to get out to the sea-shore! If I can only just get to the sea-shore!

THE GUARD. Say, you're a waitress, aren'tcha—been workin' for this party here?

BILL. Yes—I have been.

THE GUARD. Been workin' for Streetfield?

BILL. Yes.

THE GUARD. You're leavin', eh?

BILL. Yes.

THE GUARD. Well, I got orders not to let you through!

BILL. Well, why is that? I'm leaving!

THE GUARD. I got orders to keep this door closed. And you'll have to leave that baby here!

BILL. This isn't a baby: this is just my clothes!

THE GUARD. Come on, now! You got a baby in there! Can't carry no babies here!

*He wrests the package away from her and puts it under his arm.*

BILL (*stifled*). When—can I—get it again?

THE GUARD. You'll have to see the Manager about that.

BILL. Well—when can I see him?

THE GUARD. He's away now.

BILL. Will he be back tonight?

THE GUARD. We're closed tonight. We're closed half an hour ago!

BILL. Well, can I see him tomorrow morning?

THE GUARD. You'll have to get a permit from Street-field.—Come on, now: you can't hang around!

BILL. But you're going to give me a check, aren't you? I thot I was supposed to be checking it!

THE GUARD. No: we don't give out no checks!

BILL. Well, what good does it do to keep me here? I can't work for them any more!

THE GUARD. I tell yuh, this door is closed! I've got orders to keep it closed! Now, beat it, kid—don't make me get rough!

BILL (*breaking down*). Oh, they won't let me in and they won't let me out! What do they expect me to do, anyway?

# ACT II

*Gray twilight; the edge of a forest: the tree-trunks show slender and clear. Bill, still in her waitress's costume, is seated near the center at the back of the shallow scene: she is sitting on an old wooden chair with a broken back. A group of ladies and gentlemen in evening dress pass across from right to left, laughing and chattering indistinctly. They bear with them the strains of* The Sheik—*thrilling, heady and somehow sinister. One of the men stops and turns towards Bill. The others go on without him.*

THE YOUNG MAN. Hello, Billy: aren't you coming to the party? (*He is a pug-nosed tight-muscled boy, who wears a bandage about his temples.*)

BILL (*getting up and coming toward him*). Hello, Ted! What's the big idea?

TED. Aren't you coming to the party?

BILL. I guess not: I haven't had a bid. What party is it?

TED. Why, it's a party that's being given for dead people. I guess you can't qualify yet.

BILL. Oh, Gee! You're dead, aren't you? I forgot! I haven't seen you since the smash!

TED. Gosh, it's lucky you weren't killed yourself! That was some gruesome smash! Twenty feet—right off the Boulevard!

BILL. I jumped out when I saw we were going off and I landed on the grass.

TED. I got caught under the car. They had to scrape me off with a spade.

BILL. Oh, Ted: it was all my fault! I ottn't to have let you drive so fast!

TED. You couldn't have stopped me: I wanted to. I guess you know why I did it. I wanted to do something you'd get a kick out of and that was the only thing that seemed to work.

BILL. Oh, I know! I felt just terrible! I was just sick about it! You were one of the richest boys in Pittsburgh!

TED. I hope you don't think I was happy just because I had a lot of money: if I'd lived, I'd never have been happy—not without you. Everything was just awful before I died. Every night that I didn't have a date with you, I'd go out and ride around the park all alone, and I'd have a kitten every fifteen minutes thinking I saw you with somebody else. And when I'd stay home in that great huge house with the iron fountain on the lawn, I'd just go absolutely nuts! It looked like an institution, and it was a mad-house for me all right! Fifty-nine magnificent rooms and all of them absolutely empty!—empty because you weren't there!

BILL. Oh, Teddy! I'm so sawrry! I didn't know you were reelly lonely like that.

TED. Even when we were together, half the time I couldn't feel you cared anything about me. I knew that I didn't have any hold on you, and I wanted to make you feel my strength. You used to get excited when we'd go like hell—so one night when I was good and stewed, I forgot to keep on the Boulevard and I just crashed off into space!

BILL. But you did have me—you know you did. You tok like I'd held out on you!

TED. Yes: I know: but that doesn't mean so much by itself, because it doesn't last. It would almost be worse afterwards.

BILL. Oh, Teddy! If you only hadn't done it, I might have loved you reelly!

TED. You never would have: it can't be done—I bet it

was a big relief to you when I was bumped off for good—
and I don't blame you!

BILL. Oh! Teddy, that's terrible to say that! I liked you
a whole lot!

TED. Say: why don't you come out with me tonight?
I don't have to go to the party.

BILL. Oh, I'm sawrry, Teddy! but I reelly can't. I've
got a date with somebody here.

*A wolf howls in the wood.*

TED. It's another fellow you're waiting for! It's somebody you're crazy about!

BILL. It's just a friend of mine.—Oh, Teddy! does it
hurt even now that you're dead?

TED. Gee, I'm glad I did it, after all!

BILL. Cheer up, Teddy! The laugh's on me now. This
time it's me who's in love!

TED. Yes: I knew I'd have to hear it some time! I knew
I was right when I did it!

BILL. You did it on purpose then! You wahnted to kill
yourself!

TED. There's no way to end it but that!

BILL. You wahnted to kill me, too! Oh, Ted, how
terrible!—Oh, Teddy: I'm sawrry you loved me so
much!

TED. Never mind!—it's all over now.—Well, I must
go! I don't want to crab your date.

BILL. Goodby, Teddy dear. I'm sawrry! (*She kisses him.*)

TED. Thanks, Billy dear.—Goodby.

*He takes her by the hands and kisses her, then goes out at
the right. The wolf howls close at hand. Bill stiffens and looks
about. Simon, lean in a wolf-skin, darts in from among the
trees. He is tense and hollow-eyed. He throws himself down
at her feet.*

BILL. Oh, Simon: where have you been?

SIMON. I've been running with the pack, and just now

they turned on me! They would have chewed me up like
a rabbit!

BILL. You're all bloody!

SIMON. That's just the brambles. But I'm all shot!
nearly ran my damn legs off. My nerves are being eaten
by fire—and oh! I could fly out of my skin!

BILL. If you did, you'd be a man.

SIMON. I don't want to be a man! I want to be what
I am. (*Clasping his hands to his ears*) Don't you see that
big black bird, flapping around my ears? For God's sake
beat it away!

BILL. I don't see any bird!

SIMON. Look! Look! It's sailing around my head! Get
it now!—There it goes!—It's gone— No: it's perched up
there in the trees!

BILL. Why don't you lie down and take a rest, Simon
dear?

SIMON. I can't stay here! I must go!

BILL. Why have you got to go right away?

SIMON. What is there to make me stay?

BILL. Don't you wahnt to sleep a little? You're all tired
out!

SIMON. Sleep? *I* can't sleep! If I slept, they might come
and kill me! Or men might catch me and ship me away!
I have to keep awake all the time! I'm trying to stay behind in the country that everyone else has left. They found
they'd bought their tickets in their sleep and woke up to
see the boat pulling out and their passages taken for a
journey that they never meant to make. And their press-
gang would be shipping me after them, if they could only
catch me asleep!

BILL. I'll watch to see nobody comes. You'll have to
get some sleep some time.

SIMON. Don't tempt me! I'm weak already: I dream of
sleep with tears! I shut my eyes and I long to drop away

in some unfathomable pit of mist—I long to leave my nerves like old telegraph wires tangled in the upper air— I long to shed passion like the clothes of the dead! Oh, to sink softly—pillowed in vapor—down, down, down! Oh, to lie safe at the core of the earth—then I should sleep at last! Great statues would stand guard above me, ponderously cloaked in stone, and nothing would matter to them. The wars would spend themselves in silence; the cities go mad without noise; the collapse of great nations come as softly as the falling of winter leaves. I shouldn't hear even the insults of lovers tearing each other's hearts! And no breath would ever reach me there of happiness or greatness again!

BILL. Oh, Simon: I'm so sawrry for you!

SIMON. I don't want you to be sorry for me!

BILL. It's nice and quiet here: I just saw an old turtle go to sleep under the leaves. We could do like that.

SIMON. I can't stay here: it's all wet! This is just a place where tramps come and people throw things! Don't you see all those old tin cans soaking in the water over there? That old chair that you're sitting on is something that's been thrown away!

BILL. Oh, I'm sawrry: I forgot!

*Another party of people comes by, blown in on a gust of jazz.*

ONE OF THE PARTY. Hello, Simon! Coming to the dead party?

SIMON. Save a drink for me, will you?

BILL. What happens at a dead party?

*Simon merely laughs.*

BILL. Oh, Simon, don't go to it—stay here! I wahnt to give you peace.

SIMON. You lie: you want peace yourself!

BILL. Listen, Simon: I wahnt to tell you something: I just saw a disappointed girl.

SIMON. She'll get over it!

BILL. You don't know what she was disappointed about. She thot she was going to have a baby and she only had a Kewpie doll!

*He gives a brief contemptuous laugh.*

BILL. Don't you think that was sad?

SIMON. Why?

BILL. Kewpie dolls aren't reelly alive.

SIMON. Like the Skeleton in the Taxi, eh?

*Another party appears. The jazz which accompanies it goes crashing on to the beginning of the next scene.*

ONE OF THE PARTY. Come on, Simon—you'll be late!

SIMON (*getting up*). I'll be with you in half a minute!

BILL. Oh, Simon: please don't go! You'll get killed that way some night! Stay here and you'll be safe!

SIMON. Safe for what? Why should I be safe? Safe to live as citizens live? Safe to lock all my doors against danger and to lock out life with death? I've seen them marching to their clocks!—in and out and up and down—getting trade and taking wives and writing books! I've seen the generations topple down—each enchained to the next! And I'd rather die half a beast than thrive as a man like them! Such a fate should bring horror and madness, but they have only smiles and sober words—they smile their annihilation, and that smile has struck panic to my heart! I listened to their clocks and I thought: *That* destroys us all! But I at least will speak my defeat—I will tell what kingdom we have lost! My shame was never so great as to perish dumb like you—like bulls at the slaughter-house reeling from the mallet to the knife! I at least among you all am not afraid to *feel*. I am ready to stand alone on this perilous verge of Time with these black wings beating at my ears! (*He fends his head again.*)

BILL. But I'm ready to go there, too! I love you! I'll go anywhere!

SIMON. You can't. You must let me go!

BILL. But I love you! You don't understand.

SIMON. I can't lose my life for you!

BILL. When I hear your name I tremble and when I see you I can't tok!

SIMON. Let go! Don't hold me like that! If you stop me, I'll kill you, I'll go mad! (*The jazz grows louder; he wrests himself away and joins the group who have been waiting for him. Just before he goes out, he flings her a parting word.*) I don't think much of this baby motif anyhow.

ONE OF THE PARTY. You're a waitress, aren't you?

BILL. Yes.

THE MAN. Well, how about a little Service!

*They go out; the wolf's howling is heard and everything grows dark. The tree-trunks seem to prolong themselves upward as if Bill were sinking into the earth. Then, against a background entirely black, appears on the right a high narrow door opening out on a sky, white and sheer, which might be the infinitude of space, and framing the silhouette of a thin oldish man on a high stool behind a high desk. The desk stands between him and us, and he is beating a Devil's Tattoo on it with his fingers, but he is gazing out through the door: his profile seems turned away. Bill stands working at an enormous blackboard covered with very large chalked figures: she is trying to balance an equation. The music is still heard playing quite loudly as at the end of the scene before.*

BILL. Oh, I wish that music would stop! I can never get this equation with all that playing going on!

THE TUTOR. That won't make any difference.

BILL. Well, please make it stop: I'm sure I could get it! (*The music stops; she writes out the equation again and is seen to figure.*) Now if you only just wouldn't make that noise with your fingers! It mixes me all up!

*The Tutor stops rapping.*

THE TUTOR. It won't make any difference.

BILL (*finally breaking her chalk in desperation*). Oh, I can't make these equations come right! I try and try and try and they never come right! I can't make my side balance with Ted's side and I can't make Simon's side balance with my side! I can't find out the value of X! (*She pauses.*) I wish you'd tell me the value of X! (*She pauses, but he does not reply.*) Won't you tell me the value of X that makes the equations come out?

THE TUTOR (*still gazing out the door*). There's no value of X.

BILL. But there must be! How can you get them then? How can you make them come out?

THE TUTOR. There's no way of solving that problem.

BILL. Oh, I think that's mean giving people problems that haven't got any answers! It's just worrying them to death for nothing! (*She pauses: he makes no reply.*) —But if I tell him, won't that make it right?

THE TUTOR. It will make it worse than ever.

BILL. Well, can't I ever do anything then to make it come out right?

THE TUTOR. No: you can do nothing.

BILL. Bitter, bitter, bitter!—what does that word mean —bitter? When the bees ate the wrong kind of clover, the Commodore was bitter!

THE TUTOR. That word has no meaning here.

BILL. What is this place, anyhow? I thot it was the room where I tutor.

THE TUTOR. This is the bottom of everything.

BILL. Well, that isn't where I'm supposed to study! I've got to get into college, and this stuff is no good for college: it's just suffering, and it's driving me cuckoo, and I'll never get into college, and yet I can't get away from *them*!—and if Simon doesn't wahnt me, I don't know what I can do—I'll just have to turn on the gas! What else is there for me to do?

THE TUTOR. You must make them suffer instead.

BILL. But that's not right that the only way that I can get
something myself is just by making other people suffer! . . .
That's not right, is it? . . . Why don't you answer?

THE TUTOR. That question has no meaning here. (*He
gets down from his stool and puts on a black derby.*) You must
kill if you want to live.

BILL. I know: but I can't feel right about it! (*A breath of
jazz is heard; the Tutor moves toward the door.*) Are you
going to the dead party, too? . . . I guess you must be
dead. . . . Are you dead?

THE TUTOR. Death and life mean nothing here.

BILL. Well, what are you? . . . Let me see your face!
You've never let me see your face. . . . I wahnt to see
what you look like!

*He turns around: his face is perfectly blank. She gives a cry.
He steps out through the door, and darkness covers everything.*


*When the light comes on again, it reveals the Streetfields'
sitting-room. Everything is the same as in Act I, except that
the table appears in the place where it was supposed to have
been before Miss Streetfield had it moved: against the left-hand
wall to the front; its leaves have been taken down. The room
is brightly lighted, though the lamps are not seen to be on.
The blinds of both windows are open, showing blackest darkness outside. Miss Streetfield stands in front of the fire. Cousin
Serena, crocheting, sits beside it on the right. Mr. Streetfield,
further forward on the same side of the room, is stretched stiff
and askew in his chair, as if he had been stricken by paralysis:
his lips are parted and show his teeth, and his eyes have a kind
of glazed glare. Juliet Raybold is seated between Mr. Streetfield
and Cousin Serena; and, further forward and further right than
Mr. Streetfield, Anna, the Swedish maid, is sitting down among
the rest: she wears a fixed acquiescent smile.*

*They are talking in a conversational murmur. Bill comes in*

*from the dining-room, still wearing her waitress's costume. Sh*
*halts and stares at the Streetfields; then gazes about the room*
*as if to make sure it is the place she knows.*

COUSIN SERENA. The old clothes-press and Arthur's deatl
and Evadne had been asked and she not and when Aur
Harriet came to the funeral she really looked charming.

JULIET. And the bees, Cousin Serena, do tell us abou
the bees.

COUSIN SERENA. I saw one, so old and feeble that sh
thought it was a conspiracy against her.

MISS STREETFIELD. I know: it's quite worried me.

*Bill, deciding that all is as it should be, has begun to com*
*forward into the room. As she approaches Mr. Streetfield, h*
*suddenly gives a horrible hawking gasp, accompanied by a spas-*
*modic movement of his body, as if he were straining to speal*
*Bill starts back.*

MR. STREETFIELD. Ahk!—ahk!——

COUSIN SERENA (*looking up and speaking with more dis-*
*tinctness*). Poor Schuyler! he wants so to speak, but h
cannot because he is dead!

MISS STREETFIELD. Yet he dresses and comes to the table

COUSIN SERENA. He sits with us at cards in the evening

JULIET. We take him for walks in the garden.

COUSIN SERENA. What a splendid spirit he shows!

MR. STREETFIELD. Ahk—ahk!——

MISS STREETFIELD. It's Elizabeth's presence that upset
him.

ANNA (*confidentially to Bill*). You don't need to worry
it'll all be all right if you yust don't touch the table.

*The grandfather's clock begins to chime, its sweetness slightl*
*jangled.*

COUSIN SERENA. It is time for the entertainment, is it not

*Strains of music are heard, the sounds of an orchestra tuning up*

MISS STREETFIELD. Yes, Anna: go and tell them we ar
ready.

ANNA (*to Bill, without getting up, but still smiling*). All ready, Miss Elizabeth!

JULIET. What is it going to be?

COUSIN SERENA. A string quartette, is it not?

MISS STREETFIELD. No: McGee the Magician.

COUSIN SERENA. Dear me! that doesn't sound very cultivated.

MISS STREETFIELD. I'm afraid we'll have to sit through it on Elizabeth's account: McGee is Elizabeth's father.

BILL. He's the biggest magician in the country! My father's a big man!

*A flourish of music: McGee makes his entrance from the dining-room door. He is more debilitated than ever and wears a shabby dress-suit with a cracked shirt-front. He comes forward with an obsequious smile and bows very low to the Streetfields. He has a conjuror's wand in his hand.*

*From the moment he begins talking, the Streetfields become motionless like waxworks.*

MCGEE. Ladies and Gentlemen, with your kind permission, I will endeavor to present before you here tonight a few simple experiments in the art of legerdemain, or, as it is sometimes called, sleight-of-hand—by which I hope to convince you that the quickness of the human hand may ofttimes deceive the human eye. First, allow me to present to you my little coadjutor—and Lady of Mystery —Miss Billy McGee— (*A flourish: Bill leaps forward with a bright variety show smile*) Miss Billy is just as quick and alert as a little trained fox-terrier, and I'm sure will appreciate any applause you may be kind enough to give her! —And now, Billy, will you just please be good enough to bring forward that little table?

*Bill, compelled by some deadly hypnosis, goes over to get the table; the Streetfields, with the exception of Schuyler, all turn their heads to watch her.*

MR. STREETFIELD. Ahk!—ahk!——

ANNA. Oh, you mustn't touch the table!

*When Bill puts her hand on it, there is a loud peal of thunder, and the stage flashes black.*

McGEE. Don't be alarmed, Ladies and Gentlemen! It is just a little stage thunder— (*Bill takes hold of the table again, and there is another thunder-clap.*) It has nothing to do with the table! (*She tries again: thunder again.*) Only a little stage thunder!

*A terrific crash: Bill relinquishes the table and walks determinedly over to the dining-room door.*

BILL (*speaking through the door, as if out the wings of a theater*). Hey, Al: that'll do for the thunder! (*The rumbling ceases: she looks defiantly at the Streetfields and moves the table out, so that it stands, facing them, in front of the sofa.*)

MR. STREETFIELD. Ahk!—ahk!——

COUSIN SERENA. Clara, she has ruined the room!

BILL. Well, *I* didn't move it out! It was Miss Streetfield did it herself!

*The Streetfields sneer in unison. Bill, however, carrying on, takes up her position for the conjuring performance. She stands at attention and supplies McGee with his properties, which she produces promptly from behind the sofa or out of the pockets of her apron, displaying them first to the audience. She simulates appropriate surprise and delight as the entertainment proceeds. The invisible orchestra plays very badly Weber's* Invitation to the Dance.

McGEE. My first experiment, Ladies and Gentlemen, will be performed with the aid of an ordinary deck of cards—a real deck of cards, you see—not prepared in any way—fifty-two cards in the deck and every card different! Now will some kind lady or gentleman in the audience be kind enough to take a card?—will some kind lady or gentleman take a card?— (*He offers the pack spread fanwise to Miss Streetfield.*)

MISS STREETFIELD. His dress clothes do not fit him!

McGEE (*to Cousin Serena*). Any card at all!—any card in the deck!—

COUSIN SERENA. He smells of scented soap!

McGEE (*offering the cards to Juliet*). Will you take a card, Madame?

JULIET. He has dandruff on his coat!

McGEE. Just please to take a card, that's all—any card in the deck!

MISS STREETFIELD. Will you take a card, Anna?

ANNA. I yust as soon. (*She takes one.*)

McGEE. Thank you, Madame.—Now look at it, if you please, and reeplace it in the deck.—Thank you. But please don't forget what it is—please reetain the card in your mind. I know that ladies' memories are sometimes very ickle—*la donna è mobeel*, if you will pardon my French!—but just please to reemember what it is.—Now, you see I place the deck of cards on the table in full view of you all—I have no idea what card you chose.—Now will you please to name the card, Madame?

ANNA. It was the Jack of Hearts I took.

McGEE. The Jack of Hearts? Thank you, Madame!—And here is Jack himself at your service! (*He produces the Ace of Spades from the air.*)

ANNA. That is not the card I chose!

McGEE. Jack has given us the slip, the rascal!—he has changed into the Ace of Spades! A regular, lightning-change artist is Jack—I would almost call him a turn-coat! (*He proceeds hastily to the next trick.*) And here, Ladies and Gentlemen, we have a dice—an ordinary solid wooden dice—not prepared in any way. (*Bill hands him a gigantic wooden die, which he knocks against the table.*) I am sure that none of you ladies ever play dice, but I hope you will not be offended if I make so bold as to play with this one!—In the other hand, you see, I hold a handkerchief (*a large square of red plaid cloth as large as a table-cover*)—an

ordinary pocket handkerchief, free from trickery of any
kind. And I drop the dice into the handkerchief—just as i:
I wanted to hide it from the police! (*He shows the shape
of the die inside, then suddenly shakes the handkerchief out.*
And presto change!—lo and behold: the dice has disappeared!—Where can our dice have gone? Nothing ir
the handkerchief, you see!—Nothing inside or out—nothing in my hands! Where can the dice have gone? (*H*
*flourishes the handkerchief to show there is nothing in it, bu*
*it flies out of his hand like a comet and falls with a thud a*
*the Streetfields' feet. Bill snatches it up at once. The audienc*
*offers its first response to the entertainment in the form of*
*short contemptuous laugh. McGee runs on ingratiatingly.*)—
And now, Ladies and Gentlemen, for a very pretty tricl
—a trick which I call the Mysterious Bird-Cage. For thi
trick I must request some kind lady to lend me the loar
of a ring. Will some kind lady loan me a ring?—

COUSIN SERENA. I haven't found this very interesting!

McGEE. What lady will loan me a ring? I shall reequir
a lady's ring!—

JULIET. *I* think it's a dreadful bore!

MISS STREETFIELD. Never mind: it's Elizabeth's father
and we don't want to hurt her feelings!

McGEE. A lady's ring, if you please!—

MISS STREETFIELD. Anna, will you lend him your ring

ANNA. I yust as soon. (*She gives him a ring.*)

*Bill takes the candle in the brass candlestick from the le*
*side of the mantelpiece and, while her father is talking, lights i*
*The Streetfields turn their heads and watch her in apprehen*
*sion, not paying the slightest attention to McGee, as he con*
*tinues with the trick.*

McGEE. Thank you, Madame! I shall reeturn it un
harmed.—Now, watch closely: I take this lady's ring an
I place it upon the table in full view of you all. Now
watch closely: I take this lighted candle—a genuine lighte

andle, one of your very own, you see—and, by gently
troking the flame—watch closely—I pluck— (*He burns
is fingers and snatches them hastily away.*) I pluck out these
retty streamers—first, a red— (*He pulls out a red ribbon.
He has become more gingerly about the candle, as if he were
fraid of being burnt again.*) Then a white—er, a blue— (*as
a blue, instead of a white one appears*) And lastly but not
astly—lastly but not leastly—Why, something seems to
e wrong!—Oh, I see! I have been using my left hand—
hings can't possibly go *right*! I stroke the flame with my
ght hand and lo and behold! a blue—a white streamer!
Red, White and Blue, you see!—Now, I place the red—
he white—and the blue—streamers in this empty kitchen
anister. (*He drops them into a large black cylinder, which Bill
as handed him. He rattles his wand inside it, but does not
t the audience see in.*) An everyday kitchen canister, for
offee or other spices. Now, watch closely: I will give
his canister to a lady in the audience to hold. (*He hands it
o Anna.*) Thank you, Madame!—Now, here we have a
retty little jewel-case, an ordinary little jewel-case, free
rom trickery of any kind—and I place the little jewel-
ase in this bird-cage— (*He is about to put the jewel-case
n a highly suspicious-looking bird-cage with a large handker-
hief over the top; but Bill prompts him that this is wrong.*)
No: the lighted candle in the bird-cage! the lighted candle
n the bird-cage! I place the lighted candle— (*He blows it
ut*) —in this ordinary unprepared bird-cage. (*He drapes
he cage with the handkerchief and sets it on the floor.*) And
place the bird-cage on the floor, in full view of you all! I
must admit, Ladies and Gentlemen, that this may not
e the cage of a bird; but I think you'll agree, before
e've finished, that it's a regular bird of a cage!

MR. STREETFIELD. Ahk!—ahk!——

BILL. Well, Gee Whiz, Mr. Streetfield: I don't think
ur jokes are so good!

McGEE. Now, I want to call your attention to this pretty little Japanese cabinet.— (*He holds up a cabinet with eight doors, four front and four back, and four corresponding compartments inside.*) A delightful little Japanese cabinet, but quite empty, as you see! (*He rattles his wand in the compartments; the doors flap open on both sides.*) Now, watch closely: I will place this little jewel-case into this pretty little Japanese cabinet, and I will lock it with this little key. (*He locks the door in front with his right hand and immediately afterwards, in plain sight of the audience, takes the jewel-case out through the door in back and hands it behind him to Bill who disposes of it behind the sofa.*) And I will place the little cabinet on the floor, in full view of everybody!—And now the chafing-dish, if you please! An everyday chafing-dish, you see, free from trickery of any kind! What will you have, Mr. Streetfield?—an omelet?—a Welsh rarebit —An omelet? Very good! Mr. Streetfield prefers an omelet. (*He breaks an egg into the chafing-dish and pours in a small glass of alcohol; Bill throws in a lighted match and the alcohol bursts into flame.*) Though perhaps a Welsh rarebit would be more appropriate to a practiser of the Black Arts like me: I have heard it called an invention of the Devil!— And now, watch closely: I drop the key to the cabinet into the magic chafing-dish—there it goes, the key in the chafing-dish! (*He claps the lid on the chafing-dish.*) And now— (*He seems to feel that he has committed an error and hesitates as to whether to open the chafing-dish again, but finally decides to proceed.*) Yes: the key in the chafing-dish!—And now for a trial of marksmanship! (*Bill hands him a big funnel-barrelled magician's pistol, which he exhibits to the audience.*) Here I have an ordinary fifty-five caliber revolver, which I will load, in the ordinary way, with the lady's ring. (*He stuffs the ring into the barrel, wadding down with colored paper and using his wand as a ramrod.*) Do not be alarmed, Madame: I will return it completely unharmed! (*He stands back and aims at the objects on the floor.*) I know that some of you expect sharp *practice* from a magician—well, I hope to prove to you that a magician may also be a sharp-*shooter*!

COUSIN SERENA. Do you think this is safe, Clara?

MISS STREETFIELD. He is going to be arrested soon!

*McGee pulls the trigger, which clicks. Then a shot is heard from behind the scenes, which makes the magician start.*

McGEE. And now, let us see the far-reaching effects of the shot from the magic pistol! What have we in the bird-cage? (*He lifts the handkerchief to look in but immediately drops it again.*) What have we in the canister, Madame? Will you open the canister, please? (*Anna wrenches at the canister.*) You saw me put the streamers in the canister—the red, the white, and the blue! I shouldn't be surprised if, by this time, they had changed into the Stars and Stripes!

ANNA. I can't get it open!

McGEE (*taking it from her*). Our country's colors—the Stars and Stripes! (*Finding it impossible to open the canister, he hands it on to Bill, who also wrenches at it in vain and finally secretes it behind the sofa. McGee hesitates a moment toward the cabinet; but finally passes enthusiastically to the chafing-dish.*) What have we in the chafing-dish? The Stars and Stripes! (*He uncovers the chafing-dish and stands baffled for a moment.*) Why bonn-bonns, I declare! Our omelet has been changed into bonn-bonns! Spirit bonn-bonns, Ladies and Gentlemen! Try a bonn-bonn made by the spirits! (*He tosses handfuls at the Streetfields, who pay no attention to them.*) And now for the lady's ring! (*He makes vague movements toward the different objects and looks furtively on the floor—then he lifts a handkerchief lying on the table, and a playing-card falls out. He picks it up.*) The Jack of Hearts, I declare! That was the card you chose, wasn't it Madame? I told you we should see him yet! He has been trying to hide from us, the rascal!

COUSIN SERENA. What a wretched charlatan!

MISS STREETFIELD. What a lamentable fiasco!

JULIET. I think it's perfectly pathetic!

MR. STREETFIELD (*struggling*). Ahk!—ahk!——

McGEE (*plunging desperately into a last effort*). And now, Ladies and Gentlemen, with your kind permission, I propose to perform before you here tonight what is without question the most baffling escape ever offered to the American public—a feat which has puzzled scientists and eminent churchmen all over the United States!

JULIET. Is he going to do another? I can't bear it!

ANNA. He didn't give me back my ring!

McGEE. I propose to make my unassisted get-away, in the space of fifteen-sixtieths of a minute, from the most hampering set of bonds ever devised, under the most difficult set of conditions discoverable!—First, I must ask some gentleman in the audience to step up and be a witness to all I do. I want some gentleman to come up and tie me. I want you to be satisfied that I am reelly tied.—Will some gentleman step up and tie me?—A sailor, if possible! Is there a sailor in the audience?

ANNA. You must give me back my ring!

McGEE (*feverishly*). First I want you to examine these handcuffs and be satisfied they are the genuine thing! Handcuffs of the very exact description, Ladies and Gentlemen, that are used in Sing Sing Prison today! (*The music becomes fast and melodramatic.*) Ladies and Gentlemen, I propose to make my escape from a triple pair of these handcuffs—from a set of leg-irons, from a gag, from ten feet of sailor's rope, from fifty pounds of iron chains and from a double-thickness strait-jacket! I propose to perform this modern miracle when locked in a safety deposit vault descending at topspeed in a moving elevator!! submerged under eighteen feet of water!!!

ANNA. He is keeping my ring, Miss Streetfield!

McGee. Such an escape has never been effected by any other magician in the world! Seven imitators of mine have been killed in the endeavor to reproduce it!—Will no gentleman from the audience step up and make sure that there is no fraud?

*Two Policemen come in through the dining-room door and seize McGee on either side. They snap handcuffs on his wrists. The music abruptly ceases.*

First Policeman (*with the voice of the Guard*). Sorry, Ladies—but we've got to arrest this man for fraud!

Second Policeman. He cashed a loaf of bread without flour on the Merchants' and Mechanics' Bank of Cincinnati!

Juliet. Oh, how dreadful!

Miss Streetfield. A criminal!

Cousin Serena. He has a dishonest face!

McGee. This is very humiliating!

Bill. Come on, Father: do your escape! Don't let these bulls tie you up!

First Policeman (*to Bill*). Say, cut it out! We're watching you, too!

Second Policeman. She stole the electric-light fixtures for immoral purposes!

McGee. I'm just a poor old bozo that can't put anything over any more!

First Policeman. That'll do: come on now, bozo!— D'yuh want me to wrap a nightstick around your bean?

Bill. Never mind, Father: I thot you were slick. You didn't get a square deal!

Second Policeman. Shut up now or we'll give you the bum's rush—the both of yuh!

McGee. I appeal to these kind ladies here among these cultivated surroundings!

Miss Streetfield. We know nothing about him, officer. He was never invited here.

BILL (*turning upon the Streetfields*). Oh, I think you might stand up for Father! You know he wouldn't do any harm! You don't need to treatum like a bank-robber just because he's old and a little bit balmy! I hate you for the way you act!

*In the meantime, the Policemen have led out McGee— shuffling miserably in his shackles—through the dining-room door. The light has turned cold.*

COUSIN SERENA. We hate you, too, you may be sure!

JULIET. We hate you because you are not one of us!

MISS STREETFIELD. We hate you because you say *ree-member*!

COUSIN SERENA. We saw you when you tripped on the rug!

MISS STREETFIELD. We saw you when your shoulder-strap came down!

JULIET. We saw you when you kept drinking water —you didn't know how to eat the anchovy toast!

MISS STREETFIELD. Her accent breaks the vases!

JULIET. Her manners wreck the tea!

COUSIN SERENA. Her movements afflict the furniture!

MISS STREETFIELD. And we hate you for your lover!

COUSIN SERENA. We know about your lover.

JULIET. We know about the ruined bath-house!

MISS STREETFIELD. We know about the back seat of the Buick!

JULIET. We know about the pink room at the dance!

ANNA. I couldn't do a thing like that!—a nice clean Swedish girl like me!

BILL. I don't see where you get that stuff—to treat me like an alley-rat! Well, you don't need to tok about me like I was some kind of delinquent girl! We used to have everything nice and we always knew decent people!

*An apparition suddenly presents itself at the open window on the left—a dowdy furtive-looking girl with a hard plain pasty face: behind her appears, not the seascape of the Sound, but a dingy suburban backyard, shut in by yellowish frame houses.*

THE APPARITION. Hsst!

COUSIN SERENA. What a degraded-looking creature!

BILL. Listen, Mahd: I can't see you now!

MAUD. Say, what are yuh tryin' to do?—shake your old friends? I guess you and me was pretty thick once! I guess you used to come and stay at our house when your old man was dodgin' the cops!

JULIET. I don't see how a girl can be so *hard*!

BILL. I'll meet you outside in just a minute!

MAUD. I guess you wahnt to shunt me off!—don't wahnt to be bothered by me!—Remember the way I died!—all alone in a furnished room! Not a stitch only the dress I had awn and my face all blue with the gas! *With ferocity*) I turned on the old leaky gas-jet. Suicide: I killed myself!

MISS STREETFIELD. What a wanton destructive act!

BILL. Well, what is it you wahnt of me, Mahd?

MAUD (*now becoming less diabolical and more like a human being*). Say, couldja lend me a coupla dawllars? We're just completely broke at the house!—I guess you didn't hear what happened?

BILL. No: what?

MAUD. Aileen's beat it off!

BILL. Who with?

MAUD. With the otto salesman—canya imagine that! I hate to say it of my own sister but she played us a damn dirty trick! Why, he hadn't hardly done nothing for us, yet! She'd only haddum a week. Why, Ed Fairbanks furnished the whole ground floor, and Bud Maclean bot the davenport—and we was just getting ready to make a strike and get a nice new bath-room outa this one. And then what does she do but run away withum!—and just leave

me and Mother flat! And poor Mother so stewed for
week that she couldn't hardly feed herself!

MISS STREETFIELD. We have studied the problem of gir
who come to grief through lazy or dissipated parents, an
we have discovered that in many cases the motive is
craving for luxury.

BILL. Well, that's darn hard luck, Mahd——

MAUD. I'm just at my wits' end! The butcher won
give us no more credit. I just sold ol the bawttles in th
house—but they only give me three-fifty for 'em. I wheele
'em down to Schmidt's in the old baby-carriage—cany
imagine that? (*Bill is seen to become thoughtful.*) Well, it
back to the Westinghouse for Mahd! I mighta known w
couldn't depend forever on a girl with a shape like Aileen's

BILL (*lowering her voice*). Say, listen, Mahd: I don't sup
pose you wahnt that old baby-carriage any more?

MAUD. Gawd, Bill: don't scare me like that!

BILL. Well, listen: you let me have the baby-carriage
and I'll give you the two dawllars.

MAUD. Well, congratulations! I hadn't heard!—

BILL. Don't say a word! I can't talk to you now! Th
Streetfields here mustn't hear!

MAUD. You sure are a good sport, Bill! And the be:
of luck to you and yours! I sure am——

BILL. All right: now you go along! I'm busy in her
just now! (*Bill turns to the room.*)

> MAUD (*chanting derisively after her*).
> Maggie mind the baby!
> Maggie mind the child!
> Wrappum up inuz overcoat—
> The son of a bitch is wild!

*She disappears, and the window shows black again.*

COUSIN SERENA. What an unspeakable neighborhood!

JULIET. My clothes are all covered with soot!

Miss Streetfield. The garden is a cinder-pile!

Anna. I find chewing-gum under the chairs, Miss Streetfield!

Mr. Streetfield. Ahk!—ahk!——

Cousin Serena. Poor Schuyler! he wants to say he hates her because she is so hideously ugly!

Miss Streetfield. Your presence in the house, Elizabeth, has been like a long illness to Schuyler, and your accomplice, Simon Delacy, delivered the mortal blow!

Cousin Serena. We hate you because you killed Schuyler!

Bill. Well, you don't need to talk, Mrs. Middleton: you poisoned my old dog named Ginger!

Cousin Serena. His hair was falling out in great wheezes!

Miss Streetfield. They are murderers! They murdered Schuyler!

Juliet. A crime!

Cousin Serena. In the Whistler Room!

Bill. We killed him because we had to live!

Juliet. How horrid!

Cousin Serena. How ill-bred!

*Simon appears in the window; he is now wearing human clothes, but has still his hollow-eyed wolfish look.*

Simon. Yes: I dealt him the death-blow at the dance, when he ritzed me about the match! But who are *you* to persecute *us*?

Miss Streetfield. We are too proud to say!

Simon (*advancing into the room*). Who are *you* to be proud? Who are *you* to speak like our masters? Your pride is sold out, you capitalists! We have all the same masters now! Our masters squat on the western hills with their bowels about their bellies: where they breathe the very skies are blasted and the daylight shrivels to ashes. Who are you whose slaves stoke their blasts to blame her if she is black?

189

COUSIN SERENA. How insolent!

MISS STREETFIELD. How unsound!

JULIET. Simon Delacy is not a gentleman!

MISS STREETFIELD. To kill my brother Schuyler in cold blood!

SIMON. What difference does it make if he's dead? Who said he was ever alive?

*Mr. Streetfield lifts his paralyzed arms and, with an effort, succeeds in finding utterance. He speaks in a silvery far-away voice, as if from the tranquillity of another world. As he proceeds, his frozen hands loosen into elegant gestures.*

MR. STREETFIELD. Did you think I was never alive? That is false: I had once my life!—a lovely serene life, all my own, all my own! I wove it of Whistler's line—of the veils of April skies—of the white silver-shadowed cloth where the candle-light of dinner falls. If you never perceived my life, your eyes were too gross to see! In the morning I read the news and I smiled at the President; all day I relived the days when gentlemen served the State. At evening I walked in the garden remembering my grandmother's garden: its roses, its rusty asters, its spaded beds at dusk! And at night I would drift asleep, after Saint-Simon or Jane Austen, my mind making exquisite shadows of beings already shadows—or perhaps with some charming memory—an odor, a glimpse or a sound—some cool little court in Paris borne in by the freshened night— in Paris in '85—the ferns all vivid green, the pavement shining with wet—we drove in the Bois with the Prince —my father's friend, the Prince! I, too, was a sort of prince, and I liked to think of that!—Did you think I was never alive? My life was more lovely than a flower! But it fades like a flower of frost before your obdurate breath!

SIMON (*as if to himself*). An artist!—a genuine temperament! He has been betrayed like me!

BILL. Well, Gee! I don't think he can be so good if he's killed as easy as that!

MR. STREETFIELD. Make no mistake, my child! that crystal was beyond price! Those fragile sprays had been forged on the anvil of war and pain! Many ages of life had distilled me with an effort astounding thought. My case was a holy thing: you should see in me a priest of beauty. But now you dispute my place, and where you come I must die, and without me, your world will be too hideous even for you to bear!

BILL. "Even me!" You think I'm ugly! Well, you don't know what ugliness is! You don't know what it is to be stuck for life in a little lousy street! You don't know what it is to live in a house like the Wrath of God hit with a brick! You think I don't notice things like that—you people seem to think that ugliness is something you've discovered all by yourselves! Well, I always did notice it, I can tell you, and I have to carry it around for keeps. It seems to me you have it pretty soft: you've got a lotta nice things to remember—you've only got to see it on the *outside*; but I've got it *inside*, too!

MISS STREETFIELD. So I feared: there can be nothing done! Inside and outside, too!

SIMON (*who has withdrawn to the right, further forward and to the right than Anna*). But don't you see that she and I have been betrayed like you?

*Anna, Juliet and Cousin Serena suddenly rise at the same time; Miss Streetfield advances a step. The light becomes more and more unnatural; their voices are inhuman and harsh.*

JULIET. We'll make you hard!

COUSIN SERENA. We'll make you small!

MISS STREETFIELD. We'll give you an ash-can for a soul!
*Each advances as she speaks.*

SIMON (*still brooding*). But who was it who betrayed us? Was it Carnegie? Or was it Bessemer?

BILL. Oh, what do you know about souls? I haven't
got any soul-aura like Mr. Streetfield says he has: those
auras get busted like soap-bubbles out where I come from
We get held right down to the old grindstone till there's
nothing left but the hard core. But that's something that
you're not strong enough to break and you haven't got
the heat to melt, and you'll just have to drop it like an iron
pig when it gets too hot to hold!

SIMON. Was it Hearst? Was it Henry Ford? Was it
Wrigley's Chewing Gum?

MISS STREETFIELD. And we'll make you ashamed of the
child!

JULIET. We heard what that creature said!

COUSIN SERENA. Such an annoying little girl!

MISS STREETFIELD. She came on from Kansas City
alone!

COUSIN SERENA. She wanted me to read her the comic
strip!

MISS STREETFIELD. As is usual with girls of that class
her teeth were in dreadful condition!

*They are pressing close about her like fiends, hypnotizing
her to destroy her: she gives way before them slowly, as i*
*rooted by a spell. The room is darkening; only the Streetfield*
*and Bill are visible in a greenish light.*

BILL. Did you hear what they said, Simon? Did you
hear what they said about our child? We've got to go up
against them now!

SIMON (*oblivious*). Was it Whitney, who invented the
cotton gin in 1794?

BILL. Oh, help me! They're closing in on me! Can't
you fight them like you did at the dance? (*They draw
nearer.*) Oh, oh! I can't breathe!

MISS STREETFIELD (*with intense ferocity*). We don't want
to stifle you, Elizabeth—we want to strengthen and enrich
your spirit!

SIMON. Was it a Nation of Pioneers? Was it giving verybody the vote?

BILL (*still breathlessly falling back, inch by inch*). But this all a dream!

MISS STREETFIELD. What does it matter? You can't wake!

SIMON. I've said to myself often, This is only a dream!— ut it usually isn't true!—That's a very clever remark.

BILL. Oh, Simon: you've got to help me!

MISS STREETFIELD. We'll make you a college girl!

BILL (*who has entrenched herself, gasping, behind the table nd now faces them from across it*). I *won't* be a college girl! nd I *won't* be a waitress! (*She tears off her waitress's apron nd flings it down across the table.*) Stop there! You'll stop ow! You can't go up against me! I'm stronger than you! —You can't frighten me! I know what you all are! (*With terrific effort, she forces herself to meet and measure herself gainst each one, reducing them to their proper statures.*) Cousin erena's just a catty old dame!—Juliet's just a virgin who oesn't know anything!—and, Mr. Streetfield, you're a ind of a fake just like Father is!—and I guess you got a um deal in love, Miss Streetfield, just the way I did!—

*The Streetfields are seen to fall back a moment; then the om becomes suddenly dark, save for a blue shaft of light from e window, which now frames a blue nocturnal sea. Bill is anding alone in this light; the Streetfields have disappeared.*

SIMON'S VOICE. Was it Jefferson? Was it Rousseau?

BILL. Oh, I thot I was speaking to people! I thot there ere people here!

SIMON'S VOICE. Betrayed! We have been betrayed!

BILL (*gazing about and going to the window*). Oh, they're one! they're gone! We're free!

# ACT III

*A room beside the sea, of which only an angle is presented:*
*there is a doorway, without a door, in the wall on the right*
*hand side. Blue ocean in bright sun; an interminable urgent*
*murmur. The walls of the room are yellow. On the right, there*
*is a wicker couch made comfortable with a blue cushion and,*
*to the left of this, a wicker table, with an empty plate sitting*
*on it. Simon, in a gray suit of knickerbockers with pale blue*
*plaid stockings, is sitting on the couch with a little girl. He*
*looks fresh and handsome now: all traces of the wolf have dis-*
*appeared. The little girl is black-eyed like Bill. Bill herself im-*
*mediately enters, wearing light summer yellow, and in a high*
*serene state of joy.*

BILL. They're gone! I drove them away! (*He enfolds*
her in a long embrace, at once ecstatic and solemn.*) They
couldn't go up against me! (*She kisses the child.*) Hello,
Peggy: have you been a good little girl or have you just
been a little pest?

THE LITTLE GIRL. Been a good little girl.

SIMON. She's been a little pig, that's what she's been!

BILL (*looking at the plate on the table*). Did she eat up
the jelly sandwiches?

SIMON. I'm sorry: I wasn't looking.

BILL (*embracing her*). Oh, cute! She ate up all the jelly
sandwiches!

THE LITTLE GIRL. Wanta go out on the beach!

BILL (*sitting down on the couch and taking the Little Girl
on her lap*). All right! we'll go out on the beach—we'll
go out and play in the sand.

THE LITTLE GIRL. Wanta see the little sandpip-ers!

BILL. Shall we see those cute little sandpipers beating it along on their little stiff pins?—and all those cunning little sand-fleas with their great big blue eyes? (*Hugging her*) She thinks that's pretty nice to go out beside the ocean!

THE LITTLE GIRL. Wanta go now!

*A Nurse appears at the door, white-capped and white-aproned—an elderly Irish woman of ideal amiability and competence.*

BILL. Maggie will take you out now, and I'll be along pretty soon.

*The Little Girl makes for the door.*

SIMON. Goodby, Peggy.

BILL. Say goodby to Father, Peggy!

THE LITTLE GIRL (*on the wing*). Goodby, Father!

BILL. You must make her be polite, Maggie.

THE NURSE. Yes, Ma'am; and I make her say things right.

BILL. You must teach her not to pick up her cards till after they've all been dealt out.

THE NURSE. Yes, Ma'am: she knows that already.

BILL. And don't let her hog the seats on the train.

THE NURSE. No, Ma'am: she never does.

BILL. But I don't see why she shouldn't read the funny-papers. (*To Simon*) Don't you think it's all right, Simon, for her to read the funny-papers?

SIMON. Up to the age of eight.

THE NURSE. Very well, Ma'am.

BILL (*to the Little Girl*). All right: run along now.

*The Little Girl goes out with the Nurse.*

BILL. We're free now! We're free! We don't have to think about anything!

SIMON (*embracing her*). We're here together at last!

*They sit down on the couch.*

BILL. We can just stay on now for ever! the Streetfields have all disappeared!

SIMON. We'll have dinner right in here and watch the sun go down on the ocean.

BILL. Isn't the old bath-house swell today!

SIMON. I've ordered a nice sirloin steak, with French fried potatoes.

BILL. Oh, boy!—and some slick corn-fritters?

SIMON. Yes—and banana and nut salad.—And I've ordered champagne and some cocktails mixed at Sherry's before the war.

BILL. I thot there was Prohibition.

SIMON. That's all over now—didn't you know? You can get any liquor you want.

BILL. No, I didn't: I can hardly believe it! Oh, Simon, it's all just wonderful!

SIMON. See how big the ocean is!

BILL. Say, it makes you feel entirely different to see so much open space!

SIMON. And the color is pure joy—the bright blue sea sizzling white on the bright yellow sand!

BILL. Gee, I never saw it so bright!—bright yellow and bright blue!

SIMON. And white gulls diving in the air.

BILL. What's that land over beyond?

SIMON. That's Europe. I'm going there soon.

BILL. But you're going to take me, too?

SIMON. Yes, of course: we're going together.

BILL. And you'll buy me a lotta nice things?

SIMON. All kinds of beautiful things—seven dozen sheer silk stockings.

BILL. And a slinky chinchilla cloak!

SIMON. And a snappy maroon-colored roadster that you can drive yourself.— (*She makes the gesture of turning the wheel with a broad smile of delight.*) And a red ostrich feather fan.

BILL. And a German police-dog named Ginger!

SIMON. And a big box of foreign chocolates with different kinds of liquor inside.

BILL. Oh, Simon! you're so wonderful!

SIMON. We'll go to Paris first of all.

BILL. I guess I'll have to get a lotta trick dresses to compete with those Paris dames.

SIMON. Oh, you'll knock 'em all cold!—When the head waiter shows us to our table, you'll hear all the people saying, "There goes the smart Mrs. Delacy!"

BILL. All the Pittsburgh millionaires go to Paris. I guess I might see some there.

SIMON. You won't go out with anybody but me?

BILL. You didn't think I'd let you take me over and then go out with other men?

SIMON. Well, you never can tell, you know, with a fearless living force like you!

BILL (*putting her arms around him*). I wouldn't double-cross you, dear!

SIMON. Then, from Paris we'll go to Germany. That's the place where they have the beer: oh, boy! And when they blow the foam off the top, they sing German drinking-songs. It's the most wonderful thing you ever heard! And they have big romantic mountains with ancient ruined castles on them.

BILL. And I'll go zipping along the mountains in my little maroon-colored roadster, and all the Germans will say, "Some pep! There goes the American girl!"

SIMON. And, after that, we'll go to Italy.

BILL. That's where they make a lotta love!

SIMON. Yes: Italy's the country for love. That's all they do there—just make love. The days are humming with passion and the nights are heavy with love. Every night you can hear them serenading their girls in gondolas out on the water. We'll be able to hear them singing from the room where we're making love!

*The day begins to fade.*

BILL. In a big magnificent bed we'll be!

SIMON. In a palace full of golden mirrors!

BILL. And you'll buy me a red Italian shawl!

SIMON. You'll be a knock-out in a golden mirror, walking down the great staircase of the palace in a red Italian shawl!

BILL. We'll have breakfast every morning in bed!

SIMON. You must tell me everything then!

BILL. You must tell me things, too.

SIMON. You'll tell me how lonely you were——

BILL. How did you know I was lonely?

SIMON. Oh, I knew it because I loved you. I've known what it was to be lonely, too. I've known what it was to lie awake at night, violent with desire—ready to burst the world!—and then to see the walls of the day close in on me like a jail. I've known what it was to have spring come in, not welcome, but like an enemy, and make me afraid to hear the boats on the river or smell the trees in the park.

BILL. I used to lie awake and listen to the trains in Pittsburgh and wish I was a million miles away—but they just went on screeching and screeching, and it seemed like never went!

SIMON. Well, we'll never have to miss each other now. We can never be lonely again. Do you remember how we used to dread the darkness because it loosed all the frights of the mind and how the light would jolt us back to pain? Well, neither darkness nor light can make any difference now. We can lie on together for ever and nobody will ever break in.—Look: the twilight's drifting in like a shadow.

BILL. The gulls have all gone home.

SIMON. The sea's all lilac out there, with a path of silver-leaf.

BILL. The sun looks like silver, doesn't it?

SIMON. Say, wouldn't it be great to go swimming in that lilac-colored sea!

BILL. All right! Let's go in!

SIMON. You'll look like silver in the water!

BILL. Can we go in just bare-naked like that?

SIMON. Sure: the whole beach belongs to me!

BILL. Oh, Simon! you're the only person I've ever reelly loved! (*She embraces him.*)

SIMON. Listen, Bill: what do you say we start out and swim right over to Paris! We could make it just in time for dinner at some swell hotel on the shore!

*Distant music comes floating in:* The Blue Danube Blues. *He begins untying his tie.*

BILL. But we won't have anything on!

SIMON. Oh, they don't mind that over there! You know what Paris is!

BILL. All right!—I think that would be slick! (*She begins taking off her shoes and stockings.*)

SIMON. We'll strike right out in the sunset with the whole ocean to ourselves!—

BILL. I bet that stuff is cool and nice!

SIMON. Wait till you see the Paris board-walk with all the fountains playing!

BILL. How will we know where to hit Paris?

SIMON. Just follow the silver-leaf trail!

*The darkness hides them.*

*When the light goes on again, we see the Streetfields' sitting-room. It is morning: the dream has faded; the horizons of day are fixed. The window-blinds are open. Simon's voice is heard outside.*

SIMON'S VOICE. Oh, Bill!—Hey, Bill!— (*He comes in through the right-hand window. He is wearing the clothes that Bill saw in the dream but looks pale and has circles around his eyes.*) Oh, Bill!—

*Bill appears from the hall, in the yellow dress she has been dreaming about.*

BILL. Oh, I didn't expect you so early!

SIMON. Say, honestly, Bill, I'm terribly afraid I can't make it this afternoon.

BILL (*muting the percussion*). You can't!

SIMON. No, I'm just a wreck: I'm going back to town. If I did stay, I wouldn't be any good.

BILL. Oh! . . . Are you sick?

SIMON (*sinking to the sofa*). I'm completely shot. Last night was the finishing touch.

BILL. Oh—were you—out last night?

SIMON. I went to the most nauseating party I think I've ever known!

BILL. I thot you were going home—I thot you were going to get some sleep.

SIMON. Oh, Gosh! I was so depressed that I would just have gone crazy alone. I drove over to Floral Gardens, to see a man I knew over there.

BILL. Oh—you did?

SIMON. He's a gentleman bootlegger: his name is Max Fleischman. He lives like a millionaire. Gosh, I haven't seen so much to drink since Prohibition. I've *never* seen so much to drink! Chartreuse—absinthe—everything! Madge Fox, the movie actress, was there—she's a mess: she's got pink hair—and the man who produces the wise-cracks for the Merry-Go-Round Revue. I got in dutch, of course!

BILL. You did?

SIMON. Well, Fleischman was making a damn ass o. himself, bragging about how much his tapestries were worth and how much his bathroom was worth and how he never wore a shirt twice—and he had a revolver studded with diamonds that he insisted on showing everybody And he finally got on my nerves—I was a little bit stewed

—and I told him I wasn't impressed by his ermine-lined revolver: I told him he was nothing but a bootlegger, no matter how much money he made. Of course that made him sore as hell, and he ordered me out of the house. I told him I never would have come into his damn house if it hadn't been to be polite and that it was torture to stay in a place where everything was in such terrible taste. I walked out with a magnificent gesture; but when I was going across the lawn, I fell into the sunken Italian garden and passed out cold.

BILL. Oh, did you hurt yourself?

SIMON. Not much; but I lay there till daylight.

BILL. You might have died!

SIMON. I feel as if I had. I feel just like a ghost!

BILL. Wasn't there anybody with you?

SIMON. No: I went alone.

BILL. I thot I saw somebody out there in the car.

SIMON. Oh, that's just Katherine March. I picked her up on the way: she was going in my direction.

BILL. Oh! . . . Do you like Katherine March?

SIMON. Yes, I really like her a lot. She sort of awed me when I first met her, but she's really a lot of fun. She's got the most wonderful amiable smile! And this morning when I offered her some gum she took it and chewed it in a perfectly natural way. I suppose when you're really at the top, you don't care whether you're vulgar or not.—

BILL. I didn't think you'd fall for a great big dumb-bell like Katherine March!

SIMON. She's not a dumb-bell at all! She's really like some sort of goddess—one of those goddesses that's half an animal. She's so natural, and yet so dignified. She doesn't give a damn about anybody! She just rides around with her dogs—absolutely independent!

BILL. That's all she can do—ride around!

SIMON. Well, it must be a wonderful life down here—

don't you think so, in a way? It must be great to own
a lot of land! I suppose that that's the only kind of
freedom that nobody can interfere with!

BILL. You can't tell me you just met her by accident!
You're taking her out for a drive! Well, you better go
back to her: she won't wahnt to wait!

SIMON. I know—but the trouble is this morning that as
soon as I sit down anywhere, I feel as if I could never get
up—my limbs dissolve in languor!—It's funny how faint
things seem when you've been drinking a couple of days.
This whole room seems to me dim; even you seem dim:
I feel like a toy balloon floating around the place—bumping into things and bouncing off!

BILL (abruptly). Listen, Simon: I'm going away myself.

SIMON. Oh, I wouldn't do that if I were you.

BILL. I've got to.

SIMON. Why?

BILL. I'm going to have a child!

SIMON. What?—Why, Good God!—Am I responsible?

BILL. Who did you think was responsible?

SIMON (getting up from the sofa). But you never said anything about it! I had no idea!—

BILL. I wahnted to wait till I was sure.

SIMON. Are you absolutely sure now?

BILL. Yes: as far as you can be.

SIMON. Well, that's the final blow!

BILL. I'm sawrry: I've done everything I could.

SIMON. Well, I suppose there's only one solution!

BILL. I suppose so.

SIMON. I don't want to seem cold-blooded about it, but
we might as well face the situation. It can't be done, can
it? I haven't got any money—or at least not enough—and
neither of us wants to get married.

BILL. Well—I'm leaving right away. I'm going back and
stay with Father: I askedum about it when he was here.

SIMON. No, no: you mustn't do that! You must come up to New York with me! You can stay at a hotel——

BILL. No: I'm going back to Father!

SIMON. Now, don't be so bitter about it!—I can have it fixed up perfectly easily. You drive right up to New York with me——

BILL. I wouldn't have you miss your drive with Katherine March.

SIMON. Now, please don't take that attitude! It hasn't been anybody's fault. And now that it's done, we'll have to act: we certainly don't want any children! You've got to go to college, and I've got to be a writer, and that means that I've got to be free and not have to support a family—and you can't be having babies at Vassar!

BILL. Well, that's that! Now you must go!

SIMON. I'll have to take Katherine home—but I'll be back here right away! And you must get ready to leave. You must make some excuse to the Streetfields. You could be back here in a few days!

BILL. I'll never come back here!

SIMON. Why not? Don't you want to go to college?

BILL. I wouldn't have time to prepare. And, besides, I don't like it here: I can't be myself!—Now, you go on!

SIMON. I'll be back right away!

BILL. I'll be gone before you come.

SIMON. Now, please don't behave like that! Don't make it worse than it is!

BILL. That's just it: I don't wahnt to get you in a jam.

SIMON. Promise me you won't go till I come back!

BILL. I'm going right away, I tell you! I can go through with it by myself.

SIMON. Oh, don't be so damn unreasonable! You're just asking for unnecessary agony!

BILL. You go on about your business now. Don't worry: I'll be all right!

SIMON. You must promise——

BILL (*pushing him out through the window*). Look out—here comes Miss Streetfield!

*Miss Streetfield comes in from the hall.*

BILL (*beginning immediately*). Miss Streetfield: I'm awfully sawrry, but I'm afraid I can't stay here any longer!

MISS STREETFIELD. Why, Elizabeth—what's the matter?

BILL. I can't explain! I'll just have to go.—I'm awf'ly sawrry to give college up. I feel terrible to have to act this way after all the trouble you've taken for me.

MISS STREETFIELD. Now, you mustn't talk like that, my dear. You know, I didn't mean to scold you last night. Of course, I don't want to criticize your friends or to interfere with you in any way. I want you to do whatever you think right. I only want to help you as best I can.—Now, you must tell me what's the matter. (*She makes her sit down beside her on the sofa.*)

BILL. I'm sawrry: I can't explain; I'll just have to go.

MISS STREETFIELD (*putting her hand on Bill's*). I wish you could feel that I am really your friend and that you can talk to me quite freely. I know that some things are hard to talk about and that you are the sort of girl who doesn't like to talk about herself. I was just like that, too: I would never tell anyone anything. And I went through some very trying experiences that a word from some older person—someone who had the strength of religious certainty and yet sympathized with young people's problems—might have made so much easier! Now you have no mother, my dear; and I wish you could be willing to look to me for the kind of understanding and help that a girl may expect from her mother.—I have no children.

BILL. I know: you've just been wonderful to me, and I just feel terrible about it, but——

MISS STREETFIELD. I'm afraid that I've frightened you off by lecturing you too severely: you must think me a very censorious person. But, believe me, I realize very keenly how cruel life can seem—how perplexing—how heart-breaking sometimes—we may feel its dilemmas are! (*With intense earnestness and feeling*) I know that one can reach a point where it seems as if one's very life would stop if one were not able to have something that one wanted very much—a point where one is almost ready— not only to abandon all one's habits and plans—but even to desert one's most solemn duties and to violate one's most sacred obligations! But those are the moments that test us. You know what Robert Browning says:

> "When the fight begins within him
> A man's worth something."

And that's true of a woman, too. When we've withstood the ordeal of our own passions—of the most violent impulses of our own hearts—only then, for the first time, we find our real strength—such a strength as nothing else can give us!

BILL. I know—but I'm not having any struggle: I'm just doing the only thing I can!

*Mr. Streetfield and Cousin Serena come in from the hall. Mr. Streetfield carries the morning* Times.

MR. STREETFIELD. Good morning.

MISS STREETFIELD. Good morning.—Good morning, Cousin Serena.

COUSIN SERENA. Good morning, Clara.

MISS STREETFIELD. I hope you feel rested this morning.

COUSIN SERENA. Yes, thank you: it's so peaceful down here.

*She goes straight to her chair and settles herself; Mr. Streetfield sits down on the sofa and begins to read the paper.*

MISS STREETFIELD. I know that you didn't sleep well, Elizabeth, because I heard you crying out in the night. That's probably one thing that's wrong with you: you haven't had enough sleep.—Now, why don't you go right back to your room and lie down and sleep all day? I'll telephone the tutor you're not coming.—Anna will bring you a bromide.—You know the fatigue toxins in the blood may set up a condition of nervous excitement that makes it very difficult to rest.

MR. STREETFIELD. I see that Mr. Edison says that we shall soon be able to do without sleep altogether. Perhaps Elizabeth is a pioneer.

BILL. All right: I reelly don't wahnt any breakfast.

MISS STREETFIELD. Yes: go in and go to bed right away. And don't worry about anything till you've had a good rest!

BILL. Don't bother about the bromide. (*She goes out through the hall.*)

MISS STREETFIELD (*to the others*). Well, shall we go in to breakfast?

MR. STREETFIELD. A lovely, lovely morning!

*They go into the dining-room. Simon reappears through the window and looks about for Bill, who comes back with her hat and coat on and carrying a rather battered suitcase.*

SIMON. It all came to me just now as I was driving!—what you said about not being yourself! We can neither of us be ourselves down here!—and we must both get out as soon as possible!

BILL. I told you I was going alone!

SIMON. No, you're not: we're going together! You and I must stand together!

BILL. What does that mean? You wahnt us to live together, huh?

SIMON. Why not? We'll find some absolutely cheap place—some place that costs us practically nothing! An attic in the Woolworth Building or a house-boat on the Hudson or something. We'll be the talk of the town!

BILL. I don't see how we could live on a boat!

SIMON. Why not? What is there to prevent us? You mustn't think that things that sound fantastic are necessarily impossible to do. If people don't do fantastic things, it's not because they can't be done, but simply because very few people have enough imagination to think them up!

BILL. *You* didn't think of this—you're being forced into it!

SIMON. But I freely accept it now!—Think of the marvelous possibilities of a house-boat! Think of the summer evenings floating down the Palisades!—The people in the big houses would wake up and hear us playing jazz!

BILL. Aw, you're just trying to show me a good time because you got me into trouble!

SIMON. Listen, you must see life in terms of dreams. That's the only way you can conquer it!

BILL. Well, I did have a dream like that last night, and I wish it had been actually true but, now I'm awake again, everything seems pretty sour.—Say, we better go outside: the Streetfields'll be back in a minute!

SIMON. I don't care! Let them come! They could only throw me out again, and I'm getting used to that. If they didn't feel that I was formidable, they wouldn't take the trouble to do it!—You and I are the bums, Bill!—we're the people who always get put out! But the future belongs to us!

BILL. Gee, I thot when I was dreaming last night, that I was telling them all where to get off. You know I thot that you and I had murdered Mr. Streetfield. But this morning they're all alive—and they've got their own ideas!

SIMON. You and I have the same ideas! I've told off the whole of America! And you've never been buncoed by it! You have rejected both the drudgery of the slaves and the dismal salvation of the masters! You and I stand apart from this race! We must found a race of our own!

BILL. You wahnt to have the child, after all? Is that the idea?

SIMON. Why not? Somebody has to have them! And

think of the advantage to the child of having me for a
father! (*With a gesture*) Farewell! house of starvation and
decay! We leave you for a house of our own!

BILL. Aw, I think you're stuck on it here!

SIMON (*kissing her*). I'm stuck on *you*!

BILL. Look out: here come the Streetfields!

*She snatches up her suitcase, which he takes from her, and
they hurry out through the window on the left. The Streetfields
come back from the dining-room.*

MISS STREETFIELD. I must go in and see how Elizabeth is!
(*She crosses to the hall door and goes out.*)

MR. STREETFIELD (*sitting down on the sofa again and taking
up the paper*). Well, the revolution doesn't seem to have
materialized. It seems to have been postponed for another
year at least.

COUSIN SERENA (*about to sit down in her accustomed place*).
Revolution? What do you mean?

MR. STREETFIELD. Yesterday was the first of May—a
great occasion for the radical gentry. All sorts of bombs
and things were predicted. But the Government still seems
to be standing—such as it is.

COUSIN SERENA (*beginning to crochet*). I certainly saw no
disturbance.

MR. STREETFIELD. I think that the importance of these
radical activities has been greatly overestimated.

*Miss Streetfield comes back, perturbed.*

MISS STREETFIELD. Elizabeth isn't in her room: I wonder
where she can have gone!

MR. STREETFIELD. I heard a motor driving off just now.

MISS STREETFIELD. Whose was it?

MR. STREETFIELD. I don't know.

MISS STREETFIELD. You don't suppose she can have gone
off with young Delacy!

MR. STREETFIELD. She seems to have an incurable weakness for him!

MISS STREETFIELD. I'll ask Anna. (*She hurries out through the dining-room.*)

MR. STREETFIELD. I do think that table ought to go back. It's really not useful enough out here to make it worth while spoiling the room. I worked out everything so carefully for the Whistlers twenty-five years ago. (*To Miss Streetfield, as she returns*) I really think you must let us put the table back, Clara. It's not a success out here.

MISS STREETFIELD. Very well: do as you please.—Anna says that Delacy was here, and Elizabeth has evidently gone off with him.

ANNA (*appearing from the hall*). Her suitcase is gone, Miss Streetfield.

MISS STREETFIELD. Then she's gone! She's gone for good!

MR. STREETFIELD. Anna, will you stay a minute and help me to move things around?

ANNA. Yes, sir. You want to move the table?

MISS STREETFIELD. I can't understand it at all!

MR. STREETFIELD. Why, Clara, if you feel so strongly about it, I'll leave it where it is for the present!

MISS STREETFIELD. Oh, it's not the table! It's Elizabeth! Something dreadful will happen to her! That Delacy boy is such a blackguard!

MR. STREETFIELD. Oh, I shouldn't worry about her, if I were you. She's a pretty sharp little customer, and she knows how to take care of herself, I guess!

MISS STREETFIELD. And I wanted so much to help her! But I never seemed to be able to touch her! I don't think she ever really liked me!—But how could she behave like that? I really don't know what to think.—She must surely have left some sort of note! (*She hurries out through the hall.*)

MR. STREETFIELD. Dear me! Clara's quite upset! I'm afraid she's going to have one of her nervous crises! I haven't seen her stew so much about anything since her unfortunate *entêtement* for Rodney Drake!

COUSIN SERENA. Did I tell you I saw his wife at the wedding? I thought she looked very worn—she used to be such a pretty girl! Rodney has arthritis, you know. I believe he suffers dreadfully!

MR. STREETFIELD. And now, Anna, will you help me for a moment? We're moving the little table back. (*They let down the leaves of the table and carry it to its place against the wall.*) Thank you, Anna! (*He adjusts it very carefully, then contemplates it with satisfaction.*) See how perfectly it falls into place!

COUSIN SERENA. Yes: it seems much more natural.

*He comes forward and gazes about the room. The clock begins to strike nine. He walks up to the painting above the mantel.*

MR. STREETFIELD. How adorable she looks in the morning light—our little cockney lass!

COUSIN SERENA (*looking up*). Yes: what is she called? I forget.

MR. STREETFIELD (*with tenderness*). Little Liza of Lyme Regis.

# This Room and This Gin and These Sandwiches

# SCENE 1

*A dim room, in which the early light of September, coming through two windows in the right-hand wall, barely reveals two people in bed. The bed, which has no foot-board and is really a day-bed, stands at the center of the back wall with its head against the wall. Chairs with clothing on them are just visible. The window farthest from the bed is partly open.*

HE (*on the right of the bed, softly*). Are you asleep?

SHE (*loudly and distinctly*). No.

HE. What are you thinking about?

SHE. My part.

HE. I thought you were.

SHE. Give me a cigarette. (*He reaches for them on a table to the right of the bed, gives her one, lights it and takes one himself. We see the two glowing tips in the darkness.*) I think I'm going to be good, you know.

HE. I *know* you're going to be good.

SHE. There was a moment when I thought perhaps I wasn't.

HE. What ever made you think that?

SHE. Dan Frink raised hell with me two days ago: he said I didn't put Dionysus into it.

HE. You can't say Dan doesn't put Dionysus into it— I should think you'd all be groggy from his breath coming over the footlights. (*She laughs; he laughs; they laugh together.*) He's just sore because you won't let him make love to you.

SHE. No: I was really pretty bad that day.

HE. He just likes to get drunk and bully the actresses. Nine-tenths of Dan Frink is pure hot air.

SHE. No: only about two-tenths. The rest is the real thing.

HE. There's something real about him, I grant you; but there's an awful lot of phony, too.

SHE. His feeling for the theatre's not phony. After all, Dan was the person who got up the Beech Street Players, and he's kept it going six years. No matter how absurd he seems at times, he's really been the soul of the theater. I owe him a lot—we all do. And I'm very fond of Dan.

HE. He *has* been one of your lovers!

SHE (*after a brief pause*). You mustn't ask me questions like that.

HE. It's very natural.

SHE. I know, but you have no right to.

HE. Don't rub it in that I have no rights to you: I've accepted that. I just want to know where I stand.

SHE. Well, here you are!—Your standing is good.

HE. All right, my dear.

SHE. But I *have* been pretty flat at rehearsals lately. It's been so damn cold in that theatre—you have no idea what a cold blast of air comes across the stage from those wings whenever anybody opens the front door. Dan said I had all the sparkle of a glass of fizzed-out ginger ale. The truth is I've been getting a cold. It's none too warm here either.

HE. Marry me, my dear, and we'll have some heat!

SHE. I can't marry you, Arthur—I've told you.

HE. But why can't we live together?

SHE. We do: you've been here every day for the past two weeks.

HE. I shouldn't interfere with you in any way—you could go on doing everything as you do now.

SHE. You *do* try to interfere with me.

HE. If we lived together, it would be different.

SHE. No it wouldn't: I know what happens—I've tried it, and you just bust up quicker that way. I'm very well satisfied with things as they are.

*She sneezes.*

HE. No, you're not: half the time you're miserable. You're coming down with grippe this minute.

*She sneezes again.*

SHE. No, I'm not.—I must get up and study my lines.

HE. You won't be able to do them justice, because that noisome gas-heater will asphyxiate you.

*She sneezes again.*

SHE. I shouldn't want to move away from here—I like it.

HE. I like it, too, because you live here—I even have a certain affection for that horrible death-dealing heater because you've sat with your little feet under it. But I don't think it's the place for you to live.

SHE. My feet aren't little.

HE. Yes, they are: they're darling.

SHE. My dear, you're very sweet: you flatter my defects.—Sometimes I love you very much. (*He puts his arms around her and kisses her—hitherto they have been lying on their backs. After a moment*) Will you give me another cigarette?

*He turns toward the table. She sits up. He gives her one and lights it, but puts his own out in an ash-tray and does not take another.*

*It is light enough to see the room. In the back wall to the right of the day-bed, there is a door which leads into the hall. Above the bed is a large modern painting, in which erotic and fleshy female contours seem to be combined with machinery. In the right wall are the windows with a window-seat under them. Outside, one sees the three or four-story mixed brick and brown-stone fronts of the region around Washington Square in New York. In the corner, between the window-seat and the door, is a table with an electric cooker and, above it, some shelves with dishes. In the left wall to the front is an old-fashioned coal grate, with a mantel and a piece of batik hung above it. In the corner, there is a closet opening into the back wall, near which, against the wall on the left, has been set a small dressing table, more or less concealed by a screen. The gas-heater, high, narrow and ugly, is between the closet door and the bed. On the table to the right of the bed are plain tumblers, three ginger-ale bottles and a half-emptied bottle of gin; also, the pocket-book and change of the young man. Cups, dishes, etc., unwashed, on the window-seat, which has miscellaneous pillows but no cushion. A guitar lying in a chair. A shabby old comforter on the bed. During the conversation that follows, the light from the windows grows brighter.*

HE (*sitting up in bed beside her*). You love me *sometimes*. I always love you.

SHE. I'm terribly fond of you always.

HE. Why don't you live with me then?

SHE. I've told you: I don't want to live with anybody. I want to be by myself.

HE. You're very far from being by yourself at present: you have all kinds of people coming to see you morning, noon and night.

*A handorgan starts up in the street; a merry Italian tune, succeeded by* Sole Mio *and a new Broadway song or two.*

SHE. If you live with somebody, it's different: you get on each other's minds. And you can't do that with love. Even keys to the same apartment can kill it. Love ought to be all meetings and partings—partings as much as meetings.

HE. I'd be out at the office all day.

SHE. I know, but you'd be on my mind just the same.— Isn't that hurdy-gurdy marvelous! That's one of the best features of the Village: hurdy-gurdies in the early morning.

HE. Yes, but I can't hear music.

SHE. Why not?

HE. You ought to know.

SHE. On account of me?

HE. Yes.

SHE (*taking his hand*). Oh, I'm sorry, my dear: it makes me feel so mean when you say things like that.—Perhaps you oughtn't to see me any more.

HE. It was the same way during the War. I used to lie awake at night in that hospital in the Vosges, and there would be nightingales singing outside, but I couldn't really hear them. I couldn't on account of the War.

SHE. You're so sensitive, Arthur!—Were you in the hospital long?

HE. Almost five months. But it wasn't that I was suffering particularly. It was just that everything was wrong. I couldn't even say to myself, what a beautiful day this is!—I'd say, what a beautiful day this would be if only it weren't for the war!

SHE. It wasn't like that for me. The people I knew down here were bitter about the war, but they managed to keep outside it—they had to *fight* to keep outside it. We still had music—and poetry, and painting.

HE. That must have been more satisfactory than taking part in it half-heartedly as I did. Here's a poem that I wrote about it:

> We bear, unload, bring back and bear anew
> The endless litters of war-broken men.
> The summer clouds catch sunset in the blue,
> But when shall I ever see the sun again?

SHE (*touched*). That's a very sweet poem.—You're so funny when you recite your poetry, Arthur. You sound as if somebody else had written it—and as if you didn't approve of poetry anyhow.

HE. I don't believe in being too soulful about it.

SHE. How strange that pain should make you blind! It always intensifies things for me. I'd have heard the nightingales more clearly.

HE. I can't see or hear when things are wrong.

SHE. That's Puritanism.—You're a dyed-in-the-wool Puritan, Arthur.

HE. Why do you say that?

SHE. Because you make beauty depend on whether things are right or wrong.

HE. My feelings about you haven't got anything to do with moral right or wrong.

SHE. Oh, yes, they have!—the reason you're always unhappy with me is really that you think the situation's immoral. You want to get me respectably married in an apartment with nice steam-heat and a doorman in a lot of upholstery to keep out my non-respectable friends!

HE. I wouldn't live where there was a doorman for anything!—I've pulled out of all that forever!—I made my mind up about it during the war—that same time I was in the hospital. It was the first chance I'd had to think; and I suddenly realized then that I couldn't go back to the way I'd lived. The war made me see what a fraud it all was and that everything that was worth anything had to be done outside all that. That respectable life is a living death!

SHE. Why can't you get away from it then?

HE. I do.

SHE. Why aren't you happy then?

HE. Because you and I aren't really together. *You* represent the only morality that I can care anything about. The only real morality and the only real beauty!

SHE. I sound like an allegorical monument!—what about Agriculture and Industry?

HE. It's true, though—I've never thought anything like that about any woman before. The first time I ever met you after I'd seen you act, I knew that you were the person I'd been waiting for—you were the thing I wanted that I'd never found.

SHE. But now that you've found me, you're gloomy about me.

HE. Yes, I am.

SHE. Maybe it's death in *you*.

HE. What is?

SHE. Maybe you have death in you somewhere that keeps you from enjoying things.

HE. I do enjoy things when they're right.

SHE. But they never do seem to be right—and of course things never *are* right. They never are right for *anybody*—"Ay, look: high heaven and earth ail from the prime foundation!" Pain and death are around us all the time. They're waiting at the end of every street, at the opening of every door! The only thing we've got is our courage to dare to be happy in spite of them; and if death gets into that, we're done for. (*She coughs.*) Hand me a handkerchief, if there is one there.

*He gets up to get his own handkerchief out of his trousers. He is wearing expensive pyjamas.*

HE. This one of mine's pretty clean.

*He hands it to her.*

SHE. Thanks.—Why don't you give the organ-grinder a penny?

*She blows her nose.*

HE (*taking a coin from the table*). I still won't be able to hear him.

SHE. He's doing his best to keep death away!

*He throws the coin out the window.*

HE. I think I'd better shut this window.

SHE. No: leave it open—I want to hear him.

HE. You'd better let me close it in a minute. I'll get the heat turned on.

*He takes a paper of matches from the table and goes over to light the heater.*

*The organ-grinder makes a sudden spurt: the music becomes faster and louder.*

SHE. That's the effect of the money: we mustn't miss it!

HE. That picture over the bed gives me the creeps at this hour of the morning. What's it supposed to be?

SHE. We call it *Directions for Using the Empress.*

HE. I couldn't use an empress that shape.

SHE. It's all in knowing how to control the switches.

HE. I'm afraid I'd never master it.

SHE. You ought to try.

HE (*bending over the gas-heater*). It always takes about eight matches to get this heater lighted! (*The heater ignites with an explosion.*) Then it goes off like a gun! (*She laughs; he gets up and comes around to the other side of the bed.*) I'm going to have that fireplace fixed up for you.

SHE. The chimney needs repairs, and it will cost too much.

HE. I'm an architect, and I can get it done cheaply.— (*Seeing the bottle of gin on the table*) Well, immoral as it may appear to start drinking so early in the morning, I think I'm going to begin the day with a gin and ginger-ale! Where's your puritanism now?

*He pours the drink.*

SHE. Right where it was. (*Laughing*) Give me one, too.

*He hands her the glass he has just poured. The hurdy-gurdy music stops.*

HE (*as he pours out a glass for himself*). You see: *that's* the effect of the money! He plays very loud for a minute, then stops.

SHE. Still, we can't let him starve or he'd stop altogether.

*He goes over and puts the window down.*

HE. Why don't you take a couple of good stiff drinks and spend the day in bed?

SHE. I can't: I've got to rehearse.— (*As she takes a sip of the drink*) All the sparkle of fizzed-out ginger-ale!

HE (*coming back and getting into bed*). Don't pay any attention to what Dan says. He's always carrying on about "madder music and stronger wine." He belongs to the Omar Khayyam period.—You lie down and cover yourself up.

*He makes her do so and tucks the clothes around her.*

SHE. The princess in the play is no dancing-girl: she's something more like a swan.

HE. You stick to your own ideas about it. You were magnificent the other afternoon. So long as you're on the stage, that dismal little two-by-four stable seems as big as any theater in the world!

SHE. You have real nobility, Arthur!—not on account of what you say about me, but because you can see that the Beech Street Theater is really a big thing.

*The hurdy-gurdy starts up again, further down the street and fainter.*

HE. The only big things in the city now are the things that are happening down here.

SHE. Yes, that's true—the only things that matter.

HE (*moved to eloquence by the drink*). The people that live uptown and the people that live in the slums, they neither of them get a chance to do anything big themselves: they're carrying the big buildings.

SHE. Dan wants to declare Greenwich Village an independent republic.

HE. An excellent idea!

SHE. He wants to have a ceremony with spaghetti and red ink on top of Washington Arch and send up a fleet of toy balloons.

HE. Dan could supply the gas himself.—Why not simply send up Dan with a string to him?

SHE. We can't spare him—the string might break.

He. Yes: send Dan Frink and Fred Burroughs up as a couple of captive balloons!

*She laughs.*

She. To the music of a hurdy-gurdy chorus!

He. Have the drinking-fountain run *vin rouge*!

She. I'll go up on a wire like one of those angels that they have on Italian saints'-days—scattering paper roses!

He. Paper roses with torpedoes inside that go off when they hit the pavement!

She (*laughing*). We're getting tight!

He. The very first thing in the morning is really the time to get tight: it deprives early rising of its horrors.

She. It's so nice to lie here like this, isn't it?—just to lie here and drink and look at the light on the wall!

He. You can enjoy the sounds of morning activity without feeling that you have to take part in it.

She. Yes, isn't it nice of all those people to get up and bustle around so briskly!

He. I *am* happy when we're together like this!

She (*looking at him with a smile*). Are you really?

*He kisses her.*

He. I love you.

She. Look out: you'll catch my cold!

He. I don't care. (*He keeps on kissing her, embracing her more purposively.*) You look so alive, darling, even so early in the morning. Your eyes are so bright: let me kiss them!

She. They're the only thing, though, that can never be kissed!

He. Darling!

She (*ready to yield*). Put my glass over there. (*He sets it on the table and is just putting his arms around her again when there is a loud sharp knock at the door. He stops.*) I'd better go.

He. Oh, let them knock!

She. It might be a telegram or something.

222

*She jumps up, steps into a pair of mules and puts on a kimona from a chair. She is wearing men's pyjamas.*

HE. Who are you expecting a telegram from?

*The caller knocks again. She goes and opens the door on a crack.*

SHE. Oh, Mrs. Lowrie!

*She opens the door a little wider, but firmly stands in the opening so that Mrs. Lowrie cannot come in.*

MRS. LOWRIE (*ladylike, insistent, distinct*). I'm very sorry, Miss Voight, to intrude upon you so early in the morning —I'm compelled to do a great many things nowadays that I was never accustomed to do in the past—but I wanted to know whether you knew anything about Miss O'Boylan.

SHE. Miss O'Boylan? No: who is she?

MRS. LOWRIE. She's the young lady who's been living across the hall.

SHE. Oh, yes.

MRS. LOWRIE. —And she seems to have gone away.

SHE. I don't know anything about her—I don't know her except just to speak to.

MRS. LOWRIE. Well, she's taken her trunk and all her things. I'd allowed her to go on for three months without paying me any rent——

SHE. So you came to see if *I* was still here. Well, I am, and I'm going to pay you.

MRS. LOWRIE. I'm not used to people who don't pay their bills—I've never had to do with people of that kind —and I can't have such people in my house. I owe the tradesmen myself, and I've always paid every penny that I owe. All the years that Mr. Lowrie and I lived here— almost thirty-five years——

SHE. I'm terribly sorry about *my* rent, Mrs. Lowrie— but you see I've been rehearsing for this play, and you don't get any salary when you're rehearsing, and it's opening two weeks later than they expected it to at first—

I thought I was going to get paid this week, but now it seems they're not going to pay us for almost two weeks.—

*While this conversation has been going on, Arthur has quietly gotten up and taken some bills out of his wallet on the table. He goes over and slips them into the girl's right hand, which is holding the inside knob of the door. She suddenly pauses in what she is saying, glances aside and sees Arthur and the money.*

MRS. LOWRIE. Well, if people are not going to pay their rent, I'd really rather they left at once, even owing me, so that I could get other tenants who fulfill their obligations! It was a real wrench to rent my rooms. Mr. Lowrie and I came to this house almost thirty-five years ago—and my family had lived on Bleecker Street ever since the early fifties, when Greenwich Village was the fashionable neighborhood——

SHE. I can pay you something, Mrs. Lowrie. Let's see: I owe you for three months, don't I? three months, counting this month, September—that's forty-five dollars—just a moment—(*She retreats behind the door to examine the money, which turns out to be considerably more than forty-five dollars. She looks at Arthur, who makes gestures to give it to Mrs. Lowrie. Going back to the door*) Suppose I pay you twenty now and the rest when my play opens.

MRS. LOWRIE. Oh, thank you! I hope you won't be pinched.

SHE. No: not a bit.

MRS. LOWRIE. Well, I'm sorry to have made you get out of bed!

SHE (*smiling*). It's perfectly all right: I'm sorry I'm in arrears.

MRS. LOWRIE. Miss O'Boylan's going away had given me such a shock! It seems to me that people nowadays are losing all sense of integrity. A young man committed suicide, I understand, in one of the houses on Washington Square, owing the landlord seven months' rent!

*Arthur, for the girl's benefit, makes the motion of turning a crank.*

SHE. I must go back to bed, Mrs. Lowrie: I seem to be getting a cold.

MRS. LOWRIE. Oh, yes: go right back to bed then. You must take some phenacetin and quinine. Mr. Lowrie always took phenacetin and quinine—he used to have very severe colds——

SHE. I'm going to take some aspirin.—I'll pay you the rest very soon.

*She smiles and shuts the door on Mrs. Lowrie.*

HE. Why didn't you pay her the whole thing?

SHE. That's enough for her. I'll pay you back.

HE. Oh, don't—I ought to contribute to the upkeep here.

SHE (*coming back and getting into bed*). No, you oughtn't. —I shouldn't have taken it if she hadn't been in such a state.

HE. When Mrs. Lowrie begins talking about her family, there's nothing to do but pay the rent.

SHE. The genteel ones are worse than the tough ones.

HE (*exhilarated by his stroke*). Gentility unfits people for being decent. If you're genteel, you can only be decent with certain people under certain circumstances.

SHE. That old heater *doesn't* give much heat, does it?

HE. Let me warm you.

*He puts his arms around her.*

SHE. I must get up and study my part.

HE. You look so lovely!

*He kisses her, preparing to renew the attack.*

SHE. No, don't: lovely or not, I've got to study my part.

HE. Don't study it right away.

SHE. Yes, I must.

HE. Wait till the room gets warmer.

SHE. I'll study it in bed till it's warmer.

HE. I'll get the fireplace fixed right away—and that plaster, too: it might fall on you.

SHE. No: you mustn't do any more.—I don't want you to be keeping me, Arthur.—Give me my part, like a good boy; it's over there on the chair.

HE. You come out of this old comforter just as beautiful and just as fresh as Aphrodite rising from the foam!

SHE. I don't feel that way a bit, but I must study, so please hand me my part.

HE (*kissing her*). Darling——

SHE. No: don't kiss me anymore. Hand me my part, please!

HE. Very well, if you really think you have to.

*He gets up to get it.*

SHE. You can give me my cues.

HE. All right.

*He comes back with the part and hands it to her.*

## SCENE 2

*October: about midnight, after the opening of the new play at the Beech Street Theater. There is a party for the cast in Sally Voight's room.*

*The place, on which Arthur has been working, is in somewhat better shape than when we saw it first. A coal fire is glowing in the grate; and there are a coal-scuttle and poker and tongs, a telephone on the dressing-table and a long cushion on the window-seat. A neat china closet has been substituted for the shelves in the corner by the hall door, and the electric cooker has been put away. The day-bed has been pushed back sideways along the wall and has a cover so that it looks like a couch; in front of it is the equipment for drinks on a table with folding leaves, now unfolded; a punch-bowl, bottles of mineral water and whisky, glasses of diverse shapes and sizes. On a smaller table, near the window-seat to the front, are plates of cheese and sandwiches. Sally's dressing-table corner has been dismantled, her dressing table cleared of its things, and the screen folded up against the closet door. They have obtained the use for the evening of the empty room across the hall; and people are coming and going through the door—the sound of a phonograph playing dance music is heard.*

*The room is bright, the gathering lively. There are two evening-gowns and a dinner-jacket worn by uptown subscribers; but nobody else is in evening dress. Some of the women wear batiks; all have the short skirts of after the war. Smithy, the assistant stage manager, a former Wobbly, lean and tall, with a white shock of Wobbly hair, is talking to a pretty girl near the punch-bowl. The business manager, a young man named Harry Greenaway, immature and not so young as he looks, is*

227

*talking to the uptowners near the sandwiches. He is geni*
*cheerful and brisk, and produces an effect of hollowness. Abo*
*the fire are sitting Dan Frink, the director; Signe Angstror*
*the treasurer; Tracy Tripp, the stage manager and prompte*
*and Sophie Feinburg, who designs costumes and also ac*
*Tracy is ironic-naïve and a little feminine; he has a smoo*
*face of inscrutable age. Signe, about forty-five, is a tall busines*
*like blond Scandinavian. Dan Frink, about the same age, h*
*an orotund voice, florid face, hair which has already turn*
*silver and large mobile magnetic eyes: he might be a profession*
*lecturer or a popular Shakespearean actor, but he does not pr*
*cisely fit into any category. Tracy and Sophie are sitting*
*front of the fireplace; Dan is sitting at the side, between Sig*
*and the fire; Sally's guitar is leaning against Tracy's cha*
*Sophie Feinburg, in a sort of medieval robe de style, is sitti*
*on the arm of Dan's chair between Dan and Signe; she is*
*intense and strong-willed Jewess, passionately devoted to Da*
*All have drinks.*

*Arthur stands at the other side of the fire, leaning on t*
*corner of the mantelpiece. He wears rimless spectacles, a we*
*pressed suit, a white shirt with a soft button-down collar: t*
*dress of the young Eastern college graduate who continues*
*dress like an undergraduate.*

SIGNE. Well, it's a play we ought to have done. It's t
kind of thing we're here to produce!

TRACY. Did anybody see any of the critics?

SIGNE. I saw Hamilton Fite for just a second.

TRACY. What did he say?

SIGNE. He said he thought Sally was superb.

TRACY. The applause at the end of the Second Act w
principally for Sally, I'm sure.

DAN (*talking emphatically and resonantly*). No: the pl
itself gripped some of them!—and if we can get such a pl
over to a few people, we're accomplishing our main purpos

SIGNE. Yes: it's a play we ought to have done.

DAN. What we exist for is to release the creative currents: the non-conductors won't carry them, but the conductors will!

TRACY. Augie Blum was there, with a beautiful white front. (*To Signe*) Did he say anything about the play?

SIGNE. I only talked to him a second. He said he thought it was a play we ought to have done.—But his attitude didn't encourage me to ask him for any more money.—He said he thought Sally was splendid.

TRACY. The old goat!

ARTHUR. Does anybody know where she is?

TRACY. She said she was going out with some friends.

ARTHUR. I couldn't find her at the Green Goblin or Scarlatti's.

TRACY. I don't know where she went.

SIGNE. I do think, Dan, that the last act might be cut.

DAN. I shouldn't want to cut it with Boag away; I promised him I'd do it just as he'd written it.

SIGNE. But that scene where she wears the metal face and the philosopher talks at such length—the audience can't see Sally, and nobody understands the speech.

TRACY. She looks very lovely, though, sitting there absolutely motionless.

DAN. I consider that speech one of the great things in the play!

SIGNE. It's beautifully written, Dan, but nobody understands it.

DAN. *I* understand it: it contains the whole idea of the play.

SIGNE. What does it mean then?

DAN. It means, in a word, that Beauty has no answers for Wisdom.

SOPHIE. Beauty is a deeper wisdom.

SIGNE. Where does the egg-beater come in then?

DAN. That's not an egg-beater, my dear!

SIGNE. What is it then?

DAN. It's the essence of a scepter.

TRACY. It's an abstract scepter.

SIGNE. What does that long rigmarole mean—about "
million million immaculate beings"?

DAN. It means the dance of electrons and atoms.

TRACY (*speaking at almost the same time*). It's the Platoni
idea of souls.

*Signe and Arthur laugh.*

SIGNE. If there's as big a difference of opinion about :
as that, I shouldn't think it would do any harm to tak
it out.

SOPHIE. They can be souls and atoms both—it's a meta
physical conception.

DAN. Why, it's one of the most thrilling things Boa
has done!—he's the first writer who's made poetry out o
modern physics!—If people don't like it now, they *wi*
like it!—if they don't understand it, they *will* under
stand it!

SIGNE. Well, I always thought it was a play we ough
to do.

*Loud knocking is heard at the door, accompanied by a clankin
sound. Arthur goes over and opens. Fred Burroughs makes
tumultuous entrance, attracting, with an instinct for dramatizin
himself, the attention of everybody in the room. He is a b
large-limbed, red-faced Middle-Westerner, with his hair stand
ing out in all directions; his shirt has come open at the nec
and the knot on his necktie has slipped. He is drunk, and
brandishing a cow-bell.*

ARTHUR. Hello, Fred.

FRED. Hello, Arthur!—Listen, Arthur!—what do yo
think of my new publicity stunt?— (*Clanking the bel*
Hear ye! hear ye! hear ye! I bring tidings of the Beec
Street Players!—Hear ye! hear ye! hear ye! *The Zi*

*Princess* at the Beech Street Theater!—Listen, Arthur:
I'm going to go into all the wine-cellars and all the first-
class restaurants tomorrow night and I'm going to ring
his bell and make everybody stop eating, and then I'm
going to say, "Hear ye, ladies and gentlemen!"—or rather,
People, male and female!"—because you have to insult
them: the artist must always insult his audience—"People,
male and female, hear ye!" (*He rings the bell.*) "I summon
you to the Grove of Apollo! The Grove of Apollo, as
you may not have heard, has been moved to Number
Fifty-nine Beech Street, the home of The Beech Street
Players!—Apollo is not dead, he liveth!—You will find
him in Beech Street with his muses—with Melpomene,
and Calliope and Thalia—and Sally Voight and Sophie
Feinburg!—You will find them at the Beech Street
Theater!—the performance begins at 8:30, and the seats
are a dollar fifty each! Come one, come all, kind friends:
the poetry and the wisdom and the glory that were Greece
are at the Beech Street Theater tonight!"—Isn't that a
wonderful publicity stunt, Arthur?

SIGNE. Why don't you hang the bell around your neck,
Fred?

TRACY. Hang it around your neck and shake your head
from time to time.

FRED. You don't understand the significance of the cow-
bell, Signe: Apollo was a cowherd, you know!

ARTHUR. That kind of advertisement, Fred, would do a
good deal to keep *me* away.

FRED (*throwing his arm around Arthur*). Do you think it's
vulgar, Arthur?—do you think it's vulgar? The poet must
always be vulgar!—he's above and below the middle class:
Shakespeare held horses and got plastered in the wine-
cellars—Villon was a common yegg—Aeschylus was
brained over the head in a brawl and his friends said an
eagle dropped a tortoise on him!—all the poets are

rogues, all rogues!—A drink, Arthur!—I crave a drin

ARTHUR (*as he gets him one*). You haven't seen Sally the wine-cellars, have you?

FRED. No, Arthur: I haven't seen Sally since the play she was magnificent in it, Arthur! (*As Arthur hands h the drink*) Thanks. (*Turning to Dan*) Listen, Dan! I'm goi to write a play for you!—I want to tell you about t play I'm going to write for you! (*Going over to Dan, still holding the attention of the room*) Listen, Dan: it's a pl about Don Juan—it's a play about Don Juan coming Bethlehem.—Isn't that a wonderful idea! (*He takes a drin* Don Juan comes to Bethlehem, and he stops over night an inn, and suddenly he hears a commotion in the cou yard—he looks out and there he sees the Magi with t people all gathered around them. (*He takes another drin* There they are, the wise men who have come from East following the strange unknown star, walking in th stiff silken robes and with their gifts of frankincense a myrrh. So Don Juan goes down to see what's going on and he follows them into the stable, and there he fi them kneeling before the manger. "What's this?" he cri "some Eastern mummery?"—who *are* all these old bo with the whiskers who want him to stand aside while th pay homage to a woman and a child of the people? "Ho, father!" he cries, tweaking the Magi's whiskers ( *makes as if to tweak Arthur*)—"Ho, father: tell me wha is that thy learning teacheth thee to prize more th wanton love in a wench's arms? What bringest thee t long way in foul weather?" "Hast seen the star?" say Magi,—"The star that guided us here?"—

TRACY. "Guidedst us here," you mean.

FRED. "The star that guidedst us here." (*Laughter*) not "guidedst", it's "guided"!—Damn you, Tracy, y rogue—I can handle my own language—I speak the gr language of the Elizabethans!—"Good fathers," says D

Juan to the Magi,—"Thy purblind astronomy doteth!—the proud stars keep their courses: they disdain to direct us humans!" He's arrogant, cynical, see!—he eyes them with a supercilious smile. (*Fred illustrates.*)—And then *suddenly*: he sees the ox and the ass going down on their knees in their stalls——

*Harry Greenaway has detached himself from the group and quietly comes over to Fred.*

HARRY (*very quietly and tactfully*). I think you ought to be a little bit careful, Fred, of the susceptibilities of the uptown subscribers. I think the Sullivans are Catholics.

FRED (*louder*). To hell with the uptown subscribers if they can't look on reverently at a mystery! This is a miracle play! (*The Sullivans smile, amused.*) Don Juan sees the ox and the ass go down on their knees in their stalls—and suddenly he experiences a strange sensation—he feels the hinges of his knees giving way beneath him! He fights against it, his pride fights!— (*Fred illustrates, clenching the hand which is not holding the glass*) but he finds that he can no longer stand upright: it's as if all his sinews were turned to water! He sinks down! (*Fred sinks with a bump, still holding the glass in his hand*)—and then suddenly he recognizes the mother, and he cries, "*Mary!—Mary!*—What child is this, Mary? Can this be the child that our dalliance begot when we sported together in the hay?—*Mary! my sweet witch of Nazareth!*"—Isn't it terrific?—do you get it? Don Juan is the father of Christ!

SIGNE. The only thing I didn't understand, Fred, was whether you were supposed to be the ox or the ass.

FRED (*getting up from his knees*). That's all right, Signe: it's a tremendous thing, a revolutionary thing—it's more revolutionary than Nietzsche!

ARTHUR. And more alcoholic than Poe.

DAN. Don't let anybody kid you, Fred: you've got the vital fire!

FRED (*putting his arm around Arthur again*). A drink, Arthur!—I crave a drink!

ARTHUR. Help yourself.

*Fred goes over to the drinks. The general conversation is resumed. The door opens and Sally comes in. She is flushed and excited and looks very attractive. She is wearing an embroidered Cuban shawl, which she has put up over her head. People gather around her as she takes off her coat and puts the shawl down around her shoulders.*

THE ADMIRERS. You were simply marvelous, Sally! It's the best thing you've ever done. You could have heard a pin drop during the Second Act! You gave such a beautifully modulated performance!

SALLY. I'm so glad you liked it!—Really?—Oh, thank you very much!

FRED. Here she is: the Tenth Muse, Sally Voight! (*Holding up his glass*) I pay you homage, Sally!

SALLY (*smiling*). Thanks for your homage, Fred!

*Seeing that he can no longer hold the center of the floor, Fred turns his attention to a pretty little brunette in a red blouse and with a very red made-up mouth.*

ARTHUR (*who has come over to Sally and has been quietly standing by during the outburst of congratulations*). I haven't had a chance to congratulate you myself.

SALLY. Hello, Arthur.—Did you think I was all right?

ARTHUR. You were marvelous.—What became of you after the show?

SALLY. Some friends came to my dressing-room, and I went out with them.

ARTHUR. Why didn't you bring them up here?

SALLY. They had to get back to Brooklyn.

ARTHUR. Well, they kept you long enough. I was afraid something had happened to you.

SALLY (*controlling irritation*). Well, you mustn't think things have happened to me whenever I'm out of your sight.

ARTHUR. I just thought you might be tired.

SALLY. I am, but I can still get around.

ARTHUR. Don't you want a drink?

SALLY. I don't know.—Yes: a very little one.

*Arthur makes her a highball very carefully. The uptown sub-scribers have come over to congratulate her, Harry Greenaway in their wake.*

*Sally turns to talk to them.*

SIGNE (*to her companions by the fire*). Arthur adores Sally, doesn't he?

TRACY. She's loosened him up: he's more human than he was.

DAN. Sally gives life to everybody!—she's one of the great givers of life!

*Arthur hands Sally the drink.*

SALLY (*pleased by the uptowners' compliments*). Thank you!

FRED (*picking up the little girl in the red blouse*). Come dance with me! dance with Pan!—you have the grape-crushed mouth of a bacchante!—Come with me! Today is Satyrs' Day, and I am Pan, the shaggy-flanked goat-god! —Come with me! we will twirl the thyrsus together! Come and dance with Pan, O grape-reddened maenad!— come and twirl the thyrsus with Pan!

*He carries her out to the room across the hall.*

SIGNE. Fred is in one of his obstreperous moods tonight.

TRACY. I hope he doesn't land in the night-court this time.

DAN (*who is well charged with drinks himself and stimulated to put on a performance of his own by seeing Sally coming over toward them*). It's tonight! it's the play! it's Sally. It's the beauty we created together tonight—the beauty we created in the Beech Street Theater, with the tenements all around us and the Elevated growling at the door!—We had a success tonight, Sally!—it doesn't matter what the critics may say! it doesn't matter about the receipts at the box-office! *Something happened tonight* with Boag's play and

Sally—and with us all! New life in art has been born!—
Sally: I have a part for you: we'll do it in the spring!—
Aristophanes' *Lysistrata*!—the woman who called a
woman's strike and stopped the Peloponnesian War!

SALLY. That sounds like great fun.

ARTHUR (*who has come over and is standing on her right
a little behind her*). Greek plays are usually a bore on the
stage.

DAN. That's because they're never done the way they
ought to be!—I'll do *Lysistrata* the right way!

ARTHUR. If you did it the way it ought to be done,
you'd have to do it outdoors in a stadium.

DAN. We'll do it on our twenty-by-twenty stage.—
We'll have the Acropolis right here in Beech Street!—
The time has now arrived in the evening when we rise to
a higher level of vision and require another round of
drinks!—Let me fill your glass, Signe!

*He takes her glass and his own and goes over to the table
and fills them. Tracy has picked up the guitar and has been
strumming chords on it.*

SALLY. Sing that song about the New Orleans girls,
Tracy!

*She sits down on the arm of his chair. Arthur resumes his
place by the mantelpiece.*


TRACY (*sings*).
New Orleans girls are gettin' mighty frisky—
Take a little cocaine in their whisky—
    Oh, ho, Honey, take a one on me!
    Take a whiff on me!

You keep on a talkin' till you make me think
Your daddy was a bull-dog, your mammy was a mink!
    Oh, ho, Honey, take a one on me!
    Take a (*sniffs*) on me!

*At the second line of the second stanza, Sally has joined in
and she sings the last stanza with him, sniffing with great relish.*

> Whiffin' coke is mighty bad,
> But that's a habit I never had!
>     Oh, ho, Honey, etc.

ARTHUR. Gosh, that's a depraved song!
SALLY. I think it's a wonderful song!
TRACY. Here's another song from the South:

> Oh, love, oh, love! oh, careless love!
> Oh, love, oh, love! oh, careless love!
> You break de heart of many a gal—
> You never break dis heart of mine!
>
> Oh, when I wore my apron low,
> You'd follow me through rain or snow—
> But now I wear it to my chin,
> You'll pass my door and not come in!
>
> Oh, love, oh, love! oh, careless love!
> Oh, love, oh, love! oh, careless love!
> You break de heart of many a gal—
> You never break dis heart of mine!

SALLY (*who has been listening to the song intently*). What
a beautiful song, Tracy!—But why did he pass her up
when she wore her apron to her chin?
TRACY. The idea is, I guess, that she was pregnant and
was wearing her apron that way to cover it up.
ARTHUR. Why wasn't her heart broken then?
SIGNE. It was—but she didn't want to admit it.
TRACY. She was a modern girl. She was taking it in
her stride.

SALLY (*smiling*). She was just as careless as he was!

*There is a terrific crash across the hall, and the phonograph music stops.*

TRACY. Good God!

ARTHUR. What's happened?

*He starts for the door.*

SIGNE. It's probably Fred running amuck.

*Fred bursts in.*

FRED. Forgive me, Arthur!—I've done a terrible thing, Arthur! I've smashed your victrola!

ARTHUR. How did that happen?

FRED. I was dancing with it, Arthur!—the spirit of Pan took possession of me and, having no pastoral pipes, I was dancing with the victrola—I was fighting this mechanical age, Arthur, this age that divorces the musician from the music!

ARTHUR. You've divorced *us* from the music all right!

FRED. Don't be angry with me, Arthur!—forgive me! —It really wasn't my fault! somebody opened the door and gave me a push from behind—and the whole mighty edifice came toppling down in one stupendous world-deafening cataclysm!

ARTHUR. I forgive you, but it's too bad to stop the dancing.

FRED. Then let me have a drink, Arthur! I'm in desperate need of a drink!—I feel the way Samson felt after he'd pulled down the pillars of Gaza!

ARTHUR. We don't want to get crushed like the Philistines.

FRED. Then don't be a Philistine, Arthur!—You're a worshipper of Apollo, you know you are, in spite of the creases in your pants!—so give the Great God Pan a drink!

ARTHUR. The drinks are at your disposal, but I wouldn't drink any more now if I were you.

FRED (*pouring out a great slug of gin*). You mustn't be angry with me, Arthur!

SMITHY (*appearing in the doorway*). Has anybody got another phonograph?

DAN. We've got one.

SOPHIE. You couldn't bring it over: it's too heavy.

DAN. Come over to my place then!—Sally needs a rest anyway.

SOPHIE. You have nothing for them to drink.

DAN. I'll get something! (*Getting up from his chair and making his voice resound*) All come to my house! The Princess needs a rest. But for us the heights of the evening still rise in iridescent uplands. We must have dancing! we must have drinking! we must have high discourse! Tonight we shall look down like gods and see the world unrolled at our feet—and not only in space but in time! We shall behold the lost Atlantis—and the future of the Beech Street Players!—My place is at 18 MacDougal Street!—Don't lean too hard on the railing and ignore the smell in the hall!

THE COMPANY. Very well, All right. Fine!

*They begin to get their things and say goodby.*

SALLY. I don't want you all to leave.

DAN. You must go to bed. You told me you hadn't been sleeping.

SALLY. Yes, I should, I suppose.

*He takes both her hands in his.*

DAN. You must.—You're a great actress since tonight, and you must learn to take care of yourself: that's one of the responsibilities of greatness.

SALLY. You did most of it, Dan.

DAN. No: we all did it. But we've still got to work on it—so tomorrow at 3!

SALLY. Yes: all right.

SOPHIE (*who is jealous of Sally, trying to get him away*).

We'd better go over: they'll get there and won't be able to get in.

DAN (*to Sally*). Good night then and plenty of sleep!

SALLY. Good night, Dan dear!

*He and Sophie go. The guests depart in a mass: Arthur, Sally and Fred are left.*

FRED (*coming up as Dan goes*). Let me stay here a quarter of an hour, Sally!—I don't want to go over to Dan's!

SALLY. I've got to go to bed, Fred—I'm really terribly tired.

FRED. They're murmuring against me, Sally—they're giving me dark looks and dirty glances.—I can feel the air full of malignant mutterings!—let me stay for just one more drink!

ARTHUR. Sally's worn out: she wants to go to bed.

*During the conversation that follows, Sally says goodby to some last guests.*

FRED (*at his most plaintive*). Just one more drink, Arthur! Don't still be angry with me, Arthur!—I broke your victrola, Arthur, but something in me is broken now: when I came here tonight I was a positive force, I drew people about me like a lodestone—and now in one brief deafening crash, all my power has passed from me!

ARTHUR. You never have any consideration, Fred, for anybody's troubles but your own. Can't you understand that Sally needs rest?

*He takes Fred by the arm and pilots him toward the door.*

FRED. You're politely getting rid of me, Arthur!

ARTHUR. I wasn't trying to be so very polite.

FRED. Listen, Arthur: today is Satyrs' Day!—

ARTHUR. That's the beginning of the open season on satyrs.

FRED. I can't go over there, Arthur: I couldn't stand their silent aversion!

ARTHUR. Why don't you go home then?

FRED. I can't go home, Arthur, because it's Satyrs' Day!

SALLY. Good night, Fred: I've got to go to bed.

ARTHUR (*pushing him out the door*). Good night. Can you make the stairs all right?

FRED. Listen, Arthur: I'm no sodden pothouse sot—I'm a drunkard of classical stature!—

*Arthur shuts the door on him. Everybody else has gone.*

ARTHUR (*to Sally*). Good God! how does a person get that way?

FRED (*ringing his cow-bell outside the door*). I'm calling my satyrs! do you hear me?—I'm summoning my ribald rout of satyrs!—They're going to besiege you and drink up your liquor, so you might as well give me a drink!

ARTHUR. I've seen some persistent bores, but Fred makes them all look like pikers!

FRED (*giving the bell a last clank*). I'll send my satyrs to plague you!—damn you, Arthur Fiske!

ARTHUR (*toward the door, but not loudly enough to be heard by Fred*). Oh, shut up!

SALLY (*who has gone over and lit a cigarette and sat down in front of the fire*). He's all right when he's not tight.

ARTHUR. But he's always tight.

SALLY. Well, don't be so smug about him.

ARTHUR. I'm not: but he makes himself a damned nuisance.

SALLY. I'm very fond of Fred Burroughs: he's written some darn good poetry and he was nice to me when I first came to the Village.

ARTHUR. I suppose he's one of your old flames.

SALLY. Suppose he is.

ARTHUR. I shouldn't like to believe it.

SALLY. Why shouldn't you like to believe it? Fred's got real imagination, and he's got the courage to live up to it. And he has great sweetness really.

ARTHUR. It wasn't in evidence tonight.

SALLY. Fred was never a lover of mine. He was married to Marcella then. But he used to take me out to dinner when I was completely broke and living on oranges and milk.

ARTHUR. Very well, my dear: I won't be nasty about him.—Now you ought to go to bed.

SALLY. That superior tone of yours!—What did you ever do to be patronizing about poor old Fred? Fred had to go to work as a farm-hand before he'd finished primary school, and he was boning out Greek in the hayloft when you were having it poured into you at college—and being kept like a pet pony!

ARTHUR. College isn't so much fun.

SALLY. It's more fun than starting out in life without a cent of your own.

ARTHUR. Now you're in one of those moods when you talk as if you were a proletarian. You're not a proletarian —you've always belonged to the white-collar class. Your father was a foreman—a boss: you belonged to the upper stratum of Braxton Falls, Mass. You had a very good education.

SALLY. There's no real upper stratum in a mill-town.

ARTHUR. That's not true.

SALLY. What do *you* know about it? Do you imagine that when the mills close down, a foreman's any better off than anybody else?

ARTHUR. I'll bet my kind of people are much worse off and much worse to be with than your kind of people. You talk about going to college as if it were a great advantage: you don't have any idea of what it's like to spend four years in college, expecting to find something that's more interesting than home, and then to face the fact when you leave, that it's all been a vague dream. By that time you look forward to getting out: you think that then things will be real—but you find yourself just back at home, and you realize that four years of college have just been a preparation to come back and live like the people you've always reacted against. You look at them and think, "Oh, my God!" There are the family still sitting around with their confounded collections of things behind glass, and you look at their eyes and you see that they're glazed and that they're a collection, too—and then you realize that *you're* part of the collection yourself, that you've just been taken out and polished up, and that now you've been put back on the shelf!

SALLY. You at least had a nice quiet shelf. I never had any quiet at all. My mother used to have love affairs and take me with her and make me wait for her out in the hall, and my father would threaten to kill her, and my brother would fight with my father. *You* never had poverty and fighting at home and no prospect of ever getting away from it!

ARTHUR. You're exaggerating!

SALLY (*furious*). I'm *not* exaggerating: you don't know what life is really like, that's all. It's a desperate, disgraceful quarrel!

ARTHUR. I know: I saw the war.

SALLY. You only saw it as an officer: you don't know what it was like for the ranks!

ARTHUR. Now, you're not really excited now about what I know about life: you've been out with somebody tonight. (*She is silent.*) Who was it? (*She is silent.*) It wasn't Fred, was it?

SALLY. No.

ARTHUR. You might as well tell me about it: there's no use in concealing these things. (*She is silent.*) Is it somebody you're in love with?

SALLY. Yes.

*A silence.*

ARTHUR (*wounded, more subdued*). Who is he?

243

SALLY. You don't know him.

ARTHUR. What does he do?

SALLY. He's a newspaper man.

ARTHUR. Oh.—Is he somebody you've just met?

SALLY. No: I told you about him.

ARTHUR. The one you went away with?

SALLY. Yes.

ARTHUR. I thought you and he had parted.

SALLY. We had; but he came to the play tonight.

ARTHUR. Do you want to marry him?

SALLY. He's married.

ARTHUR. Do you expect to see him?

SALLY. Maybe.

*Silence.*

ARTHUR. You told me that affairs with married men were very unsatisfactory arrangements.

SALLY. I don't want to talk any more tonight. I've got to go to bed, and you must go!

ARTHUR. Very well.

SALLY (*getting up and taking her purse off the dressing-table*). Here's the twenty dollars I owe you.

ARTHUR. Did he give it to you?

SALLY. No.—Signe advanced it to me.

ARTHUR. I wish you wouldn't pay me back.

SALLY. I'm sorry Fred Burroughs broke your phonograph.

ARTHUR. Don't be silly.

*He takes the money.*

SALLY. Now please go and leave me, Arthur.

ARTHUR. All right.—Good night.

*He hesitates a moment about kissing her, then leans down and kisses her forehead.*

SALLY. Good night.

ARTHUR. I'll shut up the room across the hall.

SALLY. Yes: thank you for arranging about it.

ARTHUR. Shall I see you tomorrow?

SALLY. I'm going to sleep all morning, and I've got a rehearsal at 3.

ARTHUR. I'll come round after the theater in the evening.

SALLY. All right.

ARTHUR. Good night.

SALLY. Good night.

*He goes out. Left alone, after a moment's intense thought, she begins picking up the glasses and emptying the ash-trays into the fireplace. She sets the guitar in a chair.*

SALLY (*singing to herself*).

> New Orleans girls are gettin' mighty frisky—
> Put a little cocaine in their whisky!
>   Oh, ho, Honey, take a sniff on me!

*A knock on the door.*

SALLY. Hello!—Who's that?

A MAN'S VOICE. Sally!

*She goes over quickly and opens the door.*

SALLY. Oh, Bugs!

*He is a man in his middle thirties, an Irishman. He has a belted ulster and a rakish felt hat.*

BUGS. All alone?

SALLY. Yes.

*He embraces her and holds her.*

SALLY. I thought you'd gone home.

BUGS. So I did—I went and I stayed fifteen minutes and came away as fast as I could!

SALLY. Why did you do that? Wasn't your wife there?

BUGS. She was, and the way she greeted me—before he'd even kissed me—was to ask me whether I'd gotten he plumber.

SALLY (*smiling*). I bet you hadn't.

BUGS (*taking his coat off and sitting down on the day-bed*). Of course I hadn't: she's asked me so many times that ow I'm *never* going to do it!

245

SALLY. Don't you want a drink?

BUGS. Of course I want a drink!—I want to drink with you all night!

SALLY (*getting him one*). You didn't walk out on account of the plumbing, did you?

BUGS. Of course I walked out on account of the plumbing!—and on account of about a million other things—on account of the 1880 hat-rack and the 1910 phonograph records and the set of dinner-plates with gold edges that my mother-in-law gave us for a wedding-present!—I try to turn away from you, Sally—but I can't: it would be just like the sunflower turning its back to the sun!

SALLY (*smiling*). You ought to have had the plumbing fixed, though.

*She hands him the drink and sits down beside him.*

BUGS. I've been having things fixed for fifteen years, and the household's just as unsound as it ever was!—It can't be fixed—it can never be fixed!—you can't fix up those Sunday dinners when I always insult the guests!—When other people have got the leprosy, when the flesh begins dropping off their bones, you've got to make a break and get away! There's no use in being soft about it! The well and the sick can't live together!

SALLY. I know: if you try to be kind to them, you find they've wrapped their tentacles around you, and instead of your helping them up——

BUGS. They're dragging you relentlessly down—down to the dark slimy sea-floor, where the light of the sun never comes—and there you have to pal with the lower crusta-ceans and corpses that once were men!

SALLY. Do you care about me really? I didn't know after the last time.

BUGS. Sally, you're all there is in the world! I saw your face and I heard your voice all the way back to Brooklyn!

SALLY. You oughtn't to have come. It will upset your wife.

BUGS. Why should *they* keep *us* from having what they can't have themselves? Why should the lame keep people from walking? Why should the blind keep people from seeing? *Goddam* them: the lame, the halt and the blind! *Goddam* them: the cripples!

SALLY. Yes, you're right: goddam them!

*He puts his arms around her and they kiss, sitting static in a savage embrace.*

# SCENE 3

*November: late afternoon. It is dark outside, and there is a reading lamp turned on near the fireplace. The cooker is back in place and the corner with the dressing table as it was in the first scene.*

*Bugs Brophy, in one of the comfortable chairs, is sitting in front of the fire, reading the afternoon papers, which are lying around him on the floor. He throws down the one he has been reading.*

BUGS. The damned swine!

*He looks sullenly into the fire. Sally comes in from the theater.*

SALLY (*glad to get back to him*). Hello!

BUGS (*glancing around*). Hello.

SALLY. What's the news from the strike?

BUGS. The news from the strike is that the picket-line was broken up this morning by mounted bulls and company thugs. One woman was beaten insensible and most of her teeth knocked out, and five men have been sent to the hospital, one of them probably dying.

SALLY. Were you there?

BUGS. Yes: I saw it, and it was a perfectly cold-blooded performance. The company had arranged with the police to put a stop to the picketing this morning. But do you think I can tell about it in the *Telegraph-Dispatch*?

SALLY. Won't they let you?

BUGS. Of course they won't let me! Look at this! (*He picks up one of the papers and hands it to her, showing her the place.*) They've actually changed my copy! They've got me saying that the pickets were rioting. They've practically got me saying that they were banging their heads against the police clubs!

SALLY. And you told about the police attacking *them*?

BUGS. Of course—and they've concocted a fairy-tale, with McCaffrey, the company's ape-man, as Prince Charming!

SALLY. How can they *dare* to do such a thing?

BUGS. It's the first time they've ever done it to *me*. I ought to have stayed in the office, goddam it, and gone to the mat about it. I knew they were going to get panicky, but I thought if I wasn't there, they wouldn't have the nerve to change a signed story.

SALLY. Can't you make them publish something correcting it?

BUGS. No: they won't confess they're lying swine.

SALLY. Why don't you write about it somewhere else?

BUGS. Jesus! You see people booted in the ribs and women with blood running out of their mouths, and you keep yourself from getting into it because you think you can tell people about it—and then the very words that you've written are made to whitewash the police!

SALLY. You can tell about it in the *Masses*.

BUGS. Yes, but who reads the *Masses*? Nobody but the radicals who write for it. The ordinary public will never be told that there's civil war going on over in Payson.

SALLY. I know just how you feel: I felt that way once when I lost out on a part that I'd been rehearsing for weeks.

BUGS. The radicals are right, though: there's only one way to fight it—go over to the other side. I *will* write about it in the *Masses* and anywhere else that'll let me—and I'll tell about what happened to my story. If they don't like it, they can can me!

SALLY. They would, I suppose, wouldn't they?

BUGS. Yes: of course.—And I might as well do it myself!

SALLY. Why don't you just go ahead and see what happens?

BUGS. No: I might as well do it myself—and I might as well do it now!

*He gets up.*

SALLY. Think it over tonight, why don't you? Maybe there's something else you could do.

BUGS. No: I'll do it myself right now. It'll give me the greatest satisfaction to pass along those kicks in the slats I saw this morning to those punks in the city-room! (*He goes to the telephone. Sally lights a cigarette and watches him.*) Hello: give me Bowling Green 6000 . . . Hello! I want to speak to Mr. Murchison . . . Hello, Charley: This is Bugs. I want to thank you for what you did to my article. It's typical of your fair-minded attitude that you should want to see the police get a break . . . Well, I'm sorry, too . . . Oh, he did? . . . Well, why didn't you get in touch with me? . . . You know I'm always either at home or at Scarlatti's . . . No, I don't exaggerate: it sounds as if I'd suddenly changed my mind and decided the strikers were bums—and it makes me write a goddam lie! . . . Only a few words? Well, it's only a difference of a few words between a decent guy and a yellow dog! . . . Well, give me Bradley: I'm following the buck . . . All right: goodby. Be kind to policemen! (*He hangs up and addresses Sally.*) They had orders from Bradley, the owner, it seems. (*He takes up the receiver again.*) Bowling Green 6000 . . . Hello: I want Mr. Bradley's office . . . Hello: This is T. P. Brophy. I want to speak to Mr. Bradley . . . Hello, Mr. Bradley: this is Brophy. My article on the textile strike was changed in the city-room today, and I was told that you'd said to Murchison that my stories had been too favorable to the strikers. . . . You want the paper to stand behind American industry, but do you want it to stand behind the Columbia Woolen Company, which is beating up American citizens for exercising their constitutional rights? . . . There's no other attitude possible for anybody covering the strike than to report the simple facts, which I witnessed: that the police and the company thugs made an unprovoked attack on the pickets . . . I don't need radical sympathies to tell what I saw happen. . . . Well, I'm through then . . . Yes, my point of view *is* different—but you go ahead and stick to yours: you stand behind American industry, and when American industry goes into a tailspin, you'll— (*Mr. Bradley has hung his receiver up.*) Hello! . . . (*He hangs up.*) He's hung up. Well, that's that.—Good Christ: I don't see what else I could have done!

SALLY. I think you did quite right.

BUGS. Good God! You ought to have heard him blah-blahing about promoting industrial peace!

SALLY. The critic on the *Telegraph-Dispatch* has always been rotten to the Beech Street.

BUGS. Of course he has: he's cockeyed all the time! He can't even see what's happening on the stage!

*He sits down in the chair again.*

SALLY. How can they allow a man like that to review plays!

BUGS. On a newspaper everybody's cockeyed: it's the only way they can stand it. It's the old drinking psychology of, "Let's pretend." You know how you can get yourself through a lousy life by getting drunk part of every day and imagining that things are different from what they are and ignoring the way things really are during the part of the day when you're sober. Well, we newspaper men have got it down to a science, so that the part to be ignored is a minimum and is ignored as completely as possible. We manage to keep ourselves in a state where we're almost persuaded that the world is the way the paper represents it. We're even able to be present at things as eye-witnesses and believe they're happening the way the paper would like to have them happen. I really failed in my duty as a newspaper man this morning when I looked on at that massacre sober, but it was too early in the day to have had a drink. None of the men from the other papers were there at all.

*Sally comes over and kisses him and sits on the arm of his chair.*

SALLY. What you did was fine: I'm glad you did it.

BUGS. Well, now I'm out of the haze and out of a job, and thank God!

SALLY. You can easily get another one, can't you?

BUGS. I don't know, but I'm not going to worry about it just now. I'm feeling so much better since I told the *Dispatch* to go to hell! I've been waiting for this, to tell the truth, every day for a week. Every day I expected the ax to fall.

SALLY. Really?

BUGS. When I handed in my story yesterday, Charley Murchison said to me: "Another bouquet of roses for Rosa Mancowitz?" She's one of the strike-leaders.

SALLY. Yes, I know.

BUGS. And now I feel a damsight better. That thing upset me this morning. It makes you feel like hell to stand by and not take part in a fight like that. But I'm jobless now the same way they are!

SALLY. Oh, you're really a fine person, Bugs.—I'm not going to call you "Bugs" any more.—I can't bear to call you that awful name—I'm going to call you by your right name, "Tom." How did you ever happen to be called "Bugs"?

BUGS. I'm supposed to be nuts, I guess.

SALLY. Well, you're not: you've simply got more courage than most people and you feel about things more keenly.

BUGS. You believe in me. Gracie doesn't believe in me.

SALLY. Why doesn't she?

BUGS. All the things that are any good about me are things that interfere with her plans.

SALLY (*smiling*). Is that so?—How did you happen to marry her?

BUGS. A co-ed college.—She'd be all right if she was married to one of these intelligent college instructors. I got her away from one and I ought to have let him have her.

SALLY. Have you been home lately?

BUGS. No—and I'm not going to attempt it as long as I'm out of a job.—Well, we'll go out and have one last good old blow-out tonight, and I can worry about the rest tomorrow!

SALLY. Don't spend all your money. Let's have dinner here.

BUGS. That's too much trouble.

SALLY. No, it isn't. I've got a lot of things and I'll cook it.

BUGS. You've got enough else to do.

*It begins to snow outside.*

SALLY. It's no trouble. I'd love to get dinner. I'll make you a Spanish omelet. My Spanish omelets are fine. I've got eggs and canned tomatoes and almost everything—and there's that bottle of red wine from last night.

BUGS. I'll go out and get some more.

SALLY. No, don't. Now that you're not working on the paper, you don't need to drink so much, you know.

BUGS. Yes: I'll get up and write something in the morning.

SALLY. Let's do that all week: let's eat at home. It's easy to get dinner for two people, and it'll take my mind off my part.

BUGS. You can't be a good cook: it would make you too good to be true.

SALLY (*laughing*). Well, we'll see. (*He kisses her, and she kisses him back. They sit with their arms around one another,*

*looking into the fire. Sally jumps up.*) Well, let's see wha
I've got. (*She goes over toward the cupboard, but stops befor*
*the window.*) Oh, look: it's snowing! Great big flakes! Dic
you ever see such big ones! I'm going to leave the shade
up so that we can see it! (*Going on to the cupboard*) Let'
see: yes, I think I've really got everything.—Everything
except a green pepper. (*She comes back to him.*)

BUGS. I'll go out and get it.

SALLY (*sitting again on the arm of his chair*). Don't go yet

BUGS. No: it's swell to be here with you.

SALLY. We'll just be here together with the snow falling
all around. Just the night to eat at home, and have ar
omelet and a bottle of wine!

BUGS. Live like the workers.

SALLY. Yes: my father was a textile worker, you know

BUGS. My grandfather began as a bricklayer. But wha
do we go and do as soon as we get hold of a little money
We dig ourselves into dreadful bourgeois domesticity—
like my goddam place over in Flushing!

SALLY. I haven't done that yet.

BUGS. You're a genius.

SALLY. How do you know you're not a genius?

BUGS. I only talk like one at times.

SALLY. You've never written the things that you ough
to.

BUGS. I know: I never give myself the time. When
get money, I blow it all in on getting away from home.

SALLY. Are you comfortable with me leaning on you
like this?

BUGS. Comfortable? I'm so damn comfortable! I'm re
laxing for the first time in a week!

SALLY. You've been under a strain, haven't you?

BUGS. That strike had me all keyed up.

SALLY. I know.

*She kisses him gently on the cheek.*

BUGS. I was ready to kill everybody in the office because I thought they were all getting against me—and now I don't feel sore at them anymore. I oughtn't to have been so damn nasty to poor old Charley Murchison: *he* needs *his* job, of course, just the same way the textile workers need theirs, and at his age it isn't much fun taking orders from a younger man. The police and the pickets and the company and the union are all the same to Charley. And Bradley is just a jackass with a quiet vein of criminal cunning: one doesn't resent such people.

SALLY. You must be tired. We'll go to bed early. You got up so early this morning I didn't even know when you went.

BUGS. Your hand looked so fine on the pillow the way you sleep with your arm under your head, and your forehead with your hair brushed away looked so noble. It was dismal as hell and I didn't want to get up, but I knew that this was going to happen this morning and that there'd be nobody there if I didn't go—and I wanted to do something that was a little bit nearer to being like your forehead and hands.

SALLY. Did you really feel like that about me?—You make me feel ashamed: I'm not noble—I'm really a bitch. (*He kisses her, and they remain in silence, with their arms around one another. A knock at the door.*) I hope that's not anybody annoying!

BUGS. Keep 'em out if it is.

SALLY. Yes, I will. (*She opens the door; Dan, Sophie and Harry are outside, snow on their hats and coats.*) Hello, Dan —hello, Sophie! Come in.—Hello, Harry. (*They greet her and come in. Harry is carrying a brief-case; Dan, a paper-bag. They greet Bugs.*)

BUGS. Well, how's *Uncle Tom* coming on?

HARRY. We believe that *Uncle Tom* is going to be a stupendous success!

255

DAN. It's always a stupendous success, but we're going to make it a great play.

BUGS. Have you solved the bloodhound problem?

DAN. We've solved it with brilliant ingenuity! In the first place, it turns out that Smithy can bay like the Hound of the Baskervilles——

HARRY. He's absolutely bloodcurdling!

DAN. —And we're going to have puppets of the dogs and throw the silhouettes on a backdrop.—And Sally's going to be such an Eliza as has never been even imagined! — (*To Sally*) I want to talk to you about it tonight.

SALLY. Sit down.

SOPHIE. We can't stay: we've got to get back for dinner.

SALLY. Is that dinner in that bag? Let me see! (*She looks into the paper-bag.*) Oh, green peppers!—the only thing I needed for my omelet! Now I'll tell you what you must do: you must all stay to dinner here! I'm going to make a Spanish omelet!

SOPHIE. We've got liver and bacon at home.

SALLY. It'll keep. Now, you *must* stay!—You're always twitting me about not being practical. I want you to see that I can make an omelet!

SOPHIE. I don't believe that cooking is your department.

SALLY (*looking into the bag again*). And lettuce and a bottle of wine! It's just like *The Swiss Family Robinson*!—Let us borrow these things and we'll pay them back! I've got a beautiful Edam cheese, too—that matches the other things! We can talk about Eliza afterwards!

DAN (*to Sophie*). Let's stay: we can go home early.

SOPHIE. It won't be early if you get to drinking and talking!

SALLY. Now, Sophie: you and Dan sit down—and Harry, help me set the table!

SOPHIE. You better let me help you with the omelet.

SALLY. I don't want you to do a thing. You sit down

256

and forget about it. I want to prove to you I'm really a cook!

*She goes over and turns on the electric cooker and has Harry open a can of tomatoes. He brings out the folding table, puts it in front of the window-seat, unfolds the leaves, and sets it. Dan and Sophie sit down on the day-bed. Sally begins making the omelet.*

DAN (*to Bugs*). What's happening to the strike?

BUGS. The thugs beat up the pickets this morning: six pickets in the hospital, one a woman.

SALLY. They wouldn't print Tom's story, so he's thrown up his job.

DAN. Did you? Good for you! I wondered how you were getting away with it.

BUGS. I'm not any more.

DAN. Good God!—the greatest drama of the time and you can't write about it in the papers!—Why don't you do a play about it, Bugs? We've never had a real labor play in America.

BUGS. I've thought of it, but I've never had the time.

DAN. You've got the time now if you've quit your job.

BUGS. I'll have to get something else right away.

DAN (*becoming enthusiastic and excited*). No, Bugs: you must write a play about Payson—you must write it right away—and the Beech Street will put it on!

HARRY. Don't be too rash with your promises, Dan! The actors didn't get paid last week.

DAN. I'll find the money myself!

SALLY. If you'll write the play, Tom, I'll cook dinner for you every night.

BUGS. That one-acter of mine you put on didn't go over so badly, did it?

DAN. It was superb! You've got the sense of the theater——

HARRY. Sophie can be Rosa Mancowitz.

SOPHIE. I wouldn't want to play Rosa Mancowitz: I know Rosa Mancowitz too well.

BUGS. Rosa's a great woman.

SOPHIE. She's a great neurotic, if that's what you mean.

BUGS. She's one of the biggest forces in the labor movement today.

SOPHIE (*at once becoming vehement*). She has the power to hypnotize the workers and to make them lay their heads down on the chopping-block. That's what she's doing with your Payson strike!

BUGS. Even a losing fight's worth while.

SOPHIE. Why is it worth while?—when the workers will be worse off than before! The union will simply throw out your Communists and then sell out to the company!

BUGS. Well, the Communists at the present time are the only group who've got any guts.

SOPHIE. They are fanatics—Rosa Mancowitz is a fanatic! She can accomplish nothing as an organizer—nothing! I used to work with her—I know all about her! I used to be a Socialist party worker.

BUGS. Well, what in God's name do the Socialists hope to gain by backing the Farmer-Labor Party? Bob LaFollette is a million miles from socialism.

SOPHIE. But if we can get Socialist candidates elected We try to do only what is possible: the Communist attempt the impossible!

BUGS. They've succeeded pretty well in Russia.

SOPHIE. Russia! There's no socialism in Russia!

BUGS. You Socialists ought to hear the news about the October Revolution!

SOPHIE. The October Revolution was not a socialist revolution. The socialist revolution has to occur in a highl industrialized country. Russia is a feudal country!

BUGS. I've heard some wild tales about Russia, but th

Socialist idea that the October Revolution is merely a newspaper story——

SOPHIE. *No!* there is no socialism in Russia!—If you think there is socialism in Russia, you don't know what socialism is; but I know, because my father was a Social-Democrat in Germany—he was a friend of Edward Bernstein and Karl Kautsky——

BUGS. Our fathers guessed wrong about a good many things.

SOPHIE. Why aren't you a Communist yourself then?

SALLY. Dinner's ready. Bring your politics to the table!

*She directs them, and they take their places: Dan with his back to the window-seat; Sally at Dan's left; Harry next to Sally on the other side; Sophie beside Harry; and Bugs, facing Sally, at the end.*

DAN. Politics is bankrupt since the War. It's a waste of time to argue about it. You've got to deal with fundamental values.

HARRY. This soup is grand, Sally.

SALLY. I think it needs a little salt.—Tom, will you pour the wine?

*Bugs does so.*

HARRY. This is all exceedingly jolly!

*Music is heard outside; it is a band playing* It's a Hot Time in the Old Town Tonight, *which passes through Beech Street under the windows. The light of torches is seen.*

SALLY. What's this excitement?

HARRY. The election.

SALLY. I'd forgotten all about it.

DAN. That just goes to prove the truth of what I was saying. I bet you don't even know the candidates' names.

SALLY. Yes, I do.

DAN. Are you going to vote?

SALLY. I didn't register.

DAN. Did anybody here register? Is anybody going to vote?

HARRY. I thought I'd take a chance on LaFollette.

SOPHIE (*to Bugs*). I suppose you're going to vote for Foster.

BUGS. I would if I hadn't been so busy that I didn't get a chance to register.

SALLY. Well, here's to the defeat of Coolidge!

BUGS. And the defeat of Davis, too!

DAN. And here's to the success of Bugs's play, which can do more to make people see the truth than any political party!

SALLY (*to Bugs, smiling*). You're going to start on it right away.

BUGS. If God spares me, tomorrow morning.

DAN. You must make people see it just as you did!

BUGS. I'll make them see how we're all mixed up in it!

SALLY. You ought to have a torch-light parade in it marching through a starving mill-town with banners about Republican prosperity.

*Sally takes away the soup-cups and gets the omelet from the cooker.*

DAN (*as the music, turning the corner, grows fainter*). I don't mind that old tune they're playing, though. It reminds me of my youth in the West. They may use it for political rallies, but what it's singing about is still our old America.

BUGS. That old America's gone. That's their marching-song now while they trample on it.

SALLY (*bringing on the omelet*). Well, they can't trample over our omelet. They can't do anything to our salad and our wine. (*She sets the omelet on the table, then turns to the windows and pulls down the shades.*) Even the snow is covering up their tracks.

DAN. Yes: they can't do a damned thing to us! They can't rob us, because we haven't any money; they can' tempt us, because we don't want what money can buy. And they can't intimidate us, because we've been beyond good and evil, and we've come back, and all we need now to make us happy is an omelet and a bottle of wine. Here's to Sally's magnificent omelet!

*They lift their glasses and drink.*

SALLY (*sitting down*). Thank you!

HARRY. I never had one with spice in it before, Sally.

SALLY. What do you mean? There isn't any spice in it.

HARRY. Don't I taste cinnamon?

SALLY. Why, no. (*She tastes it.*) I must have grabbed the cinnamon shaker instead of the pepper shaker: they look exactly alike!

BUGS. Don't worry: it gives it an exotic tinge.

SALLY. I'm afraid it makes it taste rather sickish.—Oh, I'm so terribly sorry!

HARRY. Don't worry, Sally: it's fine!

SALLY. Well, Sophie, I guess you were right. You'd never have done that, I'm sure.

SOPHIE. Just scrape the outside off, and it's all right.

BUGS. All it needs is a touch of allspice!

DAN. Don't pay any attention to them, Sally. You've created a new and splendid kind of omelet!

BUGS. We'd better get it eaten up quickly or Dan will be trying to put it on at the Beech Street!

*They laugh about this.*

# SCENE 4

*A dark afternoon in December. Tracy Tripp has dropped in on Sally. He is sitting on the day-bed, and she, further front, in a chair. There is no fire, and she has a blanket around her legs.*

TRACY. You're depressed, aren't you?

SALLY. Not exactly: just a little dreary. It's the weather, I guess.

TRACY. Isn't it horrible!

SALLY. It's so darn bleak and black: there don't seem to be any afternoons any more.

TRACY. And cold. You ought to have a fire in the grate.

SALLY. When nobody's here to attend to it, I never seem to do anything about it.

TRACY. I had a godawful fit of gloom myself as I was coming along Eighth Street just now. I suddenly remembered that I was thirty-three, and I got to thinking about all the achievements that other people had to their credit by the time they were thirty-three. Take Christ, for example: by the time he was thirty-three, he'd really done a very remarkable thing—but I don't think I've got any talent for that sort of thing.—Then Napoleon was Emperor at thirty-three—but I haven't got the nasty ruthless character.

SALLY. Have you thought about Joan of Arc?

TRACY. I'm much too sophisticated for Joan of Arc I could never take table-tipping seriously.—And I haven' got the build for a Lincoln.—I think literature would b more in my line.

SALLY. I've always thought you could write, Tracy.

TRACY. I've been thinking of doing a novel—about two old aunts of mine who used to sew their bedclothes up like sleeping-bags. It's time I did something important.

SALLY. I've been feeling I was wasting my time lately, too. I'm not really doing anything now. If we put on *Night Watch* next, I shan't even have a part.

TRACY. Harry wants to take *Uncle Tom* uptown.

SALLY. I know, but that part of mine doesn't amount to anything.—Harry's against me now. Since Sophie and Dan have broken up, she's succeeded in getting Harry into her clutches, so that Harry's against everything that Dan wants to do.

TRACY. Harry and Sophie have a hell of a lot more business sense than Dan.

SALLY. They haven't got the real spirit of the theater though.

TRACY. But Dan *is* an idiot in some ways, and the thing mightn't have lasted as long as this if it hadn't been for Harry.

SALLY. Dan knows what he's doing: he's right about not wanting to take *Uncle Tom* uptown.

TRACY. But why?—if there's a chance of a big success.

SALLY (*very scornfully*). Oh, anybody can make a success of *Uncle Tom*—the kind of success Harry cares about!

TRACY. Well, it'll all be thrashed out, I suppose, at the meeting this afternoon.

SALLY. Yes: I'm dreading that meeting. The atmosphere's been getting sort of strained lately. We're not working together the way we used to.

TRACY. *You* mustn't get gloomy, though, my dear: it's all right for me to, but not for you. Whatever they do, they can't let *you* be eclipsed, because you're the principal thing they've got, and they know it.—Well, I must go over and see Sophie at the theater.

*He gets up and puts on his coat, pulling the collar up— wears no hat.*

SALLY. It was nice of you to come in, Tracy: you' cheered me up.

TRACY. Has Bugs Brophy gone away?

SALLY. He's been looking for a job.

TRACY. I haven't seen him around for a couple of wee

SALLY. He had to go out of town about it.

TRACY. He's been doing a labor play, hasn't he?

SALLY. He didn't have any money, and he thought ought to make some before he started.

TRACY. That's a hard line to stick to, labor—even mo unprofitable than art.

SALLY. He's more or less known as a radical now, a the editors are getting afraid of him

TRACY. That's another man I never could be: Len The only time I ever tried to use a phony name, registered at a hotel, and when they called me up fro downstairs and asked for me as Mr. Whoozis, I told the he wasn't there.—Well, I'll see you later at the meeting

SALLY. Yes. Goodby, Tracy.

*She goes to the door with him and holds it open as he leav*

TRACY (*out on the landing*). Hello, Bugs. Good God, y must have found Success!

BUGS (*appearing at the door in an enormous new fur co* Announcing Mr. Charles E. Mitchell of the National C Bank!

SALLY. Oh, Tom, where did you get that coat?

BUGS (*embracing her*). The better to hug you with, r dear!

*He has had some drinks, is in a state of exaltation.*

SALLY. But where did you get it?—Let me see.

*She turns on the switch by the door.*

BUGS. I stole it.

SALLY. Have you got a new job?

SCENE 4

Bugs. I've got a new job; but I stole it.

Sally. What do you mean? Did you really?

Bugs. I did. I stole it direct from the maker—and the manufacturer stole it from the fur-workers—and I'm going to give it back to the workers.

Sally. You're drunk.

Bugs. I'm exhilarated. There's nothing so exciting as stealing!

Sally. But you don't mean it really, Tom—tell me really, what have you done?

Bugs. Well, in the first place, I've done some articles for *American Success*—on leading industrial sons-of-bitches. —That's why I didn't come back before—I didn't want to see you till I'd finished them.—But I delivered the first two today—I thought I'd kept them objective and gotten in the labor angle, too—but by the time the editor had gone through them, I realized that I'd just contributed a couple more bucketsful of slush to the glorification of American business.—That was the first crime I committed; and the second I committed to atone for the first!

Sally. What do you mean?

Bugs. Well, I walked away from the office with the check for $1500 in my pocket, and I began to think about buying a fur coat—I've always wanted a fur coat, and yet at the same time the idea revolted me—they're what all the big business pirates wear. They skin them off the sweat-shop workers, and I said to myself that when I took money from a magazine like *American Success*, I was receiving their stolen goods! I said to myself that I was yellow, that I didn't have the guts to do my own stealing. The professional thief takes a risk, but when I write for a thing like *American Success*, I'm received by pretty girls in tony offices, and everybody is oozing good humor. Well, I used to know a professional fur-thief one time when I was writing a crime series, and he told me the way he used to

do it. So I went over to the fur district in the West Thirties
and I went into one of the biggest places and I said I wanted
to buy a coat and I talked about it and looked at coats
and kept on looking at coats till they got sick of me and
left me to myself. Then I went into the store-room at
the back and hid there behind one of the fur-racks, and
I stayed there till the shop was shut up. Then I opened
the window and grabbed a coat and got away down the
fire-escape.

SALLY. You're absolutely crazy, Bugs!—You see you've
got me calling you "Bugs" again.

BUGS. I'm not crazy, whatever you call me: you have
to do something to compensate!—I had a great feeling of
triumph when I got away with this coat. I'd been lurking
half-smothered in there with the smell of the hides of all
those poor damn muskrats and skunks that had been
slaughtered and made to masquerade as sable and chinchilla and ermine. I thought how they'd once been wild
and happy in the forest, and how they'd been killed to
make cheap furs for cheap people and to be hung up in
that damn stifling loft building! And the people in there
all day running the stitching machines and pounding down
the furs on the boards!—they use up the animals for their
skins and the human beings for their skill, and they shut
them all up in these loft buildings or in offices that might
as well be lofts! When I looked out the window at the
back, there was nothing but the blank wall of the next
building, and the walls of the stock-room were blank
the same way—and I felt the negation of the city—the
negation of everything that's human!—the burden of
deadness and boredom that the people work harder
than the beavers or the squirrels to pile up on their own
backs!—

SALLY. Oh, I know: it's horrible, it's hideous! That's
just the way I've felt today!

BUGS. I felt when I broke out of that fur-loft that I was breaking out of the whole goddam system!

SALLY. But suppose you'd been caught!

BUGS. I'd have said that I was just a reporter doing a story on how easy it was to steal.

SALLY. Suppose they find out about it.

BUGS. They won't. It'll be a long time before they miss one coat, and I'm going to give it to the charities. I stole it to give it back to the people who made it.

SALLY. You can't steal them all and give them back!

BUGS. No: it's only for my own self-respect! They've taught us to treat property as sacred, and even when we think we're rebels against them, they make us protect their interests—they make us keep their laws when they don't keep them themselves! Well, I've proved to myself I'm not scared of them—to hell with their moral system!—And what you and I are going to do now is take this money that I've expiated and spend it!

SALLY. You mustn't spend it all right away: you must save it so you can write your play. If you were getting your convictions on paper, you wouldn't have to be stealing coats.

BUGS. I had to make some money, Sally. I don't mind abandoning my family, but I don't want to see them starve. —They haven't called up here or anything, have they!

SALLY. No.—Why should they?—

BUGS. Gracie usually locates me and calls me up and tells me that one of the kids is sick—and then, when I go home, the kid is all right.

SALLY. Well, you'd better get in touch with her right away. It wouldn't be nice if she came here.

BUGS. I'm going to, and there's plenty of money for everybody, and you and I are going to take some of that money and we're going to do again the whole thing we did last summer!

SALLY. I can't get away from the theater—not till *Uncle Tom* has closed.

BUGS. Yes, you can: get somebody else to play Eliza. It's no part for you anyway.

SALLY. I might, I suppose. They're apparently going to revive *Night Watch* for the next production, and there's no part in that for me.

BUGS. You really oughtn't to be fooling around with these high-school theatricals anyway!

SALLY. It does seem rather amateurish sometimes.

BUGS. They've done some beautiful things, but the whole business hangs by a shoe-string—they never can give you a real production.

SALLY. I know.

BUGS. Let me get you a job uptown.

SALLY. I've had one or two offers of parts uptown, but I wanted to stay with the Beech Street.

BUGS. You ought to have more of a chance, though: you've stuck down here too long. When we come back, I'll get you something on Broadway. I know a lot of theater people. And in the meantime, tell them that you're leaving the cast!

SALLY. I'll ask them at the meeting this afternoon.

BUGS. We'll go up to Quebec and stay at the Frontenac.

SALLY. Why don't we go to some place in the country where you really can be quiet and work?

BUGS. I can work up there!

SALLY. You must somewhere.

BUGS. Now you go and pack your things—because we're going to a hotel tonight! It's too damned cold here.

SALLY. I've got to be at the theater at 8.

BUGS. We'll just have time. Pack your suitcase now, and while you're at your meeting, I'll go and get mine, and I'll meet you at the theater, and we'll have dinner at the Vanderpool.

SALLY. All right!

*She gets up and takes an old suitcase out of the closet and starts packing her things in it.*

BUGS. We'll go where the world is so bright inside that we won't care how black it is outside! I'll get some champagne, and we'll have it in our room!

SALLY. I'd better wait till after the show for that or I won't be able to cross the ice tonight.

BUGS. I suppose I ought to call up Gracie and tell her that some cash is on the way. She probably has the police out looking for me.

*He goes to the phone.*

SALLY. It would be fine if they found you with that coat!

BUGS. Flushing 5461. (*To Sally*) They won't.—Hello. —Hello, Billy. How are you? . . . What? . . . What did she do? What did she drink? (*Evidently shocked by what he hears. Sally stops packing, to pay attention.*) Did you send for a doctor? . . . Oh, hello, Alice: what's happened? . . . You've got a doctor there. . . . What does he say? . . . He has? . . . Yes: I'll come . . . I'll come right over. I'll be there right away! (*He hangs up.*)

SALLY. What's the matter?

BUGS. Gracie drank carbolic acid.

SALLY. Is—is she seriously ill?

BUGS. I don't believe so—they've used the stomach pump on her.

SALLY. You must go over there right away.

BUGS (*putting on the fur coat*). Damn Alice!—She's Gracie's sister: she took great satisfaction in telling me—she probably worked deliberately on Gracie's mind, making her feel how miserable she was!

SALLY. Do you think you'd better wear that coat? They won't be getting the police in, will they?

BUGS. No.—What the hell do I care anyway?—Wouldn't

it just work out like this?—That was the boy I had first on the phone. He hates me. He'll always hate me!—Well, goodby, most beautiful, most noble! (*He takes her hands, then kisses her.*) I'm sorry this has turned out so sour.

SALLY. Goodby. You better go right away. (*He opens the door and goes.*) Goodby.—Call me up and let me know how things are.

BUGS (*on the way downstairs*). I will.

*She comes back and stands a moment dazed and distressed, then begins unpacking the suitcase and putting the things back in their places. There is a knock at the door. She hastily closes the suitcase and puts it in the closet, then goes to open the door.*

SALLY. Oh, hello, Signe.

SIGNE (*coming in*). Would you mind if we had the meeting in your room, Sally? There's no heat in the place above the theater——Tracy forgot to order the coal.

SALLY. I'm afraid I can't come to the meeting, Signe.

SIGNE. You *must* come: we've got to decide about the next production and about taking *Uncle Tom* uptown. It's really awfully important.

SALLY. I know: but something dreadful has just happened.

SIGNE. What's the matter?

SALLY. Bugs Brophy's wife has just tried to commit suicide.

SIGNE. Oh?

*Sally sits down on the day-bed and Signe sits down beside her.*

SALLY. He just called up from here, and they told him about it.

SIGNE. Well, *you* mustn't feel responsible.—Is she all right?

SALLY. I don't know: she was still alive when he talked to them.

SIGNE. Any suburban housewife married to Bugs Brophy would have been sure to try to commit suicide sooner or

270

later. Sonya Katchalov tried to commit suicide when Ilya first fell in love with me, and I felt terribly about it, but now she's happily married and working in an uptown picture gallery, and she high-hats the life out of me when she sees me.

SALLY. I feel sick.

SIGNE. Of course you do!

SALLY. I don't feel like seeing people.

SIGNE. I'm sorry I told them to come here—but I think you ought to take part in the meeting.—You can't do anything about the other thing, and this will help you keep your mind off it. We need you: there's a real crisis. Harry's working openly against Dan and has more or less gotten Tracy and Fred on his side.

SALLY. I know: but I can't seem to care much.

SIGNE. You must cast your vote on our side, anyway. Sophie's attached herself to Harry since she and Dan broke up, and it's really split the group into two factions.

SALLY. That's another thing that's my fault, I suppose! Dan's been coming here tight lately because he was afraid to go home to Sophie—and Sophie's been sore at me about it. I couldn't help it: he'd come in and pass out, and I'd have to let him stay here all night.

SIGNE. Well, you must stand by Dan and me!

SALLY. It's all too silly and detestable!—I'm sick of the whole thing! The idea that people can't leave each other free!—that one person can't be different things to different people—that several people can't share one person!

*A knock at the door.*

SIGNE. Well, please stick by us today: we've got to keep the theater together!

SALLY (*getting up to go to the door*). I'm not sure there's any use is trying to have a group like this if things like that can break it up! I don't feel like standing up for anything.

*She opens the door to Harry, Sophie, Dan and Tracy. Harry, as usual, carries his brief case.*

HARRY. Hello, Sally! we thought maybe you'd have a fire. The coal supply has given out over there.

SALLY. It's not very warm here.

HARRY. Compared to the theater, it's tropical. (*He takes off his coat.*) Well, is everybody here?

SIGNE. Everybody but Fred.

HARRY. We might begin without him, don't you think?

SIGNE. No: I think we ought to wait for Fred. He'll be here: he told me he would.

*Signe remains on the day-bed, and Dan sits down beside her. Sophie sits on the opposite side of the fire, and Tracy on the nearer side. Harry remains standing. Sally stretches out on the window-seat and reclines looking out the window during the greater part of the conversation.*

HARRY. He understands the situation. We can get his vote later.

SOPHIE. I saw him going into Scarlatti's, so he's probably good and drunk by this time, and no use to anybody anyway.

SIGNE. He promised me to keep sober.

HARRY. Fred's promises, I fear, are writ in water—or rather, in alcohol.

DAN. I think we ought to wait for Fred, Harry.

HARRY. We mustn't take all night this time, however.

DAN. Why shouldn't we take all night, if we need to?

SIGNE. Yes: there are some very important questions to be decided.

SOPHIE. The great curse of this group is too much talk we talk when we ought to be working.

DAN. I'm not sure we don't work when we ought to be talking, Sophie! There are some things that have to be settled before there's any point in working at all, and they can only be settled by discussion.

HARRY. It's just that we sometimes tend to get a little metaphysical, Dan—and tonight we ought to think about practical matters.

*Fred's loud knock at the door.*

SIGNE. Come in.

*Fred comes in.*

FRED. Am I late? I'm sorry!—I'm sober though!—I just refused a double cognac, offered me by a prospective patron!— (*He sits down next to Sophie, at her right.*) I'm trying to sell him the idea of translating Rabelais into modern American slang. Don't you think that's a wonderful idea? He really seems very much interested. He took me out to Scarlatti's and——

SOPHIE. Is that the cognac you refused I smell?

FRED. No, that's the cognac I drank, but I refused the second one—really I did! I refused a double *fine* that was offered me by this wealthy connoisseur who's making overtures to be my Mæcenas!

SOPHIE. How heroic!

FRED. Don't insult me, Sophie! I've got a lightning brain, you know, even when I'm intoxicated!—

HARRY. Well, let's proceed with the business of the meeting. (*General silence*) First I want to lay before the group a statement of our present financial situation. (*He produces a slip of paper from his pocket and refers to it.*) We started the year with $1964.75—almost $2000—and we lost on the *Zinc Princess* $1160.55——

SIGNE. It seems to me, Harry, that if any financial statements are going to be made, *I* am the person to make them. I'm the Treasurer.

HARRY. In my capacity of Business Manager, I was just summing up the general situation.

DAN. I think that any financial statement ought to come from Signe, Harry.

SIGNE. It's true that we lost money on *The Zinc*

*Princess,* but we're making money on *Uncle Tom*——

SOPHIE. The question is, why ask for another big loss by putting on a Greek play?

DAN. That's just what we're here for, to take losses, Sophie.

HARRY. Well, now, Dan, just let me say a word about that. The Beech Street is an idealistic organization: we all know that. That's why we're interested in it, that's why we stick by it, that's why we're willing to take losses, if we have to. Well and good: that's as it should be. But why should we take losses when we *don't* have to? If we go on putting ourselves in a hole, we'll have to quit altogether.

SIGNE. What makes you think we won't put ourselves in a hole if we take *Uncle Tom* uptown? That theater will cost $600 a week, and if we don't fill it every night, we'll be in a worse hole than ever. We'll simply have two money-losing theaters instead of one.

HARRY. Eddie Applebaum says that we've got an excellent chance of success, and he's about as hard-boiled as they come.

DAN. Eddie Applebaum be damned!—the Beech Street Players was founded to get away from the Eddie Applebaums.

SIGNE. Everybody's sick to death of *Night Watch*—this would be the third time it had been revived.

DAN. *Night Watch* is a good honest little play, but we've produced it and put it over, and we're done with it. We've got to go on to something else.

SOPHIE. Tell them your proposals, Harry.

HARRY. Well, what I was going to propose was simply this: Why not take *Uncle Tom* uptown—why not try it for a week or two, anyway, and—put on *Night Watch* down here, with Fred's *Don Juan in Bethlehem* for a curtain-raiser——

FRED. I've got to play Don Juan, Harry!

HARRY. That's up to Dan.

DAN (*sulkily*). Thanks.—I've got to see *Don Juan* re-written before I want to see it played at all.

FRED (*aggrieved*). You don't appreciate my blank verse, Dan!

DAN. I appreciate your blank verse, Fred, but I don't approve of Marlowe's blank verse when it turns up in your plays.

FRED. I'm the reincarnation of Marlowe, Dan. Why is it strange that we should think the same thoughts and even express ourselves in the same tropes?

HARRY. Let me go on with what I was saying. I was suggesting a revival of *Night Watch*. Now, there isn't any part for Sally—there's only one woman's part——

SIGNE. Sophie's part: yes.

HARRY. But I've got a really brilliant idea! Why not have Sally double in *Uncle Tom*?—Why not have her even do *three* parts if she feels she can take them on?—She might do Eliza and Mrs. St. Clair and Simon Legree's girl-friend, all three. She'd make a brilliant job of it, I'm sure. Think of the range you'd have, Sally!—And another advantage would be that it would enable us to save a couple of salaries, since everybody's getting paid the same amount.

SIGNE. I don't think we ought to just shove Ellen Winters out.

HARRY. She's really inadequate for the part—she was the only member of the cast who got bad notices.

SIGNE. I don't approve of doing things in that way.

DAN. Most certainly not! Every actor in the Beech Street Theater has a right to the part he's rehearsed and opened in.

SALLY. I wouldn't take Ellen Winters' part for any-thing! She has one of the most beautiful voices I've ever heard, whatever the reviewers may say!

DAN. There's one reason which we haven't discussed

why I'm absolutely flatly opposed to taking *Uncle Tom* uptown, and that is that if it's done on Broadway, it'll be done there as a burlesque. I'm absolutely opposed to burlesquing it, and I have been all along. *Uncle Tom's Cabin* is a serious play—it had a part in changing the course of this country's history—and it can still be made a powerful play. I *made* it a powerful play, and the audiences in the first week were moved by its pathos and horror. There was scarcely a titter or a giggle throughout the whole performance. But something has happened to it—I don't know who's responsible, but now they laugh at every other line. As I say, I don't know where the inspiration for this horsing and clowning has come from, but I feel pretty certain that the actors haven't been playing for laughs like that without the definite encouragement of somebody!

HARRY. You haven't been around, Dan: when we wanted you to jack things up, you weren't there.

SOPHIE. You've been off on a spree for three weeks. Somebody had to attend to the production!

DAN. Well, somebody debauched and debased it! Somebody betrayed me and betrayed the Beech Street and betrayed everything the Beech Street stands for! Somebody betrayed our vital relation to the history of America itself!

HARRY (*facetiously*). Is General Benedict Arnold among us?

SIGNE. Dan's right—he's absolutely right about the burlesquing business: the performance has lost all its dignity!

HARRY. Well, the issue seems to be clearly drawn, and I suggest that in order not to waste further time, we take a vote on the two programs immediately: on the one hand, to move *Uncle Tom* uptown and put *Night Watch* on again down here; and, on the other, to put on *Lysistrata* and to take *Uncle Tom* off—even though it may be running to capacity houses. That's your idea, isn't it, Dan?

DAN. My idea is that the Beech Street Theater should

stand as a positive force that loses, if need be, against all the negative forces that gain!

FRED. Damn it, Dan: you've got a great spirit!—but you think that art's got to be unsuccessful. Shakespeare tickled the groundlings: why should I be contemptuous of Broadway?

DAN. You're tickling them the wrong way, Fred: they think your Simon Legree is funny.

SIGNE. Why not have two Topsies the way they do in the tent-shows?

HARRY. Well, let's vote on it. Are you ready to vote on it, Fred?

SIGNE. I'm not going to let this question be put to a vote till I've had a chance to express myself!—

SALLY (*sitting up on the window-seat*). And before we go any further, I want to say very definitely that unless Dan's program is carried out, I resign tonight.

HARRY. The understanding was, Sally, that every program was to be voted on.

SOPHIE. We didn't realize that some of our members might put their personal ambitions above the good of the organization!

SALLY. I don't care about *Lysistrata*—play it yourself, if you want to!

HARRY (*tactful*). Of course we understand, Sally, that your feeling is perfectly disinterested——

SALLY. It *is* disinterested, Harry: I care about the theater much more than about playing any particular part.

HARRY. But I really can't see, Sally, that there's anything particularly sinister about moving *Uncle Tom* to another theater.

SALLY (*more and more in earnest and excited*). What's particularly sinister about it is that, as Dan says, it's cheapening *Uncle Tom*. We don't want to cheapen anything! This whole world we live in is cheap enough already, and what we ought to be doing is trying to give people some image of the dignity and beauty of life!—

DAN. And that's why we want to do *Lysistrata*.

SALLY. Yes: that's why we ought to do *Lysistrata*—we've got to fight for life itself against all the ugliness and deadness the way Lysistrata did!

DAN. We've got to fight for the intellectual light that comes down to us from ancient Greece through all the darkness and wreckage of history, and which will still be burning when Broadway and its works are deader than the Coliseum!

SALLY. Yes: we've got to fight for those things against this black overpowering city. We've got to show people that life wasn't always like this and that it doesn't have to be always like this—because human beings are able to create something better than these great square mountains of stone with wretched squalor down in the cracks between them—and banging typewriters and squealing motor-horns and silly electric signs. Everybody else is caught in all that; but we've got to manage to keep out of it. There are lots of people in a place like New York who want to do fine things and brave things, but they can't because they're already involved—they're like animals caught in bear traps, trying to drag the traps and only skinning their legs to the bone. And *we've* got to keep out of the traps!

DAN. Every second-rate ambition is a trap!

SIGNE. And all this personal business is another kind of trap!

SALLY. And we've got to watch our step every moment!—

DAN. Because all the great artists who are dead depend on us to see through what they worked for!

SIGNE. And when young boys of genius like Boag and Keith Mitchell have only got us to give them a hearing!

SALLY. When all the human life that's been imprisoned and degraded and harried around in a city like this depends

278

on us to speak for it and to help it to speak for itself!
*There is a moment's silence.*

FRED. You make me ashamed, Sally!—You make me feel that I've been a bemused egoist!—You and Dan are absolutely right: we've got to bring fire like Prometheus: the Eighth Street car-tracks are our Caucasus and the Sixth Avenue El is our vulture!

SALLY. Why don't *you* play Lysistrata, Sophie?—you'd be better than I would, I think: you've got a more impressive presence.

SOPHIE. I don't want to play it, thank you: I'm not bawdy enough!

SALLY. Well, why not do Keith Mitchell's play next, then? There's a splendid part in that for Sophie—and a part for me, too.

SIGNE. Shall we put Sally's proposal to a vote?—Keith Mitchell's play and we close *Uncle Tom.*

HARRY. I don't want to seem indifferent to Sally's eloquence—and to Dan's eloquence—because as a matter of fact I've been very much moved by them—but I have certain doubts about Keith Mitchell's play——

DAN. So have I, Harry, but we'll get him to fix it up—and I think that's the real solution. We can do *Lysistrata* in the spring.

SIGNE. Let's vote then. All in favor say, "Ay." (*Dan, Signe, Tracy, Fred and Sally hold up their hands and say, "Ay".*) Very good: that's the program then! (*She gets up.*) Listen, Dan: I want you to call a rehearsal tomorrow and put the performance back the way you want it to be.

DAN. I will: I shouldn't have let it slump.

SIGNE. Are you doing anything for dinner, Sophie?

SOPHIE. I'm having dinner with Harry.

SIGNE. Let me butt in on it, will you? I've been wanting to talk to you both.

*Signe, Sophie and Harry leave. Fred and Tracy have gone*

*over to talk to Sally. Dan remains standing in front of the fire.*

HARRY (*waving as he goes*). Good night, Sally!

TRACY. You certainly rebounded after touching bottom —I mean, after this afternoon!

FRED. That was true greatness, Sally!—greater than any part you ever played on the stage!

TRACY. Good night, my dear. (*Kissing her*) I'm going to be a better boy all the rest of my life, and the change in my character will be all due to you!

SALLY (*grinning*). I hope you will, Tracy.

FRED. My Mæcenas is waiting for me with a double *fine*: I mustn't let him down! Good night, Sally!

SALLY. Good night, Fred!

*Smiling, she sees them out the door.*

DAN (*when they have gone, as she comes over toward him*). You were wonderful, Sally: you turned the meeting.

SALLY. I don't think Fred and Tracy would have voted against you.

DAN. They would have if it hadn't been for you.

SALLY. Dan: why did you break with Sophie?

DAN. Oh, I don't know: it got to be impossible.

SALLY. You must be nice to her. You mustn't let her hate you. You must make her be good in this play.

DAN. I will, if she'll let me.—Sally!

*He kisses her.*

SALLY. Oh don't, Dan: I don't want you to do that! I don't want to be made love to: I've had enough of love!

DAN. This is for the prophetess and the artist—for gratitude and in deep humility.

SALLY. Oh, Dan: I kiss you like that, too!

*She returns his kiss with emotion.*

# SCENE 5

*February: a dreary and damp afternoon. The heater is on, but there is still no fire.*

*Sally is lying on the day-bed, earnestly studying her part. A knock at the door: she gets up and opens it.*


SALLY. Oh, Arthur!

ARTHUR. Hello.

SALLY. Come in.

ARTHUR (*shaking hands with her, a little awkward*). How are you?

SALLY (*smiling*). I'm fine.—How are you?

ARTHUR. All right.—How are you getting along with *Lysistrata*?

SALLY. Pretty well, I guess. It's a marvelous part.

ARTHUR. I know it—and you're just the person to do it.

SALLY (*going back to the day-bed*). Oh, Arthur, I'm glad you came! I was afraid I was never going to see you again!

*She sits down on the day-bed, and he sits down beside her.*

ARTHUR (*a little less constrained*). I'm awfully glad to see you.—You're not free for dinner tonight, are you?

SALLY. Why—yes, I think so.—Dan Frink may come in.

ARTHUR. I see.—Are you living with Dan now?

SALLY. No: I'm living here alone.

ARTHUR. I see.—Well, do have dinner with me, won't you, if you can?

SALLY. All right.

ARTHUR. What happened to your newspaper man?

SALLY. Nothing. He's all right.

ARTHUR. He's gone away, I hear.

SALLY. Yes: he had to go to Havana.

ARTHUR. He's gone back to his wife, I understand.

SALLY. She's been ill, and he had to take her away.

ARTHUR (*who has been prowling around the room as he talks*). You ought to have a fire. Doesn't it work?

SALLY. I'm all right with the gas-heater: it's getting warmer. (*He looks into the coal-scuttle, which is empty.*) How did you get along with that house on Long Island you were doing?

ARTHUR. Very unsatisfactorily. The people are absolute idiots. We had to make three different sets of plans, and the ones that they finally approved were cockeyed. The architect has no more chance than anybody else when it comes to working for stupid rich people.—I haven't had any fun out of my work, and I've missed you perfectly frightfully.

SALLY. But your brother must have been relieved that you haven't been hanging around Greenwich Village?

ARTHUR. To hell with my brother! I've resigned from the club, so I never have to see him at all.

SALLY. You shouldn't have done that, should you? You'll miss it, won't you?

ARTHUR (*seeing a glass jar full of large pills on the table by the day-bed*). I know what those pills mean!

SALLY. You notice everything, don't you, Arthur?

ARTHUR. That looks ominous: I think I ought to know about it.

SALLY. No: it doesn't concern you at all.

ARTHUR. How do you know?

SALLY. Because I know.

ARTHUR. What will you do if it doesn't work?

SALLY. None of your business, Arthur.

ARTHUR. After all, it's a pretty serious matter. You must be beyond the stage for pills. Have you been to see a doctor?

SALLY. Yes.

ARTHUR. What does he say?

SALLY. He's going to do something about it, if necessary.

ARTHUR. Who did you go to: Hirschbein?

SALLY. Yes.

ARTHUR. Good God! I wouldn't trust him to dress a scratch. You'd better let me send you to a place I know.

SALLY. Don't worry. I'll be all right.

ARTHUR. Your other boy friend's no help if he's gone away to Cuba. You can't even pay for it, can you?

SALLY. He's going to send me money.—He may even be back now.

ARTHUR. Oh.—But suppose he doesn't come back and suppose he doesn't send you money. He's a bum, I understand.

SALLY. No, he's not: he's in a difficult situation.

ARTHUR. So are you. You'd better let me take care of you.

SALLY. You're very sweet, Arthur, but I don't want you to help me any more.

ARTHUR. Why not, when it may be my fault?

SALLY. The only thing is that if I'm going to do it, I suppose I ought to get it over before *Lysistrata* opens.

ARTHUR. You should! If you're ill, you won't be able to open. Let me find out about that place from this friend of mine.

*He starts to go over to the phone.*

SALLY. The phone's cut off. (*A knock at the door.*) See who it is, will you, Arthur?

*Arthur goes over and opens the door for Signe. She carries a cash-box under her arm.*

ARTHUR. Hello, Signe.

SIGNE. Oh, hello, Arthur! I haven't seen you for ages!— Hello, Sally: how are you?

SALLY. All right, I guess.

ARTHUR (*to Sally*). I'll go out and call up about that and then come back.

SALLY. No, don't: stay here now! You can do it when we go out later.

SIGNE. Yes, stay here, Arthur: I want to see you.

SALLY. Sit down, both of you. All I've got to offer you is gin. I haven't even got ginger ale.

*She goes over to the closet and gets out a couple of tumblers and a bottle of gin about half full.*

SIGNE. Just give me a little straight.

*She takes off her coat and sits down on the couch.*

SALLY. How are things at the theater?

*She pours out a slug and gives it to Signe, then looks at Arthur, who nods. She pours out two more shots.*

SIGNE. Not so good.

SALLY. What's the matter?

SIGNE. The same old situation, only worse. Harry and Sophie have combined again, and they're working against Dan and me. They want to revive *Uncle Tom* and do it in an uptown theater. (*She tosses off the gin.*)

SALLY. I thought we'd fought that all out.

SIGNE. They're threatening to do it on their own.

SALLY. How can they if the rest of us stand out against it?

SIGNE. The atmosphere at the theater is bad. Everybody's getting demoralized. I can't get anybody to talk any sense. Dan's tight, and Fred's tight—and Fred believes he's the Messiah, so he's no use at all any more. Harry has been telling everybody that the trouble is all my fault, because I've been mismanaging the finances.

SALLY. What a worm Harry is!

SIGNE. Of course the actors haven't been paid for four weeks. But then I haven't been paid for six and neither has Dan.

ARTHUR. Harry Greenaway's a terrible type: he's the

professionally affable guy who gets to be class secretary at college.

SIGNE. He's completely lost faith in Dan since Keith Mitchell's play's done so badly, and Sophie is sore because she got bad notices.

SALLY. She wouldn't let Dan direct her.

SIGNE. I know it: there ought to be a rule in little theaters that every member of the group has to sleep with the same person all season.

*A knock. Arthur goes to the door. Sally looks nervously expectant.*

SIGNE (*to Sally*). Bugs Brophy hasn't come back yet?

SALLY. I don't know.

ARTHUR (*at the door*). Hello, Tracy.

*Tracy comes in.*

SALLY. You're still with us, aren't you, Tracy?

TRACY. What do you mean?

SALLY. You haven't joined the Greenaway faction?

TRACY. Oh, no: certainly not. But I'm afraid I'm leaving the theater altogether.

SALLY. What do you mean, Tracy?

TRACY. I'm getting married.

SALLY. Why, Tracy?

SIGNE. You oughtn't to spring a thing like that on us right out of a clear sky!

TRACY. It happened very suddenly.

SALLY. Who is it, Tracy?

SIGNE. Tell us!

TRACY. A girl named Dianthe Sayre. You don't know her: I only met her last week myself.

ARTHUR. I know her: but I didn't know she was the marrying kind.

TRACY. She's not: this is merely a friendly arrangement. She wants to go abroad to meet a girl friend, and her family, being stuffy, won't let her travel alone—so she has to do this to get away. I'm going to spend the summer in the other girl's villa at Villefranche while they take a trip to the Congo.

*He sits down in a chair on the left of the day-bed.*

SALLY. Why, Tracy! A villa at Villefranche is the only thing you've needed to make you perfect!

TRACY. You must all come over and see me.

SALLY. But what are we going to do without you?

TRACY. I'm sorry: I don't want to desert you, but I've been knocking about like this for so long, leading this Bohemian life, that it's high time I settled down to some kind of respectable existence.

SIGNE. You'll just be being kept, Tracy!

TRACY. Not at all: I'll have to work extremely hard— I'll have to spend the whole summer writing letters from Dianthe to her family, telling about our life together at Villefranche. It will tax my creative powers to their limit.

*Fred's knock at the door.*

SALLY. Come in, Fred!

FRED (*bursting in*). Hello, Sally! Hello, Signe! Hello, Tracy! Hello, Arthur!—What do you think: I've got a convert to my religion!

ARTHUR. This is a day of great good fortune for everybody!

SIGNE. Who's your convert, Fred?

FRED. The little newsdealer on the corner: he's very much interested in my booklet!

ARTHUR. He can't read English, can he?

FRED. Damn it, Arthur! my religion's for the ignorant as well as for the lettered!

ARTHUR. What *is* your new religion?

FRED. Give me a drink, Arthur, and I'll tell you!

*Arthur pours Fred a drink, then looks at Tracy.*

ARTHUR. Tracy?

TRACY. Yes, thanks.

286

*Arthur hands the drinks. In the meantime, the other conversation goes on.*

SIGNE. I thought Harry was keeping you in drinks, Fred.

SALLY. You mustn't sell us out, Fred!

FRED. I'll soon have to be withdrawing from the theater, ally, because the influence of my religion is being felt, nd people will be coming to me, and I'll have to get way!—

ARTHUR. What is your doctrine, Fred?

FRED. Why, it's absolutely new, Arthur! It's a completely new religion I've created!—there's never been anything like it! All the religions of the past have either mortified the flesh in the interests of the spirit or have stinted the spirit in the interests of the flesh: and this is the first religion in history that has promoted the highest development of the spirit and at the same time facilitated the ecstasies of the flesh!

ARTHUR. That sounds like a wonderful arrangement.

FRED. There's never been anything like it, Arthur! and when people begin to find out about it, I'm going to have to go away because I don't want to have to manage a big religious movement! I'm going to go out to Santa Fé and get a little cabin in the desert and live there in dignity and simplicity—and if people come out there to see me, they'll just find me there in the desert, and I'll just tell them what I know patiently and simply and sincerely!—

ARTHUR. I'm afraid they'll be wearing a track to your door.

FRED. I'll just talk to them simply as I'm talking to you. No thaumaturgy! no signs and wonders!—no healing the sick or loaves and fishes!—though I really have a sort of mesmeric gift which might make it possible for me to do some of those things—you know, I really feel sometimes, Arthur, as if I did have a sort of an occult power!—used to hypnotize Marcella, you know—when we were

first married, that is—I wasn't able to later on, becaus
she'd oppose her will to mine.—But sometimes I've actu
ally felt as if I could make the crippled walk—and caus
people to see spirits and have visions!—And yet I know
it's wrong!—I mustn't do it!—my religion must succeed
without miracles!—it must impose itself upon peopl
through its inherent divine harmony!—and I sometime
think that my supernatural power must come from som
evil Demiurge who is trying to get possession of me!—
Wouldn't it be terrible if some malignant Demiurge shoul
secretly enter into me and compel me to perform miracle
of black magic—and if I should become drugged wit
power and allow all my influence for good to be turne
into an influence for evil!—if I should use my extra-huma
powers just to make people give me money and compe
women to yield to me!—Wouldn't that be terrible!—
and yet sometimes I feel, when my evil Demiurge come
muttering in my ear, that it might really happen if I don'
look out! (*He picks up the gin bottle.*)—Do you mind if
finish this, Sally?

SIGNE. You *have* got an evil Demiurge, Fred, and hi
name is Harry Greenaway!

FRED. Harry wants to put on my miracle-play, Signe—
and you and Dan scoff at it and want me to emasculat
it. Yet my play *Don Juan at Bethlehem* is an integral pai
of my religion: it's a symbol of the flesh and the spirit!

SALLY. You know very well, Fred, that this religion o
yours is just an alibi for fear your new play won't pa
out! The last play you wrote, you had prize-fighting fo
an alibi, and you nearly got yourself killed.

FRED. Yes, there's danger! there's danger!—The Theo
sophists will be wild!—they may try to do me physica
violence!—I may become a martyr to my own religion

ARTHUR. It's much better to have other people be th
martyrs.

288

FRED. You rogues: you don't take me seriously!—but 'll drink with you just the same!—

*He sits down on the window-seat. Dan Frink comes in without knocking.*

SALLY (*cordially*). Hello, Dan.

ARTHUR (*coming to shake hands with him*). Hello, Dan.

DAN (*shaking hands but not paying much attention to him: he has been drinking*). Hello, Arthur.— (*Addressing himself to Sally*) I'm going to have a real Acropolis!—Smithy is going to build one on the stage—and when you make your great speech about war, you'll seem to be standing on the peak of the world!

*He sits down at Sally's right on the edge of the day-bed. Sally has moved back and put pillows behind her. Signe is sitting on the edge at her left.*

SIGNE. Is it going to cost any more money?

DAN. No: he's going to make it out of old lumber. But I want a concrete dome for the sky, Signe! I can't get the deep blue I want with an ordinary canvas backdrop.

SIGNE. Don't talk about concrete domes! We'll barely make the grade as it is.

DAN. How are we off?

SIGNE. Very badly. The actors haven't been paid for four weeks——

FRED. We got paid today, Signe.

SIGNE. What do you mean? You didn't get paid.

FRED. Harry paid us.

SIGNE. Harry paid you? Where did he get the money?

FRED. I don't know, but he paid us a week's salary.

SIGNE. *What?* (*To Dan*) Did you know about this?

DAN. Not a word.

SIGNE. That just shows you how things are going! Harry has no right to pay salaries without consulting us. I had to go uptown this afternoon, and I left him and Sophie in the box-office, and they just took advantage of

my being away.—I'll bet they used the gate! (*She take*
*a key out of her purse and opens the cash-box in her lap.*
They've taken all the cash!

DAN. Is it empty?

SIGNE. There's a few pennies and nickels!

DAN. Well, this means just one thing: Harry and Sophi
leave the group! Pay them their own salaries and let the
go. We'll have it out with them tonight.

SIGNE. We can't pay them. We've got practically noth
ing in the bank. How could they have paid a week's salary
Fred? We couldn't have taken that much in. Were ther
many in the house this afternoon?

FRED. The house was a gaping void, Signe—but Harr
must have got hold of some money, because he offere
to pay the cast every week if they'd come uptown wit
*Uncle Tom's Cabin.*

SIGNE. What!

FRED. The actors have got to live, Signe! I've been abso
lutely destitute myself! I've had to exert all my person
magnetism to prevent my Hogarthian landlady from hur
ing me into the street. If I hadn't talked to her about m
religion——

SIGNE. Oh, forget your religion, Fred! Why didn't yo
tell us about this?

FRED. I thought you knew about it, Signe. He call
the whole cast together and talked to them——

DAN. What did he say precisely?

FRED. What it came down to, Dan, was that we cou
come uptown with him and get paid or stay down he
and work for nothing.

SIGNE. And you were ready to go, I suppose?

FRED. I was going to talk to you and Dan about it, Sign

SIGNE. And were the rest of them ready to go?

FRED. They were debating it.

SIGNE. Where did he get the money?

TRACY. From Eddie Applebaum, I imagine. He's the person who's been egging Harry on.

DAN. Very good: we end the group today!—and we organize another group with nobody we can't depend on! We'll start again from scratch!

SIGNE. We've done that so many times already!

DAN. There's no reason we shouldn't do it every year! Let Harry go about his business. When he came to us, he was a second-line dramatic critic on a second-rate evening paper. Let him be a second-rate producer!

SIGNE. What about actors, though, if he takes them all away with him?

DAN. Some of them will stick with us—and besides, there are always plenty of actors—get them off the streets —that's the best way—the way the Abbey Theater did! —They talk about a bigger theater!—Why, what we need is a *smaller* theater! How about that room above Scarlatti's?

TRACY. Scarlatti's not going to have that place next year.

SIGNE. No: his landlord has played him a dirty trick: he's let him increase the value of the place by making all kinds of improvements, and now he's going to turn him out and get a higher rent for it.

TRACY. It seems that the Village landlords are making a practice of that—and if you can't live cheaply down here, there's no point in living here at all.

SALLY (*scornfully*). You and your rich Lesbian!

ARTHUR. Why don't you get Dianthe Sayre to put up little money for the Beech Street?

SIGNE. How about it, Tracy?

TRACY. I'm afraid I don't know her well enough yet.

ARTHUR. Speaking of Scarlatti's, Sally, how about a little dinner?

SALLY. I don't want to go out now, Arthur: I think we ought to talk about the theater.

ARTHUR (*rather pleased with the situation and knowing that the others will have to go presently on account of the evening performance*). All right. Suppose I go out and get some sandwiches.

SALLY. Yes, why don't you do that?

FRED. And some gin, Arthur! Get some gin!

ARTHUR (*to Sally*). What would you like?

SALLY. Oh, let me see!—Chicken and tomato, I guess.

ARTHUR. O.K.

*He puts on his hat and coat and goes out.*

FRED. Listen, Dan: I'll tell you what to do! I'll tell you how we can get a theater cheaply!—Rent a haunted house!— (*To Arthur*) Don't forget the gin!

DAN. Why a haunted house?

SIGNE. Isn't the Beech Street spooky enough?

FRED. Because the rents on haunted houses are always low!—they're glad to have people live in them!—I lived in a haunted house once, down on Minetta Lane: the Italians wouldn't live in it, but I lived in it!

SALLY. Did you see any ghosts?

FRED (*springing to his feet*). Let me tell you about it!— There was supposed to have been a murder committed there. An Italian girl who'd lived in the house was engaged to be married to a man—the story was he'd knocked her up and didn't want to marry her. So on the day when the wedding was to have taken place, instead of marrying her, he came and stabbed her—and her ghost is still supposed to be seen there in the white wedding veil and the wreath of flowers, saying, "*Ahimè! Ay di me! Santa Maria!*" (*He impersonates the ghost.*) Well, I took a room there— for a dollar a week. Nobody else was living there, so actually I had the whole house. The first night or two nothing happened—I simply sat there writing and nothing happened. Then one night I was lying in bed reading——

*Signe has begun to weep, and Sally interrupts Fred to speak to her.*

SALLY. Oh, don't, Signe dear!

SIGNE. I'm sorry!

*She dries her eyes.*

DAN. Don't worry about the theater, Signe! What can those small-souled people do to us?

FRED (*who has paused momentarily*). —I was lying in bed one evening reading Ariosto in the Italian, and I heard a sound like people talking, and so I——

SALLY (*coming forward on the day-bed and putting her arm around Signe*). Now, don't, my dear!

SIGNE. I'm sorry—I'm tired, I guess—and I had a letter from Ilya today.

TRACY. What does Ilya say? I haven't heard much about him since he was deported. He's been in Russia, hasn't he?

SIGNE. He's left. He didn't like Russia.

TRACY. Yes: it's no place for Anarchists, I understand— the Communists hate 'em worse than they do the bourgeoisie.

FRED. So I was lying in bed in this house reading Ariosto in Italian—and I heard what sounded like people talking Italian—and I thought right away that it sounded like Italians jabbering at an Italian wedding!

SIGNE. Say what you like about the Anarchists, Tracy, they had something that we haven't got now and that we need!

SALLY. I know: Tom Brophy had that—he'd do things and wouldn't give a damn!

SIGNE. It wasn't only that they didn't give a damn: they had loyalty among themselves. They'd bump off members of the ruling-class, but they wouldn't double-cross one another. The people who are outside it all have enough odds against them as it is. They've got to be able to depend on one another.

DAN. *We* depend on one another—I mean, we here in this room!

SIGNE. You weren't square with Sophie Feinburg, Dan. If you had been, this might never have happened: Harry would never have had the initiative to go ahead with this by himself.

DAN. Certain emotions can't be policed. The Anarchists certainly didn't think so.

SIGNE. No: I know they didn't. Ilya's living with another woman already.

DAN. Did he write you that?

SIGNE. Yes.

*She begins to cry again.*

FRED. Listen, Signe—listen to this story—it will take your mind away from your troubles!—I heard this sound of people talking—and the idea suddenly came to me that it sounded like the guests at the wedding!—the guests at the wedding of this Italian girl who'd been murdered by her lover who didn't love her!—

SALLY. Long stories make people nervous, Fred.

SIGNE. I'm sorry to be so silly. I've never been like this before!

SALLY. You're tired: you've been working too hard. Take another drink and you'll feel better.—Give her another drink, Dan!

*Dan obeys.*

SIGNE. Well, you can't have the whole of love and the whole of revolution at the same time. And that applies to us, too: you can't have the whole of love and the whole of art both. The trouble has been with us down here that we've tried to have the whole of everything.

DAN. Why shouldn't we, Signe?

SIGNE. Because it's as much as anybody can do to have anywhere near the whole of anything.

DAN. If we are whole ourselves, we can have everything whole!

TRACY. That's just metaphysical piffle, Dan!

SIGNE. Well, it's a good thing as far as the theater goes anyway, because I'd been intending to draw some of my back pay and go over to Europe to see him, and now there's no reason for my going, so I won't need to draw on the treasury.

SALLY. Oh, Signe, there's nobody like you!

SIGNE. I'm sorry to have behaved like this!—I've never done it before.

*Dan takes her hand. He and Sally are sitting on either side of her.*

DAN. You've got it coming to you, my dear—you've been working harder than any of us. You've worked your head off raising money, and you've given us a kind of moral support that nobody else could have done. It's you who's kept us up: without you, we could never have done anything.—Here's to Signe! Let's drink to her: (*raising his glass*) the mainstay, the genius, the darling! Let's all drink to Signe, who's given us her strength and her brains and her enthusiasm and her love! (*He kisses her.*) Drink to Signe! (*They drink.*)

SIGNE. I'm very much obliged. I wish I had all those things to give.

FRED. Listen, Signe: the spring is here! Did you know that? I felt it just now as I was walking in University Place! You may not have noticed it yet—but I have a peculiar sensitivity to the seasons, and today as I was walking in University Place staring down at the pavement (*he acts it out*) —trudging along sullenly as one does in these dull leaden days—suddenly I felt a sort of lightness! (*he illustrates, rather like an acrobat skipping after a difficult feat*) as if the darkness and weight of winter had lifted. I looked up, and there was the street full of slush and the clanging

clanking car-tracks—the ugly old city seemed just as sub
terranean, just as fuliginous, as ever!—the air was stil
tarnished with February! But some message from th
summer had reached me!—from that moment I believe
in the summer!—I knew that we'd soon be hearing th
melodious murmur of boat-whistles, that we'd soon b
drinking wine out of doors; I believed in the resurrectio
of spring!—and you must believe in the spring, Signe!—
because when the spring arrives, the heart becomes whol
again!

SALLY. That's beautiful, Fred.—I hope it's true!

FRED. Of course it's true—everything I say is true! (*A
he pours himself another drink*) Gosh, I'll have to stop drink
ing when my religion begins to take hold! If I got caugh
in any outrageous escapade, how the sensation-monger
would pounce on it! I can see the headlines in the papers
"MESSIAH IN DRUNKEN BRAWL"!

*Tracy has picked up the guitar and begun to strum it.*

SIGNE. Yes, sing something, Tracy, do!

*She gets up and goes over to the dressing table and freshen
her face and arranges her hair. When she comes back, she si
down near the fireplace.*

*Tracy sings, and while he is singing, a knock is heard at th
door. Sally gets up and answers it. It is a telegram: the bo
asks whether Miss Sally Voight lives there; Sally says th
she is Miss Voight, signs the slip, takes the telegram and ope
it. Fred goes over and stretches out on the window-seat an
immediately goes to sleep. He breathes heavily and soon begir
snoring.*

TRACY (*singing*).
Oh, love! oh, love! oh, careless love!
Oh, love! oh, love! oh, careless love!
You break de heart of many a gal—
You never break dis heart of mine!

Oh, when I wore my apron low,
You'd follow me through rain or snow.
But now I wear it to my chin,
You'll pass my door and not come in!

*Sally comes back.*

SIGNE. No bad news?

SALLY. No. (*She shows her the telegram.*) Don't sing that, Tracy: I'm tired of it.

TRACY. What shall I sing?

SALLY. You might sing something amusing.

*She lights a cigarette. A silence, into which Arthur breaks, coming back with two paper bags, from one of which the necks of bottles protrude.*

ARTHUR. Sandwiches for the hungry! Gin and ginger ale for the thirsty.

SALLY. There's nothing to do, I guess, but get tight!

ARTHUR. It's horrible outside: it's sleeting.

*In setting the bags on the table, he lets one topple off on the floor.*

TRACY. Oh, oh!

SALLY. That wasn't the gin?

ARTHUR (*picking it up*). No: the sandwiches. (*Smiling a little bleakly, as he tries to enter into the spirit of the company*) I'm tight myself, I guess. I had a couple of drinks while I was waiting at that bootlegger's.

DAN. I'm surprised at you, Arthur: I didn't know you ever lost your equilibrium!

ARTHUR. I occasionally make an ass of myself just the same way that you do, Dan.

*He busies himself with the sandwiches and drinks.*

DAN. Your whole way of life makes an ass of you. When you put on that stiff collar in the morning, you're assuming the badge of the ass!

ARTHUR. As a matter of fact, I usually wear a soft one!—

*Tracy and Signe talk together, tactfully withdrawing from the conversation. They are evidently discussing songs: Tracy hums tunes and twangs his guitar.*

SALLY. Dan and Arthur: you're both asses! I won't have you being hateful to one another. If it's on my account, you might just as well be nice, because I don't belong to either of you! We're all independent people, and the Greenaways haven't got us yet! We may not have the whole of everything, but we've got something precious at this moment—we've got this room and this gin and these sandwiches, and we've got each other's very agreeable company! Arthur and Dan, I adore you both!

DAN. I'm sorry, Arthur: I didn't mean to be invidious. I used to be the damnedest ass imaginable myself. I used to be a college instructor in a great big stiff white collar about twice the size of yours!

ARTHUR. I wish to withdraw anything I said which Mr. Frink may have taken in bad part, and offer him a liverwurst sandwich—or would you rather have chicken or cheese?

DAN (*taking it*). Thank you.

ARTHUR. Here's your chicken and tomato, Sally. (*As he hands it to her, he looks at the money order in her lap.*) You got a wire?

SALLY: Yes: some money.

ARTHUR. Fifty dollars won't go far!

SALLY. It's all I need.

ARTHUR. I called up about that place I told you about.

SALLY. I'll be all right. Never mind.

ARTHUR. You're taking a terrible chance.

SALLY. You mustn't read my telegrams.

ARTHUR. I couldn't help seeing it. (*Going over to Signe*) What will you have, Signe?

SIGNE (*still a little maudlin*). Anything, Arthur—it doesn't matter.

ARTHUR. Chicken and ham?

*He gives her one.*

SIGNE. It was nice of you to get these, Arthur!

ARTHUR. Tracy?

TRACY. Have you another chicken? (*Taking it*) Thank you.

*Arthur looks around and goes over to Fred on the window-seat.*

SIGNE (*to Sally*). Well, cheerio!—fifty dollars for death and not a nickel for art!

SALLY. That's all right: they haven't got us yet!

ARTHUR. Hey, Fred!—how about a sandwich?

*He shakes Fred gently by the shoulder.*

FRED (*waking up*). Hello, Arthur! Did you bring the gin? The spring is coming, Arthur! (*He sits up on the window-seat.*) Spring is coming to the Village! There it lies, all fuliginous and tarnished—but it's going to look just the same again as it did when I first met Marcella! We'll be waking up soon again to the glory of Greenwich Village mornings, with the windows wide open and the streets wide open and life wide open before us!

*He begins to recite Keats, acting it out. He loves English poetry and reads it well, and there is a silence while the others listen.*

"Soon they awoke clear-eyed: nor burned with thirsting,
   Nor with hot fingers, nor with temples bursting:
   And springing up, they met the wondering sight
   Of their dear friends, nigh foolish with delight,
   Who feel their arms, and breasts, and kiss, and stare,
   And on their placid foreheads part the hair.
   Young men and maidens at each other gazed,
   With hands held back, and motionless, amazed
   To see the brightness in each other's eyes;
   And so they stood, fill'd with a sweet surprise,

Until their tongues were loosed in poesy.
Therefore no lover did of anguish die:
But the soft numbers, in that moment spoken,
Made silken ties, that never may be broken."

ARTHUR (*after a moment's silence*). That's wonderful, Fred
—and very true.—Don't you want a sandwich?
FRED. A drink, Arthur! give me a drink!

# SCENE 6

*April: a fine morning, sun from the windows on the window-seat. Arthur and Sally come in. She is pale and weak, and he is supporting her.*

ARTHUR (*helping her off with her things*). How do you feel?

SALLY. I'm all right.

ARTHUR. Did it tire you much to come upstairs?

SALLY (*sitting down on the day-bed*). A little: not much.

ARTHUR. You'd better lie down.

SALLY. No: I'm all right.

*She gets out a cigarette, which he lights for her.*

ARTHUR. You lost an awful lot of blood, you know.

SALLY. Yes: I suppose I did.

ARTHUR. The doctor told me that it was a very lucky thing that I got you to the hospital when I did.

SALLY. You've been very sweet.

*He kisses her.*

ARTHUR. I ought to go to the office for a little while. Will you be all right alone?

SALLY. Yes, of course: I'm afraid you've been neglecting your work. You mustn't bother about me anymore.

ARTHUR. Oh, I can always get away.—Well, I'll go now and be back at lunch-time—(*glancing at his watch*) about twelve.

SALLY. Why do you bother to come way down here?

ARTHUR. You've got to have lunch. If you feel strong enough, we can go to the Brevoort; if you don't, I'll bring something in.

SALLY. I'll go out.— (*Smiling*) I'd like some Eggs Bene
dict—I kept thinking about Eggs Benedict in the hospita

ARTHUR. Fine: we'll go to the Brevoort.—Wel
goodby, sweet. (*He kisses her.*) If you should want any
thing, call me. This is the number. (*He takes an envelop
from his pocket and writes it down.*) Your phone's workin
now.

SALLY. Is it?—Did you pay the bill?

ARTHUR. Yes.—Look: will you think about something
—if you feel as if you could think about anything.

SALLY (*smiling*). What?

ARTHUR. About—what we talked about the day yo
came back from the doctor.

SALLY. About getting married?

ARTHUR. Yes.

SALLY (*smiling*). Yes: I'll think about it. (*She puts a sligh
emphasis on "think."*)

ARTHUR. Well, goodby.

*He kisses her again.*

SALLY. Goodby.

ARTHUR (*on his way to the door*). It's a beautiful day t
come out of the hospital. Why don't you lie over on th
window-seat in the sun?

SALLY. Yes, it *is* beautiful. (*She remains where she is
Arthur goes out. She is about to stretch out on the day-be
when the telephone rings: she gets up and answers it.*) Oh
hello, Dan! . . . Yes, I just got back . . . I'm fine. I'm s
anxious to talk about the play. . . . Yes: I'm perfectly al
right! . . . Yes, come over. (*She hangs up the receiver an
goes to touch up her make-up in the mirror. A knock at th
door: she goes to open it. It is a shock to see Bugs outside, an
she hesitates as to how to receive him.*) Oh—hello.

BUGS. Hello! (*He puts his arms around her and kisses her
he is a little constrained himself.*) How are you?—all right

SALLY. Yes.

*Bugs has been transformed: he is wearing a well-pressed blue business-suit, a black derby, a stiff white collar and well-polished shoes. He is carrying a spring overcoat.*

BUGS. I didn't hear from you—I didn't know what had happened to you!

SALLY. I'm all right.

BUGS. I called here twice on my way through and couldn't find you—I left a note.

SALLY. Yes: I got it.

BUGS. You're out of your jam all right?

SALLY. Yes.

BUGS. I was sorry I couldn't send you more money—but I had to pay debts to make Gracie feel better, and then I'd used up most of the rest on the trip.

SALLY. That was enough. I got along all right.—What did you go out West for?

BUGS. Immoral purposes. Don't ask!

SALLY (*smiling*). What was it?

BUGS. Ghost-writing for a prominent motor king for a prominent five-cent weekly.

SALLY. And those are the clothes you do it in?

BUGS. This is the uniform!

SALLY. Why, you look like a capitalist!

BUGS. It's my funniest act. You ought to see me come into an office! For everybody except the king-pins, I keep the dip on, see! All office-workers are poltroons, and all you have to do to impress them is to come in and talk emphatically.

SALLY. Is it interesting out there?

BUGS. It's colossal! It's the technological masterpiece of the world! Of course, humanly, it's hell on earth; but I concentrate on the technological side.

SALLY. I see.

BUGS. I decided that, instead of sulking in a secondrate newspaper office, I might just as well get in on some of the good things that are going. Why should the muckers get all the dough when I can spend it so much more intelligently? The radical movement's dead—and somebody's got to ghost-write the old motor magician.—It's really a hell of an exciting story!

SALLY. Yes: I suppose it is.

BUGS. In his peculiar way, he's a genius.

SALLY. Is he?

BUGS. He has qualities of actual greatness—so that the job's worth doing for its own sake.—And it's a life-saver for me, because it gets me out of debt and out of Flushing.

SALLY. Yes: that's fine.—Where are you going?

BUGS. I've taken a place at Great Neck.

SALLY. Yes: that will be pleasanter, I suppose.

BUGS. I've got to do something about Gracie and the kids, and I'll be happier about them if they're happier.— But what about you?—How's the work?

SALLY. I'm going to be in *Lysistrata*—we start rehearsals tomorrow.

BUGS. See here, Sally: why not take a couple of weeks off and come away with me for awhile? I'm free, because Gracie thinks I'm still in the West, and you need a vacation, I can see it. I've got money now to do anything we want.

SALLY. I can't because I've got to start rehearsing.

BUGS (*taking her hands*). I have a desperate need to see you! All the time I was out in the West, in exile among those inchoate creatures, I'd keep thinking, Sally Voight still exists, and I'm going to see her again!

SALLY (*yielding to his charm again*). Did you?

BUGS. What's a month of stone and concrete and conveyor-belts and goddamned hypocrisy if it buys a few moments of freedom and joy? That's all we can get out of this world—a few free and happy moments—and we're fools not to pay the price for it!

## SCENE 6

*A knock at the door.*

SALLY. Come in.

*Dan enters.*

DAN. Hello, Sally. Hello, Bugs. (*They greet him; he takes Sally's hands.*) How are you?

SALLY. I'm splendid now—I've felt terribly about holding up the play.

DAN. I hope you won't be terribly disappointed, Sally—as much disappointed as I am: but I'm afraid we aren't going to be able to do it. I've just been talking to Signe about it, and the loss of funds and break-up of the company seem to make it pretty impossible. That doesn't mean we won't do it later!

SALLY. You think it's completely impossible!

DAN. I'm afraid so.—You're not really well yet, besides. (*Bugs looks at her.*) And for that part you ought to have all your strength.

SALLY. I'm all right now, I really am—I'm perfectly well able to do it. I was counting on it. I shan't know what to do with myself!

BUGS (*to Sally*). I made a suggestion, you know. (*Dan looks at him.*) —Well, you and Dan want to talk theater, and I must go along. Why don't you have dinner with me tonight and we can talk about that other matter?

SALLY. All right.

BUGS. I'll come for you here about 7.

SALLY. All right.

BUGS. Well, goodby for the present!

*He briskly picks up his coat and waves his derby and goes.*

DAN. What in God's name has happened to Bugs Brophy? He looks like a high-pressure bond-salesman.

SALLY. Yes: he's turned into a go-getter.

DAN. You love him still, don't you?

SALLY (*after a moment's pause*). Yes.—Poor Bugs!

DAN. He's caught in his trap, isn't he? just the way you said that night? He'll never be able to get away.

SALLY. Not for long.

DAN. He can only pretend he's free; and he doesn't really want to be free or he would be. It's all more or less of a fake with him, and he has to keep finding new people who haven't found out yet it's a fake. When you've found him out, he'll get somebody else.

SALLY. I've always felt that Tom was real.

DAN. It's you who endow him with reality.—But then, you do that for all of us.

SALLY. Do I? (*Smiling*) Maybe that's why I feel so tired.

DAN. People exist through you, Sally—you create them. Look at Arthur: you've made something like a genuine person out of a pair of spectacles and a pressed suit.

SALLY (*smiling*). Arthur's not so bad as that. He's really a fine person.—Arthur wants to marry me.

DAN. But do you want to marry Arthur?

SALLY. I don't think so. But what you say about my doing things for people may be true to some extent of Arthur: he wants me to make up for some lack in himself.

DAN. And you need all of yourself for the theater. If you marry him, he'll take it all!—Why don't you come up to Woodstock with me, Sally? As long as we can't do *Lysistrata*, I'm going to get out of the city right away. We could work on it together up there.

SALLY. You're simply going to close the theater?

DAN. It looks as if that was all we *could* do.

SALLY. It seems a pity we can't last the season.

DAN. I'm afraid it's out of the question. Tracy's getting married and sailing next week—and Fred says he's going away, too. He says he's discovered the real Arcadia: the St. Pierre Islands.

SALLY. What are they?

DAN. They're off the coast of Canada, it seems—

and the thing about them, according to Fred, is that they bring you wine in milk-bottles every morning.

SALLY (*laughing*). Why is that an advantage? I'd rather have my wine in wine-bottles.

DAN. I suppose it gives you a reason to start in drinking at dawn.

SALLY. The kind of place I'd like to go to would be somewhere very clean where nobody drinks at all—except maybe a little at dinner!

DAN. We could lay off altogether in the country this summer—we could just sun ourselves and study. I've got a fine little house on a hill. I'll cook all the meals so that you can rest. I'm an excellent cook, you know.

SALLY (*smiling*). Are you really? You evidently remember my omelet!

DAN. We'll live with the grass and the stones and the stars—we'll forget about Harry Greenaway and his Tom show, and we'll make plans for our next season.

SALLY. But you know I love somebody else.

DAN. Love whom you please: we both love the theater!

SALLY. Oh, Dan! you're the only one of them all who wants to give people something for nothing! And you can keep on doing it because you're a man, but I'm a woman and sometimes I feel that I'd like to have other people give *me* things for once—women are supposed to be given certain things.

DAN. You're an artist, and you're not an artist in order to do the things that other women do.

SALLY. Yes, I know—and I suppose that what that really means is that I'm no good at real roles in life. In that way I'm something like Bugs—I'm only good at putting on a show. (*A knock*) Come in.

*Arthur enters.*

ARTHUR. Hello, Dan. (*To Sally*) How are you?

SALLY (*smiling*). Fine.

ARTHUR. Well, are you ready for your Eggs Benedict?—
I came back a little early because I thought you might be
hungry.

SALLY. You know, I *am* rather hungry.

*She goes behind the screen to make up. Dan and Arthur, left
together, become covertly antagonistic.*

ARTHUR. I just saw Signe outside, and she told me you
were dropping *Lysistrata*.

DAN. We're going to do it next fall.

ARTHUR. It's just as well, I think: Sally's hardly strong
enough yet.

DAN. We'll be working on it during the summer.

ARTHUR. She ought to have a rest, I think.

DAN. I hope she'll come up to Woodstock. (*As Sally
reappears*) Well, Sally, I must be getting on.

SALLY. Come in again soon!

DAN. You bet!

*Dan goes out, gesturing farewell to Arthur.*

ARTHUR. Goodby, Dan. (*Sally goes over to arrange her
hat in the mirror. Arthur, pretty well satisfied with things,
walks to the window and looks out. A man selling flowers is
heard outside.*) There's a man selling daffodils!

SALLY. Oh, is there really?

ARTHUR. I'll buy you some.

SALLY. Don't buy me anything more: you've bought
me too many things.

ARTHUR. Daffodils are no very great extravagance.

SALLY. Think of spring's having arrived, after all! (*She
turns around from the mirror, smiling.*) There were moments
when I thought they'd given up the idea!

ARTHUR (*as he helps her on with her coat*). I've got tickets
for the Kneisel quartet tonight. We don't have to go if
you don't feel like it, but I thought you might like to hear
some music. They're playing one of Beethoven's late
quartets.

SALLY. I'd love to hear it any other time, but I don't think I want to do anything like that tonight.

ARTHUR. Very well: you don't have to go out at all. I'll bring dinner in to you here if you want.

SALLY. I've made a sort of engagement for dinner.

ARTHUR. Oh. (*A tense pause: he stops, constrained.*) With Dan?

SALLY. No.

ARTHUR. You didn't tell me.

SALLY. I didn't know then.

*She begins pulling on her gloves.*

ARTHUR. You've made the engagement since I saw you?

SALLY. Yes.

ARTHUR (*cold and dry*). Well, are you ready?

SALLY. Oh, don't get grim about it!—I can't stand it!

ARTHUR. It makes me feel grim.

SALLY. Oh, don't—everything's horrid enough already! I'm nervous and tired, and I can't stand it.

ARTHUR. It's just that it's unexpected: we talked about spending the evening together.

SALLY. I'm sorry, but it's somebody I've got to see.

ARTHUR. I see.—I suppose I know who it is.

SALLY (*sitting down on the day-bed*). Oh, don't!—you mustn't always be checking up on me!—you make me feel so guilty all the time!—I'm fond of you, you know that—but you don't own me! I've still got a right to see whom I please—and to go where I please and do what I please!

ARTHUR (*sitting down beside her*). I'm sorry, but I get to feel as if you were married to me——

SALLY. But I'm not!

ARTHUR. But I feel as if you were—I can't help it—I love you—I feel as if I'd grown together with you—and then when I find all of a sudden that you've barred me out of your life, it's as if half myself were cut away. I stagger around, feeling horribly, as if I'd had some kind of amputation—without any anaesthetic. I know that you don't understand that kind of feeling——

SALLY (*suddenly, bursting into tears*). Oh, I do! I do understand! It's horrible for me, too!—all these abortions and mutilations!—I've been hurting you and killing your love every day that we've been together! Have you ever been happy with me a single moment?

ARTHUR. Yes: a great many.

SALLY. So have I been with you—but I've been hurt myself!

ARTHUR. Yes: I know it.

SALLY. You've given me something that nobody else has—you've given me a kind of repose. But people have to fight against relaxing——

ARTHUR. You've got to have some relaxation.

SALLY. And when I fight it, you're always there and you have to take all the blows!

ARTHUR. Your courage is one of the things I love you for.

SALLY. You mustn't think that I don't care about you! —I do care about you—*deeply!*

*He puts his arms around her and kisses her; a long silence. The hurdy-gurdy strikes up outside, playing the same tunes as the autumn before.*

ARTHUR (*releasing her enough to speak*). Why don't you marry me?

SALLY. I don't know . . . I don't think——

ARTHUR. Why don't you?

SALLY. I don't know how it would be——

ARTHUR. It would be fine!

SALLY. It might be nice.

ARTHUR. It would be perfectly wonderful. Will you?

SALLY. I don't know—maybe——

ARTHUR. You will, won't you? Say yes.

SALLY. All right.

*He kisses her.*

ARTHUR. I'll look for an apartment right away. How would you like to live in the Judson?

SALLY. I told you last fall, do you remember? that you wanted to get me into an apartment house with a uniformed doorman at the door.

ARTHUR. A doorman can be a very useful thing: he can keep away the wolves and the bar-flies.—Gee, that's come just at the right moment, hasn't it?

SALLY. What do you mean?

ARTHUR. The organ-grinder.

SALLY. Oh, yes.

ARTHUR. Do you remember I said last fall that I couldn't hear the hurdy-gurdy when I was with you, because everything then was so wrong? Well, I can hear it now distinctly, and it seems to me perfectly marvelous!

SALLY. Can you, dear?—Do you remember how you gave him some money, and he made one short spurt and then stopped?— (*Standing up suddenly*) Well, let's go out to lunch; I'm hungry. (*He stands up.*) —You can hear it, but now I can't hear it.

ARTHUR. Why can't you? What do you mean?

SALLY. Why— (*she pauses, then thinks how to put it*) because it means this street and everything.

ARTHUR. But why can't you hear it, then?

SALLY. Because something that was here has gone.

*Beppo and Beth*

# ACT I

*Beppo Miles' duplex apartment in the Richelieu-Versailles apartment-hotel. At the right, an open door into a hallway that leads to the apartment-door; in back, at the right, a door into the library, and at the left, a door into the dining-room; at the left, a large window. There is a balcony above the doors in the back wall, with stairs coming down at the left: these lead to the upper floor of the duplex, which consists of two bedrooms with doors opening onto the balcony; at the right, at the end of the balcony, is a door into an upper hall.*

*The place is in process of being sumptuously done in the style of the Italian Renaissance: walls in Venetian blue, red brocades, high brocaded chairs, candelabra, etc. The left-hand wall, however, has not yet been decorated, and it remains bare and white. Left-center there is an old-fashioned American sofa with a high comb-scalloped back—a low table in front of it and a chair behind the table. A medley of ornaments and furniture: a tapestry between the two doors in the back wall and, in front of it, a small table with a drawer and a Mexican bank in the shape of a cow; a great carved grandfather's clock; a painted screen; a victrola; a lamp of which the base is a green glass jar full of water; a floor lamp behind the sofa in the shape of a bronze female nude, which holds up the bulbs and shade; caricatures of Beppo and modern paintings; modern ash-trays that stand on the floor. Some of the things have not been arranged yet but simply pushed over against the unstippled wall. Two telephones: an outside phone and a house phone.*

*A Chinese boy with horn-rimmed glasses is filling a fancy cigarette box. The door-bell rings, and he goes out to answer it. He comes back with Beth Badger.*

CHANG. I go and tell Mr. Miles you're here.

*He goes upstairs and knocks at the first door on the balcony. Beth, a woman in her middle thirties, smartly dressed with the accent of a positive personality which is at the same time a little eccentric, stands looking around the room with swift sharp professional glances. At the sight of the nude wall, she smiles. Beppo Miles follows Chang downstairs. He is a man in his early forties, in a gaudy and luxurious dressing-gown. Chang goes into the dining-room.*

BETH. Hello! I just came in to see how the apartment was going! (*She speaks rapidly, emphatically and loudly— nervous energy and nervous strain.*)

BEPPO. It's all right as far as it's gone. But you people have been holding out on me. Why in Heaven's name don't you finish it?

BETH. Do you consider that screen "all right"? It looks like one of those seascapes of Naples on the walls of Italian speakeasies!

BEPPO (*who has now descended the stairs and comes over and shakes hands with her*). Well, it's swell to see you!— sit down and have a drink, won't you? (*He goes to the dining-room door.*) Will you bring in the cocktails, Chang?

BETH. Do you consider that lamp "all right"? (*Pointing at the floor-lamp with the statue*) It looks like a fine old piece out of a high-class Saratoga gambling-house! I suppose you think those Frank Lloyd Wright ash-trays strike an appropriate note! You told us you wanted this room to impersonate the Italian Renaissance!

BEPPO. I don't want to *reproduce* the Renaissance—I want a place that's *me*. A touch of the gambling-house is all right!

BETH. And a little touch of the Aquarium! (*Indicating the water-jar lamp*) It's a wonder you don't keep gold-fish in that lamp. I never knew you had the soul of a Sixth Avenue auction room! That Tiffany clock looks like one of those things that they hide the body in in mystery plays!

BEPPO. Look, my dear: we're not married anymore, so
hy not let me have things the way I want them?

BETH. I still care enough about you not to want to see
our place look like hell.

BEPPO. If we can't be polite about each other's tastes,
hat's the use of being divorced?

BETH. You know you trust my judgment—don't be
lly!

BEPPO. My worst eye-sore here is that wall. When are
ou people going to finish the job?

BETH. When we see a little remuneration for what we've
ready done!—After all, I've kept Ada Force from soak-
g you. You're getting the whole thing for twenty
ousand!

*Chang has brought in the cocktails and puts the tray down
the little table in front of the sofa. Beppo sits on the sofa,
eth on the chair beside it. He pours out the drinks.*

BEPPO. You're just being bitches: you know that I'll
y you! I've been terribly hard-up lately: I took an
vful beating on the market. My General Tires has shrunk
about a sixth of its former dimensions, and since *Art
d Fashion* folded up on me, I've hardly been able to
y the rent. But I'm going to sign the best contract I
er had: I'm going to be rolling in money!

BETH. What is it?

BEPPO. A big syndicated feature in the Gibbs papers.
erman Godbrow Gibbs has been calling me up every
y and telling me he's got to have me—he says he's got
l the best talent but me. It's a question of doing a daily
rip with the same little tigers I did for *Art and Fashion*.
nly they go around and look into conditions and tell
ople to cheer up—that the depression's just a state of
ind.

BETH. That's hard on your little tigers—they always
ed to be furiously cynical!

BEPPO. Well, they've got to be optimistic now, and I'м
nothing if not optimistic. I'm going to ask for thirty thou
sand. Then I'll be able to pay you for the apartment an
have Mimi finish at Miss French's—and I'll get to Bud
pest in the spring: I had to miss Europe last summer.-
He's a remarkable guy, this Gibbs! He claims he can tur
public opinion in a month, and when you think of all th
people he reaches——

BETH. He's just a riproaring ranting old bounder wit
a face like the rear end of a blue-behinded ape! I sat ne:
to him once at dinner and he tried to make me betwee
the celery and the soup!

BEPPO. I've never met him—only talked to him on th
phone. He has a Napoleon complex, I know—but ther
he's got a right to it, I suppose. He's one of our conquero
in a sense.

BETH. All right, if you can work for those creature
*I* can't!

BEPPO. How are you getting along with Ada Force?

BETH. Rottenly!

BEPPO. What's the matter?

BETH. Why, I don't like it and I can't do it and I *won*
do it! I'm absolutely not able to play up to the kept ladi
of cloak-and-suit kings who want to pose as Madame
Pompadour! I can't kiss the rumps of people who ord
thirteenth-century Spanish refectories as ping-pong room
on top of the Herschell Building! When Mrs. Felix ]
Hagenpecker comes to me and tells me she wants me t
design her a boudoir in the spirit of the Seventh Plane
Yogi, I know I ought to smile very sweetly and equi
her with the Chamber of Mirrors out of an old-tin
New Orleans bad-house—but what I do is simply sa
*Merde!*—Ada is able to truckle to them because sh
hasn't got an atom of taste herself—but it's too much f
Beth!

BEPPO. It's a good job, though: what do you care, if ou can do what you want outside your work?

BETH. I can't stand it—it drives me frantic. I've dis-overed I've got a mother-complex, and Ada brings it ut!

BEPPO. Have you been psyched?

BETH. I had a psychoanalytic beau—and he showed me ow my whole childhood had been dominated by my fear f my mother. That's what keeps me under Ada Force's 1umb. I don't think I ever told you what my mother was :ally like——

BEPPO. You always seemed immensely impressed by her.

BETH (*with violence*). Well, what she really was was a arsh—*domineering*—*arrogant*—*nagging* old harridan! She rought me up in such deadly terror of her that I've been ringing and wincing ever since. When anybody says any-1ing the least bit sharp to me, I crumple up like a little :ared child! I've been creeping and crawling before people ll my life! I go around Ada Force's shop like a poor itiful little whimpering whipped puppy!—the flabby-)wled money-goofy old horror!

BEPPO (*smiling*). There's no question about it, Beth, ou're the little shrinking violet of the world!

BETH. Shut up! It's absolutely true!—And not only am an abject coward—I'm a miserable ignominious prude! still think God is going to strike me dead if I do any of 1e things Mama disapproved of——

BEPPO. Good Heavens, Beth—she must have been pretty dvanced!

BETH. She was hideously Puritanical, and that's the :ason I'm so brazen and exhibitionistic! Every time I eep with somebody or get blotto, I have to do it in a )irit of bravado!—I have to be saying all the time to Aama, "Look at this: you brutal old bluenose—I'm going ) be just as loose as I please!"

BEPPO. I've been getting psyched lately, myself—the doctor in the hotel here has been analyzing me.

BETH. You must be a rich subject!

BEPPO. It's really done a lot for me, I think.

BETH. I always used to tell you you weren't on to yourself.

BEPPO. I know it: as I look back now, I can see that what was wrong between us was really my sister-fixation. At home I'd been an only son, and I expected anybody who loved me to do what my sister had done—wait on me and pay me homage——

BETH. You picked a poor partner for a homage-payer!

BEPPO. I'd been utterly dependent on my sister, and no other eligible girl had ever been able to get me away from her, and the result was I'd go out for my fun with the little floozies of the town. So that when I was married to Mimi's mother and afterwards to you, I developed a sort of incest-taboo about you and took to going out with the floozies in Paris just the way I'd done back in Galesburg.

BETH. That floozy who finally grabbed you off would certainly have been right in her setting in any small-town drug-store!

BEPPO. Well, you see I was trying desperately to get away from my sibling-relation with you.

BETH. You got royally rolled, I hear.

BEPPO. Rolled and rooked and reamed. That's the only time in my life I was ever left stranded by a woman with no money to pay the hotel bill!

BETH. I knew you were headed for destruction, but it's your inappeasable appetite for *chi-chi*.

BEPPO. Well, I think I've come to terms with my sister complex. I've finally discovered somebody who combines the sister with the floozy.

BETH. Who is she?

BEPPO. Nobody at all—a little girl who plays the piano in

he Purple Hour night-club. But she's a darling—she gives
me something that I've never had from any other woman.

BETH. What is it?—unqualified admiration?

BEPPO. No: she's really less interested in me than a more
sophisticated person might be——

BETH. Beppo, you're still one of the world's most price-
ss people!

BEPPO (*paying no attention*). But she's so simple and
natural and sweet! You feel with a person like that that
you've gotten back to something basic that the modern
woman has lost!

BETH. Big behinds?

BEPPO. No: on the contrary, she's slim. But she's a
natural woman, that's all! (*Becoming enthusiastic, he pours
t new drinks.*) She has no education at all, but she's never
r a moment cheap. It's because she's got Europe so close
behind her—her people were Polish peasants.

BETH. Is that Europe?

BEPPO. She hasn't been New-Yorkized yet. You know
ere's something in me that still goes back to the West
d that makes me like natural homely things.—I'm going
try to hook up that feeling with the faith in American
business—in this series I'm doing for Gibbs.

BETH. Beppo, you're a riot! I suppose it was your great
ve of simplicity that inspired this sumptuous Florentine
tch-all!

BEPPO. I'm complex—that's what makes me interesting.

BETH. You ought to get yourself disentangled. Find out
hat your real need is and then make yourself damn well
cept it. That's what I'm doing.

BEPPO. What do you mean?

BETH. I'm stalking an Englishman!

BEPPO. Really?

BETH. A splendid simple clean-limbed Englishman!

BEPPO. Marvelous!

BETH. I may be deluded about him, but he seems t keep taking me out and telling me about his place in Her —which needs a mistress, he says. He keeps saying I'm n at all like an American and that I'd be very much at hon in England. I wouldn't be hard to persuade!

BEPPO. That's splendid.

BETH. I've always been weak as water where Englisl men were concerned. My father came from Boston, yo know, and anyone with an English accent has always bee able to fascinate me. Papa had a big place on Long Islar till Mama drove him insane, and we had to go and li in a boarding-house. And a big English country-hou has always been my favorite fantasy!

BEPPO. What's your Englishman up to over here?

BETH. Making business connections, as he says. Tryin to be a business man, poor dear!—He's got the loveli English buck-teeth!

BEPPO. It's not a chap named Horseley Longbroke, is i

BETH. Do you know him?

BEPPO. Yes: he's a charming fellow. As a matter of fa he's coming to dinner.—I guess that country place of I is in pretty bad condition, though.

BETH. I know; but he makes you feel that you could have a nobler aim than to restore it to its original grande —that the fate of the British Empire depends on getti the roof mended and seeing that the garden is right—a in a sense it does, of course! I'd much rather help a dece Englishman put his ancestral house in order than to but up a lot of old tarts who think they want to be interic decorated!

BEPPO. You always were a snob, Beth.—Well, my de I wish you luck!

*The telephone rings, and Chang, who has just come in w clean ash-trays, answers it at once.*

BEPPO (*apprehensively*). That's not Mr. Gibbs, is it?

CHANG (*at the phone*). All right. I tell him. (*Hanging up the receiver, to Beppo*) It was Mrs. Salzburg: she telephoned to say that she and Mr. Salzburg can't come tonight. Mr. Salzburg has collapsed.

BEPPO. Collapsed? What was the matter?

CHANG. She didn't say: she only said that Mr. Salzburg had collapsed.

BEPPO (*to Beth*). I suppose that's the penalty of being a broker.

*Chang goes out.*

BETH. I think it's his wife, too.

BEPPO. Does she cheat on him?

BETH. No, but she'd like to—so that she's probably harder to live with than if she did. She kept going to the trial of that woman who murdered her husband in the bath-tub, and then she'd come back home, he told me, and hypnotize a little pet alligator. The alligator got limp and died!

BEPPO. Look, Beth: why don't *you* come to dinner?— since your friend Longbroke's going to be here——

BETH. I'd be charmed to! Will I have time to go and dress?

BEPPO. Yes, lots of time: dinner's not till 8. I've asked Godbrow Gibbs, if you don't mind that—I thought it would be a good idea to get him on my own ground instead of trying to cope with him on his. He insists on having my decision tonight.

BETH. Very sagacious, no doubt!

BEPPO. And Chet and Charlotte are coming—you don't mind seeing Chet, do you?

BETH. No, of course not—I don't mind any of my old husbands. Chet and I see more of one another nowadays than we used to when we were married and went out to parties separately.

BEPPO. —And my little girl-friend, June.

BETH. What fun! Your little night-club buttercup?

BEPPO. I want you to tell me what you think of her.

BETH. All right, I will, my dear!

*She kisses him.*

BEPPO. It's swell to see you, old thing—I see you so little nowadays.

BETH. I don't know whether it's really safe to meet a prospective fiancé in the presence of two ex-husbands— but I'm trusting to you and Chet to give me a good character with Horseley. Try and convince him, will you, that the only thing that ever was wrong with me was that I didn't have a country house!

BEPPO. I'll make love to you, as if I regretted you.

BETH. You don't need to go so far as that.

BEPPO. Maybe I do regret you! It seemed for a moment just now as if we were back in Paris arranging to have people in.

BETH. Usually followed by ghastly rows after the people had left!

BEPPO. Still, it was fun for a while.

BETH. For a little while.—Well, I must leap! I'll change and be back in a jiffy!

BEPPO (*going out with her into the hall*). Don't rush— you've got plenty of time——

*Chang comes back for the cocktail tray. Beppo, after seeing Beth out, returns, reading the paper, which he has picked up outside the door.*

BEPPO. "Stock Market Reaches New Low." Well, well, Chang—what's the world coming to?

CHANG. The capitalist system today is entering its final phase. The contradictions inherent in capitalism have resulted in a general crisis.

BEPPO (*looking up*). You talk like a radical, Chang!

CHANG. I am a member of the Young Communist League.

BEPPO. That's interesting. I knew you were a student, but I didn't know you went in for Communism.

CHANG. A Chinese student who is able to think must inevitably become a Communist.

BEPPO. Are there many Chinese Communists?

CHANG. In China a great many, yes. In the capitalist press they call them bandits.

BEPPO. You say "contradictions in capitalism." What do you mean by that?

CHANG. It is inevitable that under the competitive system, which prevails in the capitalist countries, there must continually take place a seeking for cheaper methods of production. This stimulates increased efficiency; and the more completely is industry rationalized, the fewer workers are needed—so that the better can capitalism produce, the worse can people consume. This is a contradiction.

BEPPO. What then?

CHANG. The capitalist system today has accomplished its historical function. The system of ownership by the few gives rise to its opposite, Communism, and the dispossessed proletariat takes over the means of production and the government.

BEPPO. God forbid! The present government is bad enough!—No, Chang; the general run of humanity are no more fit to govern than they are to do anything else that calls for imagination or intellect——

CHANG. It is clear that you do not understand the basic class nature of government——

BEPPO. I don't believe in that kind of classes, Chang—I recognize only two classes: the vast undistinguished mass and the small civilized minority, and we of the civilized minority have no concern whatever with politics. Politics is a dirty game—amusing, if you like low comedy, but not a thing in which a civilized person can take the faintest interest.

CHANG. *Bourgeois* politics is a dirty game——

BEPPO. Good Heavens, my dear boy: how dreadful to hear you spouting that jargon! You Chinese are probably the most civilized people left in the whole world!—You've got centuries of philosophical serenity behind you!

CHANG. The mandarins in China—the civilized minority, as you call them—have betrayed the Chinese masses to foreign capital——

BEPPO. But what have you got to do with the masses?— You're a mandarin yourself, Chang—you know it!—Contemplate the world and laugh! To understand is to laugh!

CHANG. The class-conscious Chinese student does not study to be a mandarin.

BEPPO. But that will never do! We must have mandarins!—otherwise where would we get mandarin coats? They'd have nothing to hang on the walls in Hollywood! —There'll be eight for dinner, after all, Chang. You'd better make fresh cocktails.

*Chang picks up the cocktail tray and goes back into the dining-room. Beppo looks after him a moment.*

*Mimi appears from her room on the balcony and comes down the stairs. She is just over eighteen, very pretty and smart. She seems remarkably mature for her age—her manners are formal and self-assured, and she gives an impression of great sophistication. She is wearing an evening gown with a very low V-shaped back.*

BEPPO. That's a very snappy gown, my dear—I haven't seen it before.

MIMI. I know: I only got it yesterday. I'd really been economizing up to then, but I thought that as Mr. Herman Godbrow Gibbs was coming so nobly to the rescue——

BEPPO. We must get the apartment finished first, though.

MIMI. Yes, I know. Not another stitch!

BEPPO. It's a great success, however. You look like the back pages of *Art and Fashion*.

*He kisses her.*

Mimi. You don't mind, do you, Dad, if I go out after dinner tonight?

Beppo (*evidently disappointed*). I like to have you here to be hostess, you know. You're the only hostess I've got.

Mimi. I don't know whether it's really proper for a young gal like me to be hostess at an older people's party like this.

Beppo. You do it beautifully, my dear. You never take them out of their depth.

Mimi. But I think it cramps their style.

Beppo. On the contrary, it brightens them up!

Mimi. This is my last night before I go back to school, and I wanted to snatch a few last moments of whoopee.

Beppo. Who are you going out with?

Mimi. Jack Payne.

Beppo. Good heavens, Mimi! Again? That fellow is a frightful phony!

Mimi. I know you don't like him, Dad, and he does have his untutored side, but he's really awfully sweet.

Beppo. What does he do?

Mimi. He owns restaurants and things.

Beppo. He's just an ordinary Broadway heel.

Mimi. He's not: he's perfectly swell!

Beppo. I hate to have you seen with him, Mimi. Remember that, after all, you're a lady. I don't want you to be stuffy or snooty about it, but——

Mimi. You've told me yourself, Dad, that anybody who had real social self-confidence could feel free to do anything they pleased.

Beppo. I know: but it's a different matter to have a man like that for a regular beau.—You've hardly been seeing anybody else.

Mimi. I like him: Jack's a darling.

Beppo. But you mustn't take him seriously.

MIMI. Why not? He's serious about me.

BEPPO. Because I want you to do better with life than that. You're my only child, Mimi—you're the only thing I've gotten out of three marriages.

MIMI. I know.

BEPPO. I want you to *be* somebody and something. You have practically the whole world to choose from. When you and I travel together, we manage to meet all the smart people—all the swells and all the geniuses. And living the way we do, we can take our ease and watch them come and go.

MIMI. I know, Dad: I've watched them, and I feel very seriously that Jack is the outstanding applicant.

BEPPO. But he's *cheap*, my dear—he's cheap! You don't like people who are cheap. Don't you remember how you used to feel about that Belgian automobile salesman who gave you such a rush at Antibes?—the man we used to laugh about so? Well, Jack Payne is just like that, only worse!

MIMI. He's not a bit like that perfect jackass—he's really an awfully exciting person!

BEPPO. That sounds like your mother, Mimi. She always used to be trying to tell me that all the terrible people in the Village were gifted or exciting or something. It was generous and charming of her, but I don't want you to accept her scale of values.—

MIMI. I spend six months of the year with her, Dad!

BEPPO. I've tried to give you certain things that would offset the Green Tiger tea-room.

MIMI. You're so bitter about Mother, Dad! After all she *gave* you your tiger idea, didn't she?

BEPPO. I made it into something quite different.

MIMI. Some people think they used to be better.

BEPPO. Well, Mimi, you can't have everything. If you go in for the kind of thing that the Greenwich Village people make such a fuss about—or used to make such

fuss about: they don't do anything down there any more
—if you go in for working for little magazines that never
pay you anything and that nobody ever reads anyway,
you have to forego a lot of other things. And what you
have to do without is practically everything that makes
life worth living—comfort, amusements, good manners,
the whole of real civilized existence. I've wanted you to
have all that——

MIMI. I know.

BEPPO. And that's why I hate to see you fall for a man
who can't give you the real thing.

MIMI. You have your own weak moments, Dad. What
about your little night-club hostess?

BEPPO. June Macy's a fine person. She's not a hostess—
she's a marvelous pianist.

MIMI. I don't want to hurt your feelings, Dad, but,
although she's awfully sweet, I really don't think she's so
marvelous. You know yourself that some of your friends
are a little on the dese-dose-and-dem side.

BEPPO. Let me tell you, my dear: it's all right when
you're in your own house to have anybody in that interests
you, and anybody interests me who's amusing or good-
looking or has brains——

MIMI. Jack's certainly good-looking and amusing, and
if it's a question of having brains, he's certainly in the
running with June Macy!

BEPPO. Just a moment, my dear: I was going to say
that someday, when you're mistress in your own house,
you can entertain anyone you please, but that knocking
around in night-clubs with the dregs of the underworld——

MIMI. Please don't rave like that, Dad—it sounds as if
you had a daughter-complex!

BEPPO. I don't see enough of my daughter nowadays
to get a chance to have a daughter-complex!

MIMI. Well, I can't do anything about it anyway because

I've promised Jack I'd go tonight, and he's coming for me after dinner. (*She looks at the clock.*) Dad, you must rush! It's 7:30—they'll be coming any minute!

*Beppo looks at the clock and gets up and starts for the stairs.*

BEPPO (*with suppressed anger*). Well, take him out when he comes—I don't want you to ask people to meet him!

*He goes upstairs. Mimi shoots a look after him. The door-bell rings: Beppo hastens his pace, stumbling over the top step. Chang goes to the door. Mimi gives a few touches to her hair and dress. (The door-bell is loud and piercing: a continually recurring motif that interrupts whatever is going on and finally gets on the nerves.)*

*Chet and Charlotte Chives come in. Chet is a nice little man, sensitive and, in manner, naïve; Charlotte is a large practical woman who tries—not altogether successfully—to keep him from slipping her leash. Chet wears a dinner-jacket.*

MIMI. Hello! (*She shakes hands with them.*) Dad'll be right down.

CHET. You look s-stunning in that gown, Mimi. It g-goes anything I've seen one better!

CHARLOTTE (*laughing easily but a little coldly*). I've had one exactly like it all winter and you've never noticed it at all!

MIMI. They're certainly no great novelty—everybody has them this year, I think. (*As Chang comes back from the hall*) Will you bring the cocktails, Chang?

CHARLOTTE. You're not still home on your vacation, are you, Mimi?

MIMI. This is my last day. Back to the books tomorrow!

CHARLOTTE (*snubbingly—since Chet is plainly delighted with Mimi*). It seems to me that the schools give frightfully long vacations nowadays. (*With a patronizing smile*) —Not too long for you, though, I dare say.

MIMI. I don't like the tag-end of the holidays much. New York gets pretty leprous then.

*Chang brings in the cocktails and hors d'œuvre and passes them around—then goes out. The cocktails have been made with orange-juice and are served in small goblets.*

CHET (*taking a cocktail and beaming with decorous rakishness—he is already a little tight—while Charlotte stares about the room*). You don't think that at all! You think that everything's swell! It may be leprous to us but it isn't leprous to you!

CHARLOTTE (*interrupting*). This room is quite impressive.

MIMI. Don't look at the blank wall!

CHET. It sets off the view—it's a good idea! (*He goes over to the window and looks out.*) Well, there it is—that old devil city! You can see the whole Park from here, can't you?

MIMI. I always think the motor-roads from here look just like a big boa-constrictor trying to choke the trees and the grass.

CHET. That—that's just exactly what it looks like!— It's all so bleak and abstract.—And the people are drearier than ever this year! The New Yorkers have faces nowadays that seem actually boarded up!—it's as if the sky or something were shutting down on them——

CHARLOTTE (*behind them, breaking in*). The landlords and banks are shutting down on them!

CHET. —It's as if people were realizing for the first time that the city is really a prison—though I d-don't know whether they're even so human as that—they're more like a lot of little bugs that have just had the light turned out on them—they're still moving around in the darkness, waiting for it to flash on again so that they can keep on flying against it.—I've never known New York so ominous! Everything seems actually darker!

CHARLOTTE. Everything *is* darker: they're economizing on electric signs.

CHET. Of course! I hadn't thought of that!— (*Turning*

*away from the window*) Well, it's fine to be in here where it's bright!—the ladies in gorgeous new gowns, the caviar glittering on the crackers, the cocktails blooming like a bed of yellow tulips!

CHARLOTTE. You must have snitched a drink before you came.

CHET. Of c-course I had a drink before I came! One always ought to have at least two drinks before going out anywhere: it's a social obligation!—What a dandy little Mexican cow! (*He picks it up and rattles it.*) Some money in it, too! I ought to contribute my bit! (*He puts a penny in.*)

*Beppo, while Charlotte and Chet have been speaking, has hurried out of his room, straightening his tie, and now is on his way downstairs. He is wearing a deep-purple dress-suit.*

BEPPO. Thanks, Chet! That's a fund for collapsed financiers.

CHET. Hello!

BEPPO. I think that we artists nowadays can afford to give them a helping hand. (*Arriving at the bottom of the stairs and shaking hands with Charlotte, then with Chet*) Hello, Charlotte! (*To Chet*) Hello!

CHARLOTTE. You know, Beppo, I don't think this apartment is half so bad as people say.

BEPPO. It's slightly incomplete as yet, but I decided to give a party in it anyway!

CHET. It's s-swell! That b-blank wall would be fine to draw pictures on!

*The door-bell rings, and Beppo glances apprehensively toward the door. A moment's silence.*

BEPPO (*catching sight of the new arrival*). It's Longbroke! You know Horseley Longbroke, don't you?

CHARLOTTE. Yes, indeed: he's such a delightful man.

CHET. A real bit of old England.

BEPPO. The stuff that stopped the Spanish Armada!

*Horseley Longbroke comes in: beautifully tailored, buck-teeth, no expression.*

LONGBROKE (*shaking hands and grinning in what he believes to be the American manner*). Well, folks, this is so swell!

BEPPO. Delighted to see you, Duke!

LONGBROKE. It's such a kick to see you all!

CHARLOTTE (*amused*). Your mastery of the vernacular, Mr. Longbroke, is one of the most remarkable feats I've ever witnessed.

LONGBROKE. One picks it up quite naturally.

BEPPO (*handing him a cocktail*). It's a pity to spoil English English though.

LONGBROKE. American's a different language, I think.

BEPPO. Like everything else in God's country, it was designed for business, not beauty.—You're Oxford, aren't you?

LONGBROKE. No: Cambridge.—I think it's admirable for business letters, American.

CHARLOTTE. They haven't begun giving business courses at Oxford and Cambridge yet, have they?

LONGBROKE. Not yet; but it would be an excellent thing, I think. The educational system in England is quite anti-quated—except in the technical schools. It doesn't fit one for the modern world at all.

CHARLOTTE. Oh, I think it would be too dreadful to have business courses at Cambridge!

BEPPO. The beauty of the English system is that every-thing is purely gratuitous. In America we're always think-ing about what things are going to get us. But the men who go to English universities don't have to worry about results. I think that one of the most perfectly delightful and most perfectly satisfying jobs in the world must be that of an English don!

LONGBROKE. A don doesn't get much of a screw, you know—about £500 only.

BEPPO. But he has the good life!

CHARLOTTE. To live at Cambridge would be enough!

LONGBROKE. Of course there's a sort of chap who enjoys that sort of life. *I* can't say I should, though.

CHET. I've always thought being a Liberal member of parliament must be the most perfect job in the world!

LONGBROKE. On the contrary, an M.P. does even less well than a don—four hundred is all they get—and they're taking a cut with the new government. One really has to have private means for Parliament.

BEPPO. America's corrupting you, Longbroke!

LONGBROKE. What do you mean?

BEPPO. You're learning to look at everything from the money point of view.

*The door-bell rings as Beppo is speaking, and, glancing expectantly in that direction, he lowers his voice on his last words at the thought of Mr. Gibbs.*

LONGBROKE. Money? It seems to me Americans are perfectly dizzy about money! To an Englishman it seems as if Americans didn't take money seriously at all!

*June Macy comes in—very pretty, simple and quiet.*

BEPPO (*hailing her with evident enthusiasm*). Well, Beautiful!—You look pretty as a picture, as we used to say back in Galesburg!—This is Mrs. Chives—and Mr. Longbroke —and Mr. Chives. Miss June Macy of the Purple Hour.

*June shakes hands with Charlotte, but merely bows and smiles to the others. She is shy—follows everything that is said, but stands aside from the conversation. Mimi, however, comes over and shakes hands with her.*

JUNE (*to Mimi*). Hello!

BEPPO. I suppose it's no use offering you a cocktail.

JUNE (*smiling shyly*). No, thanks.

CHET (*who has been talking to Mimi but now turns his attention to June*). You're not f-fighting high b-blood pressure like so many people, are you?

JUNE. It's the figure: I get fat awfully easy.

CHET. You're absolutely right!—because you've got a figure that's worth keeping.

JUNE. Thanks!

CHET. I've studied anatomy—that makes me a judge. You've got an unusually lovely figure!

JUNE. Thank you!

CHET. Are you a dancer?

JUNE. No: I just play the piano.

CHET. You never do any posing, do you? I'm a painter, and I'll be needing a model soon.

CHARLOTTE (*cutting firmly in*). Look at these Periwinko skeletons, Chet. I couldn't see them at all in Paris, but I think these are quite swell.

CHET. Periwinko's skeletons have no figures!—Now if we could only c-combine what Periwinko's skeletons have with what Miss Macy has, we might get a real modern art! Put some living flesh on the bones!

CHARLOTTE. You're always "if-only"-ing, Chet!

*They turn toward the pictures and talk, Chet continuing to pay court to June.*

LONGBROKE (*to Beppo*). What a jolly apartment this is!

BEPPO. It was done by Beth Badger. I think you know her.

LONGBROKE. Oh, really? Yes, I do know her quite well.

BEPPO. She's coming to dinner tonight.

LONGBROKE. How jolly!—how swell!—I knew she did interior-decorating but I'd never seen any of her work. She's done you quite splendidly, I think! (*He looks around.*)

*The door-bell rings. Chang goes.*

BEPPO. That's probably Beth now.

LONGBROKE. I suppose interior-decorating is a very profitable line, isn't it?

BEPPO (*after a moment's hesitation*). Yes, in general, it is——

*Beth bursts in, in an evening gown—louder and more*

*animated than before, from the nervous excitement of hurrying.*

BETH. Hello! Hello, Charlotte! Hello, Mimi! Hello, Chives! (*To Beppo*) Back in a different costume! I hope you haven't been waiting for me and cursing me!

BEPPO. Not at all: you've made marvelous time! This is Miss Macy.

BETH. How do you do!

BEPPO. I believe you know Mr. Longbroke.

BETH. Why, Horseley—bless your heart! I hadn't expected to see you tonight!

BEPPO (*to Chet and Charlotte*). Jeff Salzburg has had a breakdown—did you know it?—they couldn't come tonight. (*Handing Beth a cocktail*) Fasten onto this, Beth.

CHET. Really? No, I didn't know. That's a d-damn shame!

CHARLOTTE. You heard about poor Willa Sprague?

BETH. Yes: I've felt as if a prop had been knocked out from under me!

BEPPO. I never expected *her* to crack!

CHARLOTTE. I don't know. Had you seen her lately? She'd been behaving very strangely.

CHET. She really had a talking neurosis.

BEPPO. What did she talk about?

CHET. The seventeenth century in France.

CHARLOTTE. You couldn't stop her once she got started!

BEPPO. What was really the matter, do you think?

CHARLOTTE. Roy Milton. She was mad about him.

CHET. And he was mad, but not about her.

CHARLOTTE. He's not interested in anything but parrots.

BETH. He says that his parrots have come between him and every woman who ever loved him.

CHARLOTTE. I understand that the parrots took to squawking about the seventeenth century.

CHET. They'd heard her at Roy's so much that they began saying "Louis Quatorze."

BETH. And that's all that's left of poor Willa!

BEPPO. Well, I for one intend to survive intact! At this moment I feel like a million dollars, and I hope to live to be worth it! (*He takes a drink.*)

CHET. If you had it, you mightn't feel so well. I think people are much better off bankrupt!

CHARLOTTE. That's all right for *you* to say: you haven't got anything to lose. How about it if *I* went bankrupt?

CHET. They're much more agreeable, anyway. They can't afford to be so snooty.

CHARLOTTE. You and I wouldn't be more agreeable if Voorhies Valves should shut up shop, and we had to live somewhere in a couple of rooms!

BETH. You're perfectly right, Charlotte, when Chet and I tried to live together in a studio walk-up on Eighth Street, he used to snap and snarl like a pet chow!—I've been married to two of these gents, Horseley: both Beppo and Chet Chives are former husbands of mine!

LONGBROKE. I see.

CHET. Well, I s-still insist that the hard times here m-made people much more human!

BEPPO. Yes, there's no question that the depression's a splendid thing and does you no end of good, if only you don't die of it first.

CHET. Well, h-here's to life!

BEPPO. Righto! Here's to life!

CHET. This is r-really the best hour of the day, you know! I'm still n-naïve enough to feel that anything may happen after 5!

BETH. It usually does with you—you get pie-eyed!

CHET. After 5, the fixed pattern of the day breaks up! Everything dissolves for a while! The soul comes out and unfolds itself—it floats above your head like an ectoplasm!

BEPPO. And then you realize the next morning that it's a mongoose that lives on the ceiling! I don't know what it is about that mongoose but he always makes me feel damned uncomfortable! He's never done anything savage —just darts around on the ceiling, but I hate to have him get behind me!

BETH. Elsie Peters used to put out milk for foxes.

MIMI. Jack Payne says that once he had three little owls that roosted in his mouth for a week. He said they were awfully little and he didn't mind having them there till they tried to bring home a house-guest.

BETH (*to Longbroke*). Are you haunted by those creatures in London as much as we are here?

LONGBROKE. We drink in England, but not so grimly.

BETH. You drink in a civilized fashion!

BEPPO. They ought to have some kind of apparatus like the machine that registers earthquakes, which would record the degrees of heeby-jeebies in the principal cities of the world!

BETH. Wally Ford tried going on the wagon for a month, but he says it makes almost no difference!

BEPPO. Well, that being so, ladies and gentlemen, let me offer you another cocktail! Say what you like: here we are at the moment, on the whole very agreeable people and doing on the whole very well! The world, we all know it, is tragic, it's terrible—but that's no reason we shouldn't enjoy our cocktail! We're not responsible for God's blunders, and we may as well get what fun out of them we can. It may be that laughter, after all, is our only compensation in this Vale of Tears! For us people to laugh among ourselves, perhaps that's the real end of existence! —So here's to the charm of the few! here's to the glamor of the moment! So long as *they* hold out, let the world be what it may!

*The door-bell rings violently.*

BEPPO. That must be Gibbs at last!

*He busies himself with filling the glasses while Chang goes*

338

*to the door. A moment's silence. A loud voice is heard outside.*

THE VOICE. What's the name of the people who live here?—Miles? Ah, yes, Miles! Is Mr. Miles at home?

*A man of about fifty, outdistancing Chang, comes in. He is fattish but flaccid-looking, his eyes, which have pouches and heavy rings, somewhat wildly staring. He is arrayed in a magnificent dress-suit.*

BEPPO (*shaking hands with him*). How do you do, Mr. Gibbs!

THE NEW ARRIVAL. Mr. Miles, I believe!

BEPPO. This is Mrs. Chives, Miss Macy, Miss Badger, my daughter, Mr. Longbroke, Mr. Chives.

THE NEW ARRIVAL. Most happy, Miss Childs, Mr. Pawnbroker, Mrs. Gibbs!

BEPPO (*with deference*). A cocktail, Mr. Gibbs? (*Offering him one*)

THE NEW ARRIVAL. No, thank you! My name is not Gibbs, by the way: it's Bostock—Luke Bostock!

BEPPO. Ah, you're the owner of the building—the owner of the Richelieu-Versailles!

BOSTOCK. I am, and I'm your neighbor across the hall. I hope you will forgive this intrusion—if I'm a nuisance, boot me out!—but I was all by myself tonight—all dressed up and no place to celebrate—and I thought maybe you wouldn't mind if I dropped in in a neighborly fashion——

BEPPO. —Not at all—very glad to know you. Sit down, won't you?

BOSTOCK. Thank you!

*He does so.*

BEPPO. Sure you won't have a drink?

BOSTOCK. Don't use it, thanks! No, I just want to see people, I want to see people just like you—gay, smart, good-looking people! I don't know what it was, but I felt kind of a malaise tonight—you know what I mean, a malaise, a feeling like all was not well—I don't know whether any of you people have ever felt anything like that?

BEPPO (*smiling*). A little touch now and then.

CHET. We know what you mean perfectly.

BOSTOCK. Well, you'll understand the situation then. My dinner engagement had been called off, and my valet was out for the evening, and there I was all alone—and then this malaise set in. But when you get among nice people you know that it was all just a mood!

BEPPO. Yes, we have our moods, too.

BOSTOCK. But it's not the fault of the place!

BEPPO. This apartment, you mean?

BOSTOCK. The hotel—the Richelieu-Versailles! If the hotel wasn't attractive, it wouldn't matter what you did to the apartment! It isn't the individual home nowadays —it's the apartment house, the hotel! What the building is, that's what your home-life is! And that's why I made this place cheerful yet restful—sparkling yet comfort-conscious!

BEPPO. I've found it delightful here.

BOSTOCK. I wonder if you've ever heard the story of how I came to build the Richelieu-Versailles?

BEPPO. No, I don't think so.—How did it happen?

BOSTOCK (*with genial enthusiasm, not drunken—he is lucid and cogent in his fashion, has none of the sloppiness of drunken-ness—but pitched beyond the normal key: as he goes on, Beth, unseen by Bostock, makes the gesture of sniffing cocaine for the benefit of the people near her*). It's really a rather thrilling story—rather picturesque, I think! A triumph of American democracy of the real old-fashioned brand! It was 1918: the War! I was a doughboy, a non-com truck-driver just down from the Argonne Forest. I went to the Ritz in Paris, and I asked the room-clerk for a room. I was a doughboy—I was uncouth and dusty—my O.D. jacket was busting its buttons and my puttees were plastered with mud. I asked for a room at the Ritz, and what do you think I got? The razz!—I was turned away! The clerk told me all the rooms were taken. A goddam lie, of course! —In a second I had that clerk by the throat and I was shaking him like a terrier shakes a rat! (*Leaping up and illustrating on Beppo*) I said, "You little weasel-faced frog!" I said. "You may not be aware of it, but I've got a hell of a big belch about you French!—a hell of a big belch! We come over here and bust our boilers," I said, "to save the sacred soil of France!—we get ourselves shot up and blown up," I said. "We sleep in the world's lousiest billets —And it's, '*Ah, nos braves alliés! ç'est vous qui nous avez sauvés!*'" (*To Beppo*) 'Member that?—the way they used to say that?—"But then when you try to put up at a high-class hotel in Paris," I said, "it seems there aren't any rooms! Well, I want to tell you something," I said, "and I don't want you ever to forget it! I won't be out of this man's army five years before I'll have a hotel of my own that'll make this dump look like a back-house!"—I'm sorry to be vulgar, ladies! (*With tremendous smiling deference*) But I was frankly indignant!—And I kept my word and here's the place!

BETH. What a magnificent story, Mr. Bostock!

CHARLOTTE. But why call it the Richelieu-Versailles if you've got such a hate on the French?

BOSTOCK. It was the Ritziest name I could think of— Ritzier than the Ritz.—But how did I do it, you're won-dering. By vision and by the readiness to take risks! I was a paint-truck driver by trade, and so I understood the building game. I knew a land speculator in the Bronx, and I got him to let me have a $10,000 plot of land for $20,000. He lent me $2,000 to start with——

BEPPO. It seems to me you lost on that deal. Do you mean to say you paid $20,000 for a $10,000 piece of land?

341

BOSTOCK. Not a penny ever changed hands except the $2,000 he gave me.—All he got was a mortgage for twenty-two thousand on the building I was going to erect —the dream erection of my vision.

CHARLOTTE. But what did the land speculator get out of it?

BOSTOCK. He used the mortgage as security to borrow fourteen thousand from a savings bank, and I went to a title company and borrowed a hundred and twenty thousand—so that everybody made on the deal.—With the money I put up a building worth a hundred and eighty thousand.

CHARLOTTE. But how did you pay the contractors?

BOSTOCK. That's just what I'm going to tell you! I owed them $60,000, and maybe you think I was bankrupt. If I'd been a goddam frog, I would have been. But I was a Connecticut Yankee—a Yankee from Stamford, Conn.!—and I went out and I got me a *bigger* plot of ground in a *more desirable* neighborhood on the same kind of terms as the first!—I don't want to bore you with this! Are all these details boring you!

BETH. This part *is* a tiny bit technical.

BOSTOCK. I just wanted you to know how I did it!— it's really a breath-taking story! The romance of American business! there's nothing to beat it in the world!—I went to this second land-gambler, and I got him to loan me money the same as the first one did, and I borrowed half a million from the title company. Then I paid the contractors their sixty thousand, so my credit was good again, and they were tickled to death to let me owe them a hundred and fifty thousand for putting up a bigger hotel. Was I bankrupt then? No! I climaxed in the Richelieu-Versailles—I was able to borrow enough money then to put up the Emperor hotel of Manhattan: a million dollar palace without a penny of my own invested!

CHARLOTTE. You owe a million dollars, so that makes you a millionaire!

BEPPO. But what do the contractors do now?

BOSTOCK. They pass the costs on to the manufacturers.

BEPPO. But what happens then? What do *they* do?

CHARLOTTE. I'll tell you what happens then! My family makes bathroom fixtures. What happens then is everybody goes bust!

BETH (*to Longbroke*). You chose rather an unpropitious moment to come over here to make your fortune!

LONGBROKE. So it seems.

BOSTOCK. Nothing in it! Don't believe a word of it! This country's as sound as it ever was! It's going to be better than it ever was! Just to show you how optimistic *I'm* feeling: I'm having the dining-room here enlarged and a new dish-washing machine put in that will do twice as many dishes and cut the kitchen staff down two-thirds!

JUNE. And they'll be eating in soup-kitchens, huh?

BOSTOCK. —That shows you how *I'm* counting on prosperity!—And here we are in the meantime in the glamorous Richelieu-Versailles—a great hotel for a great metropolis! I don't want to bore you, but silly as it seems, I'm a nut about my own hotel! It's just the very palace I dreamt of when I was throttling that room-clerk at the Ritz! In the Richelieu-Versailles, you dress for the Aubusson Room or you're not allowed to enter. My room-clerks are all college men, and if they don't happen to like your looks, you won't be able to register if you're the French ambassador himself! The carpets are so soft in the lobby that it makes people pipe down just to step on 'em—and have you noticed the Mellow-Lume lights that give that soft-flavored glow in the halls?—Though, believe me! there's a sharp-eyed old dame at the desk in front of the elevator—and she don't drink and never dozes!

—I got picked up in Denver once by one of those heavy-lidded house-detectives, and any rough diamond from the West that tries to start shenanigans in his room will soon hear the voice of a pity-less fate cracking down on him over the phone!—But once you're inside and once you're all right, *then* you're sittin' on top of the world!—now *aren't* yuh on the crest?—*aren't* yuh?

CHET. Just what you were saying, Beppo?

BOSTOCK. I'll bet you were saying so! Why wouldn't yuh? You're luxurious here—you're looked up to! You're in a position to high-hat anybody in the world! (*As Beth and Charlotte smile*) Don't laugh! Don't we all like to Ritz people? Don't we really?

BETH. Of course!

BOSTOCK. Of course we do! We all like a thing better because we know other people can't have it! And you people here—I can see it! you're just the very clientèle that I built this place expressly for!—In a way you get more out of it than I do, because I always see it behind the scenes.—Say, sometimes I've wished I was a stranger checking in here for the first time! As I walk along the halls at night and look at the slits of light, I think to myself, There's Life!—Life as it ought to be lived! Glamor! Poetry! Passion! Excitement, Beauty, Success! Charming sophisticates like yourselves—old tapestries and gloriously striped bath-towels—a service that thanks you twice and never shows surprise at anything—a radio by every bed-side, an ice-water tap in every bathroom! A really civilized atmosphere—now *isn't* it?—You've seen the real old prints of English fox-hunts and the engravings of French *grandes dames* having their fun in their boudoirs!—And say: I'm soon going to put in taps for coffee and fizzy water, too!—

BETH. What a marvelous idea!

BOSTOCK. Isn't it marvelous?—But, as I say, it's all for you! Sometimes—here's a funny thing! maybe you won' believe it but it's the fact! sometimes I feel that though I'm boss here, I'm never going to get past the lobby; sometimes I feel like my own house detective was going to jump me in my room! So it's *you* who're the real insiders here! In a way, I'm still an outsider.

CHET. We exist in your imagination.

BEPPO. And sometimes for a moment in our own.

CHET. You've had the r-really exciting life, though.

BOSTOCK. Well, anyway, the pay-off is this: today when I go to the Ritz in Paris, I've only got to give a belch and the manager sends me roses!

*The telephone rings, and Beppo answers it: an excited blaring voice is heard, so ear-splitting that Beppo has to hold the receiver away.*

BEPPO. Oh, hello, Mr. Gibbs! . . . I see—that's quite all right . . . Yes: do come in later if you can . . . Yes: I understand—I'm sorry . . . Goodby—yes: do come if you can! (*Hanging up*) That's Godbrow Gibbs, who was supposed to come: he says he's too busy to eat.

BOSTOCK. You bet he's busy! He's busy as hell! Godbrow Gibbs holds a mortgage on the Richelieu-Versailles, and he and my other creditors are working night and day right now to assemble the biggest plot of ground in New York! We're going to borrow enough money for the super-colossal hotel of the world that will meet my obligations on this one! It's Napoleonic, but I'll swing it!— (*With a glance at Charlotte*) Where's your "go-bust" then?

CHARLOTTE. Just a few weeks farther off.

BEPPO (*to Bostock*). Look here: why don't you stay to dinner? You've evidently been sent us by Heaven to take Godbrow Gibbs's place.

BOSTOCK. Why, I'd be *enchanté*! Sure you want me? It's damn decent of you to ask me when I've barged in on you uninvited like this and talked like a burst main!

*The telephone rings, and Chang goes to answer it.*

BEPPO. Not at all—very happy to have you!—

CHANG. That's for you, Miss Miles. It's Mr. Payne.—
(*To Beppo*) Dinner is ready.

*Mimi goes to the phone.*

MIMI. Hello . . . Oh: just a minute . . . (*To Beppo*) I'll
use the upstairs phone so I won't disturb you. . . . Jack's
got some kind of long story to tell.

BEPPO. Is it necessary? Well, we won't wait for you.
Don't be too long!

*She hurries up the stairs and disappears in her room.*

BEPPO. Shall we go in?

*The ladies go first.*

LONGBROKE (*to Bostock*). To a Britisher like myself that
seems rather a risky way of doing things, what you were
telling us about building hotels. Is that considered really
sound in America?

BOSTOCK. You British are too damn conservative!—it
takes Yankee initiative to put it over!— (*To Beppo, after
everybody else has gone into the dining-room*) Oh, if you'll
pardon me a moment, I ought to call up the desk and let
them know where I am. You go in—I'll join you in a jiffy.

BEPPO. Certainly: the house phone's right there.

BOSTOCK. Right-o!

*Beppo and Longbroke go in. Bostock, left alone, glances toward
the dining-room door, then in the direction of Mimi's room.
He then takes a paper of cocaine from his pocket and administers
a liberal sniff.*

*In the meantime, a silent figure has appeared just inside the
entrance to the hall—a young, pale, rather tense-looking man,
nattily dressed in a light gray suit. He is intently watching Bostock.*

*Mimi comes out of her room and starts down the stairs.
Bostock goes toward the phone. Mimi sees the man in the
doorway and recognizes him.*

MIMI. Hello, Al—it's all right—Mr. Payne just got me
on the phone——

*Bostock, hearing her voice, looks up at her. The man fires twice at Bostock, then disappears through the hall. Bostock puts his left hand to his right shoulder and collapses on the sofa, where he sits panic-stricken and gasping. Mimi, on the stairs, stands petrified.*

*Beppo comes rushing in from the dining-room, followed by the guests and Chang.*

BEPPO. What's happened? (*Bostock does not answer.*) What's the matter? Gosh, he's been shot!

CHET. Good Heavens!

BEPPO. Phone downstairs for a doctor, Chang!—tell them to call the police!

# ACT II

*Chet, Charlotte, Longbroke, Beth and June drinking highballs after dinner. A bottle of Scotch on the table.*

CHET. And w-when I w-woke up in the morning, there were five glasses of water on the table. I'd put them there before I went to bed.

BETH. You poor dear! you used to do that when you were married to me.—I think there were only three then.

CHET. And since then every time we give a party, I write a little note to myself telling myself I'm not going to drink, and I put it in my pocket and take it out and read it from time to time.

CHARLOTTE. It wouldn't be a bad plan if you did it before other people's parties!

CHET. No: the wh-whole idea of a party is that the guests are supposed to drink. You take turns being the host and keeping sober.

JUNE. We get some funny drunks at the Purple Hour. (*Giggling*) There was one woman in there the other night all dressed up in ermine like a sore thumb and she went away so plastered that she was afraid to stand up in the elevator and she hiked down the whole five flights on her fanny!

BETH. You heard about Peggy Fisher's little exploit in Central Park?

THE OTHERS. No.—No.—What?

BETH. She wandered away from a party at the Jamisons' —feeling the need of a little fresh air—and walked over as far as the reservoir, and then she heard somebody running

348

ehind her, and she looked around and saw what she took
o be a man in his BVD's coming after her with lustful
tent. She ran around the reservoir, and the man ran
ound after her. They did two or three laps before she
ot wise to the fact that he was merely a runner in his
ack pants.

*Laughter.*

LONGBROKE. Strange to think that there's just been a
hooting here! Do people always treat them so casually?

CHET. There's r-really nothing we can do about it?

LONGBROKE. Was it really a gangster affair, do you
uppose?

CHET. S-so the policemen said. This man evidently knew
hey'd put him on the spot, and that was why he came in
ere. It s-seems he'd been expected somewhere else, and
e'd evidently gotten scared and stayed away.

JUNE. I've heard about Fred Bostock: he's in the dope
acket.

CHARLOTTE. No doubt the police know all about him—
now exactly who shot him and why. But they won't do
nything about it! The whole situation is unspeakable!

CHET. And Bostock won't tell who did it—that's part
f the underworld code.

JUNE. Those cops were a couple of dumb clucks!—
hey couldn't find out anything, anyway!

BETH. I don't know—I thought the tall thin one seemed
een—but then I have a yen for slim men with prematurely
ray hair.

LONGBROKE. Really? I much preferred the other one—
he one with the big shoulders!

CHET. That shows h-how the underworld is creeping up
n us now—that we should talk about having "yens" for
eople. That's underworld slang, I understand.

BETH. Yes: people used to have "crushes," didn't they?
—crushes were sentimental.

CHET. Whereas "yen" is simply thieves' gibberish.~
And a business used to be a "game," nowadays it's alway
a "racket."

BETH. It's affecting the fashions, too. Adalbert Fishe
it seems, makes Phoebe wear white gloves, so that she'
look like a gunman's moll.

CHET. She'd h-have to get rid of that lisp before sh
could deceive me!

CHARLOTTE. That doesn't account for everything. Wh
does he make her get up at two in the morning and s
with a paper-bag over her head?

BETH. People get their fun in strange ways!

JUNE. I'll say!

CHET. That d-doesn't seem strange to me at all: if
were m-married to Phoebe Fisher, I'd think it was th
most natural thing in the world to put her head in
p-paper-bag!

CHARLOTTE. Her efforts to make him jealous are pathetic

BETH. Adalbert isn't quite bright himself. He threatene
to drown himself in Lake Placid once because I refuse
to fly with him, and I stopped him by telling him he'
be sure to catch cold.

*Dr. Tinker and Beppo come in from the hall.*

CHET. Well, how is he getting along, Doctor?

DR. TINKER. Nothing serious! He'll just have to wea
his arm in a sling for a couple of weeks or so.

BEPPO. That gunman must have been a poor shot.~
Well, it all goes to show that you can't be too carefu
nowadays about whom you invite to dinner.

CHET. I th-thought you were taking a chance.

BEPPO. I thought if I cultivated him socially, I migl
induce him to come down on the rent.

BETH. He was hopped up like a Hollywood directo
He had enough snow on the lapels of his coat to do th
big blizzard scene from *The Old Homestead*.

DR. TINKER. He's a thorough-going neurotic, but he won't let one do anything for him.

BEPPO. Dr. Tinker's by way of being an analyst.

DR. TINKER. Not a professional one: I only fool around with it.

CHARLOTTE. I don't approve of that.

DR. TINKER. I shouldn't care to be a professional analyst. I dislike so very much the class of people one would have to have as colleagues.

BETH. You must have a rich field as house physician here.

DR. TINKER. I should say that 70 per cent of the people here have more or less serious neuroses.

LONGBROKE. Really?

DR. TINKER. —And a good many of the rest have psychoses.

CHET. Gee!

DR. TINKER. The others are borderline cases. Like our poor friend Bostock here, they've taken to drink or drugs in the hope of escaping from neurotic anxieties.

BEPPO. Won't you have a drink, by the way?

DR. TINKER. Thank you, yes.— (*Beppo pours him one and he takes it.*) Last week, for example, I had a pathetic young man who used to wake up every morning and think he had to jump out the window. A plain case of conviction of guilt based on a mother complex.

BEPPO (*to Beth*). Where's Mimi?

BETH. She went up to her room. She was a little upset over the shooting. I think she's all right though. I gave her some spirits of ammonia.

BEPPO. I'll go up for a minute if you don't mind.—Why not move into the library and get away from the scene of the crime.—I want June to play you her new stuff.

CHET. Swell!

JUNE. I don't know if they want to hear it.

BETH. We're mad to hear it!

*She immediately takes command and herds June and Longbroke into the library. Beppo starts for the stairs, but is halted by the ringing of the door-bell. Chang comes out of the dining-room to answer it, and Mimi appears at her door.*

CHET (*to Dr. Tinker*). W-What did your young man with the feelings of guilt think he was guilty of?

DR. TINKER. Swindling people—selling them bad bonds.

CHARLOTTE. How do you know he hadn't?

DR. TINKER. He had, as a matter of fact.

CHET. Then h-how do you know it was a mother complex?

DR. TINKER. If he hadn't been a neurotic, he wouldn't have worried about it.

*They follow the others into the library.*

BEPPO (*to Chang, returning from the hall*). Who is it?—Mr. Gibbs?

CHANG. It's Mr. Payne for Miss Miles.

BEPPO. Oh! (*Mimi starts downstairs; he looks up at her.*) All right, but don't bring him into the library.

MIMI. Ask him to come in here, Chang.

*Beppo goes into the library. Chang ushers in Jack Payne. He is well set-up and good-looking, about thirty; wears a dress suit. With June and in the scenes that follow, he imposes himself by frankness and boldness. During his conversation with Mimi, June is heard playing jazz, lively or sentimental.*

MIMI. Hello!

PAYNE. Hello, Radiant!

*He kisses her.*

MIMI. We've just been having great excitement here.

PAYNE. What type of excitement?

MIMI. Why, a screwball named Luke Bostock—it seems he owns the hotel—suddenly erupted on us, and then somebody else turned up and shot him.

*Payne raises his eyebrows.*

PAYNE. Fatal?

MIMI. No; he wasn't badly hurt, it seems—but, Jack, I happened to come downstairs just as the man fired the shots—I was the only person who saw—and I'm sure it was Al Gammel.

PAYNE (*after a second's thought*). It could have been him. He's been over with those Second Avenue mugs.

MIMI. He's not with you any more?

PAYNE. Not since a couple of weeks. He doped so he wasn't no good no more. If he missedum, it must have been Al.

MIMI. But why should they want to shoot Bostock particularly?

PAYNE. Bostock's got delusions of grandeur—thinks he's a big dealer.

MIMI. What do you mean?

PAYNE. Gambling joint on the floor below this, with everything that goes with it.

MIMI. Really? How amazing!

PAYNE. I suppose some of those Second Avenue pansies got dissatisfied with him for some reason. He'd double-crossed them probably—tried to do business with some-body else. They're tough, those East Side hoodlums—they're the boys that shave with blow-torches. Don't let it worry you though—there's a lot of haphazard popping going on around here just now.—Police come and gone?

MIMI. Yes.—You won't get involved in it, will you, on account of Al's having worked for you?

PAYNE. I never get involved.—You didn't talk to your father about that other thing?

MIMI. I haven't had any chance. Besides, Jack, I guess that I ought to wait. He'd hit the ceiling now.

PAYNE. He's got to lose you sometime.

MIMI. After all, I'm still supposed to finish school.

PAYNE. Listen: school isn't everything. I went to school while. When my mother took up with the corner druggist, they made me go to school—I finished a year of high-school——

MIMI. And you hated it?

PAYNE. It was all right, but I didn't want no more. About the only thing I learned there that was worth anything to me was the primary rules of polite intercourse. The first month I went to school, whenever anybody made a pass at me—like in talking or handing me something, see?—why, I'd put up my mitts like this. Where I came from, you had to be ready to defend yourself against all comers—if you didn't put up your fists, you were a sap—as good as dead, see?—Well, they taught me at school that in respectable society, any pass that is made at you by anybody is supposed to be in the way of kindness. Well, a few pretenses like that, I figure, is about all an education can do for you—and *you've* got all the pretenses down perfect.

MIMI. I know: school is terribly silly—but I'm supposed to go to Mother in the spring, and it would really be easier to work it then. I could just go away with you instead. Why do you insist on going now?

PAYNE. I thought I'd told you that.

MIMI. But we'll still be seeing each other.

PAYNE. When you belong to each other, you belong to each other. You and I are nothing the way it is—neither one thing nor the other!

MIMI. We've been something to each other the last two weeks.

PAYNE. Yes, and then you get up and turn on the light, and I have to take you home!

MIMI. I know: it's perfectly heart-breaking——

PAYNE. You say your father is sore. Why not break i to him and get it over?

MIMI. I know that it would harrow him too mucl just now——

PAYNE. Say, think about *me* sometimes! I've been waiting for you all my life. You're the only girl I ever wanted to marry. I've had women I took around, but not as an equal—not like you. Some birds take these night-club hotcha girls and try to put them over on the stage—some take these cigarette and coat-room girls and try to put them over as hotcha—some take girls on their block and give them a job selling cigarettes. But not me! I wouldn't try to make nothing out of nobody! I figure that anybody who's got it has got it developed already—I don't want any woman that's got to depend on something that somebody else can do for them! I've passed 'em all up: night-club hostesses and dancers—Ritzy lady gyps! Some people will ruin themselves for a tart with a big reputation——

MIMI. Dad fell for one once—his third wife.

PAYNE. Lots do. But not me! When it comes to me, Ritz isn't enough and hotcha isn't enough—I've got to have a real natural princess that burns with her own power!

MIMI. You'll turn a girl's head with that princess stuff!

PAYNE. You know what you said that night on the boat.

MIMI. You remember what *you* said about letting me arrange it any way I wanted.

PAYNE. When you love somebody, you'd ought to be with them. Christ, what else is there to life?—The whole thing's phony if you look at it that way. What is there to it but a fight to the finish? You might be absolutely on the level—you might give everybody his due and never double-cross anybody—but ninety-nine per cent of them are ready to double-cross you. Why? Because they're naturally snakes? No: because they're ambitious just like you are. But you can't let them get away with it, and then *you're* the hard-hearted bastard. And after while you don't trust nobody that's anywhere near as wise as you are, and the people that you trust, they're not wise and you can't get interested in them. It's what I say, you want your equal! I used to have a girl that I'd take on that boat—and she was all right in a way, but I was all the time having to make her pipe down and I never gave her a third drink!—I want to have that boat with somebody that she and I can enjoy it *together*!

MIMI. It would be awful if I realized some day that you weren't offering me a third drink!

PAYNE. Why, once we get aboard that boat, we won't need to worry about nothing! A boat is about the only place, I figure, where people can really be free. We'll look the whole world over: Havana—Panama—Honolulu! You could take that boat to Europe, and we'll do it some day! We'll be King and Queen on the old *Ace of Hearts*!—just us two together! When I named her, I didn't know you, but I named her after you!

MIMI. This sounds like a musical comedy! When do we go into our song?

PAYNE. So I'm just another crooner! That's all it means to you, huh, when I tell you how much I love you?

*The sound of the piano has stopped. As Mimi is about to reply, Longbroke and Beppo come in from the library.*

BEPPO (*coldly*). Oh, how do you do, Payne?

MIMI. Mr. Longbroke, this is Jack Payne.

LONGBROKE (*shaking hands*). Not, Mr. Jack Payne, the celebrated bootlegger?

*Mimi is embarrassed, but Payne takes it humorously.*

PAYNE. Well, I don't exactly answer phone calls: I'm more in the wholesale business.

LONGBROKE. I see: American bootlegging is really one of the national industries, isn't it?

PAYNE (*smiling*). It seems to have its place in the picture.

BEPPO (*who has been looking at Mimi to see the effect of this revelation—wondering whether she knew already*). So you're in the liquor business, Mr. Payne?

PAYNE. I do some importing and brewing.

LONGBROKE. I'm surprised at your not having heard of him—Mr. Payne is a well-known person!

BEPPO. I don't follow bootlegging closely. (*To Payne*) Won't you have a drink, by the way?

PAYNE. Thank you.

BEPPO. Help yourself—you know what you like. I'd be interested to have your professional opinion on that. It's supposed to be Old Hallowell rye.

PAYNE (*tasting it*). That's not Old Hallowell. It's all right: it's not cut very much. But it's not Old Hallowell. I'll send you some real Old Hallowell, and you'll be able to see the difference.

BEPPO. Don't bother, thanks. I have a regular man, and I may as well stick to him.

MIMI. Jack's offering you a present, Dad!

BEPPO. Oh, I see: I beg your pardon. Thank you very much, but don't trouble!— (*to Longbroke*) This must all seem ghastly to you. Imagine the liquor trade outlawed and driven underground, till it gets into the hands of the criminal classes. In England, your great brewers and distillers get knighthoods; in America, they get night-clubs!

MIMI. Is that the best you can do, Dad? You'd better leave wisecracks to Jimmy Walker!

LONGBROKE. I don't believe our biggest distillers, you know, make half as much as your big bootleggers. Al Capone's income is supposed to be something like $30,000,000 a year, isn't it?

BEPPO. I really don't know——

PAYNE. It's hard to tell: you can figure out how much Capone makes, but you can't tell how much it costs him in campaign funds and things like that.

LONGBROKE. I say: I don't suppose there'd be any sort of opening for a chap like me in your racket? You people do a lot of business with our steamship lines, I understand.

PAYNE. Might be. The right kind of Englishman can get away with murder.

LONGBROKE. I'm afraid I shouldn't be good at murder. That's a department of commercial activity that we haven't done much with in England. I was thinking of the business side.

MIMI. That's just a saying, Mr. Longbroke: he didn't mean real murder.

LONGBROKE. But that sort of thing does happen—the shooting of this fellow here tonight, for example.

BEPPO. It does happen: your mistake was natural. And the liquor interests are often responsible.

PAYNE. Sometimes they're irresponsible.—You've got some swell pictures here. I do a little collecting myself—just grabbed off some Periwinkos.—What's this?

BEPPO. That's a Periwinko.

PAYNE. He must have had the rams when he did that one. Or maybe he hadn't learned to draw yet.

BEPPO. As a matter of fact, it's recent.

PAYNE. Well, Paris gets a man in the long run!

BEPPO. After all, you know, everybody in Paris isn't making whoopee all the time, like American tourists on the loose. Periwinko doesn't spend all his nights at night-clubs!

PAYNE. Paris gets a man just the same, and here's the way it gets him. Now take us Americans, for instance: whatever life offers us, we eat it up: work, play, speed, liquor, love. Whereas the French have to sniff things before they can drink them—and when they do start to drink them, they just sip them—and by the time they've finally got them down, they've forgotten it's something to drink and they're talking about the way it sniffs. And that's the reason I say that Paris is the finish of a man like Periwinko: it's got him so he only gives out whiffs. Those pictures are just a couple of whiffs!

BEPPO (*getting angrier and angrier*). No doubt of it: what poor Periwinko needs is a good souse on bootleg Scotch!

LONGBROKE. Mr. Payne takes the opposite view from our friend Mr. Bostock just now. Bostock wants to outdo the French, but Mr. Payne has the courage of his tastes.

PAYNE (*turning seriously to Longbroke*). If you get that outdoing idea, you're ruined. I say, find out what you really get a kick out of and do it for the kick!

BEPPO. It must be a great advantage to have tastes that are so easily satisfied.

PAYNE. Well, everything is bound to go sour on you if you stay around here too long—and that's why I say, get away! The time has come to pull out from here. That's why I own a boat.

MIMI. We'd better leave *here*, at any rate, if the show begins at 11.

PAYNE. O.K., Princess.— (*To Beppo, shaking hands*) Well, good night now. Nice to have seen you. (*To Longbroke, shaking hands*) Good night.

LONGBROKE. I say: don't forget my suggestion!

PAYNE. Fine: let's talk about it. Give me a buzz.

*Chet drifts in from the library, with his glass in his hand.*

MIMI. Well, good night, Mr. Longbroke. Good night, Chet. Say good night to the rest for me, will you?

CHET. Oh, are you going out, Mimi? Well, we h-hate to see you go, but our loss is somebody's gain!

BEPPO (*to Mimi*). Don't make it an all-night affair, please. Remember Miss French's in the morning!

MIMI. I came of age last month, you know, Dad!

*She and Payne go. Beppo stands looking after them, baffled and resentful. Longbroke takes advantage of the moment to go over to the cigarette box and put a supply in his pocket.*

LONGBROKE. I say: you don't mind if I lift a few cigarettes.

359

BEPPO (*to Chet*). Mimi's gone out with a bootlegger! What can you do about children nowadays?

CHET. Do-Don't worry about Mimi, Beppo!—she's a f-fine little girl! These kids know how to take care of themselves. They're not scared of life—it's swell!

BEPPO. I know, but they're so confoundedly sophisticated! No sentiment! No romance! they don't even take each other seriously. Mimi doesn't care an atom about that fellow: all she wants is some new excitement!

*Beth appears at the library door.*

BETH. Come back here, you saps!—we need men. Get away from those high-balls, Chet! Come back in here, Horseley—I want to hear your lovely voice!

LONGBROKE. Oh, come!

*He goes into the library with her. Beppo and Chet continue their conversation.*

CHET (*shaking his head*). —But the grown people aren't any better. P-People aren't human any more—they're g-getting more and more that way——

BEPPO. They're desperately unhappy most of them. Look how many are going to pieces!—Let me freshen your drink.

CHET. Thank you. (*Holding out his glass*) —I know; and that's why the only thing is to hold on tight to art! Damn it all! (*Clenching his fist in a slightly drunken gesture of earnestness*) Hold on to art! Art is the only thing left that can keep us from cracking up! When I go back into my studio every morning, it doesn't matter what I leave behind—I find something there that I can fasten on to like —like a sea-anemone blooming with the tide on his rock. Suppose it's only a jug—a white jug, say, on a white table cloth with two green tomatoes beside it. Just a jug and two green tomatoes! but *there's* something that can't disintegrate: there's form! *There's* something that can't go bilious: there's color! The sun may be rising and setting on a washed-up generation, but *there* are a few rays from it that haven't been spoiled by liver-specks dancing around in them. The light from the days that have faded is still there in green and white on the canvas—it's still there in the tomatoes and the jug. You may fade out yourself every evening, and finally you'll fade out entirely, but you've made something that lives in the world of art —you've succeeded in putting something of yourself into something outside yourself, and it may still be there when you've folded up!

BEPPO. That's all right for you, Chet—you're a painter, you can do it. But I'm not really an artist——

CHET. Of course, you are—don't be silly!

BEPPO. What can I do but draw little grotesques?

CHET. That's all that Hogarth could do—that's all that Goya was doing!

BEPPO. But I'm not in their class.

CHET. You're fine, Beppo—you're swell! You've got a bite and—and an imagination that nobody else can touch!

BEPPO. But what good will all that be when I'm working for Godbrow Gibbs? People like Hogarth and Goya didn't have to boost American business! I'm not really keen on this job! After years of doing glad girls for magazines, I thought I'd earned the right to do cynical tigers, and now I can't bear the idea of having my nasty little tigers go glad!

CHET. Don't do it!—keep them sour as hell!

BEPPO. But I can't now that *Art and Fashion* is dead!

CHET (*shaking his head*). Don't sell out! Never sell out!

BEPPO. Good God, Chet! *I've* got to draw for a living! You haven't got a daughter to provide for, and Charlotte has money of her own. I bet you wouldn't find that jug and apples were such an impregnable Rock of Ages if they were really the only support you had!

CHET. You know, if this were only Mexico, a man with your kind of talent could make little pottery figures and tiles with animals on them—you could do all sorts of charming things!

BEPPO. Yes: if I'd been born a Mexican Indian, I might have been really happy. I could have sat in my sunny little patio and made little jugs and banks and have felt myself a part of the life of the people—part of their civilization!

CHET. Exactly: what you made would be *used* for something! That's the trouble with modern art—what we do isn't ever used!

BEPPO. Good God, Chet—*that* may be true of you exhibiting artists who do nothing but adorn the galleries, but I can tell you it isn't the case with me. Once I start working for Gibbs, I'll be used and used plenty! (*Picking up the evening paper*) Look at that! that's where I'll be— just underneath the Gonk family—on the same page with one of those lousy cartoons that have everything in them but the kitchen stove! Here's Miriam Followell Forbes, you see, advising girls to do their necking in the hallways rather than ask the young men up to their rooms—and here's Herman Godbrow Gibbs emitting his daily blatt of balderdash! And here's poor old Beppo Miles with his poor little old half-hearted tigers being used to help put over Gibbs's balderdash!—Well, the Gibbses and the Paynes have won out in our world, and there doesn't seem to be anything left for *us* except to try to be as vulgar as they are, in the hope of getting some of the loot!

*The telephone: Beppo goes; Gibbs's voice again.*

BEPPO. Oh, hello, Mr. Gibbs . . . that's all right—it doesn't matter. No, come whenever it's convenient . . . I have a party here, and I expect to be up indefinitely . . . All right. . . . No: that's all right. Goodby.

CHET. My God, he sounds like a lost bull!

BEPPO. He's hot-foot after Prosperity!—Well, maybe

the old dear can snare it!—If I lend him my little tigers to smile hope and faith back into people's hearts, I'll be able to afford the luxury of spitting on their dearest beliefs!— Let me freshen up your drink.

*He does so and fills his own glass.*

CHET. If you c-could only c-combine what Gibbs has got with what the Mexican p-peasants have got! I'm going to drop another penny in that cow in honor of the Mexican peasants! (*He does so.*)

*Beth comes back from the library.*

BETH. They need drinks in there, Beppo! Why don't you look after your guests? You ought to have had him put a bottle in the library.

BEPPO (*ringing for Chang*). Do you find that Beth still tries to run you?

CHET. Of course.

BETH. Charlotte's evidently making a better job of it.

*Chang appears at the dining-room door.*

BEPPO. Bring another bottle of Scotch, Chang.

CHET. I've got a better working routine now.

BETH. And she's got an artist to go with her studio, so everything is perfectly splendid!

CHET. Charlotte has a stabilizing effect—you and I used to get on each other's nerves so.

BETH. Yes: I wasn't much of a stabilizer, I'm afraid.

CHET (*to Beppo*). One winter when we were out on the Coast, we sat through a whole earthquake and never knew whether it had really happened—we thought maybe it was just a new neuro symptom. Neither of us dared mention it to the other till we saw it in the paper the next morning.

BEPPO (*to Beth*). Were you and Chet in California worse than you and I in Paris?

BETH. You and I would never have sat and jittered—it was knock-down and drag-out with us!

CHET. Yes, you really loved Beppo—you never cared so much about me!

BETH. Have we got to go into that at this time of day?

CHET. I used to get jealous of you and wonder why Beth was so fond of you—she being so unsentimental and you such a romantic ham. Then I realized it was the ham in you that attracted her, and I knew that was something I could never give her!

*Chang has brought the Scotch and gone back.*

BEPPO. You go to hell!—you and your tomatoes! Why *green* tomatoes, anyway? Why not red tomatoes?

BETH. Let Chet's tomatoes alone, Beppo, and attend to the drink situation! Why didn't you have him take it into the library?

*June starts playing again in the next room:* Let's Put Out the Lights and Go to Sleep.

BEPPO. Do stop worrying, Beth. You're a guest here tonight—you're supposed to relax!

BETH. If your guests relaxed, there'd be no party!

CHET (*picking up the tray*). Well, go to it! *I'll* take the Scotch in. I want to hear the little jazz-player.

*He goes into the library with the tray.*

BETH. I can do without any more of her. I don't see that it's so remarkably different from putting a nickel in the mechanical piano.

BEPPO. She has unmistakable talent, I think.

BETH. She was just telling me about her relations. It seems they line up at the stage door every Saturday afternoon and make her give them most of her salary.

BEPPO. Yes: I've asked her why she lets them have it all, and she says: "Why, they used to rob houses and stick people up for *me*, so I've got to do something for them." It's a much simpler kind of morality than the kind we pretend to practice, but they come nearer to living up to it.

364

BETH. Beppo, you're full of bilge! I suppose you'll be paying her alimony soon. You're certainly God's gift to ambitious girls!

BEPPO. I'm not marrying any more.

BETH. That's good news!

BEPPO. I don't regret my first two marriages though.

BETH. How sweet of you to say so!

BEPPO. No, I mean it—I often miss you terribly still. Nobody for drinks at the end of the day—nobody to sit down and gab with!

BETH. What about Mimi and June?

BEPPO. For one thing, they're both too young. As you get older, it's not the same with people. You want people who have shared your experience. And it's funny what it does to you to split up with somebody you've loved and lived with: it's as if you'd cut off a whole part of your past—as if you couldn't use it any more. It's almost as if you could lose your youth by not sticking with the people you loved when you were young. You can never be young for new people.

BETH. So far as I'm concerned, it's an infinite relief to be with people who haven't known me!

BEPPO. Yes, I know: that's true once you've separated. Old love affairs make you uncomfortable. It's the ache in the hand that's been amputated.

BETH. The pain in the decapitated neck!

BEPPO. And there's nothing you can do about it: you can never get back to what's been broken. We just have to go on being carried along to the new girls and the new lovers with whom we can never have youth in common——

BETH. Shut up!—I'm almost eight years younger than you!—and my next union's going to be a permanent one!

BEPPO (*holding up his glass*). Here's to the next Duchess of Wormwood Scrubs!

BETH (*holding up her glass in retort*). Here's to your career as a patron of gifted night-club entertainers!

BEPPO. Hail and farewell, my dear!

BETH. Don't get maudlin, Beppo!

*June in the next room stops playing. Longbroke comes back from the library.*

LONGBROKE (*to Beth*). I was wondering what had become of you!

BETH. Oh, Horseley! I'm right here and longing for you!

BEPPO. Well, I'll leave you two young people together!

BETH. Do!

*Beppo goes into the library.*

LONGBROKE. It was so swell to find you here!

BETH. It was so perfectly glorious to find *you*!

*He kisses her, and she meets him emphatically.*

BETH. Again!

*They kiss again.*

BETH. Let's sit down.

*They sit down on the sofa.*

LONGBROKE. Well, how have you been shaping up?

BETH. Now let me advise you, Horseley: you'd much better let American alone. That isn't right at all! I'm already shaped: can't you see?

LONGBROKE. Oh.

BETH (*very animated again*). If you want to know how I've been, I've been horrid! I *hate* my apartment and I *hate* my work and I *hate* the woman I work for!—I hate everything except you! (*She seizes his hand and squeezes it with both of hers.*)

LONGBROKE. You've been such a godsend to *me*!

BETH. And my heart's not often stirred, I can assure you —it hasn't registered a tremor for ages. I haven't been able to give a damn whether I ever saw anybody's sickening face since God knows when!

LONGBROKE. I like you awfully, too

BETH. Do you really, my dear? I know you do!

LONGBROKE. Yes, truly—I'm frightfully keen on you!—
I suppose the decorating business does get to be quite
odious in the long run—though you went into it merely
for the fun of the thing, didn't you?

BETH. Fun! Do you think I kiss the asses of Central
Park West for fun? Do you imagine that anything but the
direst necessity would ever have landed me in the clutches
of that foul old harpy Ada Force?—It's no fun for me, I
assure you, to palm off Ada's middle-class excrement as
the pomp of the Medicis!

LONGBROKE. I didn't know you disliked it so—I thought
you did it more or less as a hobby.

BETH. No, my dear, it's the way I make my living!

LONGBROKE. I see.—But I suppose it justifies itself from
the remunerative point of view.

BETH. Not for me! *My* remuneration is a lousy little
walk-up on Lexington Avenue! There's an addressograph
up above me and a furrier underneath, and it sounds like
a boiler factory and smells like a million wet cats!

LONGBROKE. But your firm has the reputation of being
extremely successful.

BETH. Ada's successful—the business is successful. But
the only thing that *I* get out of it is a teeny-weeny little
salary and a commission on the jobs I bring in. And as
I bring in damn few jobs, I get damn little commission.
The idea was that I frequented social regions where Ada
didn't penetrate and that I was to go out and bag high-
class customers. But although I can be brash about anything else, I'm reduced to an abject jelly when it comes to
using social relations to put over commercial deals! It's
just too obscene and impossible!

LONGBROKE. Still, one shouldn't let such opportunities
slip.

BETH. Listen to him: isn't he sweet trying to talk like a go-getting business man! (*She kisses him.*) As if *you* could make capital out of your social connections! No decent Englishman could dream of it. *You* couldn't do it, my dear, if your very life depended on it! And in my case the final result has been that, instead of bringing back big game from Park Avenue, I find myself over in Brooklyn among the gefüllte-fish, designing bedroom, dining-room and living-room in mulberry, orchid and blue for families that live in the kitchen!

LONGBROKE. That does seem an odd occupation.

BETH. It's horrid—and that's why it's such an unspeakable relief to find somebody, my dear, like you! When I see you, all the *sordid* and *beastly* and *rancid* and *grating* things—all the *tacky ugly* people—seem just to be cleared away by a fresh gust of air from the English downs! I used to adore England!—those light feathery forests they have in Surrey and those tiny little silver rivers that look as if they'd been arranged by gardeners! And the marvelous big country houses that still look like Elizabethan England, way back behind their grounds and hedges! We don't have anything here like that! We don't have that distinction and dignity! Those places are so tranquil and so sure of themselves! They don't have to truckle and grab and scheme!—And you know that they stand for the loyalties that last for ever and ever.

LONGBROKE. My place in England just now is in frightfully bad condition!

BETH. What a perfect public school boy he is! Your house is in frightful condition!—Kiss me, you sweet thing! (*He kisses her, but she brusquely pulls her lips away.*) You kissed me coldly that time! What's the matter? What did I do to throw you off?

LONGBROKE. You've done nothing: you've been charming!

BETH. No: there's something you don't like! What is it? What did I do? Was I loud?—did my bad language jar on you? I'm really the prude of the world, you know! I'm sorry that I shot off my mouth in such a great big blat of blah! but I go around the shop all day like a little furtive mouse and I have to howl and bawl when I get away!

LONGBROKE. One does need to blow off steam, I think. —I say: shall we join the others?

BETH. Good heavens, Horseley! What is it?—I never saw such a chill descend! It can't be just my neurotic imagination!

LONGBROKE. Nothing, truly. It's just getting a bit late, and I wanted to have a word with Mrs. Chives about the bathroom fixture field.

BETH. Horseley, can it be that I've been wrong about you? Can it be that your commercial instincts are more highly developed than I thought?

*He hesitates a moment and has just opened his mouth to say something when the rest of the party come back. All except June have drinks in their hands.*

BEPPO. We've decided to play the phonograph! The evening seems to have reached that point!

*He looks through the records, puts one on the machine, winds it up and starts it.*

CHET (*to June*). You're certainly a dandy jazz-player, June! If only the serious composers had half the real sparkle in what they write that you've got just in your fingers!——

BETH (*with bitterness*). "If only"! If only people weren't such worms!

*The door-bell rings. Chang goes.*

BEPPO. I suppose it's our friend Gibbs at last!

*They all look toward the hall. Luke Bostock appears, instead. His shoulder has been bandaged up, and he wears his arm in a sling, his dress-coat with its empty sleeve draped over it. Beppo turns off the phonograph.*

BOSTOCK. Well, here I am again—the old shootee! I just wanted to tell you how damn sorry I was for the mess I occasioned tonight. It was rude of me to butt in in the first place—and it was ruder to get shot in your sitting-room! Let me offer my sincerest apologies!

BEPPO. Not at all! We're only relieved that you didn't get seriously hurt!

BOSTOCK. Just a scratch in the shoulder, that's all!—

DR. TINKER. You must look out for the psychic strain!

BOSTOCK. Don't worry about me, Doc!—I feel splendid! A little work-out with a bullet clears the brain!

BEPPO. Won't you sit down and have a drink? (*He looks toward the table, then rings for Chang.*)

BOSTOCK. No drink, thanks, but I'll sit down if it won't pester you!

BEPPO. No, no! delighted to have you!— (*As Chang appears at the dining-room door*) Another bottle of Scotch, Chang—and ice and glasses.

BOSTOCK. I just wanted to reassure you that shootings are not daily occurrences in the life of the Richelieu-Versailles——

BEPPO (*smiling*). I'm not uneasy at all.

BOSTOCK. It was a mutinous dish-washer—I'm certain of it!

BEPPO. Do you think so?

*Chang brings in the Scotch.*

BOSTOCK. No question about it! There was one that set up a howl when we put in the new dish-washing machines and had to lay some of them off—and my belief is it was him: a Red!

*Beppo, struck by an idea, looks at Chang, who is just going back into the dining-room.*

BEPPO. The radicals are popping at people, you think?

BOSTOCK. Why not? Look at everything else they're doing! They're talking against the stock market and advertising unemployment and stirring up labor unrest!—they're driving the banks to ruin by whispering insinuations against them! Look at the way they're treating religion!—blowing up churches in Russia and interrupting Bishop Manning right in the middle of his sermon!

CHET (*with ironic intent*). What about the Ohio flood?

BOSTOCK. Yes: they started that rumor, too!—But *you* don't need to worry, charming people!—us big shots are the ones that take the risks!—we shoulder the big jobs, we give the public the big values, but we got to battle to do it!—and that's where the thrill comes in! You may think that business is tame, that it's just paper-work done in offices, that we business men are just men of paper who leave the real struggle to others. But *you* don't know the romance of business!—the romance and the glory and the agony! A big business man, when he enters his office, hears more than just the racket of the typewriters—and the swish of the filing-cabinets and the ringing of the telephone bells! —he hears the clanging of armor—and the clash and the crash of lances!—the gallant jousting of the perfect gentle knights with their ladies' favors flying in their helmets— and their bucklers all bedight and their hauberks shining bright!—Why, such men as us crushed Carthage and we builded imperial Rome! To the victor belong the spoils— Caesar was ambitious, why not?— (*Abruptly changing his tone*) It's a game of dog eat dog, and the dangerous part of it is that you're liable to be bopped by any cockeyed hoodlum that happens to get a hate on you!

BETH (*laughing*). You had us all ready to leap on our chargers when you struck that sudden note of grisly realism!

BOSTOCK (*stopping them with a downward movement of the palm*). All right! all right!—but it's *us* that have got to take it! For you, the amenities of civilized living!—your money's worth of sheer satisfaction!—For you, this refuge from the struggles of the age!—For you, this Caravanserai Beautiful!—

*Al Gammel has appeared in the doorway of the hall on the second floor of the duplex. Now he steps out on the balcony and shoots at Bostock twice. Only Longbroke and Beppo are standing in a position to see him when they hear the shots and look up. Bostock crumples and falls; he puts his hands to his side and groans.*

BEPPO. Good God!

*He and Dr. Tinker rush to Bostock and open his shirt. Chang comes in from the dining-room.*

BEPPO. Call the police, Chang!—Somebody go after the gunman!

LONGBROKE. One ought to have a gun, I think.

BEPPO. There's one in the drawer of that table!

*Longbroke gets out the gun and runs up the stairs, along the balcony and out into the upstairs hall. Chang has gone to the phone.*

BOSTOCK. Not fatal necessarily, Doc! Never touched the vital organs! Just a couple of random shots in the stomach!

DR. TINKER. Go easy—we don't want to start a hemor-rhage! Yes: one of them went right through here, you see.—Lift him up—very slowly, very gently! The place to put him is on that couch in the next room.

*Beppo, Tinker and Chet lift him.*

BETH (*to Charlotte, as she goes to help*). This is beginning to get on my nerves!

*She takes one side of Bostock.*

DR. TINKER (*to Beth*). It's purely psychological—a neu-rosis that compels him to become a victim. What he needs is a thorough analysis.

BOSTOCK. The hell you say, Doc! What I need is a bodyguard!

*They carry him into the library; June and Charlotte follow.*

CHANG (*at the telephone—he has had difficulty getting the office and has been saying:* Hello! Hello, Office! *most of the time during the preceding conversation*). . . . Yes: again!— Mr. Bostock has been shot a second time! . . . Tell them to watch the doors to see that the assailant does not escape . . . He ran out into the hall . . . Yes.

*He hangs up; Beppo comes back from the library.*

BEPPO. Did you call the police?

CHANG. Yes.

BEPPO (*giving him a suspicious look and going toward the telephone*). Perhaps I'd better call to make sure.

CHANG. I called them, Mr. Miles—I hope you don't believe what he said: that he was shot by a class-conscious dishwasher. You don't consider me responsible?

BEPPO. I hope you weren't.

CHANG. Such acts are not committed by Communists. We know today that terrorism is infantile. What good would it do to shoot the Mr. Bostocks? That would not bring the Revolution! But in the meantime the Mr. Bostocks fall victims to their own inherent contradictions. Mr. Bostock's crisis here tonight is only a particular instance of the general crisis of capitalism. In fulfilling his historic role, he generates the forces which destroy him. He was shot by a business rival.

DR. TINKER (*appearing at the door—to Chang*). Will you call up the drug-store—Eldorado 5-9829—and tell them to send some iodine? (*To Beppo*) What an amazing case! A regular classic of masochism! He keeps putting himself into situations where people will try to kill him! It's no use fixing him up—he'll only go and get plugged again!

BETH (*coming to the door and taking him by the shoulder*). Come back in here! You can't psychoanalyze him now! *Addressing the people inside the room*) And everybody else get out!

*June, Chet and Charlotte obey. Beppo and the Doctor go in.*

*Chang finds the line busy and looks up another drug-store in the phone-book.*

CHARLOTTE (*to Chet*). Beth is so competent at things like that!—it's a pity that her opinion of her social position has kept her from being a trained nurse!

*Longbroke comes back from his errand.*

LONGBROKE. Not a trace of him! Absolutely vanished!

*He lays the gun on the table and helps himself to more cigarettes.*

CHET (*going over and pouring himself a drink*). Good Lord! What a t-terrible state of things! A man can't be safe in his own apartment! We're really at the m-mercy of these thugs!

LONGBROKE. The police-system over here is quite different from ours in England. Here the police, I understand, are in business with the criminal elements, but at home they try to catch the robbers and murderers and that sort of people, and see that they go to jail.

CHET. If only the American government had some of the efficiency of the gangsters!

CHARLOTTE. It's outrageous! I'm going to the police myself! I'm going to the Police Commissioner!

*Beppo comes back from the library and finds Chang still at the phone, asking the drug-store to send the iodine up. While Beppo and Chang are talking, the others talk among themselves.*

BEPPO (*when Chang has hung up the receiver*). I thought you called up for that sometime ago!

CHANG. The line was busy, Mr. Miles—I had to call another drug-store.—Mr. Miles, I request that you will not suspect me of sabotaging the medical necessaries for Mr. Bostock. I tell you it would not be correct for a Communist to proceed by this method in liquidating the bourgeoisie!

BEPPO. What did you mean just now when you said it was a business rival who shot him?

CHANG. The liquor industry, like every other, in that degree to which it becomes more highly centralized, must to the same degree eliminate more and more persons.—

BEPPO. The liquor industry? Is Bostock a bootlegger?

CHANG. This Bostock is an importer of liquor and drugs as well as a proprietor of hotels. Concentration of trade in the hands of a few is characteristic of this phase of capitalism. He has been struggling with a formidable competitor, and he seems to be in danger of becoming one of the persons eliminated by the capitalist system. Thus life becomes more insecure for the bourgeois as well as the worker.

BEPPO. How do you know all this?

CHANG. It is a matter of common knowledge to everybody but the bourgeois intelligentsia. The more powerless the bourgeoisie becomes, the more it flees from facing its predicament.

BEPPO. I didn't know that this personal criticism was part of your duties, Chang.

CHANG. I am not offering personal criticism: I speak only of the predicament of a class. The Marxist should never be personal.

*The door-bell rings. Chang goes. Beppo looks toward the hall, expecting the police.*

CHARLOTTE. If that's the police, I'm going to tell them what I think about the way they've handled this business! They left us here tonight with no protection at all!

*Mimi and Payne appear from the hall.*

MIMI. Hello, Dad!

BEPPO. Oh, hello. Our friend Bostock has just been shot again!

MIMI. Goodness! Where? Here?

BEPPO. Yes, right here again just now.

PAYNE. Police here?

BEPPO. Not yet.

PAYNE. Kill him?

BEPPO. He's still alive.

*Mimi looks significantly at Payne.*

MIMI (*to Payne*). Hadn't you better go and see if you can't do something?

PAYNE. What do you mean? No.

MIMI. Did anybody see who did it?

BEPPO. Yes: Longbroke and I saw him.

MIMI. What was he like?

BEPPO. He was a long lean guy—evidently not the same one you saw. You said the one you saw was short and stocky.

MIMI (*to the company*). I'm going to appeal to everybody here to help us to keep out of an awful jam. This shooting was really done by a man who used to work for Jack— this is Jack Payne: this is Mr. and Mrs. Chives and Miss Macy.—Jack didn't have anything to do with it, but the man who did the shooting used to work for him, and Jack might get into a lot of trouble if it was known he'd been here tonight—so please don't let anybody know!— Because, for one thing, if Jack gets mixed up in it, then we'll *all* get mixed up in it, he being a friend of mine and having been in the apartment tonight—and it might be an awful mess for everybody!

PAYNE. Here's the truth, believe it or not: this poor punk who's been flunking at target-practice is an ex-employee of mine. He'd been slipping a long time, and I fired him—he's a hophead and practically nuts. Now he turns up and plugs one of my competitors, maybe thinking he's doing *me* a favor, maybe with some grudge o' his own. But *I'm* not responsible in any way: I didn' want Bostock rubbed out. I was getting ready to quietly merge him. It's just a load of grief to me that this dop should come and spoil your party and do his best to ruin my reputation—if not, as Mimi says, some other people's reputations.

BEPPO. I don't know anything about *your* reputation, but we're not in the least worried about ours!

PAYNE (*putting one hand in his coat pocket as if he was covering them with a gun*). I ask you: even if I was the kind that goes gunning, is it likely that when I'm interested in your daughter, I'd bump off the owner of your building right in your own apartment?

BEPPO. How do I know what you're likely to do?

PAYNE. Listen: if Bostock had been put on the spot, he wouldn't have survived the first treatment! The real trained accredited gunman has got to be a crack shot. Why, they've got them working out in gymnasiums with trapezes and rowing-machines—so I understand—they keep them in training like college athletes! A real man-eating racketeer couldn't afford to run the risk of a job like this here tonight! If you saw this pansy with his pea-shooter, you must have known he was a phony!

BEPPO. I find it very hard to distinguish between one racketeer and another!

MIMI. Dad, we must have Jack go somewhere so that he won't run into the police!

*She looks around swiftly.*

BEPPO (*turning to Mimi*). Do you know what you're asking me to do? Do you know who your great-grandfather Buttonwood was?—do you know that he was the leader of the Vigilance Committee in Eagle County, Colorado, when it was nothing but a mining-camp full of cut-throats?—

MIMI. I know, Dad—but——

BEPPO. —Do you know that your grandfather, my father, was chief prosecutor for Kemp County, Illinois, and that he locked up so many robbers and sent so many gunmen to the gallows that they made him judge of the District Court, where he helped to forge the laws of this country?

*The door-bell rings*

MIMI (*opening the big clock*). Here: go in here, Jack! There aren't any works in the bottom part. Beth Badger has always insisted that it ought to be used for something like this!

PAYNE. If you'll forgive me, folks! It's your interest as well as mine!

*He gets in, and she closes the door. Chang comes through to answer the bell, paying no attention to what is happening. The company, with the exception of Charlotte, sit silent and frozen through this, afraid of Payne's gun.*

CHARLOTTE. You oughtn't to allow this, Beppo!—

*Two members of the Homicide Squad come in with Chang from the hall.*

BEPPO. Well, here you are! (*Laughing a little nervously*) You ought to have stuck around!

THE INSPECTOR. They don't usually go after the same man twice in the one night.

*The clock, its machinery shaken, strikes four times.*

THE INSPECTOR. Was the shot fatal?

*Dr. Tinker comes back from the library.*

BEPPO. Here's the doctor. He can tell you.

DR. TINKER. He seems to be doing pretty well. It's a miracle how the bullet passed through his abdomen without causing an internal hemorrhage. He likes to be shot—but only just so much.—(*To the Inspector*) However, don't question him too long.

THE INSPECTOR. All right. He's in there? (*To Beppo*) We'll question you people afterwards. Where were the shots fired?—in here?

BEPPO. Yes: from the balcony there.

THE INSPECTOR. Anybody see who did it?

378

Beppo. Only Mr. Longbroke and myself, and we had ..ly a glimpse of him.

The Inspector. How did he happen to be in here again?

Beppo. He wanted to apologize to us. The poor fellow .as evidently gaga.

The Inspector. All right, we'll go in and see him. Don't .) away, please, till we've questioned you.

Beppo. Right.

*The policemen go into the library and shut the door. The* *..ople in the room hold a low-voiced and tense conversation.*

Beppo. I can't say how humiliated I am. How can I ..en apologize? But I suppose there's nothing to be done .r the present!

Mimi. It does seem a little startling, I know—but it's ..uch the best way to deal with the situation, I think.

Charlotte. It'll be very startling indeed if we all have .) stand trial for murder!

Mimi. That's just what I'm trying to avoid.

Chet. You evidently get a different kind of training at Miss French's nowadays, Mimi, from the kind they got .hen Charlotte went there!

Mimi. Well, they're supposed to teach you poise at Miss ..rench's, you know, and that's what I'm trying to cultivate.

Beppo. Why did you bring him back?

Mimi. Why, there wasn't any reason why I shouldn't. . didn't know that this idiotic man was *absolutely* crazy .nd was coming back to shoot him again!

Beppo. But you knew that this Payne might be suspected!

Mimi. No, I didn't: I was the only person who saw the ..an who did the shooting before, and it seemed obvious ..e'd gotten away. And I think that you and Mr. Longbroke .ught to describe him the same way I did—because other-.vise there'll be a contradiction.

Beppo. No: he'll have to take his chances once he's out .f here!

MIMI. But if they do connect it with him, Dad, and
they find out that I've been seen with him in night-club
why, then your name will get dragged into it, and th
might hurt the moral influence of your funny-strip f
Mr. Gibbs. (*The clock strikes three times.*) Incidentally, M
Longbroke, one reason Jack wanted to come back he
was to ask you if you couldn't go with him on a lit
yachting party that he's having at the end of this week
if all this blows over peacefully. He took such a fancy
you—he thought it would give you a chance to talk abo
business together.

LONGBROKE. When? What day?

MIMI. He wanted to start Friday.

LONGBROKE. Oh!—Friday would be all right, I thin
I had an engagement for Saturday, but I think I can g
out of it quite easily.—Perhaps we'd better see first,
you say, how the present situation turns out.

MIMI (*smiling charmingly*). It's much more likely to tu
out well, if you say you saw a short stocky man.

BEPPO. *I* propose to tell the truth!

MIMI. Please don't, Dad! Suppose there's real troubl

BEPPO. Suppose there *is* trouble! Let this fellow g
what's coming to him! Our reputations aren't in dang
from the brawlings of degenerate gangsters!

MIMI. Mine is, Dad!

BEPPO. What do you mean? You're my daughter!

MIMI. Dad: I'm going to burst a bomb. I'm sorry th
it has to be now: I didn't want to tell you till later. B
Jack and I are married!

BEPPO. You've married him!

MIMI. Yes: two weeks ago. I didn't want to tell you t
spring, because I knew it would upset you so, but——

*The policemen come back from the library. Beth follows,
one of Chang's aprons.*

THE INSPECTOR. All right! I guess we won't need

380

ke you all separately this time. Where was it that Bostock
as standing?

CHET (*wanting to help Beppo out*). J-just about here, I
ould say.

*The clock begins to strike again and mercilessly keeps on
iking.*

THE INSPECTOR. And where was the man who fired the
ots?

BEPPO (*pulling himself together*). On the balcony—he'd
idently been watching from just inside the hall, and
en he stepped out and fired two shots and ran out the
or on the second floor. Mr. Longbroke ran after him,
t he'd gotten away.

THE INSPECTOR (*to Longbroke*). You didn't see where he
ent?

LONGBROKE. He'd had time to escape before I could
ach him. I had to go up those stairs and along the corridor.

THE INSPECTOR. You say only two of you saw him.

BEPPO. Mr. Longbroke and I were the only people who
ere facing in that direction.

THE INSPECTOR. What did he look like?

BEPPO. I should say he was rather thickset. He might
ve been the same man my daughter saw. But, as I say,
e was gone in a second.

THE INSPECTOR. What kind of a suit was he wearing?

BEPPO. Why—a dark suit—it might have been dark
own or blue.

THE INSPECTOR. Which is the other gentleman who
w him?

LONGBROKE. I had only just a glimpse of him.

THE INSPECTOR. How would *you* describe him?

LONGBROKE. A smallish man, I should say—and stoutish.

THE INSPECTOR. Did you notice the color of his clothes?

LONGBROKE. Not particularly—I couldn't say what color
ey were—but certainly on the dark side.

BETH. Beppo, that clock must be going mad like every thing else in this apartment! It's struck fifteen at least!

BEPPO (*trying to smile*). Yes, I know. . . . Yes: it's alwa doing that.

THE INSPECTOR (*seeing the revolver on the table and picki it up*). What's this?

BEPPO. That's my revolver. Mr. Longbroke took it go after the gunman.

*The Inspector opens it, examines the cartridges and loo down the barrel.*

THE INSPECTOR. Hasn't been shot off, eh?

BEPPO. No: I just keep it in case of emergency.

THE INSPECTOR. All right. That's about the story, I gues Nobody else saw anything, eh?

CHARLOTTE. No: it was impossible for *me* to see him.

JUNE. No: I didn't see him.

BETH. No: he was right above me.

DR. TINKER. We only heard the shots.

CHET. I h-happened to be right under the balcony.

BEPPO (*to the Inspector*). Any theories about who did i

THE INSPECTOR. It's a racketeering job, but I wouldn know who to go after. So many people had motives t bump this Bostock off. He probably knows, but you can gettum to tell.—Well, we won't trouble you any mor tonight. Thank you. We've got all your names and ac dresses. It was a piece of bad luck for you he was so dea set on coming to see you. Thought he'd be safer her I suppose.—Well, good night.

BEPPO. Good night. Thank *you*!

*The policemen go out through the hall.*

CHET. Th-Think of the implications of this scene!

CHARLOTTE (*squeezing his arm*). Keep still!

BETH. That clock is just too much, Beppo! Even you magnificent furniture is losing its self-control. I'm goin to make it stop before somebody turns up and shoots i

*She goes over and opens the clock before anybody can stop
r, and, seeing Payne inside, gives a cry.*

BETH. Oh!

PAYNE (*stepping out*). Yes: that clock ought to be fixed.
double-crossed us!

MIMI. This is Miss Badger, Jack—this is Jack Payne, my
isband. This shooting tonight was all a mistake, but we
ought it was just as well for the cops not to see Jack
the apartment.

BETH. Your husband, Mimi? What is this?—a rehearsal
r a surréaliste play?

BEPPO. It looks like one! You're no more amazed than
am! This piece of news has only just been sprung on me!

PAYNE (*to Beppo*). I'm sorry as hell it's worked out like
is! It's a lousy introduction to a son-in-law!

BEPPO. Perhaps now that the police are gone, you
ouldn't mind leaving us, too!

PAYNE. I wish I could do more than say I'm sorry! I
iow what a load of grief this is to you!—But thanks for
icking by me!—Thanks a lot, all of you!

BEPPO. It wasn't on your account, and you know it!

PAYNE. Well, it's just been one of those things!

BEPPO. It's just been one of those things that decent
:ople don't tolerate!

PAYNE (*finally nettled and turning on Beppo, though still
ith considerable restraint in his tone—his hand in his pocket
ain*). Are you absolutely certain of that? It seems to me
ou decent people have always been willing to tolerate
lot! Suppose I *had been* responsible for this—suppose I
d send killers after my rivals—suppose I *did* put all the
velled-headed, half-witted, half-hearted hoodlums who
y to carry on a business they're not fit for, where they
n't obstruct the traffic any more—why, I'd only be doing
r liquor the same thing that every big business has
one!—

MIMI. Why, yes! the Standard Oil people used to ser
gangs of thugs to beat up the other companies that we
trying to put through independent pipelines—and the ra:
road owners used to send men with brass knuckles
intimidate stockholders' meetings!—it's all in the histo
we have at school!

CHET. Go-Good H-Heavens, are those things in tl
history books now? They're classical occurrences, the
and we d-don't need to worry about them!

PAYNE. Why, sure: you don't worry today about ;
those unsuccessful contestants that took nose-dives out
hotel windows—and I'll bet that every person here h
got some little stocks and bonds that are the babies of tl
big dealers that put them under! You can dress right ai
enjoy the good things of life because of the way the
built up their businesses. But when we liquor men do ju
the same thing, you complain about our brutal method

CHET. There's s-something in what he says!

CHARLOTTE. Keep still!

PAYNE. However, I'll be taking a load off your minds.-
Thanks a lot again. Goodby.

MIMI. Won't you run into the police outside?

PAYNE. You look out into the hall, and if it's clear, I c;
take the elevator down and go out the side entrance.

MIMI. But what about Bostock's own detectives? The
must know what's going on!

PAYNE. They won't do anything about it. They'
known he was finished a long time. They know I'm tl
big shot here now. Some of them are on my pay-roll.-
Well, good night, folks!

LONGBROKE (coming over to him just as he is about to ;
out). I say: it was awfully swell of you to ask me on yo
yachting party. I'll try to make it. Where shall I meet yo

PAYNE. Come to my office at three. I'll drive you o
to the boat. Pleased as hell you can come!

LONGBROKE. KO! Friday at three then.

*Payne goes out through the hall, and Mimi follows him.*

BEPPO (*to Mimi*). Where are you going?

MIMI. I'm coming back.

*She goes out after Payne.*

LONGBROKE. So this is American racketeering!

BETH. Yes: it gets less and less like a crook play every minute!

LONGBROKE (*to Beth*). I say: you won't think me very rude if I don't come to the party Saturday. It's a question of a business opening that I really mustn't let slip.

BETH. Not a bit, you big Huntley-and-Palmer animal cracker! I was giving the party for *you*, but maybe we'd get along better without you!

LONGBROKE. I'm frightfully sorry, but it's really important!

BETH. I'll bet those buck-teeth of yours are bogus, too! I can see them wobble when you talk!

LONGBROKE. I must get the bridge fastened more securely.

BETH. Well, *I* must get back to my patient!—Come on, Dr. Tinker—the iodine's arrived.

*She breaks away abruptly and returns to the library, followed by Dr. Tinker.*

CHET (*shaking his head*). The end of the jazz age—Gee Whiz! this is what it was all leading up to!

*Mimi comes back.*

CHARLOTTE. Well, Beppo, it's really time we went!

BEPPO. Under the circumstances I won't urge you to stay.

CHET. W-We've really had an awfully good time, though—I haven't been to anything so exciting since the Quat'z-Arts Ball ten years ago—but you've had enough to cope with tonight—and—and——

BEPPO. You won't have a drink before you go?

CHET. No, thanks, old man—we'll clear out! And—don't answer any more bells!

CHARLOTTE. Let's hope we don't all end up in court!

LONGBROKE. I must say good night, too.

BEPPO. Sorry it turned out such a ghastly evening!

LONGBROKE. I found it most rewarding.

*They shake hands and go out through the hall.*

JUNE. Maybe I better go, too.

BEPPO. No, don't—please stay! I need you!

JUNE (*wanting to leave him alone with Mimi*). I'll go i
and see if I can help.

*She goes into the library.*

MIMI. I'm terribly sorry, Dad! I know you're furiou
with me, but I thought it would really be better to ge
married and tell you afterwards than to try to talk yo
into it!

BEPPO. Haven't I always been fair and sympathetic wit
you?

MIMI. Yes, Daddy: you have—but I felt you wouldn'
want me to get married—you never seemed to like th
idea of my being seriously interested in anybody.

BEPPO. I wanted you to use some discrimination!

MIMI. What's the matter with Jack, Dad? There's a lo
to him besides being a big liquor dealer—and anyway yo
approve of liquor—I've heard you say that bootlegger
were public benefactors.

BEPPO. You don't know what he is!

MIMI. Yes, I do, Dad. He's just as honorable and decer
as anybody!—and he's a member of the civilized minorit
that you're always talking about!

BEPPO. This is all the good it's done you to send you t
Miss French's school!

MIMI. But what I'm supposed to get there is just wha
Jack needs. What's the good of social ease and so forth if :
doesn't make life easier for other people? That's one thin
I can do for Jack——

BEPPO. You can't make a gentleman out of a mucker

MIMI. As long as you refuse to understand what Jack is really like, I don't see it's any use for me to talk to you. You and your friends are so snooty about Jack, but he's done as much to be proud of as any of you! When he was a boy, he wasn't very well off and had to work in a bowling-alley—and he had to have a lot of brains and nerve to get where he is now. He had to battle his way up! And then he had to fight the scum of the underworld and the corrupt police officials and everybody: he's been shot at five times—he's the most daring person I've ever known! And now Jack is in a position where he can control this whole section of the city, and he's trying to clean it up! If it wasn't for Jack's controlling it, there'd be twice as much crime as there is! He's taken the criminal types that used to be pickpockets and gunmen and set them to making beer and distilling and driving trucks—and you know you think beer is a good thing! I can't see that the kind of lives that people like the Chiveses, for instance, live, gives them any right to high-hat Jack! Chet Chives is awfully sweet, but he doesn't know what it's all about —I don't believe that Chet Chives has ever had his life in danger once! And as for these little college brats with their noses still practically wet who are so terribly blasé about everything—they've never done anything more exciting in their lives than play football and hockey, if that! And the dear old college football team looks like a kindergarten romp when you put it beside what a man's up against when he's fighting the New York racketeers!

BEPPO. But this man is a racketeer himself!—your ideas are all topsy-turvy! It's your mother coming out in you: she always liked bums!

MIMI. I wish you wouldn't talk about Mother like that! I'm just as fond of her as I am of you—though I know you don't want me to be! She's always been awfully sweet, and I don't think she drinks any more than you do

BEPPO. I don't want you to think——

MIMI. Sometimes Mother and I get together and w
kid the pants off you, Dad!

BEPPO. I don't want you to think that I don't——

MIMI. I don't see why you left her the way you did!

BEPPO. Let's not discuss it, Mimi.

MIMI. Why shouldn't we? Why should we have t
pretend that Mother doesn't exist?

BEPPO. I don't want to pretend she doesn't exist——

MIMI. Yes, you do!

BEPPO. —I just don't want you to accept all her stand
ards——

MIMI. If you wanted to influence the situation, wh
didn't you stick with her in the first place?

BEPPO. We couldn't get along—I've tried to tell you—
life had become impossible——

MIMI. Well, you've done your best to tear me in tw
between you! (*She begins to cry.*) —And you talk abou
your standards, Dad—but I don't think you know wha
you want yourself—sometimes you say you want mone
and society and just to know smart people, and other time
you want to reform things!—

BEPPO. Do I? I suppose I do. I do get confused. Don'
cry——

MIMI. And I'm going to have a life of my own instea
of having my life all split up between what you want m
to do and what Mother wants me to do! I'm going awa
with Jack tonight—I'd made up my mind to do it anywa
—that's why I brought him back here. I'm going to hav
a home of my own!—I'm going to live with just on
person!

BEPPO. My dear, please don't cry—I'm so sorry—I d
see how you feel——

MIMI. It'll be a load off you anyway—you know yo

don't want to do that funny-strip, and with me off your hands you won't have to!—

BEPPO. Listen, darling: working for things for you has been the only thing that's kept me going!—

MIMI. Oh, Dad, you know how fond of you I am, and I hate going away and leaving you like this!—

BEPPO. Why don't you just wait a few days—we can talk about it a little more soberly.

MIMI. No: I'm going tonight. I promised Jack I would. (*Getting up*) I'm going now! I'm going up and pack.

*She starts for the stairs.*

BEPPO. All right, but see here: why don't you put off the actual trip. It may look bad, his going away just now. Why don't you both stay in town?

MIMI. No: I promised him. I have to—and I want to. You wouldn't want me to be a coward!

*She starts upstairs.*

BEPPO (*breaking out*). You don't know the risks you're taking!—and I won't allow you to take them! If you try to go away with Payne, I'll turn him over to the police tonight!

MIMI (*on the stairs*). Is this behaving like a "civilized person," Dad?

*She goes up to her room. Dr. Tinker appears from the library.*

DR. TINKER. I don't want to intrude, but I couldn't help hearing. I thought a word from a psychologist might be helpful. These relations between father and daughter may become very serious problems, and it's important to analyze them in time——

BEPPO. In time? But it's done! it's already done!—and the only thing I can do is to say to myself—why have I let it happen? Why have I made myself such a life? Why have I forced her to live it?

*Mimi slips out of her room, with a bag and in a coat and hat, and goes quickly along the upstairs hall.*

DR. TINKER. That conviction of guilt is neurotic—you *must* try to realize that you're not to blame for everything that——

BEPPO (*looking up at the sound of Mimi darting out the upstairs door*). Was that Mimi? (*He rushes to the stairs, sees her door open and calls.*) Mimi! . . . Mimi! . . . She's gone!—But why should I expect her to stay?—I hate it all here myself!

# ACT III

*Beppo and June on the sofa. Except for the floor-lamp, the
stage is dark. Whisky on the table.*

June. Feel better?

Beppo. Yes: much better.

June. Now don't drink any more tonight!

Beppo. I'm all right—thanks to you, my dear—you're
the only thing now I've got left——-

June. Don't say that!

Beppo. But it's true: I know now I'm completely alone
—this whole thing doesn't hang together—people don't
mean anything to each other any more. I've been trying
to tell myself for years that there was some kind of sense
to the life I live, but I know now it's just a crazy party
with everybody talking about themselves, and the only
way we're able to stand each other is for all of us to get
plastered together so that nobody pays any attention to
what anybody else is saying. I couldn't even make my
daughter believe in it!—And you're the only real and
human thing I've got!

June. You've got plenty of girl-friends besides me!

Beppo. Not real girls, though, like you. You make me
feel I've known a real woman for the first time in my life.

June. What was the matter with all the others?

Beppo. They're not real women! Look at Charlotte
Chives!—look at Beth Badger! Charlotte wants to boss
everybody, and she never gives a man an even break—
and Beth is more or less the same way, and she's one of

391

these impossible modern girls who refuses to be an old-fashioned wife and yet at the same time hates like hell to work for her own living and earn her right to dodge domestic responsibility. But you—you earn your own living—you're a little free-swimming organism—and yet you manage to *be* a real woman. You're not even stuck on yourself because you can play the piano, whereas Beth who does nothing with her brains, carries on like a prima donna!

JUNE. I never got a chance to be stuck on myself. There were seventeen in my family, and I was at the bottom of the heap. I had sixteen brothers and sisters to pick on me.

BEPPO. Exactly—and Beth was an only child, and I was an only son. All of us people who come from families where there were only a few children or one and who had a lot of fuss made over us as kids are still trying to have the world revolve around us, whereas *you* knew damn well from the start that you had to do the revolving.—And Mimi, too—she's spoiled: all her life her mother and I have been competing for her affection, and now she's come to believe that she's a very important person and that everybody ought to give in to her—but with you it's natural for you to be considerate—you're modest and sweet to everybody, because you know that human beings are really very small in the world and that we're all in the same little boat.—Tell me, my dear: do you love me at all?

JUNE. Of course. (*Squeezing his hand*) But I wouldn't want to love anybody again the way I loved Al.

BEPPO (*disappointed*). You were crazy about him, weren't you?

JUNE. I don't know why I was, but I was—the dirty bum! (*She laughs.*) He was absolutely nuts!

BEPPO (*hopefully*). I suppose he really was mentally defective, wasn't he?

JUNE. He was one of the smartest guys you ever saw, but the things he did were crazy. He got fancy ideas about living in style as soon as he cleaned up a little money in Brooklyn, and he insisted on coming over to Manhattan and taking a big apartment in the Fifties. He had it specially decorated by one of these interior decorators—just like you're doing with this——

BEPPO (*with a displeased smile*). O! really?

JUNE. Yes, he had it all done in the Empire Style with green-satin-covered furniture and G for Gammel—that was his last name, Al Gammel—on the curtains and the bedspreads and everything. And mirrors!—the whole bedroom was lined with mirrors— (*she giggles*) he even had a mirror on the ceiling!—You can imagine what that was for! (*Beppo smiles wanly.*) And we were pie-eyed every night! Every night we'd stay up later and later till finally we got so we didn't get up till five in the afternoon.

BEPPO (*without enthusiasm*). That must have been a lot of fun.

JUNE. Some days we'd never get dressed at all—Al had purple pyjamas with lilac frogs on them—I was ashamed ovum at first!—the only times we ever went out were to speakeasies and night-clubs and shows—I'd never been to a real show before I married Al—and that was all we did for months. I used to get the meals—Al wanted to have a cook and a butler, but I wouldn't lettum—I thought it was too much of a waste. I used to play jazz to-um after dinner, and then he'd turn on the phonograph and make me dance. We'd be dancing there all by ourselves—by that time we'd be good and pie-eyed and he'd tell me how much he loved me.— (*Giggling*) What we didn't do in that apartment!

*Beppo, who has been looking crestfallen, pours himself another drink.*

JUNE (*looking at the drink, preventively*). Oh—oh!

393

BEPPO. It's all right: I'm past the peak—I'm tapering off now.—My dear, you fill me with envy!—I don't believe I've ever known what it was to love and be loved like that—to forget the world completely and not to care about anything but one another! I've always been too much of an egoist to lose myself in the other person—I've always wanted to put on a show, have the woman admire my personality.

JUNE. Didn't Al want to be admired!

BEPPO. Yes, but *I've* always picked out women who wanted to be admired, too—who wanted to put on a show for *me*. That's an arrangement that can't last long because each one is always trying to push the other one out into the audience and make him or her sit back and behave himself, and not criticize, and like it—and then the person that gets shoved into the audience oftenest finally becomes disgusted and walks out on the person that's giving the show.—That's what's always happened with me in the past—but I feel that it might perhaps be different with you—that with you love might make me forget myself.

JUNE. I wouldn't want to do what I did with Al again: we were like two animals in a cage. We did a lot of fighting, too—especially when Al was spending money and was drinking so he could'n work and the landlord was after us for the rent. Al beat me up one night because I toldum he ought to be working, and the next day he brought a woman home and that made me sore, and then I got a friend of his to give me a job playing the piano in a restaurant he had, and then Al got sore because he thought I was unfaithful to-um with this friend, and he twisted my wrist so I could'n play, and then we got put out of the apartment. I moved in with a girl-friend. Al had been away two nights, and I did'n even leavum word where I was.

BEPPO. Do you know where Al is now?

JUNE. I haven't seenum for a year—he used to come around and make me givum money—the last time I sawum, he told me he still loved me and wanted me to go back withum, but he'd started taking dope then, and I tried going back withum once, and it was the same thing over again, only worse, so I toldum I did'n want to seeum no more, and he went away, and I haven't seenum since.

*The door-bell rings.*

BEPPO (*starting*). Good God! and I thought things had quieted down! This place is like the Grand Central Station tonight!

*Chang comes in from the dining-room and goes to open the door.*

JUNE. What about your Mr. Gibbs?—weren't you still expecting him?

BEPPO. Yes—or it might be the doctor to ship Bostock out.

*Dr. Tinker comes in, followed by a bell-boy carrying a stretcher. Chang waits for orders.*

DR. TINKER. Well, how is he getting along?

BEPPO. All right, apparently. The nurse is in there.

DR. TINKER. And how are you?

BEPPO. Quite all right!

DR. TINKER. Look out for the downgrade on those drinks!

BEPPO. Just a small one and the last.

DR. TINKER. Well, let's see if we can't move him.

BEPPO. Fine!

*All except June go into the library. She lights a cigarette and looks toward the library door. Immediately Bostock's voice is heard, talking with animation.*

BOSTOCK'S VOICE. Hello, Doc! . . . Perfectly splendid! . . . Just one little shot to pick me up! . . . That's fine—I'll be absolutely O.K.! It's silly to put me on this thing—I'm perfectly well able to walk!—Just been lying around here waiting for you to give me my marching orders!... All right!... I can do it myself! All right, have it your own way! I'll be a babe in arms if you say so!

DR. TINKER'S VOICE. You must sit upright so as not to start it bleeding.

BOSTOCK'S VOICE. All right! You bet I'll sit upright! That's glorious! Now on with the procession!

*The bell-boy and Chang carry Bostock in on the stretcher, Dr. Tinker, the Nurse and Beppo following. Bostock is sitting up with a dressing-gown around his shoulders and a blanket over his legs. He is deathly pale now, and the circles around his eyes look darker.*

BOSTOCK. Stop a minute! Slaves, stop the litter! Caesar must thank his good host! (*They stop, and Bostock shakes hands with Beppo with his free left hand.*) I must say goodby and apologize again—and more humbly and more profoundly and more heartfeltly—for the lousy mess I've caused tonight!

BEPPO. I'm only sorry on your account.

BOSTOCK. But *I'm* as fit as a fiddle! It'll take a good deal more than a bullet or two to put Luke Bostock out of business! It's the old pioneer stock! The old pioneer spirit! The Indians couldn't kill us in the early days, and the gunmen can't get us today!—and it's the old pioneer spirit that we'll have to fall back on now!—I hope *your* people were pioneers, Mr. Miles—I hope they battled with the wolves—and the wildcats—and—and—those other wild animals!—I hope that your grandfather was one of those who built his own house with his own hands— with his ax and his hammer and his chisel—and his—and his other tools—that we other builders who come after him might erect vaster mansions for America—great comfort-happy chromium palaces with a radio by every bedside and a ticker by every bathtub—that's what I'm

going to have next summer, a ticker in every bathroom!
—and there's going to be good news on it, too!—and the
thing that's going to pull us through is the old pioneer
spirit!——

DR. TINKER. Don't tire yourself! You'd better be getting along—that hypodermic has got to last you.

*They start carrying him again.*

BOSTOCK. That's all right! I'm solid as hickory!—
Goodby, Mr. Miles, and thanks again!—Remember that
the old pioneer spirit is what'll put us back on top of the
world!—Forward in the covered wagon!—there are no
black hangings on *this* covered wagon! *This* covered
wagon is no hearse! (*They carry him out through the hallway, and his voice is still heard holding forth.*) The old
pioneer spirit!—

*The Nurse and Dr. Tinker follow them out.*

BEPPO (*to June*). Well, I hope that's the end of *that*! (*He
comes over to the sofa and kisses her and picks up his drink again.*)
What a blessed relief it is to be alone with you, my dear,
at last!

JUNE. Isn't Miss Badger still in there? She was looking
after him.

BEPPO. She went, I'm sure. I didn't see her go, but I
remember she said goodby to me when the nurse came.
(*He opens the library door.*) Yes, she's gone—Oh, Beth!—
Yes, she's gone. (*He shuts the door again and is coming back
to the sofa when two shots are heard outside. He stops short
in dismay.*) Good God! Again? (*He pauses and listens: sounds
of shouts and people running outside.*) Have we got to go
through all this again? I really don't think I can stand
it! (*Chang bursts in.*) Well, did they get him this time,
Chang?

CHANG. The gunman was inside the apartment and just
as we were going in, he shot at Mr. Bostock. I go for
towels.

BEPPO. Why don't you use his this time?

CHANG (*smiling*). I am afraid of Mr. Bostock's apartment.
*He goes out through the dining-room door.*

BEPPO. Poor bozo! He's evidently doomed.

JUNE. It must have been terrible forum hanging around
like that and knowing he was going to get it! I suppose
that's why he did so much talking—he was trying to keep
his mind off it.

BEPPO. Just like all the rest of us, eh?
*Chang comes back with an armful of towels.*

BEPPO. They don't need me in there, do they, Chang?
There's nothing I can do, is there?

CHANG. No: there are plenty of people.
*He goes out through the hall. Beppo subsides onto the couch.*

BEPPO. I need medical attention myself—I'm groggy!
I've got an acute pain in the back of my head. I can hardly
hold this glass. Be sweet to me—soothe me, dear.
*The door-bell rings: he starts.*

JUNE. I'll go! You sit there.

*He sits looking apprehensively toward the hallway. Two
policemen appear with Al Gammel. June comes in behind them
and, while the conversation that follows is going on, stands
petrified, gazing at Al.*

POLICEMAN. We caught this bird on the fire-escape. Can
you identify him as the man you saw?

BEPPO (*nervous and flustered*). Why, no—I can't say I do
identify him——

JUNE. The other man was short and stocky.

BEPPO. Yes: he seemed shorter than this man—and
broader.—Did you find a gun on him?

POLICEMAN. No: the gun was found in the apartment.
Could you be sure this wasn't the man you saw?

BEPPO. Well, it's hard to be absolutely sure—I saw him
only for a second and not distinctly—but he seemed to
me to be wearing a darker suit——

Policeman. Well, he was caught on the fire-escape out-side of Bostock's apartment—so we'll just take-um along and see whatuz story is.

Beppo. Let me know if there's anything I can do to help you.

Policeman. O.K.

*They go out, leading Al.*

June (*in a low voice*). My God, that was Al!

Beppo. What?

June. That was my husband.

Beppo. Really? Good Heavens! Well, that makes things worse than ever!

June. So he's a gunman now! Poor Al! (*She laughs sadly.*) No wonder he missedum so many times!

Beppo. Don't tell them you know anything about him and maybe they won't find out.

June. I wonder if they'd let me see-um.

Beppo. For Heaven's sake, don't try to do that! We're badly enough mixed up in it as it is. If they find out that this man worked for Payne and that Payne has married Mimi and that you were married to Al, they may accuse us of luring Bostock in here to kill him!

June. He looked like he was full of hop—he didn't even show whether he recognized me!

*Chang comes back.*

Beppo. Was it fatal this time, Chang?

Chang. They seem to have attained their objective.

*He goes out through the dining-room.*

Beppo. God, if he's actually dead, we may all be in a hell of a mess!

June. Al can get the chair! The crazy fool! he hasn't got the nerve for a gunman. That was always the trouble withum—he was smart but he didn't have the guts—he used to get scared sick the night before he had to move a load of liquor. He used to wake up in the night with the horrors, and he'd make me put my arms aroundum before he could get to sleep again. That was why he started taking dope, I guess. Poor Al! He used to talk like he was going to own the world—he was going to control all the liquor in Brooklyn, to listen to-um. And now he's just another mug!

BEPPO. Don't try to go and see him though!

JUNE. I'll just write to-um and won't sign my name— and sendum some money for prison. If you haven't got money, you're out of luck, because you aren't able to buy anything, and the prison food is terrible.

BEPPO. Better disguise your handwriting.

JUNE. I wonder if I ought to have takenum back the last time he wanted me to. He said he'd be a good boy. I feel terrible to see-um like this!

BEPPO. You mustn't blame yourself, my dear. You can't change other people's characters.

JUNE. I don't know—he said if I'd take-um back, he'd be a good boy and wouldn't drink no more. He shot at-um three times: he wanted to prove to-umself he could do it!

BEPPO. You love him still, don't you?

JUNE. Maybe I do.

BEPPO. You don't really care for me!

JUNE. Oh, yes, I do, but *you* know: the first person you love is different.—I used to cry my eyes out every night after he first left me—but I would'n wantum back now —it makes me feel terrible to think I don't like-um after the way we loved each other!

BEPPO. I know—I understand, my dear. (*He takes her hand.*) But life is very unjust—the world wasn't made for sensitive people. It wasn't made so that we could have the people we love, and it wasn't made so that they should deserve our loving them. The world is a sad, sad place, and there's nothing we can do about it—if we want to keep on at all, we have to try to forget how sad it is and enjoy the few good things while they last. For me, my dear, you're one of the few really fine and beautiful and marvelous things in the world—I know I'm not that for you, but——

JUNE. It's just that it's made me feel so blue seeing Al like that just after I'd been talking aboutum!—They beat them up terrible at the station-house. I saw him after they'd beaten him up before when he was arrested for stealing a car, and they'd flogged him with the hose and put pins under his nails and broke his jaw—and they wouldn't have a doctor to do anything forum.—Well, I'd better be going. (*She looks at the clock.*) Good Lord! it's quarter to four. (*She gets up, fixing her hair.*) I must go!

BEPPO (*taken aback and feeling miffed*). Why don't you stay here? It's so late. Mimi's gone, and I'm all alone.

JUNE. Not tonight: I want to go home tonight—I'm all worn out and upset.

BEPPO. So am I—so why don't you stay, and we can console one another?

JUNE. I'd only make you bluer! (*She kisses him.*) Don't worry about Mimi, though. If she lovesum and he's rich, what do you care? He won't get caught for this.

BEPPO. He's just what Al wanted to be, I suppose.

JUNE. Poor Al, he would have enjoyed it if he'd had it!

BEPPO. We all would—it's what I wanted, too—but I don't give a damn about it now!— (*A little bitterly*) Well, you're leaving me, are you?

JUNE. I must.

BEPPO. To go away and think of Al!—I imagined I had a little palace here, where my friends and Mimi and I could admire ourselves and make fun of the world. But the world is Payne and his kind—*they're* the real masters

of the palace—and tonight they've knocked down my
door and taken my daughter away! And even you—
I thought you belonged to me as no other woman ever
had—but you belong to them, too!

JUNE. Don't talk like that! I'll be seeing you soon!

BEPPO. It's Al that's the reality for you—not anything
I've got here!

JUNE. I love it here (*she kisses him*), but I don't want to
stay tonight. You go and get some sleep—you're tired!

BEPPO. I won't sleep—probably won't for weeks!

JUNE. Why don't you take some luminol? (*Kissing him
again*) Good night—don't worry now!

*He leads her toward the hall.*

JUNE. Don't come with me!—I'll get a taxi!

*They go out into the hall.*

*Chung comes in from the dining-room. He wears bone-
rimmed spectacles like Chang, but is elderly and has gray hair.
He collects the ash-trays and glasses and carries them out on
a tray. Beppo returns and picks up the newspaper, holding it
with shaking hands. Chung returns for another load.*

BEPPO (*reading aloud*). "Ruffles will Remedy Starvation:
American propaganda undertaken to make the Jap women
wear cotton ruffles on their panties is the only sure way
out of world depression, said Senator Hokus P. Bong of
Georgia, arriving on the *Germania* yesterday."— (*Bursting
out with nervous irritation*) Good God, I believe it's actually
true that the racketeers might run the country better than
this government we've got!—What would you Communists say to that?

CHUNG. Your statement, as we should analyze it, presents a dual aspect: it has a positive and a——

BEPPO (*looking up startled at the sound of his voice*). I don't
remember engaging *you*!

CHUNG. Chang is preparing a thesis. I take his place.
My name is Chung.

BEPPO. I see—and you can carry on the argument without the slightest break?

CHUNG (*smiling*). It is the Party analysis. Your statement, as I was saying, presents a dual aspect: it has a positive aspect and a negative aspect. The positive aspect of your statement is the contempt it shows for bourgeois institutions. We call this the positive aspect because it shows the demoralization of the owning class, who have no longer any confidence in their own puppet representatives. But your remark presents also a negative aspect: it is negative, according to our analysis, that the general crises of capitalism should be to you merely an occasion for cynicism. It is negative from our point of view that, despairing of bourgeois institutions, you should not have taken the further step of understanding that these must be superseded and that your interests as a bourgeois technician——

BEPPO (*stung*). I may be a technician, but I'm damned if I'm bourgeois!

CHUNG (*smiling*). I speak in terms of Marxist analysis, with no personal implication. I was saying that as the present crisis deepens, the technician who has been hitherto dependent on employment by the bourgeoisie, will find himself expropriated and forced down to the ranks of the proletariat, and that he should recognize his true solidarity with——

BEPPO. Well, it's a matter of opinion, isn't it?—Thank you for substituting for Chang. You Chinese are so considerate in that way.— (*As Chung begins piling the things on the tray*) Don't clear away all those things—leave the bottle and the White Rock and a glass, please.— (*He goes over and mixes himself a drink*) Don't you Communists ever do any drinking?

CHUNG (*smiling*). We have to keep ourselves in training.

BEPPO. Good God! I have gangsters on one side and Communists on the other! (*Chung smiles.*) —As you say, where do people like me come in? But *are* people really better off in Russia where they're all supposed to be working together for the same great common ideal? Somebody who'd been over there lately was telling me the other day about a girl who'd been given a job as rat-catcher. She was pleased and proud with the job because she was catching rats for the Soviets—she would diligently go to the library and look up all the books on rat-catching, and she'd started studying German to find out about the latest methods. A great big apple-cheeked country-girl just radiant over catching rats! And *that's* something—I admit it!—to feel the conviction that what you're doing is for something and somebody beyond yourself. But, damn it, I don't want to catch rats! *I'm* not a peasant! I'm a civilized modern person who likes a civilized life!—And the way they butchered the Tsar and his family!—and the way they've embalmed Lenin and have the yokels lining up to look at him!—No: the whole thing's distasteful! (*Chung smiles.*) —And those godawful names they concoct by tacking the first syllables of words together!

CHUNG. To take up the first of your objections——

BEPPO. No: don't explain, please! I'm not equal to an argument tonight.—You can take the rest of these things out. (*Chung takes the tray and starts for the door. Beppo lifts his glass and looks at it, then stops Chung just as he is about to go out.*) Don't go: stay a minute—put down the tray! (*Chung sets the tray on the table.*) I'm alone here—completely alone! I'm going to take this drink so that I'll feel there is somebody with me—myself!—This drink will make me double up, and then I'll be able to admire myself, console myself, pat myself on the back—I'll feel like my own best buddy! (*Chung smiles.*) And then in the morning when I come to again—instead of being the life of the party in my own congenial company—I'll be less than one human being!—Do you understand what I mean?—

'll be absolutely crazy!—I've been under a terrible strain.
think I'm going crazy anyway!—and there's no use just
talling it off with drink! (*In a sudden outbreak of nerves,
e throws the glass against the wainscoting and smashes it.*)
There's a gesture that you Communists ought to
approve! (*Chung smiles.*) Face the situation without liquor
and ask yourself, squarely: So what? In the first place,
nothing's a satisfaction, and it takes all the drinks you can
hold to pretend to yourself that it is!—When you're out
here in Galesburg, Illinois, you want to go on to Chicago;
then when you get to Chicago, you want to go on to
New York. Then when you make good in New York,
what in God's name, have you got? The thoroughly
depressing companionship of a lot of poor small-towners
like yourself who don't know what the hell to do with
themselves either! (*Chung smiles.*) You think it would be
better in Paris, but then when you get to Paris, you find
the same old fizzed-out people, and you decide that they're
worse than the ones at home, because they haven't got
even their small-town background to make fools of themselves against. You think you want to go back to America
and play a real role in the life at home by satirizing the
things you abominate—you think maybe it's exciting over
here, you think it must be going somewhere, you want
to see what's happened.—But then when you get back
and see your friends, you find that *nothing* has happened—
the people are still milling around in the same unsatisfactory apartments, just as unsettled as ever, still just
moving in or just moving out, still trying to make up
their minds whether they want to get divorced or stay
married, still eternally behind themselves, though you
never can tell what they're trying to catch up to, their
ideals or their standards of living! (*Chung smiles.*) —And
your homecoming's no more of an event than if you'd
just been away to the toilet!—And as for satirizing

America, the whole thing's so goddam hopeless and stupid that your little jokes seem pathetic!—Then you run into some new girl, and for a time you think you'd be really happy if you could only get her to take off her clothes—and then when you finally succeed, there you are alone again!—What you thought would be a fine new experience that would take you out of yourself is just another set of sexual organs—the same set you've known all along—you've mastered their topography so thoroughly that they seem just about as romantic as the Lexington Avenue subway!—And so, as you say, what am I? Not an artist! not a solid citizen! I'm outside that natural world that the other people belong to—if there really *is* any such world—most of my friends, so far as I can see, are just as badly off as I am—they're not part of anything either— I know it when I look into their faces—I see the same solitude, the same insecurity, the same straining for something to hang on to! You at least have an idea that's big, but I have to keep myself going with things that are so infinitely little!—a cocktail before dinner, the opening of a new revue, seeing an amusing friend, buying a new picture—I have to get myself from one to the other like Eliza crossing the ice, with panic and desperation always just a few jumps behind me!—And even things like that can't depend on: I'm always made jittery by the feeling that the party or the picture or the show may suddenly give way underneath me!—and they always turn out disappointing!—Even wearing these purple evening clothes hasn't braced me up as much as I hoped! And on the other hand, any little incident that's actively disagreeable—no matter how intrinsically silly it may be—can sink me down to the depths!—That senator and his ruffles, for instance—it made the whole world, all of a sudden, seem too drivelingly half-witted to live in!—or remembering an appointment with the dentist—I've got one tomorrow

s a matter of fact—and when I think of it, I'm suicidal.—
My God! is fighting through one's life—day by day,
minute by minute—is it worth the effort and the agony it
takes?—As soon as I'm alone in the evening, this horrible
depression comes down on me—that's why I have so many
people in—but it doesn't make any difference: I'm alone!
I'm alone! I'm alone!—my daughter and my girl have
both left me—I didn't have anything to give them!—and
I've driven three wives away!—It's all my fault!—I know
it—it's me, not them!—and now the devils of the mind
have come for me just the way the gunmen came for
Bostock!—We're all sitting alone scared to death in unsatisfactory apartments! (*Chung smiles.*) Don't laugh! It's
insanity I'm close to! I'm outside it all, all the time!—All
these things that I've chosen and bought don't really mean
anything to me—I thought I was going to get a kick out
of those highball glasses I bought in Venice—I had them
sent over here, and now they're even further away from
me than they were before I saw them in the shop!—
they're things that other people have drinks out of!—and
I hate them! (*He smashes another glass.*)—I hate it all—
everybody, everything!—it all has no relation to me!
Who are you? I don't even know you—you might be
something I'd had sent in from Vantine's!—But I hate
myself, too!—that's not me either!—I see myself doing
things, hear my voice saying things, and that belongs to
that outside world, too!—My work even—it's not me
who does it—it's like sitting behind a partition and working the automatic chess-player in one of those old wax-
work shows!—it's not going to be me who sits down to
draw those optimistic little tigers for Herman Godbrow
Gibbs!—it'll only be an empty doll with no mind and no
will of its own—without even any appetites left to want
the things that killing my self-respect will buy me!—And
when things have got to that point, it's time to put an

end to the whole affair!—As soon as you go out o
this room, I'll be left here at the mercy of something
I'll have to obey the compulsion that's pulling me over to
that table!—wherever that gun is, I feel it—there's a prick-
ing around it like a magnetic field!—If it's in the little
drawer of that table, I try to keep away from the table—
but tonight it's lying right there in front of me—this i
the hour that's been waiting for me!—As you say, I'n
a contemptible parasite! A cheap ham! A selfish ass
A case of arrested development!—and there's only one
thing I can do to prove I'm enough of a person to know it

*He picks up the revolver from the table and dashes towar
the library door; but the door suddenly opens and disclose
Beth, very pale, with her hand at her throat. Beppo stops short*

BEPPO. Why, Beth?—What's the matter?

BETH. I'm all right!

*She comes in and sinks down on the couch.*

BEPPO. What's happened to you? Did you faint?

BETH. I'm frightfully sorry, Beppo—I didn't get enough
to do the trick, I guess.

BEPPO. Good Heavens! What did you do?

BETH. Just the old manic depression. . . . Life suddenly
seemed just too horrible, so I grabbed the doctor's iodine

BEPPO. You drank it? (*Beth nods.*) Where? in the bath
room? (*She nods.*) I'll get a doctor!

BETH. No, don't: I'm all right. The bottle wasn't full
It just makes your throat and mouth burn.

BEPPO (*going toward the phone*). I'd rather have a docto
see you——

BETH. No, don't! I couldn't bear one. The only thing
they do, anyway, is tell you to eat starch. I was with
Francie Fernald when she drank it. Are there any of those
boiled potatoes left from dinner? If there are, just give
me one. That's all a doctor could do!

BEPPO (*to Chung*). Go get those potatoes.

*Chung goes out through the dining-room.*

BETH. I'm sorry I behaved so disgracefully—just when you were having such a crisis, too!

BEPPO. What was the matter, my dear?—Do you feel all right inside?—are you sure?

BETH. Yes: I'm much better since I vomited. If we could only puke up experience!

BEPPO. What was the matter? tell me!

BETH. The matter is I'm going mad!

*Chung returns with a plate of potatoes, salt and pepper and butter, knife and fork.*

BETH (*taking them*). Thank you. (*She begins eating one with her fingers.*) I'll be all right now!

BEPPO. Don't you want something else?

BETH. No, thanks—nothing at all.

BEPPO (*to Chung*). All right: that's all.

*Chung goes out.*

BEPPO. You mustn't let Ada Force get your goat!

BETH. It's not only that—it's everything! It came over me so I couldn't bear it how I'd always been such a bitch to everybody who'd ever cared about me—first you and then Chet—only to let myself be given the gate by that son of a bitch of an Englishman! It was all too complete, with you and Chet both here—it was too much, the final defeat (*laughing and crying*) on the scene of my former failures!—And then the nurse—it braced me up for awhile to pretend to be a trained nurse for Bostock, but then the real nurse came, very snooty, and gave me to understand I wasn't needed—and I felt so utterly useless!—

BEPPO. You mustn't feel that way, Beth!—everybody leans on you, don't you know it?—don't you know how strong you are?—don't you know how much you give people?—I got so dependent on you that that was really the reason I broke away, and I think now I was a damn fool to do it—I've been at sea ever since!

BETH. It was my fault—I'm impossible—it's me!—I've got an impossible conflict! My father was a sweet little man who liked to be gay and enjoy things, and I always fall for anybody who seems to be like him. But then mother comes into action and proceeds to hound the life out of father! I begin to boss and scold just like her. I can't do anything about it—the psychoanalyst said so! She drove my father insane, and now they're still fighting it out in me, and I'm going insane, too!

BEPPO. My dear, you don't know what it is *really* to feel your mind giving way! Do you know that I've been suffering for months from what seems an irresistible impulse to take my clothes off in elevators?

BETH. That's nothing, dearie!—it's all I can do to keep from smashing the Della Robbia cherubs over the heads of Ada Force's customers!

BEPPO. Do you ever have the feeling that your hands have come off?

BETH. I sometimes wear other people's faces!

BEPPO (*standing up and talking excitedly*). But why are we like that? Why *are* we? Because we really hate this world we live in! Because there's really nothing in it for us! What's the use of paying psychoanalysts for alibis to blame it on our parents? It's the whole thing we're part of that's washed up now! There's nothing behind it but graft and crime! To a young girl like Mimi today a racketeer looks like a prince!

BETH. You were telling me a little while ago how much you admired the morality of June Macy and her gunman relations. If it's cute for June to have stick-up men in the family, why isn't it even cuter for Mimi to marry Jack Payne?

BEPPO. I know: our own world has so gone to hell that we think the underworld's romantic.—Yet I try to bring June into my world.

BETH. That makes you a *grand seigneur*!

BEPPO. And this is what I expect her to be dazzled by: his idiotic mess of an apartment!—this senseless collection of knick-knacks that I've carried in here like a magpie! —the walls aren't even finished, and who the hell cares whether they're ever finished?—I don't! It's not real! it's not beautiful!—Even those Periwinkos, to hell with them! *He rips one off the wall and throws it after the glasses.*)

BETH. Don't do that! They're worth money!

BEPPO. To hell with them! The bootlegger can buy better ones than I can—he can even buy my daughter and my guests with his yacht! To hell with the yachts and the Periwinkos! I wanted them all my life—my father had the great ambition to live in a big house in Galesburg with an iron stag on the lawn. *He* got his iron stag, and *'ve* got my bronze Venus. To hell with the bronze Venus! *He picks up a cushion from the sofa and is about to hurl it at the floor lamp when Beth jumps up and seizes it.*

BETH. Don't!—don't wreck Venus! Don't be so hard on the old luxury furnishings!

BEPPO. No: you were perfectly right—they look like an auction room! I know it, yet I seem to have to have them.

BETH. Just like my country house. When I was a little girl, we lived in an enormous mansion with twenty well-disciplined servants and a picture of St. Francis feeding the birds!

BEPPO. And you ought to be very much relieved that you're not going back to it with Longbroke.—When I first knew you years ago, you thought you were revolting against it.

BETH. It does seem a long time ago we were revolting!

BEPPO. Do you remember the P. L. M. Express? My first finding you in that compartment is still one of the most exciting things in my life! You were sitting there in

your smart little dress with your little black eyes a॑
snapping!

BETH. I was reading a book by Cocteau.

BEPPO. I'd never known a girl so insolent to life—th॑
girls of my own age weren't like that.

BETH. You were only my second lover, and the firs॑
one hadn't been good.

BEPPO. We went practically from the station to the bed॑

BETH. In the middle of the afternoon—and then whe॑
we went outside, everything was dreamy and vague, an॑
we got into that fantastic party in that cellar where the॑
were drinking calvados.

BEPPO. How delighted with ourselves we were then॑
We thought that we'd finally gotten away from every॑
thing we'd hated at home!

BETH. And look at us!

BEPPO. Yes: how did we land here?—Good Heavens॑
when we were living in Paris, I thought that I *was* some॑
body in particular, but now in New York, I know dam॑
well that I'm nothing but a well-known name among ॑
lot of other well-known names, where it's the name tha॑
counts and not the work. What a lousy culture! Goo॑
God!—no craftsmanship, no real ideas, no genuin॑
integrity of the spirit! We're all just empty distracte॑
people, hopping around, as my mother used to say, lik॑
a hen on a hot griddle!

BETH. When you go on like that, Beppo, you remind m॑
of my own mother bawling out Papa for his frivolous life॑

BEPPO (*getting up again*). Well, why should we b॑
ashamed of our Puritanism, now that we've broken th॑
rules and only feel glummer than ever? Our Purita॑
tradition of protest is perhaps the one sound thing we'v॑
got. Why, in God's name, *don't* we protest instead of tryin॑
to drug ourselves like Bostock and going down with hi॑
rotten collapse?

BETH. When you take to smashing Periwinkos, I suppose it's the old ripsnorting Cromwellian righteousness knocking the spires off cathedrals!

BEPPO (*carried away*). Wreck the cathedrals! Why not? Tear down all these trappings that hide the truth! Let's take our world for what it is! Let's take ourselves for what we are! Tear down all the phony tapestries! Let's protest against *ourselves*! (*He pulls the tapestry down, so that it falls on him and covers him up: he stands a moment enveloped in its folds. The door-bell begins to ring. He emerges, disheveled and looking foolish. A moment's terrible silence.*) That must be Gibbs—I'd forgotten about him! (*He disengages himself from the tapestry and smooths his rumpled hair.*)

BETH. Here, I'll fold the tapestry up, and you go and answer the bell!

BEPPO. I'm not going to answer it—to hell with him!

BETH. You'd better go—it's your bread and butter!—

BEPPO (*stopping her as she is trying to fold up the tapestry*). No: to hell with it! I'm not going to answer it! It's either Gibbs or Bostock's ghost, and they both mean the same old fake!—Beth, let's get married again!

BETH. Don't be silly—answer that bell!—I'll answer it, and you go and brush your hair.

*The door-bell rings with redoubled violence. She starts to go, but he stops her, takes her by both arms and holds her.*

BEPPO. You *won't* answer it! Marry me, Beth!

BETH. So that we can finish each other off!

BEPPO. Save each other!

BETH. You'll need Mr. Gibbs just the same!

BEPPO. Mr. Gibbs would make life not worth saving!— You know it: it was always you who used to insist on my taking myself seriously. And I need you: we were always something more together than either of us could be by himself!

BETH. It's all been destroyed now.

BEPPO. It can't be or I wouldn't feel the way I do—
I wouldn't feel such awful twists at my heart every tim
I see you again!—Don't you ever feel anything about me

BETH. I almost did this afternoon.

BEPPO. What did you feel?

BETH. I don't know: sadness, I guess. That was wha
made me sarcastic. I saw the little ash-trays we bough
in Paris.

BEPPO. And every time we meet again like this and pre
tend to be sophisticated and formal, we're murdering some
thing we made. It must be real or it wouldn't rebel—i
wouldn't hurt us so! (*The door-bell gives one last prolonge
ring: Beppo intensifies his eloquence.*) It must be the onl
thing real we've got left—it's the only thing that isn't self
conscious. Our other emotions are all trumped up—they'r
things we try to talk ourselves into. And that pain is a
we've got now for love. It's still living, whether we wan
it or not—it's still alive, in spite of everything. It mean
that we used to be happy together.

BETH. I used to be so horribly nasty!

BEPPO. You used to make all the false part of me seen
false, and I couldn't stand to be without it, so I went bac
to living with it. But now I'm so disgusted with it tha
I'd rather have you back and feel like a fool now an
then! You've got me breaking my furniture already, yo
see!

BETH. I really like the ham in you, as Chet Chives say:
I'd never been the kind of girl that men get romanti
about, and when you called me a "little brown maenad,"
you thrilled me to the core.

BEPPO. I remember, and you said, "Don't get literary!
(*She laughs, and he seizes her and kisses her.*) We'll ge
married again tomorrow, and we'll take the first boat t
Mexico!

BETH. Why Mexico?

BEPPO. Because Mexico's the wonderful place where they make those little pottery animals!

BETH. You broke the little bank just now when you pulled the tapestry down.

BEPPO. I know: I want to get a new one!—The train to Mexico City will be our P. L. M. Express! We'll revive the old rebellion!

BETH. You'd better pick up those pennies: we'll need them!

# The Little Blue Light

*The Little Blue Light* was produced in Cambridge, Massachusetts, on August 15, 1950, by the Brattle Theater Company at the Cambridge Summer Playhouse, under the direction of Albert Marre and with the following cast:

| | | | | |
|---|---|---|---|---|
| The Gardener | . | . | . | ALBERT MARRE |
| Judith | . | . | . | JESSICA TANDY |
| Gandersheim | . | . | . | HUME CRONYN |
| Frank | . | . | . | PAUL BALLANTYNE |
| Ellis. | . | . | . | ROBERT FLETCHER |

It was later produced in New York, on April 29, 1951, by Quintus Productions, at the ANTA Playhouse, under the direction of Albert Marre and with the following cast:

| | | | | |
|---|---|---|---|---|
| The Gardener | . | . | . | MARTIN GABEL |
| Judith | . | . | . | ARLENE FRANCIS |
| Gandersheim | . | . | . | BURGESS MEREDITH |
| Frank | . | . | . | MELVYN DOUGLAS |
| Ellis. | . | . | . | PETER COOKSON |

The text included here is not the same as that previously published, nor is it the same as the text used in either of the stage productions. I have made a new version that seems to me an improvement on any of these.

The victory of the Republicans at the last election has upset one of the specific prophecies of *The Little Blue Light*; on the other hand, it may be worthwhile to quote from the New York *Herald Tribune* of July 4, 1951, the following curious item:

St. Petersburg, Fla., July 3 (UP).—Police and fire authorities were at a loss to explain today how Mrs. Mary Hardy Reeser, sixty-seven, apparently burned to death.

All they found when they broke into Mrs. Reeser's slightly damaged apartment yesterday was a charred skull, shrunken to the size of a cup, a piece of backbone and a suede shoe for the left foot. These remains were lying on the floor before an overstuffed chair that was burned down to the springs.

The remains were not identified positively but were presumed to be those of Mrs. Reeser.

Local funeral directors said it would require a constant 2500 degree fire for three to four hours to consume a body as completely as that found in the apartment.

However, the one-room apartment itself was barely damaged. Only the electric light switches were melted. Below them, wall plug electric outlets were in good working order. Paint on the wall behind the burned chair was unmarked. A stack of newspapers atop a water heater standing near the chair was unscorched. So were sheets lying on a daybed five feet from the chair.

Fire Chief Claud Nesbit discounted a theory that lightning might have struck Mrs. Reeser. All electricity in the apartment, except for the switches, was in perfect working order, he said. An electric clock was stopped at 4:20, but worked perfectly when plugged into another socket.

Mrs. P. M. Carpenter, landlady of the Allamanda Apartment, discovered something was wrong and called firemen when she went to Mrs. Reeser's apartment to deliver a telegram at 8:27 a.m. She said the door handle was so hot she couldn't hold it.

Mrs. Carpenter said she smelled smoke earlier when she arose to get the paper but thought it came from a defective water pump, which she turned off. Otherwise no one in the building saw smoke or fire from the apartment.

The landlady said Mrs. Reeser seemed despondent Sunday night, apparently the last time she was seen alive.

Mrs. Reeser came to St. Petersburg four years ago from Columbia, Pa. She was the mother of Dr. Richard Reeser here.

420

# ACT I

*The back lawn of a country house about an hour and a half by train from New York. It is a late mid-September afternoon in some year of the not-remote future. One corner of the house is visible at the extreme left of the stage, revealing it as one of those monumental but clumsily-planned piles that were popular in America in the eighties. A porch runs around both sides, heavily screened by vines, with a short flight of steps that leads down to the lawn from the side that faces the audience, in such a way that it is seen sideways from the front of the stage. Above the porch, on the second floor, on the side that fills the left side of the stage, is a bow-window that swells out in a lump from the yellow wooden surface of the house. At the right of the stage, a wall, too high for passersby to see over, against which China roses are blooming, shuts the garden in from the street. High lilac bushes close in the back of the stage. In the middle of the lawn are four chairs and a little round table, all made of forged iron and painted white: two of the chairs are the upright kind and the others low lounging-chairs with wheels on the back legs. They are arranged around the table, the upright chairs facing the audience and the other two drawn up on either side.*

*A gardener, old and stooping and with longish hair, is standing, with his back to the audience, trimming a rambler vine on the side of the porch that faces it.*

*A woman comes out from the porch and starts down the steps but stops half-way. She is a handsome brunette, in her early thirties, but got up in such a way as not to bring out her feminine attractiveness. She wears a kind of brown business suit with a buttoned jacket, and her hair, parted straight in the middle, has been tightly stretched back and done up in a bun. She is tense, with an habitual tensity that never completely relaxes*

JUDITH. I thought that they were going to be beautiful when they bloomed the second time, those roses. The rose bugs messed them up in the summer, and I'd been hoping they'd be perfect this fall—but they're obviously going to pieces without ever having amounted to anything. They're stunted! I don't want to go near them. Nothing I have is ever right! Why can't I have flowers like other people?

THE GARDENER (*presenting himself readily and speaking eagerly, a little overacting his part*). Dey're not in de full bloom, *signora*.

JUDITH (*looking around*). Aren't they?

THE GARDENER (*coming forward*). You wait—you will see: in a day or two, they will be *molto belle, bellissime!*— Come and look. (*She comes down the steps and follows him over to the rose-bushes.*) See: de leetla mossa rose, she just begin to open wide.

JUDITH. You're sure they're really going to pan out?

THE GARDENER. Of course, dey panna out, *signora*—letta me showa you de Golden Dawn.

JUDITH. That name is so mushy!

THE GARDENER (*exhibiting a rose*). Eccola, graziosa signora just lika de morning sky before de sun showa himself all yellow wit' just a pale pinka flush.

JUDITH (*looking at another blossom above it*). There's something the matter with this one.

THE GARDENER (*nipping it off with his shears*). You know what maka dat, *signora*? A leetla spider—so small you can hardly see him. He eata up all de juice of de rose, and by-and-by she turna brown.

JUDITH (*as if to herself*). I don't like to hear about things like that.—I knew there was something wrong. (*She looks at the roses with distaste and apprehension.*)

THE GARDENER. Dat's de only one dat hava dat.—You wanta me to picka you some?

JUDITH. It's not too soon? Suppose they just die when I get them in the house in a vase?

THE GARDENER. Don't be afraid, *signora*. (*He begins clipping them off.*) For dem it is right now de besta moment. (*Showing her one*) *Ecco*. It is for de roses just lika for de udder tings: if you tasta de besta moment, it lasta you all de life—if you don't tasta, de moment never come!

JUDITH. I have to have things absolutely perfect—otherwise I can't enjoy them.

THE GARDENER. *Corpo di Bacco, signora!* Nutting in all de world is absolutely perfect by itself. We must not expecta God to give us de perfect tings ready made to enjoy, to admire, to love. We must maka de life perfect by bringing to it de love and de art.

JUDITH. But if they've got spiders in them, they'll just turn brown and horrible, anyway.

THE GARDENER (*holding up a flower*). Look here: dissa rose is notta perfect—but if you wear it lika dis (*holding it against his coat*) and putta de badda part behind, you will maka de perfect rose. (*He offers it to her.*)

JUDITH (*refusing to take it*). No, I don't want it: it's blemished.

THE GARDENER. *Ah, porco Iddio, signora!* to maka de beauty from de tings dat are damaged, dat is de greatest triumph for de man.

JUDITH (*taking the roses from him*). I'll just take the good ones—thank you.—You might paint the chairs and things now that we don't use them so much. They look terrible. And I must get some cushions for the big ones! They're not comfortable a bit like that. They've been making me absolutely miserable!

THE GARDENER. Ah, *signora*, it's not de cushions dat cura de misery—it's de happiness dat maka de comfort.

JUDITH. You ought to write those moralizings down.

THE GARDENER. *Grazie, signora.*

JUDITH. They mightn't sound so sententious on paper.

THE GARDENER. *Scusi, signora.*

*The door in the wall opens, and a gentleman appears. He is a man in his early forties, pasty and partly bald, dressed dandiacally but in rather bad taste. He wears a light gray suit, with spats, a dark green Homburg hat, a violet tie on a lighter purple shirt and a handkerchief to match sticking out of his breast-pocket. He carries a light cane.*

THE VISITOR (*taking off his hat*). Please pardon me for coming in like this. Is this Mrs. Brock?

JUDITH. Yes.

THE VISITOR. Well, I'm the person you're renting this house from.

JUDITH. The agent?

THE VISITOR. No: the owner.

JUDITH. M. S. Ferguson?

THE VISITOR. Yes. (*Shaking hands with self-conscious urbanity*) It's nice to meet you at last.

*The Gardener, who has watched his entrance, now turns to go back to his work and as he does so faces the audience.*

THE GARDENER (*winking at the audience and dropping his Italian accent*). Just a few old platitudes!

*He returns to trimming the ramblers and gradually works offstage at the left.*

THE VISITOR (*going on to Judith*). I hope you don't mind my appearing by the back way like this. It's so natural for me and it's shorter from the station.

JUDITH. I thought you were in Europe.

THE VISITOR. I was, but I suddenly found I couldn't stick it and I hopped a plane and came back.

JUDITH. Won't you sit down? I'm afraid that these chairs are inexcusably uncomfortable—they're supposed to have cushions.

# ACT I

THE VISITOR (*sitting down in the upright chair at the left and putting his hat on the table*). They're delightful! How well you've kept things up!

JUDITH (*sitting down in the other straight chair*). I've had the garden attended to. It was in very bad shape when we came.

THE VISITOR. Really?

JUDITH. Yes: absolutely a jungle. Your caretaker hadn't done anything about it—so we got a regular gardener.

THE VISITOR. Oh, dear: really? Did he neglect the pigeons, too? I didn't see them as I came by the stable.

JUDITH. They had some kind of disease, and most of them died.

THE VISITOR. How heartbreaking! I wanted to keep them. They were a part of the old stable and made it still seem alive. I hope you haven't minded my insisting that it shouldn't be used as a garage.

JUDITH. We did what you suggested: we rented the garage across the road.

THE VISITOR. I was sure they'd let you have it—that place has been empty, too.—You don't keep horses?

JUDITH. No; but we've had the stable repainted.

THE VISITOR. Just a shade too bright, perhaps.

JUDITH. We tried to get the same color. In a year or so it won't look so glaring.

THE VISITOR. It had a quality, I always thought. You haven't cleaned out the stalls? (*Smiling with a shade of deprecation*) I liked to have some oats in the mangers.

JUDITH. We haven't touched it, because you asked us not to.

THE VISITOR. Don't think I'm finding fault. Everything that I've seen looks splendidly. One never knows what to expect of one's tenants, and I'd never even met you, you know.

JUDITH. So you came out to check.

425

THE VISITOR. I just wanted to meet you and see the place and find out how you were getting along.

JUDITH. My husband's reading proofs. In a few minutes, I'll let him know you're here.

THE VISITOR. Don't disturb him! I just dropped in.

JUDITH. Do tell me about Europe. Is the situation really worse?

THE VISITOR. Not exactly worse, perhaps, but you get to feel it more if you stay there a long time.

JUDITH. There's still not much food or coal?

THE VISITOR. Oh, there's plenty of food in the good hotels, and they manage to heat them more or less. It's the atmosphere—the whole state of mind.

JUDITH. Pretty tense?

THE VISITOR. Not only tense but inhuman, in a very disconcerting way. One used to feel here in America that the people were becoming dehumanized—with all the offices and factories and subways—but now in Europe, in a different way, they're losing their individuality. You remember how they used always to be fighting for their various national cultures? The Frenchman wanted to be a Frenchman; the Czech wanted to be a Czech; the inhabitants of every little province wanted to keep their own traditions, if it merely meant putting on some old peasant dress and celebrating a local feastday. Well, the only thing they struggle for now is to perpetuate some system of slavery that is going to make them all alike. One feels that they're just clustering like iron filings on these big concentrations of power.

JUDITH. In the countries we dominate, too?

THE VISITOR (*smiling ironically*). In the countries the United States dominates, we've gotten ourselves into the position of backing reactionary movements that are using all the methods of fascism. I'm a conservative, but the kind of thing we're doing over there is absolutely

426

n-American. We began by fighting the Reds, but we don't realize that their enemies are just as undesirable as they re. We've never understood Europe—at least our worthy presidents never do—and the result is that we're now being swept along by the hideous subhuman power that's wreaking havoc all over the world.

JUDITH. What power do you mean?

THE VISITOR (*as if his answer were more or less self-evident and revealing a touch of madness which makes Judith look round at him*). Why, the demiurge that's running amuck, devouring civilization.

JUDITH. Do you identify him with anything in particular?

THE VISITOR. I identify him with almost everything!

JUDITH. Oh. (*After a moment's pause*) Has your demiurge got a name?

THE VISITOR. He's got a thousand names—you've heard them: Belial, Moloch, Kali—call him Nobodaddy, like Blake—call it the Second Coming, like Yeats, with a wild beast instead of a savior—call him Shidnats Slyme, the Monster God.

JUDITH. You're a Gandersheim addict, I see.

THE VISITOR. Well, not precisely an addict—though I know his work pretty well.

JUDITH. If you can read him at all, you're an addict. I'm one of the people that *can't* read him, but my husband is crazy about him.

THE VISITOR. I suppose I must make a confession so that we shan't go on talking on a false assumption. I *am* Gandersheim.

JUDITH. You're not really? I knew it was a pseudonym, but you're not like the descriptions of him.

GANDERSHEIM (*grinning slyly*). That's just our publicity—mystification!

JUDITH. The photographs are hoaxes, too?

GANDERSHEIM. A friend of mine posed for them all.

JUDITH (*looking over to study him*). But I see that you are like him in some ways. Are those the violet eyes that sometimes fade to the invisible color of ultra-violet rays?

GANDERSHEIM (*rather pleased*). Perhaps.

JUDITH. And you're wearing a violet tie.

GANDERSHEIM. There *are* certain points, I think, where he and I fuse with one another.

JUDITH. But where's the Brazilian butterfly that you're supposed to wear in your buttonhole? and the mystic ring of priceless old jade?

*He holds out his left hand, on one finger of which is a large jade ring.*

GANDERSHEIM. And I do happen to know something about butterflies.

JUDITH. Is it true that you drink nothing but Armagnac from the cellar of the Comte de Germain?

*Frank Brock comes down the steps from the porch. He is a loose rangy man of forty-three, dressed in a business suit of something less than the best urban cut and with shaggy undisciplined hair. He wears spectacles with dark rims and a wide razzle-dazzle tie. He is carrying the afternoon paper.*

GANDERSHEIM. That's mythical, I'm afraid—but I have had some rather choice Armagnac. It has a flavor of violets, you see—violet and beyond, again.

JUDITH. Here's my husband.

*Gandersheim gets up.*

JUDITH (*to Frank*). Who do you think this is?

FRANK (*apprehensively, stopping in his tracks as he looks at Gandersheim*). I haven't the slightest idea. (*He has a thickly Middle-Western voice and an emphatic Middle-Western way of talking.*)

JUDITH. Gansvoort von Gandersheim.

FRANK (*after a moment of sizing up Gandersheim and deciding it is not a joke*). No! (*Coming over and shaking hands*) Say, I'm a fan of yours!

JUDITH. Frank used to subscribe to *Gruesome Tales* just to read the Shidnats Slyme stories.

FRANK. And now the goddam *Metropolitan*—which is otherwise a lousy magazine!

GANDERSHEIM. I'm also, under my other name, the person that you're renting this house from.

FRANK. The hell you are!

GANDERSHEIM. I just dropped in to see how you were getting on.

FRANK. Sit down! (*He throws himself into the lounging-chair on the left, as Gandersheim resumes his seat.*) Well, for goodness' sake!—and I never knew about it!

GANDERSHEIM (*pleased*). I always use my real family name, of course, in connection with personal business.

FRANK. Say, tell me: what happened to that chemistry professor when he finally got hold of the formula so that he could summon up Shidnats at will? Was he so scared by what happened the first time that he never tried it again, or did he turn all the demons loose on that academic cabal that was trying to block his promotion?

GANDERSHEIM. Ah, that story hasn't been written, and I'm not sure that I can give you an answer.

FRANK. I don't want to ask indiscreet questions——

GANDERSHEIM (*smiling*). Oh, it isn't a question of that. My contract with *Metropolitan's* running out, and I'm not sure they want any more stories—so I really haven't thought about what happened next.

FRANK. I don't know how I can bear it if you don't go on. I want to know whether the Shidnats adepts were able to utilize his power without blowing out their fuses.

GANDERSHEIM. It *is* rather risky, of course—it's probably safer to let it alone.

JUDITH. Mr. Gandersheim thinks that his demiurge is the dominating influence in Europe.

FRANK. I shouldn't wonder if you were right at that.

GANDERSHEIM. You know there *have* been some rather odd coincidences between certain incidents in the stories and some of the things that have been happening lately.

FRANK. What's an example?

GANDERSHEIM. Did you happen to see one of my tales called *The Octagon Building Conspiracy*?

FRANK (*nodding*). About the Shidnats cult in the war.

GANDERSHEIM. That came out before the spy revelations.

FRANK. Yes, by God, it did!

GANDERSHEIM. I sometimes have a queer kind of insight. It came to me almost like a vision. I had no private information, but one day I conceived the idea of young scientists and government officials—absolutely the conscientious type, the kind of people one would never suspect—falling under some sinister influence and betraying their country to a foreign power. It was incredible, and yet it happened. And my stories usually pass for fantasy!

FRANK. That's right! The way things are getting, it's actually easier to swallow your goblins than a lot of the real stuff that's going on. That's the reason you go over the way you do: you feed people horror in homeopathic doses so that they're able to face the things that are happening, and that they can't seem to do anything about or even begin to grasp. Your shudder stories deal more or less with the same elements of murder and espionage, but the reader can get through one in three-quarters of an hour and everything is perfectly logical, and the wind-up gives him some sort of satisfaction.

GANDERSHEIM. It's gratifying to hear you say that. I've always felt my work was modern.

JUDITH. With a good allowance of old-fashioned Gothic.

GANDERSHEIM. Alas, for the Gothic! It's done for, I'm afraid. One misses it in post-war Europe. There are more ruins, of course, than ever, and one can't say they aren't sometimes grisly, but it's hard to attune oneself to the older reverberations. Germany today is a limbo, full of beings that have never been really born—they're such gibbering specters themselves that they make the Wild Huntsmen and the Lenore bridegrooms seem as solid in retrospect as the old beer and pumpernickel.

JUDITH. But *Italy's* still romantic?

GANDERSHEIM. The landscape but not the life. There's plenty of crime, to be sure—sometimes ferocious enough—but it's mostly quite wholesale and sordid: just a routine slaughter of hostages. Nothing could be more remote from the magnificent outrages of the Borgias and the gamier days of the Papacy. In England, the big country houses that have always been so marvelously haunted have been confiscated by the wretched Labourites and turned into administrative centers. Last summer I went to Glen Murtagh Castle, the Earl of Medard's place—which I've always wanted to see: it's supposed to have had a Man in Armor, a charming Woman in White and a recurrent hereditary monster—and what did I find but a rationing bureau! When I asked about the current monster, I was told by a horrid little clerk—obviously lower middle class—that it had been sent by the Earl to the United States to get it away from the Blitz and that "we"—meaning the Labour people—had decided not to bring it back.

JUDITH. How pathetic to be robbed of one's monsters!

GANDERSHEIM. Oh, there are monsters enough—and the new thing, of course, has its own kind of beauty. There *is* a real thrill in destruction—and destruction has never been achieved on such a gigantic scale and so completely without inhibitions. The godlike irresponsibility of it!—you're sitting up there in the clouds and (*illustrating by snapping his fingers*) you just go click, click, click! and you pulverize whole cities—men and women and children are crushed or roasted to death, and palaces and public buildings—the big shells that they put up for show, the pedestals to make themselves important—they're all flapped away in great sheets of flame, along with the poor man's hovel and the shop that sells fish and chips—while the bomber sails along overhead as nonchalant and unremorseful as if he'd just lit up an autumn bonfire. And (*smiling*) there *were* some wonderful touches!—the tigers and snakes and apes that were let loose when the zoos were bombed and went wandering about the streets! (*Judith gives him a sharp look.*) But when one comes to it a few years later, the results do seem rather bleak. A house that's been shattered by bombing shows nothing but naked plaster—the rooms don't preserve their bad memories as a rugged old castle can do—unless, of course, it happens to be a room where people have been shot against the wall or a torture chamber stained with blood. But even with a place of that sort it would take at least fifty years to make it glamorous with a patina of legend, and in the meantime it may be rebuilt —or destroyed by another bombing.

JUDITH. I can see you found it disappointing.

GANDERSHEIM. It's quite creepy enough in other ways. I was quite unnerved when I left. One day I started talking to a man on the train—I couldn't make out his nationality: he spoke English with some sort of accent—and he turned out to have read my books. I thought he knew them a little too well—as if he might just have got the subject up. It occurred to me that he might be a spy——

FRANK. Why would anybody want to spy on you?

GANDERSHEIM. I'd been telling people how I felt about what was going on in Europe; and it made me a little nervous when it turned out we were stopping at the same hotel—so, instead of getting off at Genoa, I went right on through to Florence, and there, lo and behold! in my pension I found myself sitting at table with another mysterious creature—a woman with an obvious wig—who talked to me about my writings——

FRANK (*grinning*). You're just world-famous, that's all. It's what I tell you: a lot of people have read you because they've got the same jitters you have.

GANDERSHEIM. Well, in any case, Europe was getting me down—I had a night of abject panic, and then I jumped on a plane for home. And very happy I am to be back, I can tell you!

FRANK. How long have you been away?

GANDERSHEIM. I went over the second spring after the end of the war.

FRANK. Well, I hate to hand you a wet blanket the moment you get off the boat, but you don't want to have any illusions about the kind of U.S.A. you've come back to!

GANDERSHEIM. You sound frightening. What do you mean? It's true I'm rather out of touch.

FRANK. Don't imagine that we haven't got plenty of spies!

GANDERSHEIM. Hardly on the same scale, surely!

FRANK. I don't know: it seems to me nowadays that every other person I see is some kind of goddam agent!—

GANDERSHEIM. But what is it they're agents of?

FRANK. Why, of all these damn pressure groups!—the same thing you have in Europe, only not operating quite so openly.

GANDERSHEIM. How disquieting!

FRANK. It's gotten to the point where I can hardly get my magazine out. I'm constantly pursued and persecuted by the lobbyists of all these groups, these various political and religious organizations, and more than half the time they're under cover.

GANDERSHEIM. I didn't realize that *Spotlight* dealt with controversial subjects.

FRANK. Hell, fifteen years ago it wouldn't have been called controversial, but today, good God! it takes all a man's strength to stand up for an independent

433

factual article that doesn't even try to draw conclusions!

GANDERSHEIM. But how can that be?

FRANK. It can be because what used to be everybody's privilege, that Americans took for granted—free press and free speech—has now gotten to be nothing short of a heroic individual exploit.

GANDERSHEIM. But the Bill of Rights is still in order, isn't it?

FRANK. It's still in the Constitution, but everybody wants to ignore it.

GANDERSHEIM. The radicals and the reactionaries, you mean?

FRANK. That line-up is obsolete now.

GANDERSHEIM. I do wish you'd fill me in. I'm quite ignorant about what's been happening. I couldn't make anything of the political news when I read it in the Paris *Herald*.

FRANK. It certainly isn't the politics you knew, if you left as long ago as that, and you may have some pretty severe shocks in store for you. The most important fact of the last ten years—that you'll have to begin by grasping —is the virtual disappearance of the old two-party system. What happened first of all was that, beginning with the New Deal, the Democrats swallowed everything; but by that time the Democratic Party was a collection of special interests that were competing with one another like hell —so that it got to be simply a question of which kind of Democrat you were going to elect. What it finally came down to was a scrimmage between a whole lot of organized groups, each trying to get control of the government and resorting to every kind of skulduggery—bribery, blackmail, violence—to get themselves into office.

GANDERSHEIM. But what are they?—the Reds, I suppose—but what other groups have we here?

FRANK. Well, I'll give you the political picture—reading

from Right to Left. First of all, you have the Reds—they're the extreme Right: they want to institute state slavery, abolish civil rights altogether and have the country run by an oligarchy. Then you have the New Federalists—they want to restrict the vote to big employers of labor and incomes in the upper brackets. Next come the Constitutionalists, who are the nearest thing we've got to a Left: they want to keep the Constitution. All of these have political programs—they're the only big groups that do. But that doesn't tell the whole story, because there are all the other groups that function without programs but work for their group interests. The strongest one now is Labor. The politicos try to exploit it, but usually it exploits them. Then there are the Children of Peter, with their religious organization behind them. Actually the objectives of the Peters are just about the same as the Reds', and their methods are about the same. The only difference is that the Peters are directed from Madrid instead of from Belgrade, and that they make use of father confessors instead of third-degree police. But both the Reds and the Children of Peter want to put the brakes on education and to keep the working class down. They both organize their own unions as an obstruction to the legitimate unions that are fighting for the interests of Labor. Last and most disgusting perhaps is the new group of Yankee Elitists, our indigenous variety of fascists. They're mostly just small-time snobs with the usual careerist aspirations, who go along with the Big Business party—though, if they think they can gain anything by it, it's not at all unusual for them to turn into Reds overnight. They've combined with the Southern Dixiecrats, who want to keep the Negro disfranchised in the interests of old-time Southern chivalry.

*A young man appears from the house and comes over toward the group.*

435

GANDERSHEIM. You appal me: I came back from Europe, really *warm* about the Statue of Liberty, and you tell me we're caught in the same trap!

FRANK. Well, it's not quite so bad, even so, as what's happened to the rest of the world. There are still a few Americans left who don't want to take dictation from these mass-produced power-units. (*Getting up and raising his voice in his earnestness*) The main stimulus to the founding of the American Republic was disobedience to the King of England, and the mainspring of American vitality has always been our refusal to let anybody tell us what to do. The thing that can save us today is the thing that has made us great. We've got to have the guts to think for ourselves and act on our own ideas!

GANDERSHEIM. Hear, hear! How splendidly you say it! It quite rouses my Revolutionary blood! I date from the *Mayflower*, you know. (*Judith looks at him, and he adds, smiling.*) No, but I really do!

*The young man has stopped modestly at Frank's left, so as not to intrude on the group. He is Frank's secretary Ellis, an erect clean-cut fellow of twenty-six, a product of the best education, quiet and well-bred but with a perceptible tone of conscious superiority.*

FRANK (*turning to Ellis*). Did you get rid of them?

ELLIS. They've left, but they're sure to be back. They insist they've got to see you personally.

FRANK. Oh, God! What's biting them now? (*To Gandersheim*) This is just what I was telling you about! It's the Reds who have got some squawk. (*To Ellis*) Go ahead and tell me: I want him to hear.

ELLIS. It's that piece about the maraschino cherry-pickers. They say that our running it puts us in a class with the worst type of Yankee Elitists.

FRANK. How do they figure that out?

ELLIS. Their point is that maraschino cherries are an article of upper-class luxury——

FRANK. What's behind it?

ELLIS. What's evidently behind it is that the pickers belong to a union that's been fighting the Red infiltration.

FRANK. So what?

ELLIS. That links us with the Elitists. They serve manhattans at the Elitist banquets.

FRANK. So what?

ELLIS. They'll denounce us as Elitists and ruin our circulation among the small-income groups.

FRANK. Unless what?

ELLIS. They've left us an article setting forth the Red point of view on the crisis in the fruit-pickers' union—and they say they expect us to run it.

FRANK (to Gandersheim). There you are! That's what I'm up against!

JUDITH. You might introduce Ellis!

FRANK. I'm sorry. (To Gandersheim) This is Ellis, my trouble-shooter. (To Ellis) This is Gansvoort von Gandersheim.

ELLIS, What, really?

*The visitor gets up and shakes hands, with a slightly Mephistophelean smile in character with his Gandersheim role.*

JUDITH. Mr. Ferguson.

GANDERSHEIM. Oh, I don't mind—though of course it's a ridiculous name—a mixture of German and Knickerbocker Dutch. I made it up when I was just a kid, and I signed it to the first story I ever sold.

ELLIS. I see.

JUDITH. Don't you want to sit down, Ellis?

*He poises on the left arm of the other lounging-chair. Gandersheim and Frank resume their seats.*

GANDERSHEIM (to Frank). That first story was written right here, and the name was somehow a product of the atmosphere of this queer old house.—I was rather surprised, by the way, that an active man of affairs like yourself should have chosen such an old-fashioned place—and so far away from New York, in such a deserted neighborhood.

FRANK. It was just exactly the kind of thing I was looking for. I wanted to get away from town—out of reach of these goddam propagandists.

GANDERSHEIM. But you don't direct your magazine from here?

FRANK. I do, by God! I have an office in town, of course, where they handle the business end, but most of the editorial work is done right here in this house—done by us three!

GANDERSHEIM. Really? I'd imagined something on a bigger scale.

*During the speeches of Frank that follow, Ellis and Judith, who have evidently heard all this before, talk to one another, smiling, like young people relaxing from their elders.*

FRANK. Hell, you don't need a big staff if you know exactly what you want and have the self-confidence to make your own decisions. All these (*underlining the words with irony*) *editorial conferences* and *rewrite men* and enormous *research departments* are just ways that editors have to try to make themselves feel important because they haven't got any ideas. They try to find out what the *readers'* ideas are—they're always worrying about *circulation.*—And then —when they've worked out the formula for a standardized machine-made product that their readers will always take —they sit down and try to figure out how they can appeal to a still lower grade of readers without losing the original lot. The result in the long run is just the same as in radio and television: they're creating an artificial market for a mechanical mass-culture that depends on reducing the public to a lowest common denominator. You get something just as lifeless and boring as the movies were before they went bankrupt. The old yellow journalism was bad enough, but it at least had a certain vulgar gaudiness, and competition kept it lively. Today you get a processed commodity so completely devoid of flavor or of any emotion or meaning whatsoever that the only way you can force it on the customers is by killing the better grades of goods.

GANDERSHEIM. But *Spotlight* has not been eliminated!

FRANK. American journalism today has gotten to be just like the horsemeat that they put up in cans for dogs!— So long as they aren't given anything else, the Sealyham has to eat it just the same as the mutt.

GANDERSHEIM. But *you* give them something better.

FRANK. I do—and I've definitely proved that there still exist a whole lot of Americans who aren't satisfied with this goddam kennel food. I go on the opposite theory: I don't worry about the reader. I assume that any article that interests *me*—on any subject whatever—will interest a lot of other people. And I'm right!—by God, I'm right! I started out with *Spotlight* on a shoestring—it was practically a little magazine—and in four years and a half I've scared up a circulation of almost three hundred thousand. I've always maintained, and I've proved it, that there are still plenty of people in this country who like to read decent writing, who are actually famished for edible print—and I believe there are lots of people who don't want their thinking done for them—especially by these damned authoritarian groups that aim to stamp out thought altogether!

GANDERSHEIM. It's heartening to hear you say so. But what is *Spotlight's* own point of view?—simply that of independent critic?

FRANK. What's our point of view, Ellis?

ELLIS. Liberalism, I suppose.

FRANK (*going on to Gandersheim*). It's not exactly what

439

you might think of as liberalism, though—it's something older than that. My idea is simply the old-fashioned one that everybody's got a right to look at the world from the corner he's sitting in—and to yell about anything he doesn't like.

GANDERSHEIM. So you're always treading on people's toes?

FRANK. So the various pressure publicists are alway raising a howl against me—and I'm also beginning to worry the big circulation boys. It's driving them crazy to realize that there's somebody who still has the self-assurance to print whatever he pleases and who can actually make it pay. I've even swiped some of their writers, because I let them sign their names and write in their own style.

GANDERSHEIM. That's what I find so annoying with the *Metropolitan* people: they want to rewrite all my prose.

FRANK. And *what* prose they put out, huh? It's like some kind of cheap cold cream!

GANDERSHEIM. But you never take sides about anything

FRANK. I never plug a political point of view, like the liberals in the twenties did. My contention is that the abuses of the world—at least, the majority of them—have no more to do with political systems than the big acts of disinterested virtue. They're just special cases o human weakness. Take these exposés by Percy Gilman He's doing the undertakers now. Did you ever realize how the undertakers make a practice of exploiting people' grief to induce them to buy fancy coffins and all kinds o unnecessary fixings?

GANDERSHEIM (*smiling*). How scandalous! And that, o course, has no political implications.

FRANK. It's not part of an organized system! It's simply a petty swindle on the part of the undertakers—and there've always been petty swindles since the days o Ananias and Sapphira.

JUDITH. I don't agree with Frank about this.

*The Gardener appears from the porch.*

THE GARDENER (*to Frank*). Bertha aska me to tell you de Archbishop want to speak to you on de phone.

FRANK (*to Ellis*). What have we had about the Peters lately?

ELLIS. I don't think we've had anything for months.

FRANK. Well, see what he wants, will you? (*Ellis starts toward the house.*) Tell him I'm out of town!

FRANK (*to Gandersheim*). You can be sure he's got some gripe about something!

THE GARDENER (*to Judith*). You wanta me to mova de hydrangeas?

JUDITH (*to Gandersheim*). I really ought to consult *you* about this.

GANDERSHEIM. You thought of doing something with the hydrangeas?

JUDITH. I'd thought of moving them back near the stable.

*Frank looks at the first page of his paper.*

FRANK. Well, I'm damned! (*He reads an article with concentrated attention, presently turning the pages to get at the continuation.*)

GANDERSHEIM. You don't like them on the front drive?

JUDITH. They're so badly discolored. If they're meant to be blue, I'm afraid they've degenerated. They're all sort of greenish and spotty.

GANDERSHEIM. Oh, you have to put iron in the soil. They used to be very handsome.

JUDITH. I don't know what to do about them.

GANDERSHEIM. But your man here does, I'm sure. (*To the Gardener*) Sei italiano?

THE GARDENER. Parlo italiano, signore.

GANDERSHEIM (*to Judith*). You're fortunate. They make marvelous gardeners. (*To the Gardener*) Di dove vieni? Da che paese?

THE GARDENER. *Da un paese antichissimo, signore.*

GANDERSHEIM. *Ma da quale?—dimmi. Conosco l'Italia bene.*

THE GARDENER. *Non è propriamente in Italia.*

GANDERSHEIM. *Dove dunque?*

THE GARDENER. *Non lo so più nemmeno io, signore.*

GANDERSHEIM (*to Judith*). I know Italy pretty well, but I can't identify his accent. He doesn't want to tell me where he comes from.

JUDITH. But about the hydrangeas——

GANDERSHEIM. Yes?

JUDITH. Would you mind if I moved them back?

GANDERSHEIM. Why not try to revive the color? They're very much out of fashion, I know, and some people consider them ugly, but I assure you they can be perfectly magnificent. In my mother's time, they were one of our glories: great rich round fleshy clusters that varied from blue to violet or from pink to a flushed kind of purple— and the petals had fine little veins that made them look like—like Albrecht Dürer's drawings.

JUDITH. We could work on them after we'd moved them.

GANDERSHEIM. But the approach to the house is quite fine in its way—I hope you appreciate it! Hortensias, umbrella-trees, elephant ears—all those ornamental plants of the McKinley period!—and the big silver ball in the middle.

JUDITH. We had to put the ball away.

GANDERSHEIM. Really? Why?

JUDITH. It was terribly stained and tarnished.

GANDERSHEIM. Well, one can't expect everybody to care for such things— (*nodding toward the Gardener*) I'm sure *he* understands they belong here. (*Addressing him directly*) This place has its style, *non è vero?* though of course it's not the Boboli Gardens.

THE GARDENER. You can see dat somebody here once has tried to make a leettle pattern.

GANDERSHEIM. Of course there's a pattern! My mother designed it, and I don't like to see it spoiled. (*To Judith*) It's wonderful the instinct they have about everything connected with aesthetics!

JUDITH (*to the Gardener*). I'll let you know later.

THE GARDENER. *Bene, signora. In ogni modo,* we could not transplanta dem dis afternoon. For de flowers it is lika for de people. You performa de operation de very first ting in de morning: den de patient have all de day to recover.

*Judith gives him a long-suffering ironic look.*

GANDERSHEIM (*fruitily*). And a deep earthy wisdom!

JUDITH (*nodding to the Gardener*). That's enough earthy wisdom today.

THE GARDENER (*retiring*). *Bene, benissimo.*

FRANK (*to Judith, holding up the paper*). Look at this: another goddam political crime! Cardinal Keenan's been murdered.

*She takes the paper from him and quickly glances through the story.*

GANDERSHEIM. Political murders, too? In the old days, we shot only the presidents!

THE GARDENER (*turning away toward the audience and walking back to the house*). *Il trionfo della morte! Avanti Savoia!*

FRANK (*to Judith*). That looks like a Red job. (*To Gandersheim*). The mystery is how they did it. He was burned to death in some way.

GANDERSHEIM. Where did they find his body?

FRANK. He was sitting at his desk in his study. It was almost as if he'd been electrocuted.

GANDERSHEIM. It's strange that electrocution hasn't been more used for murders. You can electrocute a person, you know, with as little as fifty volts and generate that much current with an equipment that you can carry in a cigarbox. Were the electrical fixtures examined?

*Ellis appears from the house and comes over toward the group.*

FRANK. He'd just been talking on the phone—the receiver was still in his hand, but the telephone seemed perfectly normal—the insulation was all right.

JUDITH. What about the burnt-out flashlight?

FRANK. That was the other side of the room—and electrocution doesn't singe the skin. The whole upper part of his body was blackened—though his clothes were only burned from the inside.

JUDITH. But you've only got the reports of the Peters. They had a chance to set the stage. I'll bet they did it themselves, just to create a martyr!

FRANK. I don't think they'd go that far. After all, the Reds in Europe have supplied them with more martyrs than they need.

JUDITH. They haven't any over here. I wouldn't put it past them.

FRANK. It wouldn't be worth it to them. The value of martyrs has slumped. Since the bombings and the concentration camps and the Stalingrad holocaust, nobody but a few old cranks cares a damn about human life. Our emotional thermometer's blown its top: we don't react to those things any more. My guess is that for some special reason the Reds wanted to get rid of the Cardinal and counted on its passing as a natural death. (*To Ellis*) What was the call about?

ELLIS. Just what you're talking about.

FRANK. The Archbishop, by God! I forgot.

ELLIS. They've arrested Percy Gilman.

FRANK. Why?

ELLIS. He's supposed to have been the last person who'd been in Keenan's study.

FRANK. What had Percy gone to see him about?

ELLIS. It seems that the Sons of Peter have funeral parlors of their own, and Gilman had gone to the Cardinal to find out whether he knew about their racket.

FRANK. Well, what, in Heaven's name, is supposed to have happened? Is he supposed to have made Keenan so sore that he had a stroke and fell dead?

ELLIS. They accuse him of carbonizing the Cardinal with some kind of canned lightning.

JUDITH. That flashlight?

ELLIS. It does seem suspicious. They can't make out how it worked.

FRANK. They're just trying to get back at *me*! Why would Percy want to kill the Cardinal?

ELLIS. They've dug up that he once lost his job in one of the public schools for saying that Jefferson and Franklin were skeptics about religion. It seems he wrote some articles then against the Peteristic influence on education.

FRANK. That was way back in the forties!

ELLIS. They're making the most of the fact that he once had a nervous breakdown and was sent to a sanitarium. They say he's a fanatic, a madman.

FRANK. What did the Archbishop want?

ELLIS. He wants you to testify that Gilman was unstable and a religious crank.

FRANK. The hell I will! He's mild as a lamb.

JUDITH. You haven't known him long.

FRANK. I could size him up at a glance. He's a typical New Deal hack: conscientious and low-keyed to a fault! He was sent me by that Teniakis Agency, and they're always absolutely reliable.—And what the hell does the Archbishop mean by telling me what to testify?—What's their blackmail?

ELLIS. They'll get us suppressed.

FRANK. Incitement to violence?

ELLIS. Yes: they say that we've always attacked them.

FRANK. Hell! didn't we run that article about that big Peter priest who plays basket ball?

THE GARDENER (*to Frank*). *Signore.*

FRANK (*apprehensively*). What is it now?

THE GARDENER. A phone call for you, *signore.*

FRANK. Who is it?

THE GARDENER. A newspaper reporter. He says he work for de *Standard.*

FRANK. Tell him I've gone out to the West Coast.

THE GARDENER. *Bene, signore.*

ELLIS. Don't you think it might be worth while to find out what the reporter knows?

JUDITH. I'd talk to him!

*The Gardener stops to see whether Frank will change his mind; but goes on when Frank begins making a speech, and disappears into the house.*

FRANK. Nowadays they never know anything! You can't find out anything from reading the papers. (*He goes on holding forth to Gandersheim, while Ellis takes the newspaper from Judith and sits down in the lounging-chair to read it.*) The audacious American journalist who dashes to the center of tension and uncovers something that wasn't known is just as obsolete today as the cracker-barrel editorial-writer who thinks up his own comments. They both subsist entirely on handouts from the various publicity departments, and the only people who really know what's happening are the top inner committees of these anti-democratic groups. I've been a journalist all my life —I spent ten years as a city editor—but lately I've had to admit that I haven't got the slightest idea about who's doing what to whom—and there are times when I'm not sure that I care!

JUDITH. I hope you're not going to capitulate this time.

FRANK. What do you mean, "this time"?

*Gandersheim, not to seem to pay attention to a conversation that shows signs of acerbity, takes the paper from Ellis, who has laid it on his knee and looked around.*

JUDITH. Well, the Yankee Elitists persuaded you to pretty much retract your statement about F. Bulfinch Boudinot.

FRANK. I'm not going to sell Percy out, and I'm not going to get suppressed.

JUDITH. What do you propose to do?

ELLIS. Hadn't I better get in touch with your lawyer?

FRANK. More lawyers: my God!

JUDITH. They certainly let you down the last time.

FRANK. Don't be so defeatist.

JUDITH. I'm not defeatist: I think you ought to fight.

FRANK. Of course I'm going to fight. I'm going to take the offensive. I'm going to find out for myself for once exactly what's happened and why.

JUDITH. Who will you get to do it? You're not planning to investigate yourself?

FRANK (*ironically*). That would be a dandy idea, wouldn't it?

ELLIS. How about that little man who did the exposé of the Trotter poll?

FRANK (*to Gandersheim*). That's something you ought to know about! It turns out that when they take these polls, they don't actually make a bona fide effort to find out what people think: they're paid by various interests to manufacture public opinion by producing the right kind of predictions.

GANDERSHEIM (*putting down the paper*). It's strange that no one heard any noise. There were several other people in the house. One can only imagine something like an enormous oxy-acetylene blow-torch.

FRANK (*to Ellis, announcing a sudden idea*). Do you know who's going after this story?

447

ELLIS. Have you got an inspiration?

FRANK. *You* are!

ELLIS. I'm afraid I can't quite see that.

FRANK (*springing to his feet again*). You're just the ideal person!

ELLIS. But wouldn't it be better to get somebody who isn't connected with the magazine?

FRANK. That doesn't make any difference. The great thing about it is that nobody will take you seriously. Don't misunderstand me, but they'll think you're a perfect ninny. You'll be obviously out of your element, and they'll think you're naïve and diffident—those professional foxes and weasels won't pay any attention to you. But the fact is—*you* know and *I* know—that you're a hell of an astute guy. You're the sharpest checker of copy and the deftest brusher-off of visitors that I've ever had working for me—and what's more, you have the qualification that your father was an Episcopal minister and that you worked for the Federated Churches——

ELLIS. I was just Father's secretary.

FRANK. But you got to know the leaders in the religious world.

ELLIS. I don't exactly like to exploit the connections I made through Father.

FRANK. He's dead now, isn't he?

ELLIS. But even so.

GANDERSHEIM (*embarrassed by the conversation, in a low voice to Judith*). Do you mind if I look at the roses?

*They go over to the wall together, and he comments on the various bushes, but she keeps an ear out for the others and sometimes glances in their direction.*

FRANK. Well, you've lost your religious faith, you told me, and I hope you've got some faith in *Spotlight*. This is a goddam critical situation: the whole issue of a free press is at stake—and it may mean saving an innocent

448

man. With the power that the Peters have now, they might be able to railroad Percy to the chair.

ELLIS. I can't imagine that I'm the right person; but if you really think I could be any use——

FRANK. You can if you start right away and get around before they've framed their case. Go to people in the other churches and find out where Keenan stood and who would have had an interest in killing him——

ELLIS. I used to know Bishop Fay pretty well.

FRANK. If possible, get something on them. If they threaten us, we'll blackmail them back.

ELLIS. I shouldn't like to betray people's confidence.

FRANK. Don't worry: *they* wouldn't hesitate. The whole Peter business is a confidence game. I've always said they ought to be hauled into court under the Blue Sky Law. They take money for priorities in Purgatory.

ELLIS (*smiling*). I'm not sure I can be that hardboiled.

FRANK. It's a matter of defending the decencies against gangs that don't give a damn for them.—Now go and grab your suitcase and catch the 5.40! (*He takes out his watch and looks quickly at it.*) You've only got twenty minutes.

JUDITH (*coming back with Gandersheim*). Are you actually going, Ellis?

ELLIS (*grinning self-consciously, but with a certain boyish enjoyment*). I feel like a character in a spy story.

GANDERSHEIM. A Galahad!

FRANK (*to Ellis*). Now scram. I'll brief you on the way to the train.

*Ellis strides off to the house.*

GANDERSHEIM (*to Frank*). I'm absolutely thrilled by this, you know! You're a real man of action, aren't you?

FRANK. And I've got another brilliant idea! *You're* going to write for *Spotlight*!

GANDERSHEIM. I'm afraid I don't have any talent for exposés and that kind of thing.

FRANK. It's your stories I want, for God's sake! I've never run any fiction, but your stories are something special. If your contract with *Metropolitan* is running out and they're harassing you the way you say, why not let me publish your stuff? Whatever they've been paying you, I'll better it.

GANDERSHEIM. I'm not happy with *Metropolitan*, it's true: not only are they ruining my prose, they've been sticking me over in the back among the body-odor ads— and at the same time breaking up my stories with the *most* impossible illustrations of athletic-looking young men and women that contradict my whole uncanny atmosphere.

FRANK. Don't worry about illustrations—I promise not to put any of your hobgoblins into bathing-suits or wooden brazeers.—We'll have dinner in a minute or two, and we can talk about terms afterwards.

GANDERSHEIM. Oh, I won't stay to dinner!—I just dropped in.

FRANK. Yes, you will—we'll be eating right away.

GANDERSHEIM (*looking toward Judith, as she does nothing to second the invitation*). It can't be convenient for you to have me on such short notice. I'll take the train with the young man.

FRANK (*to Judith*). Tell him to stay.

JUDITH. Yes: do stay.

GANDERSHEIM. I'd be charmed if it's really not too much trouble.

JUDITH. I'll tell Bertha. (*She goes into the house.*)

GANDERSHEIM (*to Frank*). Since you're kind enough to be interested in the Shidnats myth, you might like to know that it was first conceived right here in this very house.

FRANK. You don't say!

GANDERSHEIM (*nodding toward the second floor*). That window up there is the one through which Shidnats first appeared to Gandersheim. The original series of stories, you know, were told in the first person.

FRANK. You mean the window where the landscape would change and be transformed into something unearthly?

GANDERSHEIM. Yes: the runes are carved above it. Did you notice them?

FRANK. I'll be damned—so that's what that is!

GANDERSHEIM. They're not really carved, of course. I cut them out with my jigsaw when I was just a kid. That's when the whole thing got started.

FRANK. Sit down.

*Frank drops back into his lounging-chair; Gandersheim takes a seat in the straight chair at the right. It is beginning to get darker.*

GANDERSHEIM. I had rather a lonely childhood—to explain how the whole thing came about. We lived out here with very few neighbors that we particularly cared to know—this locality had already ceased to be fashionable—and I was an only child. In the summers when I was not going to school, I used to get so unspeakably bored! I'd lie up there on the window-seat and imagine that if I looked out the window at just the right moment of twilight, I'd suddenly see something different from the same old trees and fields—something exciting and troubling. Every summer we planned to travel, but we never got off on a decent trip. My mother was a professional invalid, and when the time for departure approached, she'd always turn out to be ill. I see now that she was a hopeless neurotic, so the whole thing could have been predicted—but every time it was the same disappointment—I used just to collapse with despair when I was first told we couldn't go—and then I'd resign myself, try

451

not to get too depressed but to keep myself keyed down
to our stagnant life. I had to conjure up a new country
that I could get to without leaving home—and that's how
Shidnats Slyme began: Shidnats was the god of that
country.

*Ellis has come out of the house, carrying a small and very
smart leather suitcase and wearing a summer straw-hat with a
striped blue-and-black band. Judith follows behind him.*

ELLIS. Well, I'm off. (*To Frank*) I'll need some money.

FRANK (*pulling out his pocketbook*). I'll arrange for you
to draw in town. (*Finding only ten dollars in his pocketbook*)
Wait a minute! (*He brings a checkbook out of the pocket of
his coat and, taking a fountain-pen from his breast-pocket, sits
down at the table and writes out a check.*)

GANDERSHEIM (*to Ellis*). Do I see a St. Matthew's band?

ELLIS. Yes. It's high time I got a fall hat.

GANDERSHEIM. I went to St. Matthew's.

ELLIS. *Did* you?

GANDERSHEIM. I didn't finish, but I'm proud of having
been there, and it's cheering to see that band. With so
much vulgarity rampant and the ground quaking under
one's feet, it's somehow reassuring to know that the old
school still endures.—Were you there when Dr. Parker
was still alive?

ELLIS. No, but we heard a lot about him.

GANDERSHEIM. I had a warm admiration for him. He was
a really imaginative person. He had the good taste not to
fire me when I was caught reading a book on the Black
Mass.

ELLIS. You're not Froggy Ferguson?

GANDERSHEIM. I am.

ELLIS. By my time you'd become a legend. Did you
really hold rites in the lumber-room and offer up a Second
Form boy as a human sacrifice?

GANDERSHEIM (*rather pleased*). No, of course not—that

ACT I

all nonsense. The worst thing we did up there was to burn
a few bad-smelling chemicals.

FRANK (*handing Ellis the ten-dollar bill and the check*).
Here you are. Cash this at your club.

ELLIS. Thanks.

FRANK (*looking at his watch again*). Now, let's get started.

ELLIS. O.K. (*To Gandersheim, quickly shaking hands*) Nice
to have seen you. (*Saluting Judith*) Wish me luck.

JUDITH. I do.

*He and Frank go out through the gate, Frank taking him
by the arm and beginning at once to instruct him.*

GANDERSHEIM (*to Judith*). A splendid young chap, isn't
he?—and so plucky to go off in that way! (*She is brooding
and does not reply.*) St. Matthew's *does* turn out gentlemen.
I'm sorry I didn't graduate. The old doctor didn't want
to expel me—he didn't take my Satanism seriously; but
he punished me in a crushing way that ruined my whole
spring term, and my mother was so indignant that she
wouldn't let me go back the next fall—so I had only two
years. I found myself stuck out here again. It was horrible,
all wrong—I was too old to be at home. I really got to
hate poor Mother. She had a noose around everyone's
neck—and when Father died and she was here alone, I
knew that it was out of the question for me to think of
going to college.— (*As he becomes aware that Judith is looking at him rather detachedly*) Please forgive all this reminis-
cence! Coming out here has brought it back.

JUDITH. When did you get off to Europe?

*She sits down in the straight chair on the right.*

GANDERSHEIM. Not till I was seventeen—but it probably saved me from going mad. I made Mother take me
abroad and we lived two years in Florence. Then we
came back to the States, so that Mother could get better
medical attention, and, to everybody's surprise, she died.
I'm afraid that my father had bored her to death—with

453

his stuffy old business in Worth Street and his interest in the Civil War. He did get through the Crash, though, unscathed. He left me a small steady income—and, after my parents died, I had no real ties in this country, and my great friend was living in Florence, so I went back there and stayed—till the war began making things intolerable. I'd always kept up this house. I'd thought, when I left it first, that I never wanted to see it again, but I found when I came back to the States that it was the only place I really belonged.

JUDITH. I'm sorry about the pigeons.

GANDERSHEIM. Well, of course, one can't hope to save everything—especially when one isn't here. I'm delighted —quite thrilled—as a matter of fact, at finding you people so *simpatico*. I always have a certain sinking, a sensation almost like panic, when I first get back to this house. It's the world of my adolescence—irresistible and yet repellent —and the horror of Shidnats Slyme always seems to be lurking for me here. He appeared to me first in this house, and (*with a deprecatory smile*) I still expect to find him in residence. He embodies himself sometimes in people, pretends to be a human being, but I always recognize his presence. I was telling you about my experience in Europe —my horrible qualms in that pension. And I felt a slight touch of it today when I was coming out here to see you. After all, what did I know about your husband! The editor of a popular magazine—that might mean the Monster God! I couldn't imagine why such a man should bury himself in such a place unless he were an adept of the cult —or even an incarnation——

*Frank comes back through the gate.*

GANDERSHEIM. I was just telling your wife that this house has a peculiar emotional effect on me: I can't get over the notion that Shidnats is somewhere around.

FRANK. Well, I haven't seen that noisome green liquid

oozing out from under any of the doors—though we've had some serious trouble with the plumbing.

GANDERSHEIM. *You* keep him away! You're the power that works against him—the power that works for good. I was just telling your wife how happy I was to find a man like you in possession: an unterrified champion of all the things that Americans have got to keep if they're going to hold their heads up—a warrior who is fighting *my* battles!

FRANK (*not displeased but cutting him short*). Everybody's got to fight!—Do you want to wash before dinner?

GANDERSHEIM. If I might.

FRANK. There's a bathroom at the left, right inside that door.

GANDERSHEIM (*smiling*). I know where the bathrooms are.

FRANK (*grinning*). Sorry: this business has distracted my mind. I forgot that you were in your own house.

GANDERSHEIM. I have a peculiar reason for remembering that first-floor bathroom!

FRANK. Was it a hideout for Shidnats Slyme?

*Gandersheim gives a coy and eerie laugh and goes up the steps to the house.*

FRANK (*to Judith*). By God, I'm inspired today! There was a moment when I thought it was getting me down, but then I made a big comeback!

JUDITH. *I* think you're making a mistake.

FRANK. About sending Ellis?

JUDITH. Yes—about that Gandersheim, too.

FRANK. I know you don't like his stuff——

JUDITH. He's screwy. He was going on just now in a perfectly loony way. He's got delusions of persecution.

FRANK. He's eccentric—nothing worse, I'd say.

JUDITH. You'll alienate your serious readers by printing that rubbish of his. You might just as well run a comic-strip!

FRANK. If *I* like it, why shouldn't *they*? I consider him a top-notch asset. His following's been growing steadily. There's no question about it: at the present time, he's America's Number One bugaboo-monger.

JUDITH. And Ellis isn't going to be able to do what you want him to do—even if he doesn't get murdered.

FRANK. I've got a lot of confidence in him.

JUDITH. But he just isn't brash enough to walk in where he's not wanted, and he's too reserved himself to make people tell him things.

FRANK. He's all steamed up about it—he's just boyish enough to enjoy it. His innocence is his great advantage. He'll be able to see the goddam obvious things that there's a general conspiracy not to see.

JUDITH. In the meantime, I suppose you realize that I'll have to interview all the people and take all the telephone calls.

FRANK. I'll get somebody out from the office.

JUDITH. No, you won't: you'll decide as usual that there's nobody there that can handle it.

FRANK. Don't worry: you won't have to do it.

JUDITH. *I* think it would be a lot better if you'd attend to some of those things yourself.

FRANK. Where would I get the time?

JUDITH. After all, you don't have to read proof—and it makes a bad impression on people never to be willing to see them. You seem to yourself so courageous, but you're getting the reputation of always evading and hiding—and I don't feel that I can take it again to be the person you hide behind.

FRANK. You won't have to: you can go on gardening.

JUDITH. You know that I'm no good at gardening—that old man does it all—and our friend here has done nothing but complain that things aren't the way they ought to be.

FRANK. Well, you won't have to do Ellis's work. That's that!

JUDITH. Not that I've got anything better to do. I'm sure I don't know what you think there is in this kind of life for *me*—I can tell you there isn't much.

FRANK. What's the matter? This sounds like last winter. I thought you'd been liking it here lately.

JUDITH. I *was*.

FRANK. Well, what's wrong now? Tell me.

JUDITH. It's just that you're so completely inconsiderate when you begin throwing your weight around.

FRANK. How many times do you want me to tell you that I'm going to get another secretary?

JUDITH. It isn't only that. I was just getting everything organized, and now you've sent Ellis away and spoiled it.

FRANK. It isn't as if he wasn't coming back.

JUDITH. I'd planned that party for Friday.

FRANK. Well, what's to prevent your having it?

JUDITH. I counted on Ellis for tennis.

FRANK. I'll play, what the hell!

JUDITH. No: you're terrible. Nobody wants to play doubles with you.

FRANK (*morosely, an idea dawning*). You're going to miss Ellis a lot?

JUDITH. Of course I am.

FRANK. I see.

*The dinner gong is sounded. She starts for the house.*

FRANK (*following her*). I didn't know you liked him that much. You were telling me he was too conventional.

JUDITH. I've gotten to like him very much.

FRANK. Oh, God: another crush!

JUDITH. You know that I like Ellis, and you sent him away on purpose.

FRANK. I swear I never gave it a thought!

JUDITH. It's your absolutely psychopathic jealousy—you don't want me to have any friends!

*They go up the steps, she first.*

FRANK. Oh, don't start that!

JUDITH. It's instinctive with you to cut me off from everybody I like.

FRANK. We'll talk about this later.

JUDITH. No, we won't!

*She goes into the house, and he follows.*

# ACT II

## SCENE I

*Mid-October: half-past five in the afternoon. The work-room on the second floor of Gandersheim's house, in which Frank and Judith are living. This was formerly an upstairs library but has been converted into a sort of editorial office (Frank has his own study on the floor below), and now contains an incongruous mixture of the original library furniture with modern office equipment. The walls are paneled in dark stained oak in the style of the early nineteen hundreds. On the right, toward the front of the stage, the big bow-window, which was seen from the outside in Act I, makes a recess with a wide cushioned window-seat, and the audience have a glimpse of the panes, with the frieze of jigsaw "runes" above them, but they cannot see out the window. In the middle of the back wall is a fire-place with a carved wooden mantelpiece, on which stands a clock surmounted by a small bronze figure and above which hangs a large steel engraving: the well-known nineteenth century group called* Shakespeare and His Friends. *On either side of the fireplace are bookcases that rise somewhat higher, in which the old leather-bound sets have partly been replaced by up-to-date reference books. One bookcase is ornamented with a large stuffed owl, the other with a terrestrial globe. There is a morris-chair, with a floor lamp beside it, in the corner to the right of the fireplace. In the left-hand corner, against the left wall, is an old mahogany desk, with a flap that comes down on hinges. It is open: there is a typewriter on it and a highbacked chair in front of it. Further forward along this left wall are a row of steel filing-cases and above them a bulletin board on which are tacked up schedules for coming issues of* Spotlight, *lists of*

459

*articles or ideas for articles, etc. Further forward, there is a door that leads into the hall and opens toward the front of the stage, so that the audience can see the doorway as soon as the door is opened. Stretching across the middle of the room, parallel with the back wall and further back than the bow-window, stands a long plain unfinished table, on which are papers, pencils, pen and ink, ash-trays and cigarettes, newspapers and magazines and two green-shaded student-lamps, and around which are grouped several chairs. One of these, at the right-hand end, is the mate to the highbacked chair at the desk: the others are miscellaneous —some of them old-fashioned, with cushioned seats, others office furniture, hard and stiff.*

*Judith, in harlequin glasses, a plain but smart working suit and a man's shirt with a necktie and a buttoned-down collar, is sitting in the highbacked chair, at the end of the long table, editing a manuscript with an evidently ruthless hand.*

*Ellis opens the door and comes in, leaving the door half open. He is carrying a brief-case, which he lays on the table.*

JUDITH. Oh, hello! (*She takes off her glasses.*)

ELLIS. You stood me up again.

JUDITH. I'm sorry. I missed the nine forty-five, because Frank had taken the car—as usual, without telling me— and then I couldn't get anybody to wait on me in that new Park Avenue place where they have those men's clothes for women—the sales girls are getting so snooty that they don't want to sell you anything—and then the taxi-driver took me West instead of East before I noticed where we were going—it may have been my fault: he said I told him West but I was sure I told him East. When I got to the Tally-Ho, you'd gone.

ELLIS. I couldn't wait: I had an appointment with the head of the Constitutionalist Committee.

JUDITH. I called you up, but you weren't there—then I didn't want to call from here.

ELLIS. Why? On account of Frank?

JUDITH. I'd told him I was lunching with you, and it wasn't very well received.

ELLIS. Really?

JUDITH. Have you seen him?

ELLIS. Just for a minute. He said he was busy.

JUDITH. Was he nasty?

ELLIS. The same as usual.

JUDITH. He's never very gracious, is he?

ELLIS. He's all right. They tell me that newspaper men are all more or less like that.

JUDITH. He's really full of hate.

ELLIS. Why?

JUDITH. Because he never was the newspaper man he wanted to be. He doesn't know he's frustrated, though, because he's too extraverted. He doesn't even know he's extraverted.

ELLIS. Isn't that all right for a journalist?—to submerge himself in public events?

JUDITH. Frank *doesn't* submerge himself—he's always hiding away. He always makes somebody else grapple with the actual problems—you, for instance.

ELLIS. And I've been no good at all.

*He sits down in a chair near the middle of the table, on the side that faces the audience.*

JUDITH. But you got Percy Gilman off.

ELLIS. I didn't have anything to do with that. It was all done by the Teniakis Bureau—that super-employment agency that Gilman was recommended by. They made the Cardinal's secretary testify that he'd been there through the whole interview and that the explosion or whatever it was didn't happen till after he'd gone.

JUDITH. But they accused him of laying the flashlight.

ELLIS. The secretary says that Gilman had nothing to do with the flashlight. So the whole thing is just as mysterious as ever. In the meantime, all the anti-Constitutionalist groups have been so much scared by the prospect of the Constitutionalists' winning the elections that they've all been working together to beat them, and you can't get them to talk about the murder or any delicate matter of that kind. It's really the most amazing thing how well-disciplined these movements are. Even the high-school children: if you mention any public issue, they'll reel off their latest directive, as if it were Boyle's law of gases.— So I've been a complete flop.

JUDITH. No, you haven't. Frank was just saying that for the first time you'd made him "see the picture," as he calls it.

ELLIS. He gave me a bawling-out on the phone the other day.

JUDITH. Don't take it from him. Just snap back at him, and you'll find he'll always recoil.

ELLIS. I'm not quite in a position to do that.—How's Gandersheim working out as secretary?

JUDITH. Frank thinks he's wonderful, but I think he's dreadful.

ELLIS. A little on the spooky side.

JUDITH. What I really can't stand is that he's making this place a headquarters for his nauseating brotherhood. He has hundreds of fans, it seems. He writes to them on paper with a phony crest, and they come out here to talk poltergeists with him. The truth is that Gandersheim's myth is a literary power cult—for arm-chair romantics and second-rate pansies.

ELLIS. I'd imagined that Shidnats Slyme was presented as a monstrous menace.

JUDITH. The attitude toward him is ambivalent.

ELLIS. I haven't heard that word for ages. In my child-hood people used it all the time.

JUDITH. It was indispensable then, because it gave

a certain dignity to trying to have things both ways.

ELLIS. It could even be pronounced "ambilavent."

JUDITH. And they would talk about "having a block." Are you old enough to remember that? To talk about "having a block" was a way of giving scientific standing to some humiliating deficiency—like not being able to spell—or a failure to keep some promise that you didn't want to keep.

ELLIS. That was what happened to you yesterday when you missed the train and all that.

JUDITH. I was really afraid of Frank.

ELLIS. You don't use that technique you were just recommending?

JUDITH. I didn't want a quarrel.

ELLIS. Some other day maybe?

JUDITH. Maybe.

ELLIS. How do Gandersheim's followers go down with Frank?

JUDITH. He stands for them because Gandersheim adores him. He just drools after Frank—it's sickening. But Frank thinks it's perfectly natural that people should be his abject slaves.

ELLIS. He's not taken in, though, by people, beyond a certain point.

JUDITH. I've never seen him gag at flattery.

ELLIS. Well, he's got a great deal more shrewdness—and a great deal more independence—than most of those mugs I've been seeing in town. All they want is to be yessed by their underlings, and then they yes their higher-ups. I have a real admiration for Frank.

JUDITH. Then you oughtn't to ask me to lunch.

ELLIS. I miss you a lot.

JUDITH. You don't.

ELLIS. I've realized how much you've meant to me since I've been staying up there in town.

JUDITH. Oh, no, I haven't.—What have I meant?

ELLIS. You're the only girl I ever knew who had the same kind of brains as a man and yet at the same time was perfectly beautiful.

JUDITH. New York is full of types like me. You haven't seen the latest crop of career girls.

ELLIS. *You're* not a career girl.

JUDITH. How do you know?

ELLIS. If you were, you wouldn't be out here.

JUDITH. But I don't like being out here. This isn't really my role. Now that you're away and with Gandersheim here, this place is getting me down. I'm absolutely stuffy and stale.

ELLIS. Then meet me for a drink some day. You won't have to explain about it.

JUDITH. It's too serious when you don't explain.

ELLIS. Not necessarily, is it?

JUDITH. It seems to work out that way.

ELLIS. Not that I'm not prepared to be serious.

JUDITH. It's better the way it is. What we have is a "joking relationship." Did you ever study anthropology? They talk about "joking relationships." When a Navaho Indian, for example, meets one of his aunts on his father's side, they're supposed to exchange badinage—and I guess that a boss's wife and a husband's secretary ought to do the same kind of thing.

ELLIS. I shouldn't think that would always be a good idea. It would produce too many bad jokes.

JUDITH. Thank you!

ELLIS. I didn't mean you. You're brilliant.

JUDITH. I'm not: I'm getting so stupid that I couldn't amuse a baby—though actually I don't like babies, I never know what to do about them.

ELLIS. You don't care for children.

JUDITH. No: not other people's! I wouldn't mind having

some *boys* of my own—but I wouldn't like them when they were little.

ELLIS (*after a brief pause, during which he has been asking himself whether he ought to go on with the subject*). Maybe children are what you need.

JUDITH. I don't know: I don't want them now.—It may be too late for me to have them.

ELLIS. Not necessarily, is it?

JUDITH. Oh, I don't know! How did we get on this subject? Let's drop it!

ELLIS. You're not sure you want to stay with Frank?

JUDITH. I suppose that's really it—though I usually give other reasons. I'm fond of Frank, of course, but it's not really right between us. He's so much older than I am. I began by being his secretary, and I still can't help feeling like a secretary—a secretary who occasionally sleeps with the boss.

ELLIS. But you married him.

JUDITH. It makes it easier if you're living together in the country.

*Gandersheim has appeared in the doorway and stands listening to the conversation, concealed from Judith and Ellis by the partially closed door.*

ELLIS. I thought that there was quite a lot more than that between you and Frank.

JUDITH. Oh, there was, I suppose, but—oh, I don't know!—I guess maybe it's just that nowadays I don't even have a woman-friend to get together with and beef about our husbands. I've felt completely flat since you left.

ELLIS (*getting up and coming over to her*). I need somebody to confide in, too—so why don't you meet me in town for a drink?—and be sure to make it this time!

JUDITH. I've been having awful migraines lately—and when they hit me, I can't do anything.

ELLIS (*smiling*). Psychosomatic, no doubt?

JUDITH. That's another great comforting word.

ELLIS. Like "that blessed word Mesopotamia" that the old woman found in the Bible.

JUDITH. Yes: of course "psychosomatic" is a mystical idea, isn't it?—Something like the Incarnation.

ELLIS. You're the brightest girl I ever knew.

JUDITH. Girl? I'm getting middle-aged.

ELLIS. Next Saturday?

JUDITH. All right.

*She looks up at him, and he leans down and kisses her. They remain for a moment in silence, her mouth pressed against his.*

ELLIS (*straightening up*). How about five at the Tally-Ho?

JUDITH. I'd have to make it earlier than that—I'd have to get back well before dinner.

ELLIS. Four o'clock then?

JUDITH. All right.

*Gandersheim quietly enters and closes the door behind him. He has a handful of unfolded letters. Ellis looks around and sees him.*

ELLIS (*to Gandersheim*). Have you been having an awful time with all that?

GANDERSHEIM. Oh, no: it comes quite easily. (*He goes over to the desk with the typewriter.*)

ELLIS. You're wonderful at the brush-off, I understand.

GANDERSHEIM. A touch of mystification helps.

JUDITH (*whose feelings of guilt and of fear lest they may have been overheard leads her to propitiate Gandersheim*). He's the master of the evasive answer. He doesn't just tell them that Frank is busy. He tells them something so utterly confusing that they're frightened and go away.

ELLIS (*to Gandersheim*). How would you handle a specific case?

JUDITH. Tell him how you disposed of the Elitist.

GANDERSHEIM (*coming forward to the long table*). Oh, he

was trying to pump me about Frank's politics, and I explained to him that *Spotlight's* position was that of a floating platform stabilized in interstellar space, and that Frank's point of view was that of a celestial engineer whose problem was to keep it in place by maintaining a delicate balance between the different gravitational pulls.

ELLIS. Nice work. How did he take it?

GANDERSHEIM. He asked me starkly which candidate Frank would support, and I replied that the function of *Spotlight* was not to support but to scrutinize.

ELLIS. Masterly! I envy your resourcefulness.

JUDITH. Tell him about the currency crank.

GANDERSHEIM. Oh, that was quite fantastic. A wild-eyed fellow appeared who had one of those panaceas for curing our economic ills. It was a perfectly simple device: you would issue some paper money that had double denominations—that is, there would be bills, for example, that had five dollars printed on one side and ten on the other side—and anybody who could certify that his income was below a certain level could use them for the larger amount.

ELLIS. What was your flabbergasting answer?

GANDERSHEIM. I told him that, from our point of view, all value was already relative, and that to issue a two-sided currency would only make things more complicated.

ELLIS. I'm full of admiration. I never really had the right knack in dealing with the lunatic fringe.

*Frank comes in.*

FRANK. We're scooped!

ELLIS. What?

FRANK. That murder's been pinned on the Reds.

ELLIS (*getting up*). Where did you hear that?

FRANK. On the radio. It seems that the Teniakis Bureau has been working on the case, and they've gotten the murderer's sister to talk.—You're a hell of an investigator!

ELLIS. Who is he?

FRANK. That laboratory worker who'd been to see the Cardinal that afternoon, just before Percy Gilman was there. You'll remember he'd once been a Red and then claimed to be converted to Peterism, and had come to talk to the Cardinal about publishing a repudiation of Reddism in one of the Peter papers.

GANDERSHEIM. How did he manage the murder?

FRANK. They haven't gotten him to tell yet, but he'd been working with inflammable gases.

ELLIS. Has he actually confessed to the crime?

FRANK. He doesn't need to: this sister has produced a letter he wrote her that shows he was still a Red long after he was supposed to have been converted. He and she had fallen out, because he'd gone over to Belgrade when she still stuck to the Kremlin—and that's the reason she's decided to expose him. I told you to go after their families.

ELLIS. I don't like pumping people's families.

FRANK. Hell—It's a question of public peril!

ELLIS. Well, I'm glad I didn't have anything to do with making that woman talk——

FRANK. She was evidently crazy to talk.

ELLIS. —And I doubt the value of her evidence.

FRANK. That would come better from you if——

ELLIS (*asserting himself and cutting in on Frank*). You say that you disapprove of the methods these groups are using, but one of the worst features of it is the way they work on people systematically to destroy normal human relationships. There's getting to be a premium on treachery——

*A knock on the door interrupts him.*

FRANK. Yes?

*The Gardener opens the door and, holding his old slouch hat, comes a short way into the room.*

THE GARDENER (*to Judith, with an Irish brogue*). I'm sorry to disturb you, ma'am, but did you want me to transplant the hydrangeas the first thing tomorrow morning? I've just done trimmin' them back.

JUDITH. Oh, yes! (*To Gandersheim*) I hope you approve of this. You don't mind our moving them, do you?—moving the hydrangeas to the stable?

GANDERSHEIM. Well, I do, rather. I think it would be better, as I told you when you first brought the question up, to cultivate the original color. You'd see that they belong where they are.

JUDITH. Couldn't we move them back there for a while and feed them whatever they need till they're blue?

GANDERSHEIM. I should miss them—I shouldn't feel comfortable. I know that a hydrangea border is as out-of-date now as a boa, but, after all, the whole place is "period."

JUDITH. I was going to plant a border of tulips. They'd light up all that rather bleak approach to the house.

GANDERSHEIM. Oh, I shouldn't like that at all! I'm afraid I really couldn't face tulips. I've seen them at their most brilliant in Holland, and I must say they absolutely repel me—just a regiment of brash little prongs sticking up like pins in a map. I like my flowers a little less—bouncing.

THE GARDENER. Sure, you've no need to worry about that, sir; the missus has ordered some breeds that are speckled and striped like salamanders. They're as unwholesome as anything you could wish.

JUDITH. They're deliciously morbid—you'll see. The hydrangeas are just sickly and sloppy now. Come down and look things over for once. You've never really faced it.

GANDERSHEIM. I'm afraid I must do these letters.

FRANK. Go on, Gandy—there's no hurry about those. Let's get this gardening crisis settled. It's absolutely wearing me down, and the flowers have been looking lousy—I think they're suffering from a sense of insecurity.

JUDITH (*to Ellis, sarcastically*). That's another favorite phrase from the forties!

469

*Ellis gives her a brief grin, which registers his resentment of Frank.*

FRANK. It's been a permanent condition since then!— Now, go on—go and feed your hydrangeas!

*Judith moves toward the door, and Gandersheim and the Gardener follow.*

JUDITH (*to Gandersheim*). It seems that they spray them now instead of merely putting stuff in the soil.

GANDERSHEIM. I do think he's right, you know: flowers should never be frightened.

*They go out. Frank sits down in one of the chairs on the side of the table nearest the audience; Ellis remains standing.*

ELLIS. I'm sorry you think I've fallen down—but I told you I wasn't the man for that job.

FRANK. You ought to have seen that woman.

ELLIS. I admit that I've been a failure, and I was just going to tell you that I want to quit.

FRANK. Now don't get excited—I don't want you to quit.

ELLIS. I'm no good to you as a detective.

FRANK. You're new at it, that's all. But don't worry. We can drop our own investigation. I need you here now.

ELLIS. I meant, quit the job entirely.

FRANK. Leave the magazine, you mean?

ELLIS. Yes: you've got Gandersheim, and you don't really need me now.

FRANK. He can't do everything: he's got to write his stories.

ELLIS. I understand he has an irresistible magic for exorcising unwelcome visitors.

FRANK. To tell you the truth, Ellis, this shop has been getting a little *too* four-dimensional since Gandersheim has been handling things. I like to have everything in black and white, and I miss your clear-cut methods.

ELLIS. You can easily get somebody else who'll copy out the letters in a big round hand.

FRANK. It's the *point of view* I can't get. You have the *Spotlight* point of view.

ELLIS. But what *is* the *Spotlight* point of view? It's having no point of view at all.

FRANK. I thought you were sympathetic with what I'm trying to do.

ELLIS. I am, I suppose—but good Lord, I can't see that you make much impression on the tendencies you're trying to check. You couldn't even get Gilman out of jail. It took that employment bureau.

FRANK. Yes: you have to hand it to Teniakis. He certainly looks after his people.

*Gandersheim comes into the room.*

GANDERSHEIM (*to Frank*). If you'll pardon me just a moment, I want to look something up in the gardening encyclopedia. We used to have an old one here.

FRANK. Go ahead—all your books are still there.

*Gandersheim goes over to the bookcase at the right of the fireplace.*

ELLIS (*to Frank, picking up the brief-case*). I'll just take care of this stuff I brought out. May I go down to your room, where it's quicker?

FRANK (*morosely*). Go ahead.

GANDERSHEIM (*taking down a volume*). I suppose this is quite out of date. Judith says they spray them now.

FRANK. This is a hell of a note! Ellis has just announced he's quitting.

GANDERSHEIM. I'm not entirely surprised.

FRANK. What do you mean?

GANDERSHEIM. Well, I hesitate to mention the matter— and anything I say, you understand, is said in the strictest confidence.

FRANK. Go ahead.

471

GANDERSHEIM. Well, I believe that Ellis—who is a ver~
well-brought-up young man—has a very strong sense o~
honor.

FRANK. So he was telling me.

GANDERSHEIM. Oh, I don't mean the reporting thing—
I don't mean about the sister.

FRANK. What *do* you mean?

GANDERSHEIM. Well, I don't really think that he'~
want to stay on with *Spotlight*, if—if—well, if he wa~
in a position in which he felt he was abusing your con~
fidence.

FRANK. You mean he's gone over to the Reds?

GANDERSHEIM. No, no: I meant something more per~
sonal.

*A pause: Frank stands frowning and brooding. Gandersheim
finds the place in the book.*

FRANK. You don't mean Judith?

GANDERSHEIM (*looking up for a moment, then examining
the encyclopedia article*). On his side a little, perhaps.

FRANK. What gives you that idea?

GANDERSHEIM. Well, one notices certain things—an~
quite without design on my part, I overheard a conversa~
tion just now——

*Judith comes in.*

JUDITH (*to Gandersheim*). You got away from me befor~
I was done with you.

GANDERSHEIM. I just came up here to look up th~
hydrangeas. It turns out to be rather complicated. I shoul~
have to take it up with the gardener.

JUDITH. I wanted you to go all over the place with me~
but you slipped away into the pergola, and when w~
looked there, you'd disappeared.

GANDERSHEIM (*flustered by Judith's appearance*). I'm en~
tirely at your service.

JUDITH. Don't be scared: I'm not going to try to pu~

anything more over on you. (*To Frank*) He did give in about the tulips.

GANDERSHEIM. So very few things nowadays are allowed to remain the same.

FRANK. Go on and thrash it out with the gardener, Gandy—I want to talk to Judith.

JUDITH (*to Frank*). If he succeeds in escaping me now, I'm afraid I'll never get him again!

GANDERSHEIM. I don't see that you really need me, since you've quite made up your mind about everything.

FRANK (*to Judith*). Let him alone—let him talk to the gardener: he'll get along better without you.

*Gandersheim, leaving the book on the table, goes out with a piqued air of dignity. Frank pretends to look at a manuscript till Gandersheim has left the room.*

JUDITH (*hardly waiting for the door to close*). I hope you don't think it's a treat for me to have the landlord living here with us and interfering with all my arrangements.

FRANK. He's certainly been a godsend to *me*.

JUDITH. I don't think you ought to let him do so much— especially answering letters. You've already got the reputation of being an eccentric and a crank, and now people will say you're crazy.

FRANK. It at least means that *you* don't have to attend to them. You were complaining that you'd have to do everything. In some ways he's the most satisfactory person that I've ever had in that job.

JUDITH. That's just because he turns cartwheels for you whenever you open your mouth. He's absolutely infatuated with you.

FRANK. I'm glad somebody is.

JUDITH. It it were you, I'd be embarrassed.

FRANK. The only thing I find embarrassing is having you be rude to Gandy—and openly hostile to me.

JUDITH. I'm sorry, Frank, but this whole situation has

become absolutely impossible. I was just going to tell you: I want to get a job in town.

FRANK. What's the matter now?

JUDITH. I can't go on like this. I've got nothing to do out here.

FRANK. I thought that you were just telling me that housekeeping was giving you so much to do that you hadn't any time for anything else!

JUDITH. The trouble is I'm not a housewife. I've tried it, and I know I'm no good at it.

FRANK. Yes, you are.

JUDITH. No, I'm not. I don't have any chance at all to do the kind of thing I *can* do.

FRANK. You've been wonderful with the magazine.

JUDITH. You want to be the whole thing yourself—you don't even really want my suggestions.

FRANK. That isn't true at all—on the contrary——

JUDITH. I've decided that the moment for a break has come. I'm losing all my resiliency out here. Jane Hunter was saying the other day that I'd become so suburban and wholesome that she could hardly believe I was the same girl who'd made the Dean cry at college.

FRANK. You're in better shape now than you ever were! It's the first time you've ever been tanned.

JUDITH. I'm not the type that ought to be tanned. I wanted to try this tennis-playing life, but now that I've had it, it bores me. I can't be a young country club matron —especially when you won't go near the club—and even the club out here is second-rate.

FRANK. Sit down and let's talk about it.

JUDITH. I don't want to sit down and talk about it. We've talked about it enough.

FRANK. What's the matter lately?

JUDITH. Nothing's the matter except that I've made up my mind.

FRANK. Well, you've chosen a fine time to walk out on me. Did you know that Ellis was quitting?

JUDITH. Did you fire him?

FRANK. No, of course I didn't fire him. He's gotten his feelings hurt.

JUDITH. I don't wonder, the way you've been treating him.

FRANK. What do you mean, the way I've been treating him?

JUDITH. You were insulting to him just now.

FRANK. No, I wasn't.

JUDITH. Of course you were. You're such a born bully that you're not even able to realize that you're habitually insulting to people.

FRANK. On the contrary, *you* bully *me*: you've got me afraid to open my mouth.— (*Expostulating and waving his arms*) Listen, Judy: when you and I work together, we're wonderful—we can stand up to anything. But when we break loose against one another, we simply use up all our energies and don't accomplish anything.

JUDITH. That's why I think it's so much better for each of us to be independent.

FRANK (*coming over to her and taking both her hands*). Listen, darling: you know that I can't live without you.

JUDITH. Those nostalgic clichés of yours! I wish you could get along without them when you're making your big scenes.

FRANK. You sound like one of those heroines from the "live-your-own-life" period.

JUDITH. Yes, of course: the whole thing is old hat—this is the kind of perfectly obvious situation that there's no point in making a fuss about.

FRANK. Now, look here— (*he puts his arm around her and leads her over to the head of the table*) I want you to sit down a minute and listen to me talk——

JUDITH. I've been doing that for years.

FRANK. Not many.

JUDITH. Four.

FRANK. All right, but this is not a mere oration. Sit down here.

*He makes her sit down in the first chair at the right behind the table and takes his place in the highbacked chair at the head.*

JUDITH. You're going to tell me that you divorced your wife to marry me, and that I prevent you from seeing your daughter.

FRANK. No, I'm not.

JUDITH. You usually do at this point.

FRANK. First of all, what I want to say is that you ought to know it's actually true when I tell you that I can't get along without you. It's not a cliché, it's the literal fact. You've been the mainspring of *Spotlight*—you inspired it in the first place. Everything I've done since I've known you has been done on account of you. Though I'd been a fair success before, I'd only been a glorified hack. I was an old-style newspaper man, well on the way to obsolescence—and the big turning-point in my life was that night when I lectured at your college and you came up to ask me questions, with your hair done up in a bun and your panther eyes flashing out challenge. Do you remember that you said to me that F. D. R. had the virtues of a tactful hostess?—that he knew how to diminish friction and prevent disagreeable incidents, but had no real ideas of his own? Do you remember how you said that?

JUDITH (*pleased as always at praise but not wanting to acknowledge it*). No.

FRANK. Well, it made a sensational impression on me. I was jolted and shocked at first, but then I was released, delighted. It was just what I'd been thinking myself but wouldn't have had the nerve to say or wouldn't have been able to say that well. I thought that you were the brightest girl I'd ever seen. I hadn't known such girls existed—and I don't believe they ever did before. What's always been miraculous to me and what's given me such guts as I've had lately has been just exactly that fact: that an obstinate old-timer like me, a journalist who still takes journalism seriously, an American who still believes that this country has a great contribution to make to the progress of civilization—that a person like me had made contact, an actual vital contact, with one of the most gifted young people of your nineteen-forty crop that grew up without any illusions. The thing that I was proudest of was your telling me that you had more respect for me than for the boys of your own generation. Do you remember telling me that?

JUDITH (*in a tone which implies that she remembers but is no longer interested in it*). Yes.

FRANK. I don't want to hand myself bouquets, but I think I did give you something. You kids were born into a world where the money had all blown up and nobody knew where they were at. The first batch consoled themselves with Communism, but then, when Soviet Russia went bad, they didn't know where the hell to turn. The next batch were shipped off to war, which they weren't enthusiastic about, and the later ones who'd missed the war found themselves shunted off into compulsory military training, with the prospect of another war about, which they were even less enthusiastic. Now, *I'd* had the luck to grow up in a small-sized Western city, where my dad ran an independent paper and where he'd somehow managed to survive as a ring-tailed gyascutus of Populism from the heroic Bryan period——

JUDITH. I've heard all this before, you know.

FRANK. Not so eloquently expressed, have you?—What I wanted to say was simply that you gave me the spark that ignited me—that made me flame up again when I might well have smouldered out——

JUDITH. Oh, Frank, your old moth-eaten metaphors!

FRANK (*going on even more ardently, since he knows that, in spite of her mockery, she is gratified by his admiration*). "Flame up" is the only way to say it—it isn't even a metaphor. At that time you were a burning brand, but you were just being reckless and negative—your audacity had no real object——

JUDITH. My flame has been burning so low lately that it's more like a pilot-light on one of those gas-ranges, and if I don't have a new cylinder put in, there's just going to be a faint bad smell and you'll know that the gas has gone out.

FRANK. And is Ellis your new cylinder?— (*with sarcasm*) to carry on with your up-to-date imagery.

JUDITH. I knew that was coming!

FRANK. Well? (*She does not reply: he gets up.*) You haven't answered my question.

JUDITH. There's nothing between Ellis and me.

FRANK. You were complaining that you missed him so much.

JUDITH. Why shouldn't I? He's closer to me than you are, because he's nearer my age. We can understand one another with just a look—just an inflection—we don't have to have all these long arguments and historical recapitulations.

FRANK. And that's why you want to go to town, isn't it?

JUDITH. Is what why I want to go to town?

FRANK. You've made him throw up his job! I don't think he had any idea of it when I saw him before he came upstairs. You'd talked to him in between.

JUDITH. He didn't say a word to me about his job.

FRANK. You influenced him to throw it up.

JUDITH. You influenced him yourself by being so nasty to him.

FRANK. I don't think he's sore at me. The trouble is he's interested in you, and he thinks he's being disloyal.

JUDITH (*getting up*). I won't stand for this any more! If there were no other reason for getting away, these continual scenes of jealousy would be enough.

FRANK. So you walk out on me at the worst possible moment! Just because you were deserted yourself, you try to revenge yourself by walking out on other people!

JUDITH. No one ever walked out on *me*!

FRANK. But your parents died before you were six—and you've never gotten over it.

JUDITH. This psychoanalytic routine of yours is just as old-fashioned now as your sentiments from Victorian novels.

FRANK. You can't help being bitter, maybe—but I think you ought to keep it well in mind what you're really being bitter about. It's not me—it's not anything *I've* done to you——

JUDITH. You promised me not to talk about that.

FRANK (*determined, in desperation, to make some impression on her*). You ought to be reminded of it when you're trying to blame somebody else for the fact that your parents——

JUDITH (*resisting in real alarm*). Now, don't!

FRANK. —For the fact that your parents were victims of the damned frauds and swindles of Wall Street——

JUDITH. You promised. If you break your promise, I'll never have any more respect for you!

FRANK. That your father was ruined in the Crash, and that he shot your mother and then shot himself when you were in the next room. (*She becomes pale and rigid, cannot speak.*) I'm sorry, but I brought it out on purpose—because I think you ought to face it. You're making a big mistake when you try to shut it out of your mind: that only gets you all confused. It makes you think that I'm your father,

479

so that you work up a grudge against me—a completely irrational grudge. *I'm* not your father—I'm your husband I love you—I love you, darling—and it's a hell of a raw deal for me to have to be identified with him——

JUDITH (*screaming*). Oh, how can you? How can you You promised me you never would! How can you, you great horrible lout! (*She throws a magazine from the tabl at him.*) You pretentious small-time tyrant!

FRANK (*coming over to her*). Don't—I'm sorry——

JUDITH (*hysterical, grasping his hands, as he tries to put hi arms around her*). Don't hit me!

FRANK. I'm not going to hit you.

JUDITH. You want to kill me! (*Shrieking*) Help!

*Gandersheim opens the door and enters; the Gardener hang behind in the doorway.*

GANDERSHEIM. I'm sorry. I hope I'm not interrupting.

*Judith leaves the room, weeping.*

FRANK. Judy is in one of her states. It's not so bad a it sounds.

GANDERSHEIM. Is there anything I can do?

FRANK. No, thanks. She'll be all right.

GANDERSHEIM. I was just bringing the gardener in to show him the encyclopedia.

FRANK. Go ahead.

*He hurries out.*

GANDERSHEIM (*to the Gardener*). Come in. I'll just read you what it says.

*He picks up the volume from the table and finds the plac again. The room is already half dark, and he carries the boo over to the window-seat. He is agitated but tries to hide it an sits down behind the table to consult the book. During th conversation that follows, the room is growing dark.*

GANDERSHEIM. You know, they're rather curious botani- cally. The things that you think are the flowers are actually sexless and sterile: they don't have either stamens or pistil

But they certainly make a brave showing!—that is, when they're properly nourished—and that's our problem now: to get them back to their brilliant blue. They do look rather livid now—as if the dye were all running out of them. They ought to be a brilliant rather frightening blue —I've always found blue rather frightening—and the color does have its significance in connection with my life in this house. My mother had piercing blue eyes, but it isn't only my mother's eyes. It's got something to do with the blues—I don't mean the musical blues, but what I used to call *le cafard blafard*—that's a French phrase I made up once. I thought I couldn't stand it here at first when she wouldn't send me back to school, but I managed to settle down to it and somehow nourished myself—I exploited the elements that made me blue, just as we hope our hortensias will—that's a much more beautiful name for them, I think—and I got to like the old blue border, because it represented my mood.— (*Looking up from the book*) Tell me, do you believe in dreams? I see now that you're really an Irishman—and all you Irish are great dreamers, aren't you?

THE GARDENER. Sure, I've had some quare dreams in my time, and the worst of them always came true.

GANDERSHEIM. Prophetic, eh?

THE GARDENER. I'm a bit on the prophetic side maybe. It's necessary, of course, to interpret them.

GANDERSHEIM. I wish you'd interpret this dream of mine. I've had it again and again just since I've been back in this house—and, for some reason I don't understand, it's indescribably dreadful.

THE GARDENER. If you tell me what it is, I'll be glad to try.

GANDERSHEIM. Well, I'm walking along in the street— a perfectly normal street. The sun is out, and everything is cheerful—the people are all going about their business.

I come to a house and I knock at the door. No one answers
I go in. The house is completely empty and perfectly
commonplace. But there's a *thing* waiting for me in there
—quietly waiting for me: *I* have to come to *it*. I walk
through the rooms and the hallway and out through the
backdoor—and there in the backyard, just hanging in the
air above my head, is the *paralyzing unspeakable thing*. It
makes my blood run cold just to think of it, and I haven't
even had the courage to put it into one of my stories.
It's just a little spark of blue light that might be made by
crossed electric wires—but I know that I can't resist it,
that it's certainly going to get me. I always wake up at
that point, but even then I can't shake it off. I'm trembling
—frightened to death—sunk in the most hideous despair—
and I don't know why it should be—I can't make out
where the image comes from. It's just a quiet little point
of light, but it's pitiless, it's infinitely cruel!

THE GARDENER. Would ye care to say what's frightened
ye most in your life?

GANDERSHEIM. Oh, it would be hard to say. I've always
been subject to panics of the kind that are called irrational
—as if something were going to pounce on me, to take
possession of me. I had a touch of it just now outside when
she was bullying me about the hydrangeas—and then
when we walked in on that scene, I was suddenly all
unnerved!

THE GARDENER. Would it maybe be the piercing blue
eye that you say your mother had—that little blue light
you're scared of?

GANDERSHEIM. Oh, please! I've been all through Freud.

THE GARDENER. And did you not learn anything from it?

GANDERSHEIM. I read it like fiction and got bored with
the plots—and even more with some of my friends who
fancied themselves as Freudian characters.

THE GARDENER. Sure, it's true that the case-histories

have turned into myths and that people feel they have to
act them out. But there's some truth in all great myths.
They can teach us what to expect.

GANDERSHEIM. What a knowledgeable old chap you are!
My childhood does come back on me rather here, with
everything that was nastiest about it. But I don't know
where else to go.

THE GARDENER. I'm in the same situation meself.

GANDERSHEIM. You've never thought of going back to
the old country?

THE GARDENER. To Ireland? Faith, Ireland today is as
bad as the rest of the world!

GANDERSHEIM. The Irish have at least won their freedom.

THE GARDENER. They've won their freedom the same
way as the Russians. They've lost all their men of vision.
When they were victims of a monarchical tyranny, they
had rebels, and the rebels had the luxury of heroism and
oratory, prophecy and literature. But when the people
came into their own, they were content to be tyrannized
over by police captains and politicians, paperwork-men
and priests. So I'm better off here than there. There's still
some hope in a house like this.

GANDERSHEIM. Do you think so? It's rather been getting
me down.

THE GARDENER. Don't be scared of the lady, sir.

GANDERSHEIM. My mother?

THE GARDENER. That, too.

GANDERSHEIM. You mean Judith?

THE GARDENER. She's far more scared than you.

GANDERSHEIM. You surprise me!

THE GARDENER. Sure, she's frightened of her own
shadow, for she thinks it must cast a contagion on everything it falls upon.

GANDERSHEIM. On account of that dreadful thing, you
mean?—her father shooting her mother?

THE GARDENER. It's both grievance and guilt she feels, and nothing can make up the loss.

GANDERSHEIM. One could pity her a little more easily if she weren't so extremely aggressive. I really can't take it from her! When she scored off me out there just now —when she made me sacrifice those hydrangeas—I couldn't resist my little revenge—though it may have been rather unfair—it did upset me when I heard her screaming. Not that *she* would have hesitated a moment to take advantage of *me*. She's one of these modern women who want to have equality for the sexes, but they *don't* have the same sense of honor as men, and you can't always meekly submit to being made a ninny of. There are moments in modern life when you have to fight a bitch in the same spirit.

THE GARDENER (*interrupting him*). Sure, you can't see to read by that light. (*He turns on one of the student-lamps and moves it up to illuminate the book.*) Now what has the encyclopedia to tell us about the hydrangeas?

GANDERSHEIM. Thank you. Oh, yes: let me see. Here it is: you can put iron or alum in the soil.— (*Looking up at the Gardener and smiling*) If we could really revive the hydrangeas, if we could get them to blaze a splendiferous blue, it might make that blue light burn a little bit dimmer. Do you think so?—I'm just talking nonsense—it's only poetical nonsense. One doesn't have to explain poetry to an Irishman.

THE GARDENER (*reading over his shoulder*). "Late in autumn, after frost, when the leaves have fallen, the plants may be moved to a frost-proof cellar and kept rather dry till spring. They may then be repotted with new soil."

GANDERSHEIM. I do hope they won't die in the meantime!

SCENE 2

*The same room. Early December: eleven o'clock in the morning.*
*Frank and Gandersheim are sitting at the table—Frank in the*
*highbacked chair, Gandersheim about four feet away from him,*
*on the opposite side from the audience. Gandersheim has lying*
*before him a neat pile of manuscripts, on the top page of each*
*of which has been clipped a piece of yellow paper for the editors*
*to write their comments on; Frank is sorting out a more disorderly*
*lot. He picks up a typewritten list.*

FRANK. Well, here's the contents of the first January
issue. First: *A Slap-Happy New Year*. That's an editorial
by me. My idea is that the American people have taken
such a beating in the last election that such of them as are
rejoicing over it are actually goofy with punishment. (*He*
*hands the manuscript to Gandersheim, who laughs appreciatively*
*as he lays it face down beside him.*) *The Washington Iron Cur-*
*tain*. "Iron Curtain" is a hell of an old phrase now—and
what I'd really like to call it is *The United States: Top Secret*
—but I wanted to write a leader: *Is the Human Race Top*
*Secret?*

GANDERSHEIM. That's brilliant. Why don't you save it
then?

FRANK. That's what I think I will. All right: let the Iron
Curtain go. (*He hands the article to Gandersheim, who does*
*with it as before.*) Maybe we'll think of something better
later. The next is *The Mechanical Brain and the Gettysburg*
*Address.*

GANDERSHEIM. I haven't seen that.

FRANK. It's a hell of a good article! (*He hands it to*
*Gandersheim, who glances through it.*) It shows that this so-
called machine that thinks may be able to play chess and
translate and correct examination papers, but it couldn't

produce a Gettysburg Address—that is to say, if you set it for the occasion and place and for a certain number of words, the best it could possibly do would be to string a lot of clichés together.—*Twentieth Floor Express: An Elevator-Man Looks at Life.* You've got that. Did you fix it up?

GANDERSHEIM (*taking it out of his pile and putting it with the others*). I did the best I could.

FRANK. It's interesting, though, don't you think? That impulse he has in the lunch-hour to drop the elevator with everybody in it.

GANDERSHEIM. A very pretty idea—yes.

FRANK. Next: *Pressure Personalities, Five* (*handing it to Gandersheim, who looks to see the rest of the title before adding it to the pile as before*). This one is Luke Teniakis.

GANDERSHEIM. I don't think I know about *him*.

FRANK. He's the fellow who runs that Bureau that sent us Percy Gilman—and got him exonerated. He's not an important figure, but he's a hell of an admirable guy, and I wanted to have him in. Here's a little Greek delicatessen dealer who comes over here without a cent and who builds up something unique: an employment agency that sticks by its clients—just because he remembered his own hard times.—Then here's a nostalgic piece: *When We Skated in Rockefeller Plaza: A Glimpse of Old New York.* (*Gandersheim finds it.*) O.K. Here's the first of a new series: *My Moment of Supreme Indifference.* (*He finds the manuscript and hands it to Gandersheim.*) That's the name of the series. You know there've been a couple of series like that in other magazines: one on *The Happiest Moment of My Life* and one on *My Proudest Day.* Well, I thought it would be a good idea to have people write up the moments when they felt the most complete indifference about the things that they were supposed to take seriously.

GANDERSHEIM. I didn't know about that either. Was it your idea?

ACT II. SCENE 2

FRANK. No: Judy's.

GANDERSHEIM. Oh!

FRANK. This first one's maybe a bit obvious: *When I Missed the Train for my Wedding*.

GANDERSHEIM (*smiling on one side of his mouth*). That will offend people, won't it?

FRANK. Just scandalize them a little. The others strike more of a heroic note—about people who felt perfect indifference when they thought they were falling to their deaths in planes or missing out on their Hollywood options. —Then here's the second political: *Did the Election Lose Us Our Liberties?*—And special American problems: *Can the Apache Be Saved from Extinction?* (*He looks for the manuscript.*)

GANDERSHEIM. Do you want those two question-titles?

FRANK. Right you are. (*He rewrites one of them.*) *The Twilight of the Apache*. All right. (*He hands Gandersheim the articles.*) —*When the Rue de la Paix Moved to Seventh Avenue*. That's the only article for women this month— but it'll have to be enough. (*He looks for the manuscript.*)

GANDERSHEIM. I don't think we ought to cater to them. That's the trouble with American magazines. They're all just as feminine as *Harper's Brazeer*.

FRANK. That's always been my idea. Goddam it, the very sports departments are written for women now. You've got that one, haven't you? (*Gandersheim looks in his pile.*) —Next number: *Pretzel-Bending: A Vanishing Skill*. You've got that one, too.

GANDERSHEIM (*taking them out*). You don't think we're overdoing the nostalgic note just a tiny bit this month?

FRANK. How do you mean?

GANDERSHEIM. Well, it seems to me we're saying fare-well to such a lot of things: we're kissing the Apaches goodby—and pretzels and our political liberties and skating in Rockerfeller Plaza, all in the same issue.

FRANK (*studying the list*). By God, I believe you're right.

GANDERSHEIM. I suggest taking out the pretzels and putting in *The Slot-Machine Swindle*—we've had it around for a year.

FRANK. I can't seem to bring myself to run that damn thing. It makes our exposés look so picayune. The slot-machine isn't always working, so the customer loses his nickel or doesn't get his gum—so what? But all right: put it in. Let's get it over with!—Now we come (*with his ironical emphasis*) to your *monsterpiece*, which hasn't materialized yet: *The Horror at the North Window: The Professor Faces Shidnats.*

GANDERSHEIM. I'll have it ready by the end of the week. I'm finding it more difficult than usual. I want to have Shidnats Slyme appear, and he's never been described directly——

FRANK. He'd better be sensationally horrible after the build-up you've been giving him for years.

GANDERSHEIM. It will take a little doing. I'm not really sure how he looks—whether he's frightening in an obvious way or something that seems innocent in itself—something like a little blue light.

FRANK. I thought he was a hideous monster.

GANDERSHEIM. The other thing has great possibilities— a terrible little blue light——

FRANK. That's too abstract: your readers would feel they weren't getting their money's worth.

GANDERSHEIM. That's why I must get it exactly right.

FRANK. What you've made people expect is a hair-raising demon.

GANDERSHEIM. That's just why the other would be more of a surprise. The Professor is looking out the window, and he sees what he takes at first for a star that he doesn't recognize—but then he becomes aware that it's hanging right over the garden—then it seems to be closer to the window, half a dozen feet beyond the pane. (*He turns toward the bay-window and gestures; Frank looks toward the window, too.*) The next time, it's there in the room—even though the lights are on: doesn't that give you a queer twinge?—quietly and steadily shining, but with devilish deadly intensity—with a ray like an old-fashioned hatpin that will stick you right through the brain——

FRANK. Well, that's an unpleasant thought, but it seems to me a little too special. As a Gandersheim fan, I'll be bitterly disappointed if I don't get a bang-up bugaboo with a definite personality.

GANDERSHEIM. I'm not sure that Shidnats Slyme has anything so human as a personality. He takes possession of other people's personalities. In his non-incarnate state, he's simply a force that blights and kills, the cruellest thing that exists——

FRANK. You wouldn't gather that from the name?—Where did you get that name, by the way?

GANDERSHEIM (*smiling slyly*). It's never been explained in the stories, but a few of my readers have guessed. Do you know what my initials stand for?—the initials of my real name?

FRANK. M. S.? No: what?

GANDERSHEIM. Myles Standish. (*He pauses expectantly.*)

FRANK. I don't get it.

GANDERSHEIM. Spell Myles Standish backwards.

FRANK (*grinning*). I see! But why treat a good name like that?

GANDERSHEIM. It's a real desecration, I know. I was named after Myles Standish, because he was an ancestor of mine. But it was something I cooked up as a boy. Actually, I was awfully proud of coming of *Mayflower* stock. All the people around here were much richer than we—they were all manufacturers and suchlike. My father was a business man, too, but I liked to think that we were different, because he was a linen importer, and the firm was very old, with a distinguished brass plate on the building. But what I was proudest of was my connection with Myles Standish. I thought I had the right to despise all these people we were living among out here—people, who made hardware and baking-powder—because they were parvenus—however much they might be rolling in money and however much they might beat me at tennis.

FRANK. Then why pervert your *Mayflower* name?

GANDERSHEIM. My fantasy was that I was Standish—that Standish was among them and they didn't know it, weren't able to appreciate him. They thought I was just a sissy, just a hateful little brat, but all the time I was one of the giants, the leader of the Plymouth Colony, an instrument chosen by a jealous God to make His will prevail. And yet, while Big Business prevailed, I had to work underground, I had to assume a disguise—so I turned my name around to make it sound as unpleasant and outlandish as I thought they must think I was——

FRANK. That would be a story in itself—you ought to write it someday—but in the meantime, won't you kindly get to work on *The Horror at the North Window*? Thursday's your deadline, remember. (*He goes on reading his list.*) Well, here's the sporting piece: *Muskallonge-Fishing in Michigan.* (*Finding it and picking it up*) We've got to get a better title.

GANDERSHEIM. *Unmasking the Muskallonge*?

FRANK. I don't see the point to that.

GANDERSHEIM. Well, it says that——

FRANK. *Misleading the Muskallonge*—that's no good either. *Outsmarting the Muskallonge!*—that'll do. (*He changes the title with his pencil.*) *Outsmarting the Muskallonge.*—And finally, Judy's nightlife—it hasn't appeared, I suppose?

GANDERSHEIM (*smugly*). Not to my knowledge.

FRANK. Jesus, I wish she'd at least call me up! She wanted to catch the opening of Pinky's Place, but that was two nights ago. It's a hell of a damn nuisance having your wife as a regular contributor!

GANDERSHEIM. Her articles are making a hit, though.

FRANK. I hope they're worth the price I pay for them! She stays away practically the whole week. The household is going to pieces, and if I want to see anything of her, I have to go up to town and spend an evening in some ghastly dive.

GANDERSHEIM. I don't know whether you know that she was mentioned the other day in connection with Pappadapoulos, the man who runs Pinky's Place.

FRANK (*disregarding this*). I don't see what people get out of those places! Have you been to a night-club lately? They're mass propositions now, just like everything else. They remind you of the old-fashioned beer-gardens, except that they have none of the things that used to make beer-gardens comfortable.

GANDERSHEIM. Judy seems to find them worth while.

FRANK. The kids of her age never knew a time when anything was any good.

GANDERSHEIM. No: of course, they've never known— but *we* know.—We have many things in common, Frank. I feel sometimes that you and I are different aspects of the same person!

FRANK (*not much liking this*). I don't see that entirely.

GANDERSHEIM (*slightly hurt*). Oh, I don't mean we aren't very different in a great many obvious ways. Of course I'm an Easterner, an aesthete, what's usually called a dreamer— (*Frank picks up a pile of mail and begins going through it rapidly, tearing the envelopes open, glancing at the enclosures and throwing them aside.*) I've travelled, become cosmopolitan; while you're very much the Westerner and the rugged practical man: you stick by the country and its *mores*. And yet both of us represent the same old American thing: an individualistic idealism. We're two faces of the same coin—and it was written that we should land up here, in this silly old house of mine, working on the same brave project. Deep down, we're inseparable, inextricable. Nobody who hadn't been bred in the American tradition of *The Rights of Man* could have launched a magazine like *Spotlight*; and I think I can say that no one who didn't have Melville and Poe in his blood could ever have——

FRANK (*staring at a letter he has opened*). Well, I'm a son of a bitch!

GANDERSHEIM. What is it?

FRANK. A threat, by God! An anonymous letter!

GANDERSHEIM. Let me see it. (*He takes the letter.*) How curious! It's not illiterate, as so many anonymous letters are.

FRANK (*getting up and standing behind him*). Look at the way it's written! It's as pompous as an official communication! (*Reading*) "Frank Brock is hereby notified that, as from date of receipt of this letter, he must discontinue at once the publication of his scheduled series, *Pressure Portraits*. The consequence of failing to comply with this order will be prompt incapacitation through violence, in the fullest and most definitive physical meaning of the phrase. This warning is not the production of an unbalanced individual but of a responsible organization devoted to the public interest and provided with improved equipment for the implementation of its policies."

GANDERSHEIM. "Incapacitation through violence in the fullest sense of the phrase"—do you think that means they're threatening to kill you? What a very peculiar way of putting it!

FRANK. It's simply damn badly written, in this typical bureaucratic jargon that's been rampant ever since the war. If I knew their goddam address, I'd put it into decent English and send it back.

GANDERSHEIM (*still looking at the letter*). You'd better think right away about getting police protection. I wonder what they're threatening to do. You know, I'm convinced that there's some new kind of weapon that nobody's got on to yet. We still don't know how Cardinal Keenan was murdered—and then there was that postmaster in New Rochelle who was found burned to death the other day— the papers didn't pay much attention to it, but it was queer and it hasn't been explained.

FRANK. I suppose this means a bodyguard. That's a nuisance I'd hoped to avoid—and to hell with it!—I'm not going to do a thing. I'll just go on running the series as scheduled.

GANDERSHEIM. You've got more nerve, Frank, than anybody I've ever known, and I'm right by your side all the time. If they should get you——

FRANK. Is that Judy? (*He listens intently for her step.*)

GANDERSHEIM (*finishing a little lamely*). —They'd get me, too.

*Judith enters. She is very smartly dressed; has changed her way of doing her hair and has evidently been given the works at a beauty parlor. She has entirely dropped the magazine editor and is blooming in a new role: that of fascinating woman-about-town. Throughout the scene that follows, she puts on a great show of knowingness, self-assurance and conscious attractiveness, patronizing Frank in a way that would quickly exasperate him if it were not for the seriousness of the situation and the importance of what she has to tell him. He comes over to the door to meet her. Gandersheim nods to her curtly and pretends to busy himself at the other end of the room, then reclines on the window-seat, with his back against the wall opposite the audience, examining manuscripts.*

FRANK. I hope you've got your copy with you!

JUDITH. I haven't quite finished it yet. I was going to type it out now.

FRANK. You better get to work right away. It ought to go out by the one o'clock messenger. But before you do anything else, please find out what's wrong in the kitchen. We got a rotten breakfast this morning, and I'm not sure we're going to get any lunch.

JUDITH. I've seen Bertha. She says you've been barking at her.

FRANK. Of course I've been barking at her. She brought me coffee that was stone cold.

JUDITH. She says that you made a long telephone call after it was brought in.

FRANK. It was cold when it first arrived. She was definitely opposed to the whole idea of giving us breakfast at all.

JUDITH. You can't expect her to revel in it if you're so disagreeable to her.

FRANK. If you were here, that wouldn't happen—and if you're going to stay away, you might at least get your copy in on time!

JUDITH. I wanted to wait for the opening of the Only Yesterday Club—and it turned out to be the only one that was interesting. They sang old surrealist songs from the Lean Thirties that I could sometimes just remember from my childhood. It's incredible how they liked to talk gibberish then—it was evidently an outlet for them:

> "Oh, Mairzy Doats and Dozy Doats
> And little Lamzy Divy"—

FRANK (*interrupting*). I've just received an interesting specimen of a different variety of gibberish. Read that.

*He hands her the letter and watches her while she reads it, not without a certain satisfaction, since he expects her to be upset.*

JUDITH (*handing it back to him*). Yes. I'm not surprised. If I were you, I'd stop the series.

FRANK. You'd have me just lay down and take it?

JUDITH. If my guess is right about what this is. The next article's Luke Teniakis, isn't it?

FRANK. One of the least offensive.

JUDITH. That's where you're wrong. Teniakis is the biggest shot of all.

FRANK. Teniakis is a smart young Greek, but he isn't a big shot!

JUDITH. Yes, he is. You just don't know about it.

FRANK. What do you mean?

JUDITH. It'll take quite a lot of explaining. (*She sits down on the farther side of the table toward the left, and lights a cigarette.*) But you certainly ought to know.

FRANK. Go on.

*He sits down opposite her, toward the right.*

JUDITH. Well, I suppose you've got it in your article how he fought in the Liberation movement that was trying to give Greece a new deal and that was put down by the British with U.S. tanks.

FRANK. Yes.

JUDITH. Well, as a result of that, he lost faith in the Allied pretensions, but at the same time he was too independent to want to work for the Reds. He came over here to America and set up his Mediterranean Relief Bureau to feed and find jobs for political refugees and politically-minded D.P.'s—but he soon learned American political methods—the kind that don't have anything to do with philosophies or general principles—and he rapidly built up a machine that controlled an immense number of jobs in all kinds of businesses and institutions——

FRANK. I know all that, too.

JUDITH. What you evidently *don't* know, though, is that the Teniakis organization is now the biggest thing in the country. All the other movements are past their prime, they've been getting corrupt and porous, and Teniakis has been able to permeate them——

FRANK (*resentful at being told all this by Judith*). Permeate them with what?

495

JUDITH. Why, just with Teniakisites. He began by making petty deals with the various political and religious groups in order to get his people placed; but with his brain for intrigue—in his way, he's brilliant—he gradually brought pressure to bear on them to give his clients more and more power. He's got his key-men in the pressure groups and in every department of the government. It was Luke Teniakis who arranged the truce between the anti-Constitutionalist groups and made it possible for them to win the election, and to all intents and purposes it's Teniakis who's now in the White House.

FRANK. And why has nobody had any inkling of this?

JUDITH. *You* haven't had any inkling of it, because you hide yourself away out here and don't have any idea of what's going on. I began hearing about it before I'd been in New York a week. But there hasn't been anything in the papers, because Teniakis doesn't want publicity. He wants to be known as just the head of a relief bureau. That's why he's trying to stop your article.

FRANK. I must admit that's a damn smart idea: a movement with no publicity!

JUDITH. The age of propaganda is finished. The old groups have been making more noise just because they're losing their grip. They know that they've got nothing more to offer.

FRANK. But what's the idea behind this movement?

JUDITH. There isn't any idea. You liberals always imagine that there has to be an idea behind things. What was the idea behind Genghis Khan or Alexander the Great? The old groups haven't got any real ideas. The Reds haven't believed in their Communism since sometime in the early thirties. The so-called faith of the Children of Peter is something that no decently educated person—with the exception of a few panicky poets—has been able to take seriously since the seventeenth century. And as for the

Yankee Elitists, with all their talk about the Founding Fathers—if even John Adams turned up today, they'd denounce him as a dangerous demagogue.

FRANK. I haven't heard you hold forth so eloquently since your big valedictory oration.

JUDITH. Well, your irony is out of place. I'm simply trying to tell you the score. It may be rather hard for you to grasp it, but you know you've always said yourself that all any of them wanted was power, and what Teniakis has been doing is simply concentrating on power without bothering about ideas or policies. He says he had enough of ideologies when he saw how the Greek politicians sat around in cafés talking while the fighters were put in jail. But he believes in free speech——

FRANK. So long as nobody mentions *him*.

JUDITH. Yes: the British left the press free in Greece, and he saw that if people were at liberty to discuss their problems in print, they were less likely to make real trouble. He says that——

FRANK. You've met him?

JUDITH. Just once.

FRANK. What kind of a guy is he?

JUDITH. He's a quiet little man—well-dressed. You wouldn't be likely to notice him unless you were face to face with him, but then everything he does is so definite——

FRANK. He made an impression on you?

JUDITH. Yes—in a way, yes. He's so perfectly matter-of-fact. The point is that he gives people permanent jobs—which is, after all, what they most want. They've been over-drugged with lurid lies.

FRANK. No inspirational hokum, eh?

JUDITH. All they seem to have is their slogan—that's been passed around by word of mouth, but that's supposed to have never been printed: *Rule by the Uncommon Man in the Interest of the Common Man.* From the moment

497

that anybody whatever—no matter how mediocre his abilities are—holds one of Teniakis' jobs, he has the status of Uncommon Man and is entitled to regard other people as common men. They say, though, that, as a matter of fact, there's a pretty high level of ability among the Teniakis appointees.

FRANK. That has a familiar sound.

JUDITH. It's different from fascism, though. It has no social or political program—and it isn't patriotic.

FRANK. You can't tell me he does it all without any kind of personal cult!

JUDITH. Well, they sometimes call him the greatest Greek since Pericles—but he doesn't encourage that.

FRANK. And you think I ought to knuckle under to the greatest Greek since Spyros Skouras without even putting up a fight?

JUDITH. I don't see what else you can do.

FRANK. Hell, I can't refuse a challenge like that! If what you're telling me's true, it's the greatest story of all time. Not to break it would be journalistic suicide.

JUDITH. If you try to break it now, it'll be actual suicide.

FRANK. Why should they go to such lengths?

JUDITH. Right now is the critical time. If the rank and file of the Peters and the Reds and all the rest of the ideological groups were to find out that their top leaders didn't take the groups' doctrines seriously but were really Teniakisites, there might be a violent reaction.

FRANK. All the more reason to set off the bomb!

JUDITH. It would mean putting an end to my articles, but of course you don't care about that! There's no other magazine that I could write in the way I do in *Spotlight*, but you never consider me!

FRANK. Well, I'm not going to suspend publication, and I don't want to get murdered. But there's a high wall around this place, and there's no reason I can't barricade myself. I'll take it up at once with the Chief of Police.

JUDITH. He may be one of Teniakis' men.

FRANK. Out here?

JUDITH. Why not? He has them everywhere.

FRANK. I can always get people I trust.

JUDITH. You've made Bertha so sore at you now that I wouldn't trust *her* not to betray you.

FRANK. She's all right: I'll charm her again.

JUDITH. Your charm! Do you think you can depend on it?

FRANK. Yes. And then, that old gardener——

*Gandersheim, who has been staring out the window, now suddenly jumps up from the window-seat and speaks in great excitement.*

GANDERSHEIM. The gardener!—here he comes now. Listen, Frank: I see the whole thing! I've really been expecting all this—I've had the sense of it ever since I came here. Teniakis is the *Monster God*, and he's been lurking here all the time. He's here with us in the shape of the gardener! He's coming to us from over there! (*Pointing at the window*) Look: the landscape has changed!

FRANK (*going over to the window*). What do you mean, it's changed?

GANDERSHEIM. Those horrible little houses!—that's where he's got his own people. They'll creep in on us from there—they'll close in on us!

FRANK. That's just a real estate development—it's been there all along.

GANDERSHEIM. I'm sure *I've* never seen it before.

JUDITH (*who has come to the window, too*). You didn't see it on account of the trees. It's just that the leaves have fallen.

GANDERSHEIM. But look at that old man!—do you see him? He's coming across the fields from there, and there's something *unheimlich* about him. Haven't you noticed how strange he is?

JUDITH. I do think he's a little bit odd, but he's not really one of your goblins.

GANDERSHEIM. One can't tell who or what he is—even his nationality. I thought he was an Italian at first, and he certainly talked Italian—but then, when I spoke to him later, he seemed to have an Irish brogue.

FRANK. I noticed that, too.

GANDERSHEIM. He spoke to me here one day in the queerest, most impudent way, and somehow he got me to talk to him about all kinds of personal things.

JUDITH. He's been impudent with me, too.

GANDERSHEIM. It's Shidnats—Shidnats is *real*? When I spoke about the little blue spark, he simply turned on the light. He meant that he controlled the switch!

FRANK. He might be a Teniakis agent. (*To Gandersheim*) Go down and get him in, Gandy. He's on his way to the stable.

GANDERSHEIM. There's something wrong with the stable: all those pigeons dying!

FRANK. Take it easy: you ought to be writing that story instead of acting it out.

GANDERSHEIM. You think I'm crazy, I know, but I definitely feel he's not human. I wouldn't venture into the stable with him.

FRANK. Just ask Bertha to ring for him and tell him I want to see him.

GANDERSHEIM. All right, Frank: I may be silly, but you ought to be careful with him!

*He goes out, controlling his agitation.*

JUDITH (*when Gandersheim has left*). I don't see how you can have him around.

FRANK. I couldn't do without him now.

JUDITH. Don't you think it's rather alarming to have him fly off the handle like that?

FRANK. He's nervous and highstrung—and he's been thinking about his next story.—Tell me: who put you in touch with the Teniakis organization? Where did you get your information?

JUDITH. I got it from several sources.

FRANK. If you've met Teniakis himself, you must know some of his agents.

JUDITH. Pinky who runs Pinky's Place is one of his principal henchmen.

FRANK. You must have known him pretty well for him to tell you all that.

JUDITH. I do know him pretty well.

FRANK. I knew that those nightlife articles were just a pretext to go on the loose!

JUDITH. It seems to me I've done pretty well by you. If I hadn't been getting around, you wouldn't have known a thing. You didn't even realize that Percy Gilman was the Teniakis man on our staff.

FRANK. What harm did Percy do us?

JUDITH. He was using you as a screen when he went to kill that Cardinal.

FRANK. I don't believe he had anything to do with it!

JUDITH. Well, he did. He and Keenan's secretary were both Teniakis' agents. Teniakis had the Cardinal killed because Keenan had gotten on to the fact that the Bureau was infiltrating the Church, and had been putting up a very tough fight.

FRANK. How was the murder worked?

JUDITH. It was the flashlight. It's a new lethal weapon.

GANDERSHEIM. An electrocution device?

JUDITH. Yes, but it's a product of brain research. It's something entirely new. Up to a few years ago, it seems, the brain research people had only been able to study cats and dogs or patients under anesthetics who were having brain operations. But lately, in some jail in Europe that was crammed with political prisoners, they began just exposing their brains and testing pain reactions. They'd found out how to use the emotions to generate electric charges, and they went the Nazis one better. Instead of just making soap and lampshades out of human fat and skin, they amused themselves by rigging up the cells with electrodes and amplifiers and having the prisoners electrocute themselves by their purely subjective feelings. They'd threaten them or disappoint them, and the apparatus would do the rest. The principle of it is something like radar.

FRANK. What did they do?—get the Cardinal over-excited?

JUDITH. Yes: the gun only works for emotions like hatred and fear and grief. They haven't got the hang of the pleasant ones, and the unpleasant feelings are the only kind that they always know how to produce. The secretary set the gun, and Percy Gilman made the Cardinal furious by accusing the Church of corruption. Then he left him, and the gun went off.

FRANK. It seems unnecessarily complicated.

JUDITH. Well, the man who made it just loves gadgets and he's an incorrigible practical joker. It was invented by a Teniakis guerrilla, who'd been in jail and had seen those experiments. It does have the advantage that the killer doesn't have to be there at all, and that when people find the apparatus, they don't understand what it is. It even aims automatically.

*Gandersheim returns with the Gardener, who is this time without his hat and looks sober and dignified.*

FRANK (*to the Gardener*). Oh, come on in.—Well, how are you getting along?

*The Gardener advances in front of the table and, as Frank resumes the highbacked chair, he turns a chair around to face him and sits down near the other end. Judith takes a seat behind the table, between the Gardener and Frank, leaving a chair between Frank and herself. Gandersheim remains in the background.*

THE GARDENER (*with a Scotch accent*). Weel enough.

FRANK. The work is too heavy for you alone.

THE GARDENER. Ah'm no owerwirket: Ah dinna complain.

FRANK. You ought to have somebody to help you, and I've got to get somebody to drive the car, now that Mrs. Brock is so much in town. I thought you might have a friend who could qualify.

THE GARDENER. Ah've no monny acquentances aboot here.

FRANK. How did *you* happen to come to us, by the way? Was it through an employment agency?

THE GARDENER. Ah've never subjected mysel' to the indeegnity o' the auction block.

FRANK. You simply turned up here, huh? How did you know we needed a gardener?

THE GARDENER. Ah'd heard that ye'd moved in here, and Ah cam' on the offchance. Ah'm condemned to such places noo.

JUDITH (*sharply*). What kind of places do you mean?

THE GARDENER. Lonesome places wi' folk like you.

GANDERSHEIM. But why are you condemned to such places?

THE GARDENER. Ah canna leeve in the great cities noo—and it seems that Ah've still monny mair years to sairve.

GANDERSHEIM. How old are you, may one ask?

THE GARDENER. How auld would ye think?

GANDERSHEIM. Why—I'd say in your late sixties.

THE GARDENER. You'd be a long way short o' the mark.

FRANK. This is getting away from the subject. (*To the Gardener*) Do you happen to know anything about the Teniakis Bureau?

THE GARDENER. Not from pairsonal experience. Ah've heard of it.

FRANK. You're a naturalized citizen, I take it.

THE GARDENER. Ay.

FRANK. What *is* your nationality?

THE GARDENER. Technically speaking, Ah'm just an American—if that's a nationality.

GANDERSHEIM (*coming over to Frank and speaking in a low voice*). He's got a Scotch accent now. (*He sits down in the chair between Judith and Frank.*)

FRANK. Sometimes you sound like an Italian—sometimes you sound like an Irishman—right now you've got a burr like a Scotchman.

THE GARDENER. Ah'd leeved for conseederable periods in a variety o' deefferent countries before Ah cam' to the United States, and noo that Ah'm auld, Ah meex them up.

FRANK. Where were you born?—in Europe?

THE GARDENER. Eh, mon, Ah hardly ken. 'Twas somewhere near the Mediterranean, but Ah canna te' ye where. Mah faither was an eeteenirant cobbler, an' mah family were always on the move.

FRANK. You say that you've heard about the Teniakis Bureau. Would it be a good place, do you think, to get a reliable man?

THE GARDENER. Ah'm sairtain that anyone they sent ye would be verra *un*reliable for *you*.

FRANK. Why?

THE GARDENER. Wi' your eendependent magazine and your ambeetion to stick by your preenciples, they'll do ye whatever meeschief they're able.

FRANK. What do you mean?

THE GARDENER. Eh, ye maun ken what Ah mean, seence ye've ca'ed me in here to question me.

FRANK. How do *you* come to know so much about it?

THE GARDENER. Ah've a special knack o' kennin' such matters.

FRANK. That's what I thought.—Listen here: you might just as well tell me right now—because otherwise

I'll find out for myself: What kind of an agent are you?

THE GARDENER. Ah'm not an agent in your sense o' the worrd. If Ah'm an agent, Ah'm God's agent.

GANDERSHEIM (*struck with panic*). What God are you the agent of?

THE GARDENER. Not your God, Meester Gandersheim—for he's nothing more nor less than the auld Presbyterian Devil—ye got them meexed up in your childhood. In this country, ye began with the Puritan God—the hateful auld jealous Jehovah that folk had read about in the Bible. Ah believed in him once mysel', but later Ah cam' to tak' account that ye need not make God a tyrant to maintain a streect regard for your duties. An' when God is a hanging judge, wi' the Devil to ply the gallows, there's like to be hardly a pin to choose between the judge and his hangman. Tak' my word for it: the fear of a cruel God will mak' ye as cruel as the God ye fear.

GANDERSHEIM. Please mind your own business!

THE GARDENER. Dinna fash yersel'——

FRANK (*to the Gardener*). Never mind: I didn't get you in here to preach to us. I just wanted to ask your advice about hiring another man.

THE GARDENER. Ah'll help you, sir, in any way Ah can. Ye can count on my loyalty at a' times, if that's what ye want to make sure of.

FRANK. I can, eh? (*He looks at him searchingly, impressed by his tone of sincerity.*)

THE GARDENER. Ay, why should ye not? Ah'm on the same side o' the struggle as you.

FRANK. What struggle?

THE GARDENER. Ay, what, indeed! It's no verra easy to say. We can hardly talk noo aboot Recht an' Wrong, for it's that that's made our hanging judges, an' put the whole world at their maircy, till there's been nothing but hanging judges wi' no releegion behind them.

FRANK. What the hell? haven't we got to believe that the things we want to do are right? I hope you think that this tough Greek is wrong!

THE GARDENER. Ay, but the most we can say for ourselves is that we're conscious o' representing forces that Teniakis doesna ken, and that we hope he's meescalculated and that what *we* represent will prevail.

FRANK. What forces do you mean exactly?

THE GARDENER. Why, the forces alive in this house. The godlike imagination that recreates life through art— Meester Gandersheim has his share of it, though the quality is puir today—and the weell to comprehend and to speak the truth—deteriorated though *that* is—that ye've tried to poot across in *Spotlight*.

JUDITH. I suppose *I* don't contribute anything!

THE GARDENER. You've something to contreebute, if ye will. You've the spirit of a fighter, if ye'd fight for a cause, instead of just wi' eendividuals. 'Twas women like you that won the vote and that took your sex out of the keetchen to use their brains for themselves—but today you'll neither carry children nor carry the banner of freedom.

JUDITH. I *am* free.

THE GARDENER. Free for how long and for what?— Wi' the rest o' the wairld enslaved?

JUDITH (*to Frank*). You see what a self-righteous old bore he is?

FRANK. After all, we more or less asked for it. (*To the Gardener*) All right: thank you.

THE GARDENER. Dinna distrust me—dinna be feared to call on me. Ye might care to know Ah've never yet died —so, presumably, Ah canna be keelled.

*He goes out. They watch him to the door.*

GANDERSHEIM (*still rather nervous*). What did he mean by that?

JUDITH. He's obviously cracked.

FRANK. I don't know.

JUDITH. He's most obnoxious, in any case.

FRANK. He may be some kind of religious fanatic, but I don't see that he's necessarily crazier than anybody else out here. Gandy has got us surrounded with the demons of Shidnats Slyme! You come and tell me I'm caught in the toils of a super-dictatorship that's super-secret and super-sly, so that it's hopeless even to struggle—and how do I know that *that* isn't a product of *your* imagination?

JUDITH. Thank you for your opinion of my judgment! You see that your friend the gardener knows about Teniakis. In the meantime, you're confronted with that letter.

FRANK. I'm going to give it to the police right away.

JUDITH. If I were you, I'd hold out that article.

FRANK. I hate like hell to yield to threats! There's something in what the old man says: we've got to hope we're stronger than they are.

JUDITH. But in this case we're definitely not—and you're putting *me* in danger, too. They might kidnap me and hold me as a hostage.

FRANK. Yes: you better stay down here.

JUDITH. And both of us get killed together?

FRANK. Well, I can't just weakly submit. You've never wanted me to in the past.

JUDITH. It's never been a case of life or death.

FRANK. Or of your brilliant journalistic activities.

JUDITH. It's so characteristic of you that you should try to make it a question of my vanity when I'm actually in serious danger!

FRANK. Well!— (*He picks out the article from the pile and throws it on the table.*) I won't send it down by this messenger. I'll hold it out for the present and take the matter under consideration. (*He picks up the manuscripts.*) But don't tell me later on that I haven't got any guts.

*She makes no reply. He hurries out.*

GANDERSHEIM (*to Judith, with bitterness*). You want to destroy his manhood!

JUDITH. That's something you'd sympathize with, isn't it? (*She lights a cigarette.*)

GANDERSHEIM. I certainly sympathize with Frank for everything you've been trying to do to him—to humiliate him and break down his confidence.

JUDITH. Do you want him to be actually killed?

GANDERSHEIM (*agitatedly getting together his manuscripts*). I've got my own suspicions about all this!

JUDITH. What do you mean by that?

GANDERSHEIM. I wonder how you ever came to know so much—and you're a friend of Teniakis, it seems.

JUDITH. I suppose you think you're going to tell Frank that I'm in on the conspiracy to shut him up. If you do, *I'll* tell Frank a few things about *you* that I heard at the Punchinello Club.

GANDERSHEIM (*getting up from the table, with his papers*). Frank is a very broadminded and understanding person!

JUDITH. His broadmindedness has limitations.

GANDERSHEIM (*escaping from the room*). Well, we'll see who wins out!

*She looks after him with a malevolent smile.*

# ACT III

*The workroom in the late afternoon of the day before Christmas. On the window-seat is a "gift-wrapped" Christmas package. On the table, a tray with a bottle of Scotch, a bowl of cracked ice, highball glasses and a bottle of soda-water. Frank has pulled out the morris-chair so that it stands in front of the table on the right, and he is sitting in it, reading what looks like a leaflet. The day has been dark and is growing darker, and he has turned on one of the student-lamps. He looks up quickly and apprehensively, as he hears a step on the stairs, then stands up, drops the leaflet on the table and covers it with some other papers and, putting his right hand in the pocket of his coat, points a revolver through the pocket toward the door, at which he gazes impassively but intently.*

*Judith comes in. She is now cultivating a different style, that of intriguing femme fatale: pale and handsome, hair done up on the top of her head, eyebrows completely plucked and false ones drawn on as supercilious arches, a close-fitting dark suit. She carries in her left hand, her arm dropped down at her side, a Christmas wreath tied with a large red ribbon.*

FRANK. Hello.

JUDITH. Hello.

FRANK. I didn't expect you.

JUDITH. I said I was coming for Christmas.

FRANK. It's a week since I've heard anything from you.

JUDITH. I've been busy. I didn't know just when I could come.

FRANK. I haven't done anything about Christmas dinner.

509

JUDITH. I thought you were going to ask the What's-Their-Names and those other people for tomorrow afternoon.

*She goes over to the mantelpiece and sets the wreath up in front of the clock.*

FRANK. I hadn't heard anything from you.

JUDITH. I told you I was coming.

FRANK (*watching her with the wreath*). That's cockeyed. Get the ribbon on the bottom.

JUDITH. Why not at the top?

FRANK. Well, get it in the middle, anyway! (*She arranges it with the bow at the bottom.*) That still isn't straight.

JUDITH (*turning around and coming over to get a cigarette from the table*). You can't make it stand straight if you have the bow underneath.

FRANK. The What's-Their-Names have asked us to their house for dinner tomorrow night.

JUDITH. I have to go back tomorrow night. I'm going to dinner in town.

FRANK. I told them I didn't know whether you'd be here. Why, as a matter of fact, did you think it was worth while to come at all?

JUDITH. It wasn't if you're going to behave like this.

FRANK. This is a hell of a merry Christmas! If I'd known you weren't going to take it seriously, I'd have arranged to spend it with Francie.

JUDITH. Why didn't you?

FRANK. You left it up in the air. You said you'd call me, then never did, and I've had enough of calling you and being told that you're not there. Do you realize that you've succeeded in preventing me from seeing my own daughter on Christmas Day every Christmas for the last three years?

JUDITH. I told you I'd be glad to have her here.

FRANK. The Christmas she spent with us was a nightmare!

JUDITH. I'll go right back to town!

FRANK. Sit down and have a drink, now that you're here.

*She goes over and stands in front of the fireplace. He puts some ice into one of the glasses and pours in a dose of whiskey.*

FRANK. You don't like soda-water, but I didn't know you were coming.

JUDITH. This is a delightful reception. You haven't even got a fire in the fireplace.

FRANK (*moving toward the door*). I'll get Bertha to bring some regular water.

JUDITH. Never mind: I'll drink it straight.

FRANK. Sure you want it that way?

JUDITH. It's all right.

*He hands it to her and pours a drink for himself.*

FRANK. The truth is you can't take Christmas. It always gets you down——

JUDITH. No, it doesn't.

FRANK. I don't think you've ever gotten over those perfectly grisly Christmases that you used to spend at your aunt's after your parents died—when you had to go to church in East Orange, and you said that about the only present you got was the popcorn they gave you in Sunday School.

JUDITH. You never hesitate to remind me of the unpleasant things in my life, do you?

FRANK. You remind me of them yourself—but by all means let's forget about them. (*Going over to the window-seat*) I got you a present. I hope you'll like it, because it's something you said you wanted.

JUDITH (*looking toward the package, her childish curiosity and greediness rising to the bait*). What is it? (*As he brings it over to her, resuming her former attitude*) You shouldn't give me a present: I didn't expect you to.

FRANK. Why not?

JUDITH. Our relations have deteriorated so. (*She unties the ribbon, opens the box and takes out the object inside.*)

FRANK. Not fundamentally, perhaps.

JUDITH (*unwrapping a large jewelled comb of the kind that is supposed to be worn in Spain*). It's too big: I'd·look ridiculous.

FRANK. It's just exactly what you said you wanted.

JUDITH. It's too flashy for my present style.

FRANK. Those are real emeralds.

JUDITH. Are they?

FRANK. I got them to match your eyes.

JUDITH. You should have kept it till tomorrow morning. This is only Christmas Eve.

FRANK (*giving up*). Well, you can't win: it's hopeless! It's what I told you—though you don't like to hear it: when you were little you never had a decent Christmas— so you always have to be disappointed!

JUDITH. It's just that, under the circumstances, I don't like to have you giving me presents.

*She lays the comb back in the box and puts it on the table.*

FRANK. But why, for God's sake?—What circumstances?

JUDITH. Oh, you know.

FRANK. You mean you've been cheating on me?

JUDITH. What you agreed to when I went to New York was really a separation.

FRANK. That wasn't *my* understanding!—Well, who's the boy-friend: Ellis?

JUDITH. I don't see Ellis any more.

FRANK (*snatching at this*). I couldn't imagine you'd find him very thrilling.

JUDITH (*with a little smile, as if to herself*). He has his points, though.

FRANK (*losing his temper*). Oh, what the hell do I care? Sleep with a different man every night! You don't need to come out here at all! You'd better keep away from me, anyway, if you want to go to any more night-clubs.

JUDITH. Is that a threat?

FRANK. No, it's not a threat: it's a statement of the simple truth! I'm just about to break the story on Luke Teniakis.

JUDITH. Right away?

FRANK. Yes.

JUDITH. In the next number?

FRANK. January 14.

JUDITH. You haven't advertised it, have you?

FRANK. Of course not. It isn't even listed in the contents.

JUDITH. I think you're crazy. He won't let it get on the stands.

FRANK. He won't find out about it.

JUDITH. He must have a spy at the press.

FRANK. It hasn't been set up at the press.

JUDITH. How are you handling it, then?

FRANK. I've set it up out here with my own hands. I learned typesetting as a kid, you know, and I got hold of an old hand-press that they were keeping as a curiosity in the local newspaper office. I bought it and set it up here in the stable. I've printed the article myself, and I'm going to drive into town with it, and Gandy and I are going to work all night putting the pages in every copy.

JUDITH. He'll stop it right away on the newsstands.

FRANK. He won't be able to do anything about it before a lot of people have seen it. It will have gone out to all the subscribers.

JUDITH. And how will you dodge the rap?

FRANK (*exalted by desperation and by the stimulus of his drink*). I'll go up to town and live at the Plaza——

JUDITH. You better not take a room too high up!

FRANK. —I'll damn well make a point of being seen in all the most conspicuous places, and I'll just wait for the blow to fall—if they've really got the nerve to kill me. I'll go to nightclubs and shows every night—and I'm going to get a girl to go with me who'll say thank-you for Christmas presents! If they get me, maybe somebody will write on my tomb: *He died for American journalism!*

JUDITH. How did you get your facts?

FRANK. That I'm not telling anybody. But there's a damsight more dissatisfaction with Teniakis and his conspiratorial methods than you seem to realize.

JUDITH. It'll be the end of my articles! Even if *Spotlight* goes on, they'd never let me into the night-clubs. Half the nightlife in New York now is controlled by Teniakis.

*Gandersheim enters.*

GANDERSHEIM (*to Judith, with perceptible condescension*). Oh hello! (*To Frank*) The printers are on the phone.

FRANK (*nervous*). What do they want?

GANDERSHEIM. I don't know: they insisted on talking to you.

*Frank goes quickly out. Gandersheim walks over to Frank's end of the table and starts checking up on the papers to make sure that nothing dangerous has been left there.*

GANDERSHEIM (*to Judith*). It's nice that you could get out. We weren't certain you were coming.

JUDITH (*observing his anxiety*). Don't worry about the article: Frank's just told me about it.

GANDERSHEIM. Oh? (*Looking up at her*) We're in your hands, then.

JUDITH. Don't worry.

GANDERSHEIM. I'm not. (*Attempting to propitiate her*) You'll look stunning with that Spanish comb.

JUDITH. Poor Frank! He has no taste about such things.

*She goes over and takes it out of the box, examining it again, to find out whether it is really expensive, and wondering whether she can wear it. Gandersheim, hearing the back-gate click, looks nervously out the window, sees something that arrests his attention and leans across the window-seat.*

JUDITH. What do you see now, Sister Ann?—another bogeyman from Ghoul's Row?

GANDERSHEIM. It's Ellis.

JUDITH. No! (*She comes over quickly, with the comb in her hand, and looks out at Gandersheim's right.*) Please don't tell him I'm here: I don't want to see him!

GANDERSHEIM. Frank will tell him.

JUDITH. Well, *you* needn't.

*She goes out hastily, still carrying the comb, to shut herself up in her bedroom. Gandersheim looks after her a moment, then, coming in front of the table, moves toward the middle of the room.*

GANDERSHEIM (*soliloquizing*). She's played him some dirty trick—or maybe he's found her out. He wouldn't be able to stand for her long. Such a nice clean good-looking young chap!—he had such a fine sense of decency that he wouldn't go on working for Frank when he was having a love-affair with her. That's something that's so very rare nowadays: an old-fashioned sense of honor! Our good old St. Matthew's School does really count for something still! Old Dr. Parkes at Morning Prayers and the poetry he used to read: *Say not the struggle naught availeth; Play up, play up and play the game!; Amici usque ad aras:* one always knows where one is with a person from one's own background. I had a moment of terror just now when I thought it was some stranger coming—but, thank goodness, it's only Ellis. I hope he's not still after Judy! If it's his loyalty to Frank that has brought him back, what a help he could be to us now!

*Ellis appears at the door, immediately followed by Frank. Ellis has left his hat downstairs but has brought up his brief-case with him. Frank leaves the door partway open.*

ELLIS. Hello, Gandersheim.

*Gandersheim, smiling, shakes hands.*

GANDERSHEIM. It seemed so delightfully natural to see

THE LITTLE BLUE LIGHT

you coming through the back-gate with your briefcase!

ELLIS (*to Frank*). This isn't really a social call. I want to talk business with you.

FRANK. Go on. Sit down. What's on your mind?

*He sits down at the head of the table, and Ellis takes one of the chairs on the side that is nearer the audience, standing his briefcase on the table in front of him.*

ELLIS. I'd like to talk to you alone, if you don't mind.

FRANK. Gandy sits in on all my conferences.

ELLIS. I'd rather see you entirely alone.

FRANK. That would have been all right when you were confidential secretary here—but now you're just a complainer or a favor-asker, like any other visitor.—Which are you?

ELLIS. Both.

FRANK. Shoot.

*Gandersheim retires to the window-seat.*

ELLIS. First of all, I'll have to explain that I'm representing an organization that I don't think you knew I was connected with: the Luke Teniakis Relief Bureau.

FRANK. I wondered what you were doing.

ELLIS. What I came to see you about is the article on the Bureau that you're planning to run.

FRANK. In the *Pressure Portraits* series? I've cancelled it.

ELLIS. I mean the other article—the one you want to bring out in this issue. (*He unfastens the briefcase, opens it and takes out a copy of the insert, leaving the briefcase, open, on the table.*)

FRANK. There isn't any other article.

ELLIS (*grinning*). I mean the one you set up in the stable —this one. (*Holding it up*)

FRANK. I've been seriously disappointed in you, Ellis, but I didn't expect to see you turn spy!

ELLIS (*smiling*). I'm not in the Intelligence Department. Haven't you been rather furtive yourself?

FRANK. There's nothing in the laws of the United States that says a man can't set up his own newspaper!

ELLIS. We think that a public-spirited citizen won't want to do anything on his own account that's not in the public interest.

FRANK. Who the hell is "we"? Who says what is or isn't in the public interest? I've got a damsight more right to judge that than any racketeering delicatessen-dealer.

ELLIS. There's no racketeering in the Bureau. Teniakis is strict about that. The main thing, however, is that we want you to hold out the article.

FRANK. If I won't, what does your (*ironical*) *organization* propose to do about it?

ELLIS. What we propose to do is to explain the situation more fully, in the hope that you'll see it our way.

FRANK (*turning around toward Gandersheim*). I'll be damned: he's coming out here to high-pressure me!

ELLIS. I knew you were going to say that, Frank—but this is not the same thing at all as the propaganda groups who've been after you. What *we're* after isn't publicity but for the press to take no notice at all of us, so that Luke can go quietly on building up the essential services. And seriously, Frank, I can tell you that the Relief Bureau *is* getting things done. The Teniakis appointees have the know-how and the know-what, as we say.

FRANK. I seem to have heard that before. I suppose you'll be telling me next that the Long Island Railroad is running on time!

ELLIS. So it is. Didn't you know?—But there's one thing that's running damn badly, and it's something that we'd like to get your help with.

FRANK. Now comes the bribe! Go on: I'm fascinated!

ELLIS. The fact is the matter came up before any-body knew about your article. The situation is that *Dopesheet*—you know *Dopesheet*, the racing journal

—has got into an awful mess. McGonegal is resigning.

FRANK. Why?

ELLIS. I won't go into that now.

FRANK. I see!

ELLIS. Well, the paper isn't exactly, of course, on the very highest level of journalism, but it's always been a little more than just a racing sheet. It's always stood up for the Common Man——

FRANK. And encouraged him to throw away his money. —Go on: I wouldn't miss a word of this!

ELLIS. It has real possibilities, Frank—and Luke himself has had the idea that you'd be just the man to remake it— (*As Frank seems about to explode*) Don't answer till you've thought about it. It's more interesting than you——

FRANK. Listen, Ellis: what interests *me* is to know how a guy like you who's been brought up as a perfect gentleman can be hypnotized into falling for this mug. I'm not exactly surprised, because you can't be surprised by anything nowadays——

GANDERSHEIM. I am: I'm absolutely shocked!

FRANK —But I feel a certain curiosity as to precisely how the feat was accomplished.

GANDERSHEIM. The man is an illiterate gangster!

ELLIS. We call him the greatest Greek since Pericles and the greatest American since Andrew Jackson.

FRANK. Why Andrew Jackson, for goodness' sake?

*Judith appears in the doorway and stands listening behind the door.*

ELLIS. Jackson was an early example of the Teniakis principle of Rule by the Uncommon Man in the Interests of the Common Man.

GANDERSHEIM. What would Dr. Parkes have said if he'd heard you compare Teniakis with Pericles?

ELLIS. Something very stuffy, no doubt. You have an exaggerated respect for St. Matthew's, Gandersheim—

perhaps because you didn't finish there. If you'd been through the whole mill as I was, with Princeton and Oxford on top of it, it wouldn't have very much glamor for you. I don't doubt that those places meant something in the fairly remote past, when they trained what were known as "the better people." Even as late as my father's day, it was possible to cherish the illusion that there still existed a world in which social distinction and scholarship and the practice of the more serious professions had some kind of real importance. But by the time *I* went to St. Matthew's, the headmaster was merely a money-raiser who had memorized a few lines from Wordsworth, and the fathers of most of the boys were nothing much more than money-raisers either—people who thought they ought to be rich but who'd been driven to desperation by the Government's inroads into business. When the parents—who were invariably divorced—came up to see the boys for weekends, they were usually as jumpy as Mexican beans from having had to skip an evening's drinking.

GANDERSHEIM. There is still such a thing as a gentleman!

ELLIS. Where? There's no class of gentlemen now that counts. The ideal of public service that was a part of the upper-class tradition is only kept alive today by the fruit-dealer Teniakis, who was trained in the Greek Resistance —and if somebody like me who's been trained in those obsolete schools of conformity can help to make Luke's contacts smoother by a little St. Matthew's suavity, I'll consider that my education has not been entirely wasted. (*To Frank*) Does that answer your question?

FRANK. It answers my question, old bean, with a frankness I'd hardly expected. And now I'm going to ask you another: What does your public-spirited leader propose to do if I fail to be won by your suavity?

ELLIS. I'll answer that question frankly, too: the article won't be distributed.

FRANK (*springing up from his chair*). By God, they can't prevent me from talking, if it's the last thing I ever do!

ELLIS. Don't kid yourself, Frank—and don't do anything foolish. I've come as a friend, believe it or——

FRANK. I anticipated something like this, and I know what to do about it. Go back and tell that smart Greek louse who's taken you on as an errand-boy that your mission was completely fruitless.

*Judith comes in from behind the door, but walks around the end of the table, so as to pass on the opposite side from Ellis.*

ELLIS. Don't you think that your language is rather strong for the weakness of your position? We've taken our precautions, too——

JUDITH. Hello, Ellis: what an exciting surprise! Is this a Christmas visit?

ELLIS (*looking around and rising, but greeting her rather stiffly*). Hello: I didn't know you were here.

*He shakes hands with her across the table, and while this is going on, Judith, with her free left hand, quickly picks up the unfastened briefcase and, stepping back from the table and holding the briefcase away to the right, pulls out of it a large flashlight.*

ELLIS (*rising and putting out his hand*). Please don't fool with that: it's broken.

*She whisks it away and darts over between Frank and the window-seat.*

ELLIS (*moving toward her end of the table*). Look out: it may give you a shock!

JUDITH (*to Frank*). Don't let him get it back—it's the thing they kill people with!

*Frank pulls out his revolver and, stepping behind the table, stops Ellis at about half-way its length. Gandersheim has jumped to his feet and stands behind Frank. Judith gets as far away as possible, at the extreme right of the stage, with the table between her and Ellis.*

ELLIS. Don't be silly! It's just a broken flashlight.

JUDITH. I know what it is! (*To Frank*) This is the thing I told you about—the thing that they used to kill Keenan.

ELLIS. You'd better leave it alone!

JUDITH. Nonsense: I know how it works. It isn't even set to go off.—Well, a fine knight-in-armor *you* turned out to be!

ELLIS. I didn't know you were out here. You were supposed to be in town today.

JUDITH. So you came here to kill Frank!

ELLIS. I came out to try to prevent it.

FRANK. Hadn't we better get rid of it right away?

JUDITH. It can't go off now.

FRANK (*to Gandersheim*). See if the gardener's still out there.

GANDERSHEIM (*looking out the window*). Yes.

FRANK. Call him in.

*Gandersheim knocks on the glass and gestures to the Gardener to come up.*

FRANK (*to Judith, in a surly tone*). How do *you* know so much about it?

JUDITH. Somebody explained it to me.

FRANK. Who did?

JUDITH. I wouldn't want to tell.

ELLIS. *We* know, though.

JUDITH. No, you don't.

*Frank, still covering Ellis, opens with his left hand a drawer in the end of the table and takes out another revolver.*

ELLIS. If you care about saving your friend, you'd better give back that gun. You know I couldn't use it now, even if I wanted to.

*She shoots him an ironical look.*

FRANK (*to Ellis*). Well, this is a hot one! I send you up to town as a tried and trusted henchman to investigate a murder and you come back with the murderer's weapon, all ready to roast me to a cinder!

521

ELLIS. I'm sorry, Frank: I was trying to save you. They'd have simply bumped you off before now if I hadn't volunteered to come out here.

FRANK. You didn't come exactly unarmed!

ELLIS. It's the most humane way: I didn't want them to do any of the other things.

*The Gardener enters.*

FRANK. That was darling of you!— (*Addressing the Gardener*) Mr. Ellis, I'm sorry to say, is no longer in sympathy with us. He's come back here as an agent of the gang we want to expose.

THE GARDENER (*crossing himself*). *Bozhe moy!*

FRANK. He came here to kill me, in fact. (*Holding out the revolver, but not turning away from Ellis*) Take this and stand by the door. Shoot him in the leg if he tries to rush us.

THE GARDENER (*coming forward*). Please forgive, little father. I can only help to fight with words. It is forbidden me to fight with weapons.

FRANK. Do you mean it's against your religion?

THE GARDENER. Yes, gracious little father.

FRANK. Good God, he's gone Russian on us now!— All right. (*Handing the gun to Gandersheim*) You take it and go over there. (*Gandersheim complies, passing in front of the table.*) Keep an eye on the door, too.

GANDERSHEIM. I will, Frank.

*He comes forward so that he can see into the hallway.*

JUDITH (*to Frank*). They must have thought you were an easy victim. Ellis told them how bad-tempered you were, and he came out to get you worked up and then leave you to storm and fume and eventually set off the gun.

THE GARDENER (*crossing himself again*). *Spasi, Gospodi, i pomilui!*

FRANK (*to Ellis*). Offering me the editorship of *Dopesheet*, huh?

ELLIS. I'd like to say that Judith's point of view on this is a very much distorted one.

FRANK. Distorting your behavior, Ellis, is the same as painting the lily. But the problem is what to do about you. (*Indicating the morris-chair*) Why don't you sit down while we talk about it? (*Ellis complies.*) Don't you want a drink?

ELLIS. No, thanks.

FRANK. Never drink while on duty, eh?

JUDITH (*to Frank*). I don't think you ought to hesitate to shoot him—if we could be sure of getting rid of the body.

FRANK. Let's not resort to their methods. (*To Ellis*) How would you like to give me your word of honor that you'd get out of the country and stay?

JUDITH (*sneering*). Ellis hasn't any honor—his word isn't worth a thing! He'll even lie out of a dinner engagement.

ELLIS. I'm sorry about that evening: I really did have to dine with my aunt—and I resent being told that my word is no good.

FRANK. Will you swear, if I let you go, that you'll clear out and say nothing? You won't want to face them after this failure. I'll supply the money.

GANDERSHEIM. Don't let him go, Frank: it's Shidnats!

FRANK. Oh, lay off that, Gandy!

GANDERSHEIM. He came from over there (*gesturing with the gun toward the window*), just as I knew he would! It's not the real Ellis—how could it be? It's Shidnats in Ellis's body. They've murdered the real Ellis!

JUDITH (*coming over to Gandersheim*). You'd better give me that gun.

GANDERSHEIM. Please leave me alone!

FRANK. Listen, Gandy: I admit that this sounds like one of your stories, but we've got to face an actual crisis. There's nobody to watch the stable. Will you go down there and check? If you've got a good incantation, it might be helpful to get it off.

GANDERSHEIM. Don't make fun of me, Frank!

FRANK. Give Judy the gun and go out and see if things are all right.

GANDERSHEIM. Whatever you say, Frank.

*Judith takes the revolver from him, transferring the flashlight to her left hand. Gandersheim, chagrined, goes out, closing the door behind him.*

FRANK (*to Judith*). Get rid of that damned flashlight.

*She crosses over, still covering Ellis, and puts the flashlight on the mantel, the bulb-end facing the stage.*

JUDITH. The idea of thinking that Ellis is any different now than he ever was!

*She returns and takes up her stand between Ellis and the door.*

FRANK. What gets me is how he kept acting as though he were so goddam scrupulous.

ELLIS. You were urging me to get rid of my scruples when you wanted to find out about Keenan—and, given your objective, you were perfectly right.

FRANK. I didn't want you to commit any murders! What beats me is how you made the jump from being a minister's son to the role of professional killer!

ELLIS. As I told you, you're quite mistaken. My idea in coming out here——

THE GARDENER (*interrupting*). Forgive me, please—but if you will permit me, I understand this very well. I can perhaps explain better than he can. I was once assassin, too. In the old days in Russia, I was Neegeeleést. I took part in Neegeeleést conspiracy that assassinated Alexander Second——

FRANK. Well, that was legitimate, wasn't it? The old regime in Russia was rotten.

THE GARDENER. From political point of view, we thought

we were doing right thing. But later I come to look at the matter from point of view of God, and I know then that we committed mortal sin. I did not throw bombs myself, but I was there when my comrades threw them. First bomb killed only Cossacks—but it was horrible to see even Cossacks die. Then the Tsar got down from his carriage to find out if anybody hurt, and I see that he is thin and old, that he is tired and sick and has many worries, that he drives in his own carriage like a prisoner, that the autocrat is less free than we. For the first time, all of a sudden, I see that he is a man and I pity him. Not only he is always in danger, but he suffers on account of our hatred. Then second bomb is thrown—it explodes and tears off both his legs, and they carry him away to die in terrible unspeakable suffering. I was student of natural science, then —I was rebel against Christian God, but I could not forget the face of Alexander Nikoláevich. Not very long after, I read the writings of Lyov Tolstóy, and I understand all our sin. I see clearly that through hatred and violence one can never cure any evil—such methods only make more evil. Through love, and only through love, can evil be turned away.

ELLIS (*clearing his throat, a little embarrassed*). What I'm trying to explain is that I don't hate Frank. He may think I resented him when I worked here, but actually I've always liked him, and——

THE GARDENER. You are convinced that world will be better off if you murder a man you like?

ELLIS. The world will be better off if it's decently run for once—and that's what we hope to accomplish. What about all the millions of people who were killed in the last two wars? If another such war can be stopped by a few quick and painless executions, we certainly oughtn't to hesitate.

FRANK. How can you stop a war?

ELLIS. The Relief Bureau is international: we've got people all over the world.

THE GARDENER. It is against law of God to kill in war, and it is equally against law of God to kill for political reasons.

ELLIS. We prefer to say *administrative*.

FRANK. You're quibbling.

THE GARDENER. It is not important what you call it. All violent acts are crimes: they are offences against Christian teaching.

ELLIS. Don't think I haven't thought about this. As Frank says, I'm a minister's son. But my father had a fashionable Episcopal church and was a passionate Anglophile, and it was brought home to me very strongly by the time I was ten years old and we were fighting the Japs and the Germans that what *you* call the Christian teaching is *not* what's taught by the Christian church.

THE GARDENER. It is true that the churches preach war, but that is not precept of Christ.

ELLIS. No, but really—aside from the churches—you can find non-resistance in the Gospels, but you can also find the other thing. One of my father's most successful sermons was based on the text from Matthew, *I came not to send peace, but a sword.* That was during the first World War, and he had the congregation so excited that, after the service was over, the women stood out on the church steps and pinned white feathers on all the men who hadn't enlisted yet. What's the point of pretending we're Christians, and that Christianity means brotherly love? It's much better, it seems to me, to do such killing as we need without rancor. The way we regard it at the Bureau: it's just a clearing of the ground to build.

JUDITH. You've got your own clichés now, haven't you?

ELLIS. You're bitter against me, Judy, for reasons that are completely irrelevant and due to a misunderstanding.

JUDITH. It would be interesting to hear your story!

ELLIS. I'd be glad to tell you, if you'd let me.

JUDITH. Look, Frank: you're not getting anywhere. This is no time to argue theology. You can see that I really know something about the Teniakis business, and I think it might be more useful if I could talk with Ellis alone.

FRANK. What light would that throw on your problem?

JUDITH. I can't explain now, but I swear to you it's really important.

FRANK. It's not important to *me* if Ellis stood you up on a date.

JUDITH. It's not that. Do leave us alone for just a few minutes. You can stand right outside in the hall. It's the only way I can help you.

FRANK. All right, but make it quick. I can't afford to waste much time. (*As he is walking toward the door, he takes the flashlight down from the mantel.*) I'll put this away somewhere.

JUDITH. No, leave it: it's safer here—because I know how it works. It's not set, and even when it is, there's a device that lets you know when it's going off. The flashlight bulb lights up and keeps burning for several minutes before the gun fires itself. That's how the killer knows when to leave, if he's had to stay in the room.

FRANK. I don't want you bumping off Ellis!

JUDITH. I won't—I promise.

FRANK. All right—better keep between him and the door!

JUDITH. Don't worry.

FRANK. O.K.— (*To the Gardener*) Come along.

THE GARDENER. I obey, little father.

*Frank goes out.*

THE GARDENER (*following Frank, but turning and addressing the audience—he speaks now with a Jewish accent*). I haven't had a scene like this since Gorki's *The Lower Depths*—and the translation is terrible!

*He goes out and shuts the door.*

ELLIS. What I wanted to explain to you, first of all, is that I did have to go to my aunt's.

JUDITH. Do you expect her to leave you money?

ELLIS. No—but she's my father's only living sister, and a formidable old lady. She doesn't invite you often, and when she does, you have to go.

JUDITH. In other words, one of your aunts would always have a priority over me.

ELLIS. That's not the way I'd put it. I——

JUDITH (*interrupting him*). I resent your whole attitude toward me. You went to the most elaborate trouble not to have me meet your Southampton friends that night.

ELLIS. I thought they'd bore you to death. All they talk about is business and beaches.

JUDITH. I thought *he* looked rather sweet.

ELLIS (*grinning*). It may have been an instinct on my part not to have you meet somebody that looked rather sweet to you.

JUDITH. You didn't care about me that much!

ELLIS. Don't you think *I've* got some cause for complaint?

JUDITH. No.

ELLIS. You wouldn't even let me talk to you on the phone. And how about Pinky Papadopoulos?

JUDITH. I don't really like him. He's too Levantine.

ELLIS. He must have been pretty crazy about you to have told you about his gun.

JUDITH. That's what I wanted to talk about. I don't want him to get into trouble. I want you to promise me absolutely that you won't give Pinky away.

ELLIS. Otherwise, what?—you'll shoot me?

JUDITH. No: I don't want to shoot you.

ELLIS. Why should I promise, then?

JUDITH. Because I want you to.

Ellis. I hope it's not really finished between us.

Judith. I didn't want it to be.

Ellis. Shall I see you again?

Judith. If you want to.

Ellis. You know I do. It was really your letting me down that made my join Teniakis.

Judith. No!

Ellis. Yes, it was: I was terrifically upset. After all, I'd only seen you twice—and I hadn't ever known before what that kind of thing—what love could be like.

Judith. It was exciting in that sordid little room up above the Tokyo Club, wasn't it? I didn't tell you then, but that's the room the professional tarts use.

Ellis. Yes: it transfigures everything, doesn't it? I couldn't get down to earth afterwards. I couldn't bear to go on as I'd been doing, just being a polite young man and doing research for their articles.

Judith. Did you actually take the oath and give them the guarantee?

Ellis. Yes.

Judith. What crime did they make you commit?

Ellis. You're not allowed to tell.—I was desperate: I wanted to be hard, like you.

Judith. I'm sorry. I'll try to make it up to you.

Ellis. Will you really?

Judith. The third time is always the best.

Ellis. How do I know I can count on you this time?

*She comes over and, sitting on the right arm of his chair, still holding the revolver in her hand, she puts her right arm around his neck and leans over and gives him a long kiss.*

Judith (*lifting her head*). Does that convince you?

Ellis. Yes.

Judith. You won't tell about Pinky?

Ellis. No.

Judith. I'm really with you people, you know.

ELLIS. Are you really? You didn't act so just now.

JUDITH. That was just because I was sore at you.

ELLIS. Really?

JUDITH. Of course—but I'm not any more: it's very much the other way.

ELLIS. What about my mission, though?

JUDITH. Frank, you mean?

ELLIS. Yes.

JUDITH. That might come out all right.

ELLIS. You think you can make him see it our way?

JUDITH. Not in his present mood.

ELLIS. What will you do, then?

JUDITH. If necessary, I'll have to do what you were going to do. In the meantime, tell him you'll disappear. Give him your word of honor.

ELLIS. I don't quite like to do that.

JUDITH. Oh, come: we've had to change our ideas about human relations, haven't we?—since that day when you were saying to Frank that these movements put a premium on treachery.

ELLIS (*suspicious of irony and giving her a doubtful glance*). Of course: an impersonal relation can be something much more sacred and binding.

JUDITH. So go back and tell your headquarters that everything's been taken care of.

ELLIS. Can I depend on you? I noticed just now that your instinct was to rush to Frank's protection.

JUDITH. Not really—it was just to get back at you.

ELLIS. What night, then?

JUDITH. Let's say the end of the week. With what's likely to happen here, I probably won't be free till Saturday.

ELLIS. You mean—Frank?

JUDITH. Yes.—Let's say Saturday, at the Tokyo, at eight o'clock. (*She moves away toward the door.*)

ELLIS. You won't shoot me if I get up from this chair?

JUDITH. What do you want to do?

ELLIS (*coming over to her, as she stops in front of the fire-place*). I just want to tell you this! (*He embraces her with his right arm and gives her a long kiss on the mouth, while with his left arm, without her seeing, he reaches to the mantelpiece and pushes a catch on the flashlight; then he relinquishes her, murmuring in a low lover's voice:*) Till Saturday—don't let me down!

JUDITH (*with a lover's look*). All right.—Go back over there.

*He returns to the morris-chair. Judith walks to the door, while Ellis looks after her with a crooked smile.*

JUDITH (*opening the door*). Come in.

*Frank appears, with the Gardener, who hangs behind.*

JUDITH (*to Frank*). He's going back and going to tell them that he's left the gun. That will give you time to get away. It wouldn't do to hold him here: they'd be right out to see what was wrong. He's given his word of honor that he won't let them know the real situation. Now, don't ask me how I did it—but I've got something on Teniakis.—Here, take this. (*She gives him the revolver and hurries out the door.*)

FRANK (*looking at Ellis intently*). Do you agree to that?

ELLIS. Yes.

FRANK. All right: be on your way! (*To the Gardener*) See him off the place. (*To Ellis, as the latter stands up*) I'm not even going to follow you with a gun. You've given me your word, and I trust you.

ELLIS. This doesn't mean, Frank, you know, that you'll be free to distribute your article. I wish you'd come around and discuss it. Teniakis himself will talk to you. You don't understand his point of view—you've written about him exactly as if he were just an old-fashioned boss.

FRANK. The old-time political bosses contented themselves

with stuffing the ballot—and sometimes having somebody beaten up. They didn't kidnap and murder people. And everybody knew who they were.

ELLIS. There never was a human society that didn't depend on force. We shoot our traitors and spies.

FRANK. Only in time of war—and the people gave our government that power. Who's appointed Teniakis to be judge and executioner?

ELLIS. The people are finding it pays to put things in the Bureau's hands. They're conceding——

FRANK. Well, here's one person who isn't! (*The bulb of the flashlight lights up with a sharp but unobtrusive blue light.*) Now, go on!— (*Turning to the Gardener, which gives Ellis a chance to glance toward the flashlight*) See him out by the back and lock the gate. I'll watch from the window.

ELLIS. Goodby, Frank.

FRANK. Goodby.

*Ellis goes out with the Gardener, the Gardener shutting the door. Frank puts the revolver on the table and stands thinking, his hands on his hips. Judith enters. She is very pale. She is wearing the Spanish comb and carrying a small Christmas package, done up with a rosette of ribbon.*

JUDITH. You'd better get away somewhere, Frank.

FRANK (*turning around*). Get away? For God's sake, I've been prepared for this! I've got a plane on call out here, and I'm going to fly over Manhattan and as many other places as my leaflets last and bomb them with the truth about Teniakis.

JUDITH. You're not!

FRANK. I certainly am!—and maybe you'd better come along.

JUDITH. They'll get you as soon as you land.

FRANK. I'm going to land in Canada, where they've only got Commonwealth Socialism.— (*Grinning*) You look wonderful with that comb.

JUDITH. I like it. I'm going to wear it. (*Awkwardly presenting her package*) I brought you a little present.

FRANK. No! You don't mean to say! (*He takes it and unties the ribbon.*) I thought you were done with Christmas.

JUDITH. I wouldn't let Christmas go by without giving you a present.

*He unrolls a gray cloth, on which are fastened a variety of enormous gold-plated tie-clips in the shape of daggers, swords and arrows. The flashlight bulb goes out.*

FRANK. Tie-clips, by God!

JUDITH. You were complaining you couldn't find them anywhere.

FRANK. A completely new model, by gracious! What is this? A dagger?—an arrow—a sword! (*He detaches the dagger and clips it on his tie.*) I'm delighted!—I never feel right without one, and I haven't had a decent one for years. Baby darling! (*He kisses her.*) This makes me feel a lot better about meeting my Maker, if I've got to. I'll at least be correctly dressed.

JUDITH. You know I'm really for you, don't you?

FRANK (*with a light touch*). There are moments when my faith in you wavers.

JUDITH. But I am—I almost always am!—Oh, everything's so horrible, isn't it? You can't live with it! Let's go to Canada! I can't stand it any longer! I hate those night-clubs and places: they cheapen you—it's all so dirty! They tried to make me talk about *Spotlight*—but I wouldn't tell them a thing.

FRANK. You must have gone pretty far with somebody to get all that information.

JUDITH (*beginning to cry*). Oh, don't!—don't reproach me: I can't stand it!—I've always been loyal to you, really. That snobby little punk Ellis!—now that he's gone bad, he's more of a prig than ever. (*Sobbing and gasping*) You know how I bought him off? I let him think that if he'd do what I asked, I'd set the flashlight for you. (*She begins to laugh and choke hysterically. The flashlight bulb goes on.*) Oh, don't look so hurt! Don't! (*As he gazes at her surprised, with a touch of alarm*) —I can't bear to have you look hurt! I know that I've treated you rottenly, but I'll try to make up for it now. I'll go up in the plane with you—it's terribly exciting. You're the only one who's really got guts! (*She throws herself against him, clinging with her hands to his shoulders. He puts his arms around her.*) That'll be a surprise for Ellis! (*She laughs uncontrollably again.*)—I hope they asphyxiate him, the way they do with their hopeless incompetents!

FRANK. By God, today is my greatest day!—the day of desperation and glory! There are times when the whole turn against tyranny depends on just one man who dares to speak!—And you're back with me! You're back to stay?

JUDITH (*between sobs*). If you want me.

FRANK (*pulling her to him*). You've always been my real strength!—I don't fear man, devil nor delicatessen-dealer!— (*He brings out his handkerchief and wipes her eyes.*) Now, take it easy, puss.

JUDITH. I feel terribly about what I've done to you!

FRANK. Today you've wiped everything out!—Now, get yourself in hand: we've got to get going.

*The flashlight bulb fades off.*

JUDITH. I'm ready.

FRANK. You'll have to pack some things for Canada. I'll go get Gandy. Meet me downstairs.

JUDITH. You're not going to take *him*?

FRANK. I *was* going to. You don't object, do you?

JUDITH (*like a sulky tearful child*). Yes.

FRANK. I don't like to leave him here alone.

JUDITH. If *he* goes, *I'm* not going.

FRANK. He'll be disappointed—but never mind. Now go on—we've got to hurry.

JUDITH. And I might as well say right now that if I'm

534

going to come back with you again, you've got to get rid of Gandy.

FRANK (*making for the door*). All right, all right! We'll talk about that later.

*The door opens, and Gandersheim enters.*

GANDERSHEIM. I came up to see what your plans were. The gardener's down there on watch.

FRANK. We'll have to go ahead with Plan Two. But Judith's going to fly with me, so you needn't come. We'll need the room in the plane for the leaflets.—But you'd better find some place to hide out that nobody but me will know.—I'm going to call the pilot now. (*To Judith*) Meet me down below!

*Frank hurries out. Gandersheim stands stunned, then casts a hateful look at Judith. During the conversation that follows, she is hurriedly going through the files and the papers on the table, collecting important things that she thinks they should take in the plane.*

GANDERSHEIM. It's nervy of you to go with Frank, but are you quite sure you want to be identified with what he's trying to do?

JUDITH. Frank and I always work together.

GANDERSHEIM. That's news!

JUDITH. You'd better think about getting away. If you stay around here, they may kidnap you. If I were you, I'd go to Mexico.

GANDERSHEIM. I wouldn't desert Frank!

JUDITH. He can't have you here any more.

GANDERSHEIM. What do you mean?

JUDITH. He won't need you any more, because I'm coming back here to work with him.

GANDERSHEIM. Does that come from Frank?

JUDITH. Yes.

GANDERSHEIM. I hope you won't mind if I say that I don't necessarily believe it!

JUDITH. Ask him.

GANDERSHEIM. You've made him do this!

JUDITH. Yes, I have.

GANDERSHEIM. You *bitch*!

*The bulb lights up.*

JUDITH. Even that old theatrical line can't make you a dramatic character.

GANDERSHEIM. It makes you a bitch.

JUDITH. It'll be enough for Frank, when he knows how you talk to me in my own house!

GANDERSHEIM. Your own house! It's *my* house, please—and I've let you play utter hob with it! Transplanting my hydrangeas and all the rest!

JUDITH. Don't give yourself away so.

GANDERSHEIM. I'm sick of your insinuations!

JUDITH. It's so obvious they're sexual symbols.

GANDERSHEIM. They obviously are to you. You can't bear to have those handsome flowers flourishing in front of the house, just because you want to castrate the men! You've done your best to ruin Frank, to kill his faith in himself—just because you can't bear to see men succeed. You made up to Ellis in the first place just out of perversity and vanity—you're incapable of loving anyone—I'm sure you've never even had a single moment of genuine physical passion! And the result was that Ellis deserted Frank. Then *you* deserted Frank. If it hadn't been for me at that time, he might never have got through this crisis—and now you're coming between us!

JUDITH. If it hadn't been for *me*, he'd never have known about Teniakis.

GANDERSHEIM (*getting more and more furious*). I won't have it! I won't permit it! Frank Brock is the finest person that I've ever known in my life, and you want to spoil our friendship—when you've never done anything yourself that wasn't destructive and hateful!

JUDITH. It takes one of you sissies, doesn't it, to be really nasty to a woman!

GANDERSHEIM. A woman! What kind of a woman are *you*? I thought you didn't want to be a woman. You won't condescend to have children—you don't even care to have a husband, except for an occasional meal-ticket and to amuse yourself by torturing him on rainy days. You want to compete with the men, yet you expect them to treat you with chivalry, and what a horrid yowl you set up when anybody tries to slap you down! The relation between Frank and me is absolutely staunch and true: we have confidence in one another, and that confidence is never betrayed.

JUDITH. But Frank doesn't want *you*, he wants *me*.

GANDERSHEIM. But you really don't want *him*—you just want to feel you can make him squirm—to titillate your own little ego!

JUDITH. Now, stop that!—I won't stand for it, I tell you!

GANDERSHEIM. You know what you are?—you're Shidnats Slyme! You're not a woman at all! You're neither a man nor a woman!

JUDITH. That's an amusing accusation from you.

GANDERSHEIM. I never thought he'd come in skirts, and that's why I didn't recognize him—but that's what's so horrible, I see it now—that's what's short-circuiting the world: the woman that won't be a woman, the woman that the men can't depend on! My mother was a thwarter, not a letter-down—but it was part of the same thing: she wouldn't let my father travel, she wouldn't send me back to school. And what good is a woman, for pity's sake, if she doesn't want to make *men*?!

JUDITH. A woman can't make a man if he hasn't got the makings of a man.

GANDERSHEIM. I was a man today all right when I

had this gun in my hand (*he picks the revolver up from the table*), when Frank and I were standing up to Teniakis!

JUDITH. No, you weren't. Put that down!

GANDERSHEIM. You're frightened of a man with a gun!
—well, that's symbolical, too.

JUDITH (*showing signs of becoming hysterical*). Put it down!
—put that gun away!

GANDERSHEIM. Your father and mother, eh?

JUDITH. Don't dare to talk about that!

GANDERSHEIM. I'm afraid it gives me great satisfaction to feel just for once in this house that I've got the upper hand of a woman! If my father had frightened my mother the way I'm frightening you, I might have had the life that I longed for. Maybe that was the way that *your* father felt when he shot his wife and himself!

JUDITH (*shrieking before Gandersheim has finished*). Help! —oh, Frank, help!

GANDERSHEIM. All right: I'll put it away. (*He replaces the revolver on the table.*) You'd better pull yourself together if you're going to go up in that plane.

*She stares at him, her mouth open, her brows contracted, in a tragic childish mask of terror. Frank comes running in. The Gardener appears behind him, but does not come far beyond the door.*

FRANK (*putting his arm around Judith*). What's the matter? what's going on?

JUDITH. He was threatening me!

GANDERSHEIM. That isn't true.

JUDITH. He was threatening me with the gun!

GANDERSHEIM. I wasn't.

FRANK (*to Judith*). Now, for God's sake don't have one of your fits—if you do, I can't take you with me—and we ought to leave—it's almost eight. (*He looks at the clock on the mantel.*) —My God, that thing's lit up!

*They all look up at the flashlight.*

GANDERSHEIM. The little blue light!—that's *it!* Shidnats is behind that, too!

*Frank quickly takes the flashlight down.*

JUDITH (*completely unstrung but trying to concentrate*). Wait a minute—I know how it works. (*She fumbles at it with shaking hands.*) There's a button, but it's not the one that looks like a flashlight button——

*Frank takes hold of the flashlight.*

GANDERSHEIM (*in a panic*). I did this! He's in *me* now— he's taken possession of *me!*

JUDITH. Make him get out—he'll set it off!

FRANK. Better throw it out the window.

GANDERSHEIM (*to Judith, as he starts toward the door*). You're setting it off yourself!

*A blaze of blue livid light, exploded from the mantelpiece, illuminates the whole room. We see Gandersheim, Frank and Judith, for a moment, with their mouths gaping open. Then Gandersheim falls back on the table, and Frank and Judith collapse in front of the fireplace. Then the flare fades out, with the other lights, leaving the stage in darkness.*

*The Gardener, his figure irradiated against an opaque black background, is revealed at the front of the stage, in the center and facing the audience. He is standing erect now, with an austere Hebraic head thrown back. He speaks with the accent and the somber tones of a tragedy in the Jewish theater.*

THE GARDENER. Like Apollo in the house of Admetus, I must depart at the advent of death—I, Ahasuerus, the doomed rabbi, the Wandering Jew. In many different countries, in many different tongues, I have played your stage gardener, your moralist. But what use for me to continue today if my words cannot influence the action? What use to play commentator merely in a world I can no longer guide? We, the Children of Israel, gave you the God of the Old Testament, and you judged and punished like him. We gave you the God of the New

Testament, and you tried to forgive and love. We gave you the Social Revolution, and you tried to judge the men of the present and to love the men of the future. But I who mocked at our prophet Christ, who told him to walk faster as he carried the cross and who therefore was sentenced to wander till Christ should return again—I have lived through two thousand years to see all these moralities fail. Even Israel has forgotten its prophets—for, goaded by the outrage and cruelty of the people of heathen lands who have rejected the laws of God, we have claimed our own land again and defended it against violence with violence. No one can reproach us now for our helplessness, our homelessness—but in that home that Israel has now regained, I no longer have any place. I cannot learn to be a patriot in Palestine. And, in your country, who will receive me?—who will recognize the sign of God? who will fight at the command of the spirit?—who will even serve the vision of Justice that has gleamed for our secular leaders? For you, God and spirit and vision are fading with the words that name them. What you trust in, for all your techniques, for all your mechanisms of industry and politics, is merely the brute vitality that animates the universe—and our own people, dwelling among you, are exchanging their traditional disciplines for the new one of electronics. So now you must make your new rules, develop your new calculations. They are based on statistical averages, and I cannot help you there, for my gospel has all been derived from the conscience, the courage, the insight, by which men of a chosen race asserted their superior authority. This household that, stranded and harried, has destroyed itself before our eyes seemed the only place left me for shelter—and whom can I work for now? My friends are few and weak—I have hardly even self-declared enemies to do honor to God's agent by hating him. (*The light on him begins to dim but leaves his face illumined.*)

540

Why must I wander still? Was Jesus deceived?—will He not come again? Am I already half a wraith that flickers for a moment still in your terrorized darkness of soul when you are tortured or tempted by the forces that are pressing you into alien shapes? Is the star of Bethlehem setting, on this night of the Holy Nativity, as the little blue light of hate?

No: even in this black night of blasphemy I cannot yet die or rest: I must go on to new unbelievers. God's hand still directs and drives me—though perhaps to the last precipice-edge above which mankind must falter. God has created the Light, and the Light will not wholly fail —I shall bear it, though the Heavens be darkened, to show where the abyss drops. Now farewell—but I shall always be with you—somewhere, at some man's side!

*The light on his face goes out.*